The Social History of Human Experience

General Editor: Neil McKendrick

Mirrors of Mortality:
Studies in the Social History of Death

Mirrors of Mortality

Studies in the Social History of Death

Edited by Joachim Whaley

St. Martin's Press   New York

St. Martin's Press, Inc., 175 Fifth Avenue, New York, NY 10010
Printed in Great Britain
First published in the United States of America in 1982

ISBN 0-312-53441-8

Library of Congress Cataloging in Publication Data
Main entry under title:

Mirrors of mortality.

    Includes bibliographical references and index.
    Contents: To die and enter the House of Hades /
Christiane Sourvinou-Inwood—Sacred corpse, profane
carrion / R. C. Finucane—From public to
private, the royal funerals in England, 1500–1830 /
Paul S. Fritz—[etc.]
    1. Death—Social aspects—History—Addresses,
essays, lectures. I. Whaley, Joachim.

HQ1073.M55 1981   306   81–18363
ISBN 0-312-53441-8   AACR2

Contents

Illustrations

Between pages 124 and 125

Notes on Contributors

C. A. Bayly is Fellow and Tutor of St. Catharine's College, Cambridge. He has published various articles on Indian politics and society and is the author of *The Local Roots of Indian Politics. Allahabad, 1880–1920* (1975). He is at present completing a study of the towns and trading communities of north India and has recently been appointed an editor of the *New Cambridge History of India*.

David Cannadine read history at Clare College, Cambridge, and received his doctorate from the University of Oxford in 1975. He is now Fellow of Christ's College and Lecturer in history in the University of Cambridge. He has contributed to a wide range of journals and his *Lords and Landlords: The Aristocracy and the Towns, 1775–1967* appeared in 1980.

R. C. Finucane held a Leverhulme Fellowship in the University of Oxford in 1970 and a research fellowship in the Medieval Centre, Reading University from 1973 to 1976. His *Miracles and Pilgrims: Popular Beliefs in Medieval England* was published in 1977.

Paul S. Fritz is Professor of History at McMaster University, Canada, and co-editor of the Publications of the McMaster University Association of 18th Century Studies. His book *The English Ministers and Jacobitism Between the Rebellions of 1715 and 1745* appeared in 1975.

David Irwin is Reader in the History of Art and Head of Department at the University of Aberdeen. His books include: *English Neoclassical Art* (1966), *Winckelmann: Writings on Art* (1972), *Scottish Painters: At Home and Abroad 1700–1900* (co-author with his wife, 1975), and most recently *John Flaxman: Sculptor, Illustrator, Designer* (1979).

John McManners is Canon of Christ Church and Regius Professor of Ecclesiastical History in the University of Oxford. He is also a Fellow of the British Academy. His books include: *French Ecclesiastical Society and the Ancien Regime: A Study of Angers in the 18th Century* (1960), *Lectures on European History 1789–1914: Men, Machines and Freedom* (1966), *The*

French Revolution and the Church (1969) and *Church and State in France 1870–1914* (1972).

Christiane Sourvinou-Inwood graduated from Athens University and received her doctorate from the University of Oxford. She held various academic appointments in Oxford and Liverpool and is the author of *Theseus as Son and Stepson. A Tentative Illustration of the Greek Mythological Mentality* (1979). She has now given up academic life to write plays and detective stories.

Joachim Whaley was educated at Christ's College, Cambridge, where he held a Fellowship in History from 1976 to 1978. He is now a Fellow of Robinson College and lectures on German history in the Faculty of Modern and Medieval Languages at Cambridge University. He is currently writing a history of religious toleration in north Germany in the eighteenth century.

Introduction

JOACHIM WHALEY

History, Hegel once wrote, is the record of 'what man does with death'. Indeed man's existence has always been characterized by an awareness of his transitory nature. It is the sense of time and hence the sense of mortality which distinguishes man from all other species. Animals may fear death and undoubtedly have some primitive consciousness of the demise of their fellow creatures. But man alone actually buries his dead and man alone has conceived of the possibility of an after-life whether by direct translation of the body or by some more complex translation of the spirit or soul. Death is a biological fact which man shares in common with all other species, but there is also a sense in which W. B. Yeats was correct when he claimed that 'Man has created death'.[1]

Hegel and Yeats both pointed to one of the most extraordinary and most prominent features of human existence—the preoccupation, almost the obsession of all societies with its termination. Some 500,000 years ago Peking Man already buried his dead. By 50,000 B.C. Neanderthal Man had created a relatively elaborate series of rituals providing for what were thought to be man's *post-mortem* needs. The emergence of *homo sapiens* in the Upper Palaeolithic era is characterized by the increasing complexity of burial customs and by the time the first civilized societies had been established ancestor worship, elaborate burial rituals and increasingly complex and massive tombs or houses for the dead had become a regular feature of all societies.

Even the most cursory glance at the relics of human history, at the most fragmentary records of even its lesser-known episodes, reveals how continuously man has been preoccupied with death. Human beings have devoted an astonishing amount of intellectual energy and artistic accomplishment to speculation about the nature of death and a possible after-life. They have created elaborate burial rites to enable the dead to progress on their journey. They have expended incredible material resources and enormous physical prowess in order to provide the dead with houses or monuments. And

[1] Many of these ideas are discussed by S. G. F. Brandon, *The Judgement of the Dead. An Historical and Comparative Study of the Idea of a* Post-Mortem *Judgement in the Major Religions* (London, 1967), pp. 1–5, *passim* and John Bowker, *The Sense of God* (Oxford, 1973), pp. 66–85.

1

although, at the most fundamental level, all this was undoubtedly designed first and foremost to aid the dead, much of it was just as important for those who survived. Rituals of translation often served to restructure disrupted social or personal relationships; burial rites frequently helped to reinforce social or political ideals, while tombs and monuments strengthened concepts of continuity, legitimacy and status. Although death is different from all other rites of passage in that the human actor is forced to relinquish his role, it is like all others in that the dead are very rarely banished from the stage. Indeed the coexistence of the living and the dead has been one of the most prominent characteristics of human society.

The recognition that death has dominated the human consciousness is not a novel one. Much of the evidence which modern scholars have been concerned to evaluate is itself testimony to this. In art, the theme of the *danse macabre* is but the most prominent and most enduring of many images of mortality which provide valuable information about attitudes to death and the dead. In literature, the long-standing tradition of the *ars moriendi*, advice to dying persons on how to die, is first found in the Egyptian Book of the Pyramids and the later Book of Coffins. Artistic motifs and literary themes concerned with mortality can be found in virtually all periods. And on occasion they have been the subject of heated debates as in the eighteenth century when men like Lessing were concerned to establish a new conception of mortality by reviving the ancient notion of death as the companion of sleep in opposition to the horrific and brutal vision of their predecessors.[2] In an intriguing and not entirely dissimilar way, the subject of death has been revived in the recent past. The publication of Geoffrey Gorer's famous article on 'The Pornography of Death' in 1955 signalled the prelude to the publication of a mass of books and articles concerned with the problem of mortality in modern society.[3] The perception and discussion of this contemporary problem has provided a major stimulus to the emergence of a body of historical literature which has attempted to analyse attitudes to death and dying in the past.

Gorer argued that the subject of death had become a form of pornography. The liberation of sexual mores had led to the suppression of death as modern society, highly mobile, prosperous and mechanized, increasingly failed to be able to come to terms with the problem of mortality. The reasons for this development are complex and not entirely understood. The decline of religion is seen to have played a central part. At the same time others have claimed that modern societies have little need for the complex social rituals which previously surrounded death. The decline of the elaborate funeral and the fact that most people now die in institutions rather than at home in the

---

[2] On Lessing and his contemporaries see essays in *Wie die Alten den Tod gebildet. Wandlungen der Sepulkralkultur 1750–1850* edited by Hans-Kurt Boehlke (Mainze, 1979).

[3] Geoffrey Gorer, 'The Pornography of Death' in W. Phillips and P. Rahr (eds.) *Modern Writing* (Berkeley, 1956), pp. 56–62.

midst of the family has meant that the means whereby grief and mourning were formerly socialized within a supportive community are now no longer available to modern man.

This has happened at a time when improvements in medical technology have ensured that more people survive to a relatively high age. It has been suggested too that other factors less capable of simple definition have played a part: some, for example, have argued that the very language with which man formerly spoke about death is in some way inaccessible to modern man since the mass extermination of human lives during the 1940s and the horrific destruction caused by the atom bombs at Hiroshima and Nagasaki.[4]

There has been little agreement on which of these diverse factors (and there are many more) has been crucial in the crisis in modern attitudes to death. Nor is there much substantial agreement on the remedy. In America the so-called Death Awareness Movement has been more active than most in its attempts to bring back the subject of death and dying. Everywhere, the literature on the subject has become immense—countless articles and books devoted to the art of dying, to the problem of coping with grief and mourning.[5] Most are characterized by the belief that it is essential for modern man to restore somehow an equanimity in the face of death, and thus re-establish a relationship both between individuals and society and between individuals and nature which has only recently been lost.

It is precisely the question of what this relationship was, how it was gradually eroded and what the consequences might be that dominated the first attempts at a history of attitudes to death in the 1960s. The most prominent pioneer in this field has undoubtedly been the French scholar Philippe Ariès whose still controversial work will be discussed below. His theme was quickly taken up by other scholars, most notably in France but also in America where David Stannard edited a volume of essays in 1975, one of whose explicit aims was to produce 'at least a partial explanation for the disturbing turns the concept of death has taken in modern American society'.[6] In the meantime death has become one of the most widely discussed issues at historical conferences, and the subject of numerous works of historical scholarship. It is a field which continues to fascinate historians and yet, in important ways, to elude them.

Despite the obvious and growing general interest in the subject it is bedevilled by obscurity and confusion. Indeed Michel Vovelle, one of the leading scholars in the field, was forced to admit in 1975 (after he had

---

[4] See the discussion by A. Alvarez, *The Savage God; A Study of Suicide* (London, 1971), pp. 197–217.

[5] Two bibliographies provide valuable guides to this literature: Albert Jay Miller and Michael James Aeri, *Death: A Bibliographical Guide* (Metuchen, New Jersey and London, 1977); Barbara K. Harrah and David F. Harrah, *Funeral Service: A Bibliography of Literature on its Past, Present and Future, the Various Means of Disposition and Memorialization* (Metuchen, New Jersey, 1976).

[6] David E. Stannard (ed.), *Death in America* (University of Pennsylvania Press, 1975), p. xi.

written no less than three books on attitudes to death in France) that it is still far from clear what it is that historians are actually trying to study when they look at death or what historical methods are most appropriately applied to such studies.[7]

Many of these problems are in a sense the product of contemporary preoccupations which had dominated the major writings on the subject. For the claim that modern man's attitude to death represents a distinct and unhealthy break from the past, implies an assumption about the way in which such attitudes have changed which it is impossible to substantiate adequately. Just as we are unsure about the nature and origins of our own attitudes, so it has been difficult to introduce any greater certainty into our analysis of these attitudes in the past.

Other difficulties involved in any general account have resulted from the sheer complexity both of the subject matter and of the evidence. The study of attitudes to death involves the analysis of death mythologies in art and literature, of medical practice and beliefs, of popular superstitions and folklore, of burial rites and customs, of ecclesiastical laws and structures, of civil law and custom, in short of virtually all aspects of human activity and most forms of human expression. The range of potentially relevant evidence is equally extensive—from art and literature, to gravestones and funeral orations.[8] These lists are by no means exhaustive. Indeed they could never be so. For the claim made by Philippe Ariès and Pierre Chaunu that it is by looking at attitudes to death that one can judge the character of civilizations must undermine any attempt to delimit either the range of questions posed or the material examined.

The only attempt to sketch a long-term history of attitudes to death has been made by Philippe Ariès. His thesis was developed in a series of articles now collected in a French edition. It has, however, been fully elaborated in two closely related works. The first of these was published in 1974 as the transcript of a series of lectures delivered in Baltimore. This relatively brief and programmatic outline was then revised and extended in a massive volume entitled *L'Homme devant la mort* which appeared in 1977.[9] As Ariès himself admits, his thesis has become more complex over the years and he himself recommends readers to look at his lectures first by way of introduction to the major statement which followed.[10]

---

[7] Michel Vovelle, 'Les attitudes devant la mort: problèmes de méthode, approches et lectures différentes', *Annales E.S.C.*, xxxi (1976), 120–32.

[8] Many of these problems are discussed by Natalie Zemon Davis, 'Some Tasks and Themes in the Study of Popular Religion' in C. Trinkaus and H. A. Obermann (eds.), *The Pursuit of Holiness in late Medieval and Renaissance Religion* (Leiden, 1974), pp. 307–36.

[9] The relevant works by Philippe Ariès are: *Essais sur l'histoire de la mort en Occident du Moyen Age à nos jours* (Paris, 1975); *Western Attitudes toward Death from the Middle Ages to the Present* (Johns Hopkins University Press, 1974); *L'Homme devant la mort* (Paris, 1977).

[10] Ariès, *L'Homme devant la mort*, pp. 596–7.

Not the least of the problems involved in approaching Ariès' work is the fact that it is not a straightforward attempt at periodization. He does believe that mental attitudes (and the most significant of these, he believes, are attitudes to death) change over time. But that is not to say that old attitudes are completely superseded—rather one should look at what Ariès calls the five major variations as a series of overlapping images often coinciding with each other and only broadly conforming to a long-term chronological development. This basic premise demands considerable mental agility on the part of the reader as the account revolves around an uncertain chronology to which Ariès is understandably reluctant to tie himself down.

Ariès' panoramic survey rests on the belief that there have been five distinct collective attitudes to death which have characterized European society during the last one and a half millennia. Although these attitudes overlap and often appear to lack a strong chronology, Ariès' whole work is based on what amounts to the general proposition that man's relationship with nature and hence with death has become increasingly distorted as a result of human progress.[11] Thus the two periods in which attitudes to death have been most problematic and least healthy or natural are the eighteenth and twentieth centuries.

The first attitude to death in Ariès' scheme is both a chronological stage and a condition which prevailed among the masses until the end of the nineteenth century. It is characterized by the total harmony of the living and the dead. Death in this condition is not a frightening event but one expected and accepted as inevitable. The act of dying itself is not dramatized in any way, and the death-bed ritual is the central and most symbolic aspect of death in a society which trusts in the ability of the Church to take care of the souls of the departed. Individuals accept death as a kind of extended sleep, confident in the ultimate resurrection of the body at the Last Judgement. This kind of natural acceptance on the part of a community able to come to terms easily with both the dying and the dead is, according to Ariès, typical of most primitive societies. But it gained special force in Europe from the early Christian concept of death. Furthermore, this attitude survived well into the nineteenth century among the majority of the population. In those peasant communities described by Tolstoy, and in similar communities throughout Europe, attitudes to death remained basically similar to those of the early Middle Ages.

The first significant change occurred amongst a small intellectual and social élite during the eleventh and twelfth centuries. Ariès relates this change to the emergence of individualism, with related concepts of personal destiny not only in life but also after death. A previously rather vague idea of a Second Coming or general resurrection is now transformed into a specific vision of the Last Judgement. The individual and his destiny take

[11] Ibid, pp. 596–607.

precedence over the community—a change reflected in the institution of requiem masses for individuals rather than occasional collective commemorations and in the new emphasis on the funeral rather than the deathbed. As funerals became more and more ostentatious, so they were increasingly used to express ideals of social status and material wealth, indicative of a fierce love of life and material welfare. This lust for life is also expressed in artistic representations of death: the soul is separated from the rotting corpse. The revulsion of the *danse macabre* is, according to Ariès, another sign not of despair generated by the Black Death but of the same lust for life. This second stage which was also studied in some depth and with similar results by Alberto Tenenti some thirty years ago, is held to have lasted until the eighteenth century.[12]

By about 1700 we thus have two prevailing attitudes to death in European society: the one a natural acceptance which characterized the attitude of the majority, the other fiercely resentful and passionately attached to the pleasures of the material world and preoccupied with the fate of individuals in the next. At this point, however, Ariès introduces a third attitude labelled *La mort longue et proche* ('protracted and imminent death') which seems to emerge in the sixteenth century and reaches its fullest and most disturbing expression in the Enlightenment. This is perhaps the most complex of all the phases in his argument and it is by no means clear how he wishes to integrate it into the overall scheme.

Superficially, Ariès claims, little changes during the sixteenth and seventeenth centuries: the *artes moriendi,* and the *danses macabres* continue to dominate the consciousness of an élite obsessed with the 'death of self'. But he claims that beneath this articulate level, deep-rooted changes were taking place which were in part a reaction against the obsessions of the élite. He finds that both Lutherans and Catholics in the sixteenth century begin to condemn excessive expenditure on elaborate burial rituals and to plead for more modest interments, a more spiritually relevant approach to dying. In some way which is never made quite clear, this attitude is transformed by the eighteenth century into what amounted to a denial of death by the Enlightenment. Enlightened medicine becomes fascinated with the biological realities of death while early health reformers begin to demand the removal of the cemeteries from the churches and city centres—the first symbolic expulsion or rejection of the dead from the community of the living. Another rather contradictory feature of this phase is the emergence of a symbolic link between sex and death as a result of the scientific preoccupation with the corpse. Death becomes 'untamed' and 'savage' since optimistic enlightened doctors gradually become afraid of the one biological state they sense they will never be able to reverse.

This third condition is then intimately linked to the development of

[12] Alberto Tenenti, *La Vie et la mort à travers l'art du XVe siècle* (Paris, 1952).

rationality and reaches its most complex expression in the so-called triumph of reason in the Enlightenment. Although not entirely coherent nor fully explained, it is an important part of Ariès' argument since he claims that it preshadows the modern suppression of death. As Ariès puts it, the enlightened élites dragged themselves and their world ever closer to a meaningless abyss, from which they were only saved in the short term by the emergence of a fourth major attitude to death during the eighteenth century.

This fourth stage, labelled 'Thy death', is more closely related to other major social changes which took place after about 1750. The emergence of the modern nuclear family and the development of an entirely new form of personal affection within it has been observed by many scholars, notably Lawrence Stone and David Stannard.[13] Their findings support Ariès' contention that these changes had an essential impact on attitudes to death. Attention is once more directed back to the individual but this time focused on the surviving family rather than on the dying individual. At the same time death was transformed into a welcome event under the impact of romanticism. The cult of the tomb and the social and family significance of regular visits to the cemetery are the prime indicators of the new emotional expression of grief which characterized the nineteenth century.

The final stage in Ariès' scheme is well known. His term 'Forbidden Death' or *'la mort inversée'* denotes that suppression of the idea of death and dying which was observed by Gorer and others. It is linked in turn to the decline of beliefs in survival after death, to the increasing medicalization of death in hospitals and homes for the dying. Just as many *philosophes* sought to deny death in the eighteenth century or at least to banish the dead from the cities, so modern man has, according to Ariès, attempted to suppress the frightening and scandalizing knowledge of his own mortality. As a result, he is now unable to come to terms with death having lost entirely that natural acceptance of biological reality which characterized the early medieval world.

Ariès concludes with some sombre judgements on this latest condition making it clear that he at least would wish to return to that more golden age. It is, indeed, perhaps not too far-fetched to see Ariès' study itself as part of a new consciousness of the problem of death and dying which might constitute an additional sixth phase to the five-fold outline provided in his work.

No brief summary could hope to do justice to this complex and diverse thesis. The argument is not only complex in its balance between a chronological scheme and a series of coexisting attitudes, but also remarkable for

---

[13] Lawrence Stone, *The Family, Sex and Marriage in England, 1500–1800* (London, 1977); David E. Stannard, *The Puritan Way of Death: A Study in Religion, Culture and Social Change* (Oxford, 1977).

the range of evidence used and the wealth of detail which is brought to bear on it. Some critics, notably Lawrence Stone, have questioned the broad structure of the thesis and its chronological progression. Stone proposes to ignore the third phase and amalgamate the second with the fourth: the rise of individualism would thus be closely linked with the emergence of the modern family in the eighteenth century.[14] But such emendations are not wholly satisfactory. It is difficult to ignore the evidence produced by both Ariès and Tenenti on the change of the later Middle Ages and difficult too to assimilate all phenomena of the eighteenth century to the rise of the modern family. Other work on the cemetery reform movement, for example, tends to relate fairly closely to Ariès' arguments about his 'protracted and imminent death' phase.[15]

The specific links in Ariès' argument will only be tested by detailed research which has yet to be done. For the moment, it is essentially only possible to raise more general questions which concern the very nature of the enterprise itself and the extent to which it is at all possible to write a history of death or of attitudes to death in the way in which Ariès has attempted to do.

In the first instance it is in fact difficult to see exactly what Ariès is trying to describe. It is never made really clear what these attitudes consist of, how they are generated or how they change. Ariès treats culture as an independent variable, refusing steadfastly to regard it as a mere reflection or agent of material forces. But despite the refreshing nature of this approach, it is in some ways disturbing that Ariès' changes are never related to any demographic or economic background. It is this methodological problem combined with the author's obvious polemical preferences which have led critics to question the whole concept of his approach. As one German reviewer argued, Ariès is engaged in the ultimately hopeless task of writing the history of a subject of which by definition there can be no history. Have attitudes to death really changed so dramatically over the last thousand years or so? Ariès, Detlef Ilmer claims, is not an historian but a moralist; his history is essentially not a work of scholarship but a 'piece of nostalgic devotional literature'.[16]

There is no doubt some truth in such views which are widely shared. It is possible to criticize both Ariès' methodology and his emotional involvement in the subject. Indeed to some extent his work can be read as an extended

---

[14] Lawrence Stone, 'Death and its History', *New York Review of Books*, 12 October 1978, pp. 22–32 at pp. 29–30.

[15] See Madeleine Foisil, 'Les Attitudes devant la mort au XVIIIe siècle: sépultures et suppression dans le cimetière parisien des Saints-Innocents', *Revue historique*, ccli (1974), 303–30; and A. Lottin, 'Les Morts chassés de la cité. "Lumières et préjugés": "les émeutes" à Lille (1779) et à Cambrai (1786) lors du transfert des cimetières', *Revue du Nord*, lx (1978), 73–103.

[16] Ilmer's review of the German edition of Ariès' essays appeared in *Zeitschrift für historische Forschung*, vi (1979), 213–15.

polemical tract for the present complicated by the addition of a mass of diverse and often confused historical evidence.

But the fact remains that different periods do seem to be characterized by different images of death and attitudes to it. These attitudes and images do appear to occupy a very central place in the thought and behaviour of widely differing societies at very different times and stages of growth. And in the last resort any discussion at the moment must reduce itself to two fundamental questions: firstly whether it is possible to discern attitudes to death in so far as they might form coherent systems at various times, and secondly, if one can, then is it possible to account for the way in which they change? There can be no certain answer to either question at this stage, for the historical study of attitudes to death, like the study of social attitudes of all kinds, is still in its infancy.

The question of whether it is possible to make effective generalizations about the character or spirit of an age as revealed in generally shared attitudes to life or death is one of the most thorny problems with which historians have been faced in recent years. An initial optimism about the possibility of a history of what were labelled *mentalités* has given way to a considerably more cautious attitude.[17] At one level it does seem possible to talk of a 'baroque attitude to death' or of a 'Victorian way of death'. But on closer examination such general images seem to dissolve, giving way to an almost infinite diversity. Attitudes to death in all ages are characterized by the most diverse emotions—fear, sorrow, anger, despair, resentment, resignation, defiance, pity, avarice, triumph, helplessness. And if fear and sorrow predominate it is by no means unusual to find complex mixtures in individuals.[18]

Precisely these individuals and the diverse emotions felt by them contribute to the formation of social attitudes which in essence represent average feelings. As Philip Greven has pointed out in his study of attitudes to children in Early America it is futile to look for one common attitude to anything in any given society. The assumption that all human beings will think the same way at any time is one which our own experience of the present should indicate is not a valid one to impose on the past.[19] The implication is thus that attitudes must be, indeed can only be studied meaningfully in close relation to specific geographical, religious, social, economic, political and psychological circumstances, bearing in mind that there is bound to be an almost infinite diversity both among individuals and also among groups in the same society. Indeed a recent study by Robert Favre of the theme of death in eighteenth-century France suggests that even

[17] See Jacques Le Goff, 'Les Mentalités. Une histoire ambigue' in Jacques Le Goff and Pierre Nora (eds.), *Faire de l'histoire*, 3 vols. (Paris, 1974), iii, pp. 76–94.
[18] John Hinton, *Dying* (Harmondsworth, 1967), pp. 21–49.
[19] Philip Greven, *The Protestant Temperament. Patterns of Child-Rearing, Religious Experience and the Self in Early America* (New York, 1977), pp. 3–5, 17–18.

by looking at the relatively limited written evidence produced by a small intellectual élite, it is possible to find a vast diversity of attitude.[20]

The second major problem raised by Ariès' work is that of the motors of change. At no point is it made clear why one prevailing attitude gives way to another. The eighteenth-century debate about the removal of cemeteries from the city centres is seen as part of a broad change in social attitudes to the dead but it is not fully related to the internal medical debate about health and public hygiene which seems to have been crucial in the long term. Just as it is difficult to assume that all individuals share one attitude to death at any given time, so it is difficult to assume that such individuals themselves hold a coherent and internally logical view of such diverse subjects as medical care for the dying, funeral practice, entombment and the prospects of an after-life. It may thus well be that one must look for more than one motor of change. But it is surely not enough simply to stress that there can be no strict material causation, that culture is an autonomous category.

Answers to some of these questions have been attempted by a group of French historians whom Emmanuel Le Roy Ladurie credited with having produced *la nouvelle histoire de la mort*.[21] Le Roy Ladurie pointed especially to the work of three scholars (Pierre Chaunu, François Lebrun and Michel Vovelle) all of whom have studied attitudes to death in France between about 1500 and 1800. In some ways they have less in common than Le Roy Ladurie suggests. Pierre Chaunu, for example, is much closer to Ariès than to Lebrun or Vovelle in his insistence that the reason why it is important to study the history of attitudes to death is that we are ourselves in the midst of an unprecedented crisis in our relationship with death. Chaunu shares Ariès' chronological scheme perhaps more explicitly than either Lebrun or Vovelle, and although he has written specifically about Paris, Chaunu seems to believe with Ariès that looking at attitudes to death is one way of evaluating the quality of a society, the extent to which it succeeds in creating a framework within which individuals and groups can maintain a healthy relationship with nature.[22]

On the other hand Chaunu fully shares the conviction of Lebrun and Vovelle that a more elaborate technical methodological approach is needed before we can either assess collective attitudes or see how they change. Chaunu in particular has stressed that the study of attitudes to death is an extension of the post-War preoccupation with demography and that similar statistical methods are involved. The study of mentalities, he has argued,

[20] Robert Favre, *La Mort au siècle des lumières* (Lyons, 1978).
[21] Emmanuel Le Roy Ladurie, 'Chaunu, Lebrun, Vovelle: la nouvelle histoire de la mort' in Emmanuel Le Roy Ladurie, *Le Territoire de l'historien*, 2 vols. (Paris, 1973–78), i, pp. 393–403.
[22] Pierre Chaunu, *La Mort à Paris. 16e, 17e, 18e siècles* (Paris, 1978), p. 28. The best introduction to this work is Chaunu's earlier article, 'Mourir à Paris (XVIe–XVIIe–XVIIIe Siècles)', *Annales E.S.C.*, xxxi (1976), 29–50.

cannot rely on random printed or manuscript material alone. Only quantification of abundant and regular sources (the most common being wills, used by both Chaunu and Vovelle) can provide the key to attitudes which were so much taken for granted that they were rarely articulated in any literary form.

In Chaunu's case the commitment to quantification is two-fold. Firstly he is convinced of the value of analysing serial sources like wills for changing formulas which might reveal new attitudes to death. Secondly he stresses the role of changing demographic patterns in the formulation of such attitudes. Crudely stated, his thesis rests on a more or less direct correlation between rising life expectancy and the increasing denial of death which has been a feature of Western society from about 1700 to the present. In the seventeenth century mortality was high and thus men were inevitably preoccupied with death. Only a few decades later mortality began to fall substantially and this was reflected in the thought of the Enlightenment which was obsessed with life rather than death. Other factors, like the decline of the belief in an after-life are also important in Chaunu's argument, but these are essentially subsidiary to the material foundation. Changing attitudes, according to Chaunu, appear first among the élite and then gradually percolate down to the deepest roots of society.

Other studies have, however, shown that the correlation between mortality figures and attitudes to death and burial described by Chaunu may well be illusory or at least only relevant for those specific areas he has studied. Attitudes to death do seem to have changed and mortality rates have declined from about 35 per 1,000 in the decade 1750–60 to about 10 per 1,000 in the decade 1950–60. But the significance one attaches to such figures is to a large degree dependent on the extent to which one believes in a contemporary crisis in man's attitude to death and dying. If on the contrary one believes that changes in attitudes do not essentially reflect anything significant about man's emotional development, then the importance of Chaunu's demographic data is rather more limited.

Indeed, François Lebrun's study of Anjou in the seventeenth and eighteenth centuries has clearly demonstrated that changes in attitudes there were not related to demographic trends. Anjou's demographic development until the French Revolution was not marked by any substantial rise in life-expectancy. Lebrun's study does relate the depressing rhythm of pre-modern mortality to a whole range of attitudes: it was, for example, easier for parents to come to terms with the death of young children since so few actually survived to adulthood or even adolescence. From the middle of the eighteenth century attitudes amongst an élite underwent the same transformations in Anjou as elsewhere: Jansenists and libertins combined to end the elaborate funeral of the baroque era while urban reformers and doctors began to demand the expulsion of the dead from the city centres. Even without significant demographic changes, the process which Lebrun calls the divorce

11

of the village of the living from the village of the dead took place in the second half of the eighteenth century.[23]

It is significant, however, that Chaunu has been one of the few to attempt a long-term explanation of change rather than a mere description. In most cases quantitative analysis of wills or other evidence has merely produced more elaborate and differentiated accounts of episodes previously or simultaneously dealt with by Ariès. But even so, the attempt to link changing attitudes to death with changing biological patterns in an essentially monocausal system has not been successful.

Perhaps the most important work of this kind has been that produced by Michel Vovelle. In a work hailed by Jean Delumeau as comparable with Braudel's Méditerranée and Goubert's Beauvaisis, Vovelle studied attitudes to death in eighteenth-century Provence using statistical analysis of wills.[24] With major qualifications, Vovelle characterized the overall development as being one of 'dechristianization'. It was a striking and even emotive term which has been subject to much misunderstanding and misinterpretation. What he is essentially concerned to chart is the decline of the militant 'total' Christianity which dominated Europe from about 1500 to 1700. The Reformation, he argued, had effectively created a form of Catholicism hitherto unknown during the Middle Ages: its absolute aspirations were ultimately impossible and during the eighteenth century its stranglehold on Western society gradually crumbled. By 1800 religion had become divorced from the state, private rather than public, the preserve of women rather than men, expressive of individual virtue and piety rather than social order.

Vovelle studied this process using the central question of attitudes to death—central both because death after all happened to everyone and because it was precisely in the translation of souls via purgatory into heaven or hell that the Church had created its most powerful lever over the minds and purses of men. Hence attitudes to death are linked to demographic trends, social structures, theological systems and a multitude of other factors. Throughout the claim is not that religion disappeared and hence death was denied, but rather that religious practice assumed different forms, became restricted to a different and less public level. Hence death too was regarded in different ways and the burial of the dead assumed a new significance.

In Vovelle's studies, the most complex and sophisticated to date, the question of death is central because of the extraordinary range of questions about which it reveals information. Attitudes to death in short are indicators of social change. They are complex, often incoherent and incomprehensible, at once meaningful and illogical. In Vovelle's account, Chaunu's material

---

[23] François Lebrun, *Les Hommes devant la mort à Anjou au XVIIe et XVIIIe siècles* (Paris, 1971).
[24] Michel Vovelle, *Piété baroque et déchristianisation en Provence au XVIIIe siècle* (Paris, 1973); Jean Delumeau, 'Au sujet de la déchristianisation', *Revue d'histoire moderne et contemporaine,* xxi (1975), 52–60.

causation is combined with Ariès' relative autonomy in a mixture which distinguishes his work as the first real attempt to look at death within the context of social history understood as the history of society.

Even so, it is important to remember that Vovelle's work is highly specific. It concentrates on the history of catholic Provence roughly between 1680 and 1800. Protestant areas of Europe might well reveal a very different set of patterns. If Philippe Ariès first pointed to the significance and centrality of death to the understanding of society, Michel Vovelle above all has demonstrated just how complex the problem is, how closely related to both social and theological variables, moulded by a perplexing mixture of material and non-material factors.

In this sense, Vovelle's work forms a bridge between recent historical writing on the subject of attitudes to death and the studies of those anthropologists and sociologists who already recognized their importance in the nineteenth century.[25] Many of them were not concerned explicitly with a descriptive account of funerary ritual but with the analysis of its functions. This occurred on two essentially overlapping levels: firstly that of belief, where an attempt is made to relate specific rituals to religious and intellectual structures; and secondly that of social function where rituals are related to social structures, political hierarchies and family formations. Both levels are equally important. But the sheer diversity of the results of such studies once more underlines the lesson of much of Vovelle's research: it is as difficult to establish general patterns over several societies as it is to find a coherent trend within individual societies.[26]

The historical study of attitudes to death is thus a relatively new field. The theses of Ariès, the methodologies of Vovelle have yet to be tested in depth. At present both are still open to criticisms of a more general nature and neither has been subjected fully to the positive test of comparative research.

The essays presented in this volume form an attempt to stimulate a more general discussion of the significance of death in human history. They do not claim to represent a unified view. Although all address themselves to problems raised in recent years by Philippe Ariès and other French scholars, their aim is not collectively either to support or to reject any overall interpretation. They deal with very different facets of these problems. While Professor John McManners examines the work of Ariès and others in its own historical and historiographical context, the other essays demonstrate the complexity of the study of attitudes to death in greatly differing contexts

---

[25] See Richard Huntington and Peter Metcalf, *Celebrations of Death. The Anthropology of Mortuary Ritual* (Cambridge, 1979); Jack Goody, 'Death and the Interpretation of Culture: A Bibliographic Overview', in Stannard, *Death in America,* pp. 1-8.

[26] The complexity of the problems of interpretation is stressed by Peter J. Ucko, 'Ethnography and the Archeological Interpretation of Funerary Remains', *World Archeology,* i (1969-70), 262-80.

ranging from Ancient Greece to Hindu north India since 1600 and Modern Britain. Similarly the scale of analysis varies from the relatively small community of seventeenth- and eighteenth-century Hamburg to a consideration of the iconographical evidence of tombs throughout Europe around 1800.

Collectively the essays point to the fundamental need for scholars to be more clear about the assumptions which underlie many of the recent attempts to study the history of attitudes to death. If Ariès is wrong and it is neither more difficult nor more painful to die today than it was some two hundred years ago, if other societies appear to have experienced changes similar to those pinpointed by Ariès in Europe, then many of the questions he has asked will have to be reconsidered. Fundamental to this revision will be the distinction between grief and the expression of grief. That men are more or less sad when faced with death is not something which historians can hope to measure. But the ways in which it is generally permissible for men to express grief are both constantly changing and linked to some of the most important characteristics of any human society.

I

To Die and Enter the House of Hades: Homer, Before and After*

CHRISTIANE SOURVINOU-INWOOD

Access to ancient Greek society is severely limited by the quantity and nature of our sources. So the study of early Greek attitudes towards death presents even greater difficulties than is normally the case in the history of collective representations; and it is necessary to use as many types of evidence and methodological tools as possible.

The collapse of the Mycenaean palatial societies, and the disintegration of the sophisticated Mycenaean civilization in the later twelfth century B.C. ushered in the Greek Dark Ages,[1] a period of impoverishment and depopulation in which writing and many craft skills were lost. In its early part there was insecurity, desertion of sites and population movements. Later there was peace, but also relative isolation from the outside world. People lived in villages—each probably ruled by an aristocratic leader and his family—separated by large unpopulated areas. Signs of recovery first appear in the late tenth century, but it was in the early eighth century B.C. that the changes took place which led to the emergence of the historical Greek civilization. A population explosion[2] resulted in an increase in the number and size of settlements. In some cases several small communities would merge into one larger settlement.[3] This demographic revolution created new problems and potentials. The vehicle through which the Greeks dealt with these and other developments was a new political and settlement unit, the city-state. Almost certainly, the city-state first emerged in the eighth century, though on the coast of Asia Minor urbanization had begun earlier. Other major eighth-century phenomena are the expansion of communications within Greece and overseas, and the colonization of non-Greek lands, all of

---

* All the translations are my own. According to the convention I have adopted here the Greek Dark Ages come to an end at *c.* 800 B.C.

[1] On the Greek Dark Ages, the eighth century B.C. and the Archaic period (*c.* 700 B.C. to *c.* 480 B.C.) see the following: A. M. Snodgrass, *The Dark Age of Greece* (Edinburgh 1971); ibid., *Archaic Greece. The Age of Experiment* (London, Melbourne, Toronto 1980); ibid., *Archaeology and the Rise of the Greek State* (Cambridge 1977); V. R. d'A. Desborough. *The Greek Dark Ages* (London 1972); J. N. Coldstream, *Geometric Greece* (London 1977); W. G. Forrest, *The Emergence of Greek Democracy* (London 1966); O. Murray, *Early Greece* (Fontana, 1980).

[2] Snodgrass, *Rise* 10–8; ibid., *Archaic Greece* 19–25.

[3] Cf. Snodgrass, *Rise* 15

which drastically expanded Greek physical and mental horizons. Another major development was the reintroduction of writing at around 750; the script, this time, is alphabetic, and was borrowed and adapted from the Phoenicians. More extensive and intensive agriculture and advances in the crafts, especially metallurgy, contributed to increased prosperity. After centuries of independent local developments and diversification, the Panhellenic inter-state sanctuaries like Delphi and Olympia become agents of a Panhellenic mentality, especially in the sphere of religion, as do the Homeric epics. The *Iliad* and the *Odyssey* were given their final form, and probably written down, in the eighth century in Ionia, and from there they spread all over the Greek world. They are the end-product of a long tradition of oral poetry which began in the Late Mycenaean or Early Dark Age period. 'Homer' is the eighth-century bard—or, possibly, bards, one for each poem—who composed the final version of the two epics.[4] The heroic deeds and wars described in the poems were believed to have taken place in the Mycenaean period; in fact the 'Homeric world', the material culture, the customs and institutions of the epics, has no counterpart in any real historical society; it is an artificial conflation of elements which had belonged to different historical societies and were combined to create this stratified picture over the centuries during which the epic material was expanded, compressed and modified by the generations of bards who handled and transmitted it.[5] This means that the collective attitudes towards death contained in the epics may also be not those of any given historical society, but an amalgam of attitudes which had characterized successive societies. And in one way this is correct. However, collective representations change slowly, and even when they do, stratifications take place, so that old attitudes survive alongside new ones.[6] And so it appears that the stratified Homeric nexus of death-related attitudes corresponds to the actual nexus of attitudes of the eighth century, when collective representations which had been static for centuries begin to show signs of movement. In Homer there is one dominant model of attitudes towards death, firmly rooted in the epic, and then signs of a tentative beginning of a partial movement away from it. The dominant model is the 'familiar' or 'traditional' type of attitude towards

---

[4] The bibliography on Homer is immense. For a general introduction and survey see J. B. Hainsworth, *Homer* (*Greece and Rome:* New Surveys in the Classics no. 3, Oxford 1969); see also: G. S. Kirk, *Homer and the Epic* (Cambridge 1965); ibid., *Homer and the Oral Tradition* (Cambridge 1976).

[5] D. H. F. Gray, 'Homeric epithets for things', *Classical Quarterly* 61 (1947), 109–21; ibid., 'Metal-Working in Homer', *Journal of Hellenic Studies* 74 (1954), 1–15; A. M. Snodgrass, 'An Historical Homeric Society?', *JHS* 94 (1974), 114–25.

In common with the overwhelming majority of scholars I consider the 24th book of the Odyssey a later addition, and so I will be excluding it from the discussion.

[6] See M. Vovelle, *Mourir autrefois. Attitudes collectives devant la mort au xviie et xviiie siècles* (Paris 1974) p. 10; ibid., 'Les attitudes devant la mort, front actuel de l'histoire des mentalités', *Archives de sciences sociales des religions* 39 (1975), 23; Ph. Ariès, *Western Attitudes toward Death from the Middle Ages to the Present* (Baltimore 1974) pp. 1–2.

16

death, a version of the 'Tamed Death' attitude analysed by Ariès.[7] In this model death is accepted as an inescapable evil, part of the life-cycle of the world,[8] and of the community, in which the generations succeed each other, and the continuity of the community is contrasted with the discontinuity of the individual. Death is familiar, hateful rather than frightening. There is no death-avoidance, either in the sense of avoiding contact with death and the dead, or in that of excessive concern with avoiding one's death. The new stirrings by contrast, some of which are also reflected in the eighth century archaeological evidence, are the first beginnings of a series of developments which will gain momentum in the succeeding, archaic period (c. 700–c. 480) during which we can detect a (partial) shift away from familiar acceptance, towards a more individual, and anxious approach towards one's own death—broadly comparable to the change which occurred in the late Middle Ages in Europe.[9] The changing demographic, socio-economic, political and intellectual realities of eighth-century Greece, in interaction with each other, affected the existing system of funerary behaviour, attitudes towards death, and after-life beliefs; they initiated a process of change, feedback and interaction within the interlocking parts of the funerary system (multiplier effect), and continued to fuel it through the following period, thanks to the continuing socio-economic and political fluidity and unrest of the archaic age, but also to its intellectual developments, themselves connected with these historical circumstances, and some also interacting with the funerary system: the first known emergence of European individualism,[10] the birth of modern philosophy, astronomy, geography, mathematics, the flowering of a distinctive art and literature.[11]

This paper concentrates on the Dark Age and eighth-century attitudes. Space allows me only to signal the changes that followed. My investigation centres on the Homeric poems which provide the richest material. But two other sources offer both information and a control for the Homeric picture:

[7] Op. cit. 2–25; *L'Homme devant la mort* (Paris 1977) pp. 13–96, 99–287 *passim*, 596–9; see also ibid., 'Les grandes étapes et le sens de l'évolution de nos attitudes devant la mort', *Arch. sc. soc. des rel.* 39 (1975), 7–10.

[8] On the cycle of life and death in Homer see also, briefly, E. Vermeule, *Aspects of Death in Early Greek Art and Poetry* (Berkeley, Los Angeles, London 1979) p. 119.

[9] See Ariès, *Western Attitudes*, pp. 27–52; ibid., *L'Homme*, pp. 99–288; ibid. *Arch. sc. soc. des rel.* op. cit. 10–1.

[10] This is at present a matter of controversy among classicists, for the old view that individualism had emerged in the archaic period has been challenged. However, it seems to me that the challenge depends entirely on a too narrow definition of the concept of individualism, on which see S. Lukes, *Individualism* (Oxford 1973) esp. pp. 40–122. In fact, the emergence of individualism in archaic Greece is, I think, in many respects comparable to that in the Late Middle Ages (see C. Morris, *The Discovery of the Individual 1050–1200* (London 1972)), with the one big difference that the archaic Greeks did not have the advantage of an earlier tradition of individualism on which to draw in order to help them express this new reality, as the Western Europeans did (cf. Morris *passim*). On the 'rise of the individual' in the archaic period see most recently Snodgrass, *Archaic Greece* pp. 160–200.

[11] Snodgrass op. cit.

archaeological evidence for burial practices, and the poems of Hesiod. Hesiod wrote his *Theogony* and *Works and Days* at around 700, a little later than the date of the Homeric composition. His viewpoint is that of the peasant, the common man, while Homer desribes the aristocratic ethos.[12] But the attitudes towards death reflected in each (where they can be compared) are the same, except that in Hesiod we find a slightly more developed version of some elements reflecting the incipient movement away from the traditional model.

I will begin with the early Greek perception of death which, like the after-life beliefs which will follow, expresses and at the same time affects the collective attitudes towards death. Death is first of all a separation. When it comes, the *psyche* (soul or shade) leaves the body and flies away; eventually it will enter Hades, the Land of the Dead. Another component, the *thymos,* primarily the seat of the emotions, also leaves the body, never to be heard of again; presumably its existence is tied up with life, and so eventually it dies. What remains is a decomposing corpse whose sinews have ceased to hold flesh and bones together.[13] It is simply senseless matter which will rot unless cremated.[14] The process of decomposition attracts no interest. The shade enters the 'house of Hades' only after his remains have been buried.

The Homeric 'system' of after-life beliefs, like the other Homeric 'systems', is conflated and artificial: a composite eschatology made up of elements which had originated in different historical societies; these were perceived, and channelled through, the viewpoint of the poet's own funerary ideology and religious/mythological mentality which provided the matrices for both the understanding, and the reshaping and elaboration, of the traditional material which Homer deployed. The divergences between the different strands of beliefs are particularly marked in the matter of the nature of the shades residing in Hades. These range from witless senseless ghosts to lively shades whose activities and disputes require the services of a judge.[15] But some beliefs are constant throughout the poems, and others constant but for a few, thinly scattered new elements, and the beliefs which are most significant from the point of view of social attitudes towards death belong to these two categories. These attitudes are apparently unaffected by the variations in the nature of the shades. Clearly, an eternity as a witless senseless ghost was not, to an early Greek, a more frightening prospect, likely to generate more anxiety, than an eternity as a lively shade. After all, the former belief is a way of visualizing and articulating the notions 'cessation of life' and 'continuing survival' in a peaceful image of the unseeable existence after death akin to 'they are sleeping'.

[12] Forrest p. 62; Murray p. 40.
[13] *Odyssey* 11. 217–22; see also J. Bremmer, *The Early Greek Conception of the Soul* (published doctoral thesis, Univ. of Amsterdam, 1979) pp. 68–71.
[14] *Iliad* 24. 50–4.
[15] see the eleventh book of the *Odyssey*, which describes Odysseus' visit to Hades—accomplished with the help of the sorceress Circe.

Sleep, *Hypnos,* is the twin brother of Death, *Thanatos,* who is a personification rather than an agent of death.[16] But, Hesiod tells us, while Sleep walks peacefully and is kind to men, Thanatos has an iron heart and a bronze spirit, and never releases his victim; he is abhorrent even to the immortal gods. This description is consistent with the Homeric adjectives of death: black, hateful, bringing bitter grief and long woe. Sleep may appear to us a natural metaphor for death, but Homer only uses it once (*Iliad* 11. 241), while in Hesiod dying as though overcome by sleep is a blessing belonging to the utopian golden race of the past (*Works and Days* 116). So the event of death is perceived in terms of hostility, with almost no peaceful connotations.

In Hesiod, Death and Sleep are brothers to black Ker, a vaguely defined personification, a death-demon whose name in Homer is normally a common noun meaning 'doom', 'fate of death'.[17] Ker is female, and a more frightening figure than Thanatos. Women in Greek mentality are represented as dangerous, evil-bringing and alien:[18] this mentality, in a polarized mythological version, lies behind the figure of Ker (or sometimes Keres in the plural), and also behind the image of the dangerous part-human death-bringing female monsters who seduce to death, as the Sirens do in Homer through their song.[19] These images fuse two fundamental male anxieties, the fear and abhorrence of death and the fear of the alien female nature.

There are also two death-bringing gods, Apollo and Artemis, but this is a reassuring rather than a frightening image. Death, especially sudden death, threatens society's defences against chaos and anomic terror.[20] The early Greek collective representations explained and articulated sudden death in terms of an intelligible and familiar mechanism, divine action: a woman who dies suddenly has been shot by the archer goddess Artemis, a man by Apollo the archer god.[21] This representation contains the threat and the terror, and also allows people to cope with them on the basis of the familiar pattern of behaviour and relationships between men and gods. Usually,

[16] See Homer, *Iliad* 16. 671–3; Hesiod, *Theogony* 211–2, 758–66; see also Vermeule 37–41.
[17] *Theogony,* 211–12; see also Hesiod, *Theogony,* ed. by M. L. West (Oxford 1966) 227; for the Homeric evidence for Ker see Vermeule pp. 39–41; 220, n.68.
[18] See Hesiod, *Works and Days* 54–105; *Theogony* 570–612; see also N. Loraux, 'Origines des hommes' (*Dictionnaire des mythologies,* Flammarion) pp. 6–8: N. Loraux and L. Kahn, 'Mort. Les mythes grecques' (*Dictionnaire des mythologies*) pp. 7–8.
[19] *Odyssey* 12. 39–46; Loraux and Kahn op. cit.; see also my few remarks in Classical Quarterly 29 (1979), 245.
[20] See P. Berger and T. Luckmann, *The Social Construction of Reality* (Penguin, 1971; orig.: 1966) p. 121; Ariès, *L'Homme* pp. 597–8; R. Huntington and P. Metcalf, *Celebrations of Death. The Anthropology of Mortuary Ritual* (Cambridge, London, New York, Melbourne 1979) (hereafter: *Celebrations*) p. 23.
[21] Artemis: *Odyssey* 11. 171–3, 197–203; *Iliad* 21. 483–4; the mythological paradigm (Ariadne): *Odyssey* 11. 324–5. Apollo: *Iliad* 24. 757; *Odyssey* 3. 279–81; 17. 251–2, 494; 7. 63–5; the mythological paradigm (Eurytus): *Odyssey* 8.226–8. Apollo and Artemis together, he killing the males, she the females: mythological paradigm: the punishment of Niobe through the slaughter of her children: *Iliad* 24. 605–6.

sudden death at the hands of Apollo or Artemis also involves the connotation 'premature death', and it is this aspect which is objectionable—apart from the mere fact of death itself. But the manner of this death is desirable: on the partly-utopic island of Syria, where there is no famine or illness, when people get old they are shot by Apollo and Artemis (*Odyssey* 15. 403–11). The mythological paradigms make clear that premature sudden death is perceived as a divine punishment. This contains the terror by making the event intelligible and 'justifiable'. Also, it provides a means of defence when the community is hit by a series of 'sudden' deaths as in a pestilence, when death spreads quickly and threatens the community's very survival. In *Iliad* 1. 9–10, 43–52 Apollo devastates the Greek camp, shooting mules, dogs and men until the Greeks take measures to discover the cause of his anger and placate it. So this mythological representation of death reflects, and is an organic part of, an efficient system of symbolic defences which keeps the terror of death at bay, and so shores up the traditional model of familiar acceptance.

'All men must die' is a constant motif in the epics. The disguised Athena tells Telemachus (*Odyssey,* 3. 236–8) that 'death is common to all men, and not even the gods can keep it off a man they love, when the portion of death which brings long woe destroys him'. Everybody dies and goes to Hades, even the children of the gods, even the great Heracles. This is a central tenet of mainstream Homeric eschatology in all its strands. However, there is a very thin, recent layer of belief, not integrated within the remaining funerary ideology, according to which a few selected people connected with the gods escape death and gain some sort of immortality. Menelaus, who as Helen's husband is Zeus' son-in-law, will go to a paradise with ideal weather, the Elysian fields at the ends of the earth. The Dioscuri, Helen's brothers, were given a kind of eternal life on alternating days. These[22] are the first signs of a challenge to the inescapable fate of death which in the following (archaic) period will grow and develop into an important new eschatological strand that will provide the common man with a model of hope for a better life after death. Already in Hesiod the theme of paradise is developed further. Part of the 'heroic' race which included the Homeric heroes went to the paradise of the Islands of the Blessed, where the earth produces crops three times a year (*Works and Days* 157–69).

We know that the shades fly to Hades, though nothing is said about the details of the journey, and that they reach it alone, without the help of a divine psychopompic figure. A river forms the frontier between Hades and the world of the living, and a shade is not allowed to cross before his corpse is buried. Once in Hades, the shades cannot cross the river again and return to the upper world. The definite division between the two worlds and

---

[22] Menelaus: *Odyssey* 4. 561–5; Dioscuri: *Odyssey* 11. 300–4. A third case, Calypso's promise of immortality to Odysseus is mentioned in a part of the *Odyssey* (23. 333–6) which is almost certainly post-Homeric.

controlled communication between them is also expressed through the image of the gates which are firmly attached to the Land of the Dead and to Hades its ruler-god.[23] More specifically, in Homer and Hesiod the gates symbolize the fact that nobody is allowed to leave Hades. Cerberus, the god Hades' dog, articulates the same idea. According to Hesiod (*Theogony* 767–73), the beast is friendly to those who enter Hades, but devours anybody trying to get out through the gate. This definite, naturally articulated division between the realms of the living and of the dead is a manifestation of an ordered and structured universe in which there are proper boundaries between life and death and the passage from one to the other is governed by fixed and strict rules which are an important part of the cosmic order.

Hades (the place) is characterized by murky darkness and lack of sun; it is joyless, terrible and dank, and even the gods hate it. This representation depends clearly on a definition of life in terms of light and sun, so that death is their absence; but it has other dimensions: the darkness inside the earth, projected from the experience of caves, and the unseeability of death. The mental attitude behind the representation is love of life.

Hades the god is not sharply characterized, as befits the god who rules over the unseeable.[24] He is hateful, the king of those beneath the earth, implacable, inflexible—the last two epithets expressing once more the inescapability of death. In *Iliad* 15. 187–93 the three brothers Zeus, Poseidon and Hades divide the world between them: Zeus got the sky and the air and the clouds, Poseidon the sea, Hades 'the murky darkness'; Olympus, the dwelling place of the gods, and the earth are common to all three. In ascribing to Hades equal jurisdiction over the earth, the life-space of men, this mythological articulation of the cosmic order reveals that same mentality about death which permeates the epics, in which death is seen as part of the life-cycle, an inescapable part of life. Hades' wife, the Queen of the dead, is Persephone, daughter of Zeus and Demeter the goddess responsible for agriculture. Persephone's usual epithet in Homer and Hesiod is 'awesome'; only once is she 'pure' and once 'noble'. The early Greek mentality saw connections between death on the one hand and the fertility of the earth and agriculture on the other, and expressed them through Persephone's close association with Demeter and the myth of her Rape by Hades. Hades himself is connected with agriculture in cult.[25] The association between death and the fertility of the earth is dependent on a mentality in which death is per-

[23] *Iliad* 6. 367; 8. 367; 13. 415; 5. 646; 23. 71; *Odyssey* 11. 277; 14. 156; Hesiod, *Theogony* 773; cf. West op. cit. 365.
[24] Hades' very name may be connected with the concept of the unseeable. On Hades see W. Burkert, *Griechische Religion der archaischen und klassischen Epoche* (Stuttgart, Berlin, Cologne, Mainz, 1977) p. 302 with bibliography. This, incidentally, is probably the best book on Greek religion ever written.
[25] See Hesiod, *Works and Days* 465. These elements in Hades' personality will be developed further in the following periods, when the 'hopeful' elements of death increase dramatically (see below).

ceived as an inseparable part of the life-cycle of men, animals and plants, and as such is accepted as a natural, inescapable event, part of the cosmic order.

Another facet of this 'traditional' attitude towards death is the collective destiny of the shades. There is no individual destiny for individual shades, no rewards or punishments for morally or otherwise reprehensible behaviour. It is only in the following period that we first encounter the concept of individual destiny and salvation; this is a fundamental eschatological change, one of the symptoms of the shift in attitudes which took place in the archaic period.[26] But the germs of this development can be found in Homer. They are not integrated in the eschatological survey of the 11th book of the *Odyssey*, but are casually mentioned in the oath which invokes as witnesses—among others—the Erinyes who punish under the earth dead men who have sworn a false oath.[27] The Erinyes in Homer appear as upholders of justice and order, which was endangered by forswearing—the oath played an important part in early Greek life. Probably, it was when life and social transactions became more complex and precarious, in the expanding communities and universe of the eighth century, that the oath acquired this eschatological underpinning in the context of a funerary ideology in which the inescapable collective destiny in Hades was under pressure.

The only people who are punished in the Homeric Hades are the three 'cosmic sinners' who offended against the gods and the cosmic order, Sisyphus, Tantalus and Tityus. Their punishment had originally taken place in some other cosmic and timeless setting and was then transferred to Hades, probably by Homer himself. Sisyphus was punished for trying to cheat death—according to later sources; Homer gives no reasons for the punishment.

There is no fear of ghosts in Homer or Hesiod. The Homeric heroes ill-treat their enemies' corpses without fear of ghostly revenge, even before the shades have entered Hades for ever. The dead are not regarded as malevolent or vengeful—whether or not they were capable of harming the living. They are 'the wasted ones', or 'the outworn ones', the 'feeble heads of the dead', not frightening alien creatures with strange powers, but diminished versions of men.

The Greek language offers a dramatic illustration of early Greek attitudes towards death: the words used to express the concept 'men', 'mankind', mean 'mortals', (*brotoi, thnetoi anthropoi*), while the gods are 'the immortals'. It is mortality that characterizes mankind. This is sad but inescapable, part of the cosmic order. In the words of a Homeric hero (*Iliad* 6. 145-9):

> Why do you ask about my lineage, great-hearted son of Tydeus? The generations of men are like the generations of leaves. The wind scatters some of the leaves

[26] For a similar development in the Late Middle Ages see H. de Lubac, *Corpus Mysticum* (Paris 1949) p. 322; Morris (n.10) pp. 144-52; Ariès, *L'Homme,* pp. 149-54.
[27] *Iliad* 3. 276-80; 19. 259-60. For the Erinyes in Homer cf. H. Lloyd-Jones, *The Justice of Zeus* (Berkeley, Los Angeles, London 1971) p. 75.

down on to the earth, but when spring comes the luxuriant forest produces other leaves; so it is with the generations of men, one grows, the other comes to an end.

This is a striking acceptance of the discontinuity of the individual set against the continuity of the species which gives it some meaning; it is a perspective of the inevitable cycle of self-renewing life, birth and death, death and birth, in which the individual death is but an episode in the history of mankind and of society.

Another Homeric concept expressing the same attitude is that of one's 'lot' or 'portion' of death, *moira thanatoio*: *moira* means first of all 'portion' and then also 'fate'. This concept of 'portion of death' which becomes 'fate of death' is firmly rooted in the epics; behind it lies the idea that death *is* the lot of man, and that each death is less a personal tragedy—sad though it is—than the fulfilment of that fate. The mentality behind this whole nexus is one which sees the world as an ordered and articulated cosmos, in which everything has an apportioned place, and each person has a portion of life, after which he gets his lot of death, and this is how the life-cycle of the universe works. An extension of this concept of portion of death is the idea of a preapportioned day of death: one won't die before that day comes, but must die when it does. This may be no more than an *ad hoc* defence mechanism against the pressures and fears of war, rather than an articulated belief. But in a few cases we do find explicitly expressed the belief that man's lot and/or his day of death is preapportioned, and also its mythological equivalent, the image of the Fate spinning one's destiny when one is born.[28] This does not mean grim predetermination. When the notion of preapportioned death is actually articulated, there is a large element of choice, and the time-spans involved are apparently flexible (cf. below). The notion of the preassigned lot of life and death seems to be one of the mental hypotheses into which the concept of portion of life and death was developed in the early Greek representations, a hypothesis neither precisely articulated nor firmly asserted, just a possibility, lightly sketched.

The acceptance of one's mortality in the framework of this traditional model of attitudes towards death has implications for one's conduct in life. Homer offers two complementary views. The first, implicit throughout the *Iliad,* is explicitly articulated by Sarpedon, who is urging Glaucus to fight bravely in the front line as is their duty as kings (*Iliad* 12. 322–8):

> If it were the case that once we escaped from this battle we would live for ever, ageless and immortal, I would not be fighting in the front line, nor would I send you into the glory-giving battle. But now innumerable fates of death lie in wait for us anyway, and no man can escape them. So let us go, and either we will give some man the glory he prays for, or some man will give it to us.

[28] Preapportioned day of death: *Iliad* 7. 44–52; *Odyssey* 5. 113–15. See also below on Achilles, for preapportioned fate. The image of Zeus' scales which articulates visually the notion of portion of life and death: *Iliad* 22. 209–14. The Fate spinning one's destiny: *Iliad* 20. 127–8; 24. 209–12; *Odyssey* 7. 192–8.

Acceptance of one's mortality and vulnerability in the face of this familiar ever-present death led to a matter-of-fact acceptance of the prospect of one's death and the rejection of death-avoidance as a determining factor in one's behaviour. The early Greek love of life did not involve obsession with life-prolongation: the prospect of dying now rather than later does not deter men from pursuing honour in battle. This is another manifestation of the traditional, familiar model of attitudes towards death. Sarpedon expressed the ethos of the aristocratic warrior-champions. In *Odyssey* 18. 130–42 contemplation of man's condition suggests a course of conduct which puts other attitudes and choices in a larger context:

> Man is the most feeble of the creatures of the earth. For as long as the gods give him prosperity, and his limbs have power to move, he never thinks of bad times; but when the gods send misfortunes, he is compelled to bear them with an enduring heart ... So, men must not be lawless, but they must accept in silence whatever presents the gods may send.

Men's total vulnerability and dependence on the gods is pushed to the back of their minds—as a defence against anomic terror; but the real guarantee and defence against the chaos of the helpless human condition is the divine order and justice, which men must therefore respect above all else. This divine order and justice is, at least partly, ethical here. The acceptance and respect for its cosmic order aspect is deeply ingrained in Greek mentality in all periods; but the perception of the cosmic order changes; in our period it still includes the inescapable fate of death leading to a collective after-life in Hades. And this acceptance explains Sarpedon's attitude and, generally, the matter-of-fact acceptance of the prospect of one's death.

Achilles, son of a goddess, had a choice between two destinies (*Iliad* 9. 410ff.) if he stayed and fought at Troy, he would die, but win imperishable glory; if he went home, he would have a long life, but lose the glory. Eventually, he chooses to fight and is killed.[29] Later (*Odyssey* 11. 465ff.), Odysseus, while visiting Hades, meets Achilles' shade, who states that he would prefer to be alive, even as the servant of a poor man, than to rule among the dead. This does not mean that Achilles is meant to be regretting his earlier choice; or that another poet—or the same one—is expressing a different view. For the premise of Achilles' decision was that eventually we all have to die. Homer is simply making him express here the early Greek love of life through this image: any life is preferable to death, a wretched servant alive is better off than the king of the dead. This deeply-felt love of life accompanies the traditional acceptance of the familiar death, here, as in other societies.[30]

The attitudes towards the death of the (important) other display the same acceptance. That death may cause deep grief, but is accepted as a blow from which one will have to recover so that life can go on. The notion of grief as

---

[29] For an analysis of Achilles' motivation see Lloyd-Jones pp. 21–2.
[30] Ariès, *L'Homme* pp. 22–3.

a (lasting) sentimental loss or a separation from an irreplaceable beloved being is not much in evidence in the epics. The emphasis is usually more on the social persona of the deceased, and the disadvantages which the bereaved will suffer as a result of the death.[31] Achilles' grief for Patroclus may have an element of sentimental loss, but it is mixed with guilt (cf.n.29). Anyway, Apollo's divine judgement is that it is excessive (*Iliad* 24. 46–9). However, Laertes has not recovered from the loss of his wife (*Odyssey* 15. 353–9): he has aged prematurely and is praying for death. And it was grief for the (presumed) death of their son that had killed her. This inability to adapt to a loss and resume normal life described here as plausible conduct indicates the emergence of an attitude in which acceptance of death is receding slightly, and the loss of the (important) other is harder to bear.

The mentality which perceives death as the inescapable fate of man, and each individual death as a moment in the history of mankind in general and the community in particular, belongs to the small stable organic societies of the Dark Ages, in which every individual had his role, and was important for the community's survival. So the other side of this traditional death-attitude is that each death was a blow for the community which therefore adopted a ritual behaviour that allowed its members to externalize this trauma, cope with it, and eventually exorcize it so that normal life could be resumed. I will now consider this ritual behaviour, both to show how they achieved these aims, and because this behaviour, properly decoded, will reveal that society's collective representations and attitudes towards death,[32] and so enlarge, and serve as a control for the conclusions reached so far.[33]

First, briefly, the process of dying. The dying man, who knows he is dying, addresses a few last words to the living. In battle these include a request for proper burial.[34] When the death occurs at home the farewell is peaceful and accompanied by physical contact.[35] These actions are a concrete and comforting expression of the continuity of life, the community and the family, which alone can make sense of the discontinuity of the individual.[36] They are a comfort to the survivors and to the dying (cf.n.35). In the same spirit, when someone has expired there are proper gestures to be performed, which also express symbolically that death has taken place: the corpse's

---

[31] See *Iliad* 6. 407ff.; 22. 477ff.; 5. 156–8; 13. 656–9; 9. 632–6.

[32] See M. Wilson, 'Nyakyusa Ritual and Symbolism' in J. Middleton (ed.), *Myth and Cosmos* (New York 1967) p. 166; L.-V. Thomas, 'Mort et langage en Occident', *Arch. sc. soc. des rel.* 39 (1975), 46, 49.

[33] The analysis is based on the Homeric evidence, checked, when possible, against Hesiod and the archaeological remains. We are only concerned with the basic structure and component elements of the death-ritual. Grave-types, the scale of offerings etc. are not relevant here, so their conflated nature in Homer does not affect the argument. Elements of conflation do appear in the death-ritual, and are themselves informative (see, for example, below on the expression of grief by the non-bereaved); but the main structure and basic ritual behaviour remain fairly constant and, when a control is possible, tally with the archaeological record.

[34] *Iliad* 16. 492–501, 843–54; 22. 337–43.

[35] *Iliad* 24. 742–5.

[36] See Ariès, *L'Homme*, pp. 21–6.

eyelids and mouth must be closed.[37] Then the death-ritual proper begins. Space prevents me from giving a detailed analysis of its elements and their interpretation on the basis of the function and significance which they have within the overall system of values and collective representations of early Greek society. I can only summarize the ritual behaviour and the results of my analysis.

The system of values underlying and articulating this death-ritual, expressed through axes of binary oppositions, is that which characterizes ancient Greek mentality in general:[38]

> Disorder — Order (a concept of fundamental
> importance in ancient Greek mentality)
> Female — Male
> Pollution — Purity
> Nature — Society/Culture
> Death — Life
> Separation — Integration

On to which is integrated the pair:

> Mourning — Burial

We can summarize and decode the early Greek death-ritual as follows:

1. After the death: Separation	Corpse: Separation from 'whole' person, and from life and community: it is washed, anointed, clothed.[39]	Mourners: Separation from 'whole' person of deceased, and from life, order and normality. Wailing. Death taken on: self-defilement (men), self-wounding (women): self-aggression: release of sorrow and anger, externalization of grief and pollution; partial identification with deceased.[40] Ritual weight carried chiefly by women.[41]	Values and Attitudes expressed: Separation Grief Trauma Pollution Disorder Death	Ritual Behaviour: Acceptance of/embracing death; playing up of its symbolic attributes.

[37] *Odyssey* 11. 424–6; *Iliad* 11. 451–3.
[38] For some of these binary oppositions see my *Theseus as son and stepson* (London 1979), pp. 9–10.
[39] *Iliad* 7. 421–36; 18. 213ff.; 24. 580–90; cf. *Iliad*. 16. 679–80. For a description of the whole death-ritual in Homer see M. Andronikos, *Totenkult, Archaeologia Homerica* vol. iii. ch. W, separately published (Göttingen 1968) pp. 1–37. For a discussion of weeping, mourning and lament see K. Meuli, *Gesammelte Schriften* (Basle-Stuttgart 1975), pp. 333–8.
[40] *Iliad* 24. 710ff.; 19. 282ff.; 18. 22–31; 22. 405ff.; 24. 160ff.; *Odyssey* 8. 523–30.
[41] See n. 40. Also, when mourning is mentioned, it is always women who are referred to as mourners: *Odyssey* 3. 260–1; *Iliad* 11. 394–5; 22. 82–9; 18. 339–40; when burial is mentioned the reference is to men: see *Iliad* 16. 674–5; in *Iliad* 24. 793–6 it is the men who collect Hector's bones from the pyre and bury them.

	Corpse:	Mourners:	Values and Attitudes:	Ritual Behaviour:
2. *Prothesis* (= Layout of the corpse): looking at the corpse: transition, adjustment; temporary suspension in a state of abnormality (disorder, pollution, grief, death).	(a) decomposing matter: symbol of corruption and death; (b) metonymic sign for the deceased. Corpse the focus of the ritual. *Shade:* Betwixt and between: between Hades and the upper world.[42]	(a) Lament; (b) Community visits to look at, and pay respects to corpse. (a) Lament: kinswomen and male professional singers; = i. emotional release, ii. articulation of the social persona of deceased (through praise, expressions of sorrow) prior to its severance. (b) i. articulation of social persona, ii. death observed. (c) Chief mourner has physical contact with the corpse; i. emotional, ii. contact with death and corruption. Men and women carry the ritual weight.[43]	A. Disorder Pollution Grief Death B. But: i. Formal patterning of ritual acts: element of Order. ii. Articulation of relationships between deceased and survivors: element of Order.	Acceptance of death, but in formalized and contained form. Death's encroachment on the community is articulated and ordered as a preliminary to severance.
3. The burial ceremony: Reintegration. Leads to the reinstatement of order and normality. Itself tripartite:		Men carry the main ritual weight.	Separation from death Order Community-ties/Group solidarity Life Vitality	Rejection of death and disorder. Reinstatement of order. Assertion of life. Play-up of group-ties and of the continuity of the community.
i. *Ekphora* (= burial procession): separation.	*Corpse/Shade:* Separation from house/community.	Procession goes through life-space of community, at daytime: death obtrudes in, and disrupts, life. Separation from deceased: mourners cut their hair and give it to deceased.[44]		

[42] Corpse: see *Iliad* 24. 50-4; *Odyssey* 11. 218-22. Shade: see *Iliad* 23. 64ff.

[43] *Iliad* 24. 720ff.; 18. 314ff., 354ff.; cf. *Iliad* 24. 35-7. On lament see M. Alexiou, *The Ritual Lament in Greek Tradition* (Cambridge 1974), pp. 12-4; pp. 102-3.

[44] *Iliad* 23. 131ff.; 24. 785ff.

27

	Corpse/Shade:	Mourners:
ii. Cremation and/or rites at the grave	in liminal burial place. In cremation: corpse in liminal state: transformation to bones	Apparently only close kin group involved. Libations, offerings of food and drink, lament.[45]
iii. Burial (of bones or corpse): reintegration	Corpse (body or bones): enclosed in grave with grave-offerings, which: articulation of social persona of dead.[46] Corpse incorporated into the earth. Shade incorporated into Hades.	Mourners: Wider group participates. Libations. Funeral meal/banquet at the grave or at home after the burial:[47] Reintegration of the kin group and of the community. Exceptionally Funeral Games:[48] Reintegration of the group.

This then is a well-orchestrated ritual of high intensity. For weeping and lamenting and self-aggression are not, of course, a spontaneous show of emotion, but a regulated symbol into which emotions of grief and sorrow are channelled when these are felt, or through which they are created when not, and in any case are amplified, as part of a release-mechanism which leads to adjustment.[49] A society may overplay or underplay the externalization of grief: the range of acceptable and/or prescriptive emotions at the death-ritual varies widely from society to society, depending on its circumstances and system of values and on the collective attitudes to death behind the ritual. The heightened tone of this ritual is possible because in these communities

---

[45] *Iliad* 23. 155ff. For libations, offerings of food and drink and other offerings, see Andronikos, pp. 93–6; Snodgrass, *Dark Age,* p. 192; D. C. Kurtz and J. Boardman, *Greek Burial Customs* (London, 1971) pp. 58, 64–7.

[46] *Iliad* 23. 249ff.; 24. 790ff. For grave-offerings see Snodgrass, *Dark Age,* p. 150; Kurtz and Boardman, pp. 39–40, 61–4.

[47] Op. cit. The Homeric picture of the funeral banquet is conflated: different locations and positions are attested, corresponding to the customs of different periods, when the meal was held nearer or further away from the grave. Away from the grave, at home/in the life-space of the community after the burial: *Iliad* 7. 476–7; 24. 801–4. Before the mound is erected, so probably at the grave: *Iliad* 24. 664ff., and archaeological evidence: Snodgrass, *Dark Ages,* p. 379; ibid., *JHS* 1974, 124; ibid., *Archaic Greece* 35; see also J. Boardman, *JHS* 86 (1966) 2. Hesiod, *Works and Days* 735 mentions a funeral banquet without specifying its location. On the subject see also Burkert p. 297. Patroclus' funeral feast is held around the corpse during the prothesis: *Iliad* 23. 29–34; the significance of this feast is different from that of the others: it refers to the community and ties with the dead, rather than those of the reconstructed group after the burial, which in Patroclus' funeral find expression in the funeral games.

[48] Iliad 23. 257ff.; Hesiod, *Works and Days* 654–7; see also Kurtz and Boardman p. 203; K. Meuli, *Der griechische Agon* (Cologne, 1968)

[49] Cf. *Celebrations* pp. 24ff.; 30–3.

a larger group than those directly bereaved participates in it. First in the sense that society is prepared to tolerate the disruption, the encroachment of death in the community's life that this version of the death-ritual entails; and second in the sense that the emotional burden, or some of it, is shared by a larger group than just the immediate family, and this allows an emotional tone too high to bear for a small group. Homer feels that the fact that grief is assumed and expressed by people not directly affected by the death needs some comment: he tries to explain why certain people weep by supposing that they remember their own sorrows, and some other, dearer dead, and that it is for this that they really lament.[50] He is right in so far as it is true that the (socially ordained) grief and lament does focus the emotions in such a way. But the fact that he felt the need to comment on it suggests that this assumption of grief by outsiders described in the traditional epic material was already less of a routine aspect of the ritual and may even have started to recede in the eighth century, at least in Ionia, an advanced region where urbanization had begun early. In the small Dark Age villages, community life was *de facto* disrupted by each death, and each dead person had inevitably had social relationships with all the rest of the community which needed severing and consequent adjustment, so the whole community was *de facto* involved in each death-ritual. Moreover, in those years, the survival of the (vulnerable and depopulated) community was the top priority. And because the whole community shared in this heightened emotional ritual, the community ties were reinforced at a time when they were threatened by death.[51] This strengthening of the group solidarity is intensified by, and given explicit symbolic expression in the final part of the ritual, when the trauma is being overcome. This part expresses and asserts the separation from death and disorder and reinstatement of order, but also the values of group solidarity and life and vitality, both supremely important for the community's survival and both threatened by death.

This death-ritual achieves its aims by first accepting and embracing death, then adjusting to, and articulating death's encroachment on life, and finally rejecting it. This acceptance of death is of course an emotionally effective way of coping with it—when the support of a larger group is available; but it also indicates, and depends on a collective representation in which death is familiar, hateful but not really frightening, in which physical contact with a corpse is not abhorrent. And conversely, this physical and other contact with corpses and death in the ritual reinforced this attitude of familiarity,[52] as the whole ritual reinforced familiarity and acceptance by reasserting them periodically in moments of crisis—deaths. More generally, in a small stable

---

[50] *Iliad* 19. 301–2, 337–8; 24. 166–8.

[51] For a comparable situation, but concerning the kinship group, see Wilson, op. cit. (n.32) p. 164.

[52] A child taking part in an eighth-century burial procession in a scene painted on a pot: J. Boardman, *JHS* 1966, 3.

society where each generation experiences closely the death and birth of others, others with whom his life has been, or will be, closely intertwined, death becomes familiar and the concept of each individual death as part of the life-cycle of the community which lives on through the generations is a living reality. This is their experience of death. Until changes in the demographic, socio-economic and political model disturbed the balance and eventually produced a shift in these traditional attitudes. What I am suggesting is that the demographic, socio-economic and other changes which led to urbanization and the city-state, and the corresponding break-up of the small tightly-knit earlier communities, led to a loosening of the community involvement in each death. The ritual would still preserve its form, still be public, but the supportive group would now be looser and less directly involved in the death, so that the burden shifts more and more on to the immediate family—except for the aristocratic families, who could call upon people belonging to their sphere of influence to provide a new supportive framework.[53] These shifts, and the loss of the small stable framework of the familiar death, the widening horizons, the mental shake-up due to the dislocation of old structures and the creation of new ones, all these and other changes altered the old stable physical and conceptual framework which had supported the traditional and familiar attitudes towards death, and began to affect these attitudes. Hence, the first stirrings of a change in the eighth century.

The form of the reintegration rites merits a brief comment. The funeral games were held in honour of exceptional dead, aristocrats, and it was probably also other aristocrats who participated in them. So here the relevant reintegration may be that of the aristocratic group at inter-community level. The values asserted are group solidarity here expressed through competition, the competitive ethos of the Dark Age and eighth-century aristocrats, and warlike prowess, though at the end of the eighth century at least a poetry competition was included. The banquet, the communal meal, was an import-

[53] There probably was, in the Dark Ages, some differentiation between the death-ritual performed for members of the leading family, or rather, just for the community leader, and that of the rest. But in a community where each death involved the whole society, such differentiation can only have been one of scale of offerings etc. (though this, to judge from the graves, was always very modest in this period), and in the involvement of other aristocrats from outside the community. The death of a leader affects a society profoundly (see Berger and Luckmann, p. 121), and this is usually expressed symbolically in the funerary ritual of leaders and kings. But obviously, the extent to which this is the case depends on the nature of the socio-political system and the function and role of the leader within a society. The evidence for ancient Greece comes from a later period, the fifth century B.C., and concerns Sparta, where the institution of kingship had survived: Herodotus vi. 58: here there is maximum and compulsory community involvement. But the nature of the Spartan state (see below) does not allow us to extrapolate and draw conclusions about the early Greek customs concerning the death of leaders who had ruled over very much smaller and less complex communities. On the other hand, the intensity of the Trojans' grief over Hector's death may have been determined by such a dimensional distinction operating in the poet's (or successive poets') mind. For Hector, though the king's son rather than the king, was a leader, and Troy's main champion.

ant part of early Greek social life, the principal vehicle for social intercourse and the reinforcement of group solidarity.[54] What is worth noting is the complete absence of the sexual/fertility dimension from these rites. Here the assertion of life does not, as in other societies,[55] involve this particular manifestation of the life principle. On the contrary, Hesiod (*Works and Days* 735–6) says that a man should not beget children when he returns from an 'ill-omened' burial and funerary feast. So the assertion of life in the face of death in purely biological terms is inappropriate; in the banquet the biological function is mediated through the social vehicle. It was probably felt that the unmediated biological function of sex and procreation was too vulnerable in the proximity of death. For it is society that sets up the defences against the harsh biological realities of which death is the most threatening.

Given the significance and function of the death-ritual, it is natural that great importance was attached to its performance. Proper burial, mourning and lament are 'the due of the dead'.[56] And this provides the main parameter determining the concepts of good and bad death:[57] the performance of the ritual which reflects, and symbolically represents, the perception of each death as a moment in the history of the community whose continuity gives meaning to the individual discontinuity. So bad death is death away from the community and/or one's friends, a lonely and unseen death, like that at sea.[58] The elements that make up a bad death outside the community are often mentioned separately: to die away from home, or without saying goodbye, or unmourned, or unburied.[59] Burial was especially important. We saw that the shade did not enter Hades until after burial. Even if the unburied dead did eventually enter Hades after their flesh had disintegrated and only bones without identity were left, this did not compensate for a proper dispatch to the Land of the Dead. To die without the assistance of one's community, without proper rites, to lie unburied and rotting is an emotionally traumatic prospect affecting a vulnerable part of one's identity; it is also a death unmediated by society, unprotected by its defences: it is to die like a wild beast. A recurring gruesome Homeric image expresses this: one's rotting unburied corpse being eaten by dogs and birds, or, more rarely, in water, fish and eels:[60] a harsh and frightening image of death, in which nature at its most savage disposes of the body. Instead of the series 'men: culture; fire and/or constructed grave: culture; burial: culture', here we have 'animals: nature; eating raw: nature; non-burial: nature'. The Homeric

---

[54] See Murray pp. 49–50; M. I. Finley, *The World of Odysseus* (1954), pp. 144–6.

[55] See, for example, Wilson, pp. 158, 162.

[56] *Iliad* 16. 456–7, 671–5; 23. 9; *Odyssey* 4. 193–8.

[57] See also Berger and Luckmann, p. 119.

[58] See *Odyssey* 1. 236–43; 5. 306–12. See also a similar concept in Ariès' 'tamed death' model; *L'Homme*, 18ff. See also *Iliad* 21. 273–83.

[59] *Iliad* 11. 816–8; 24. 742–5; 22. 82–9; 24. 33ff.

[60] Dogs and birds: *Iliad* 11. 394–5; 15. 347–51; 2. 391–3; 1. 2–5; 22. 59–76; 11. 451–4; *Odyssey* 3. 256–61. Fish and eels: *Iliad* 21. 122ff., 201ff.

heroes constantly threatened their enemies with this fate, and sometimes at least the threat was fulfilled. As in the European Middle Ages,[61] vengeance did not stop at death. The enemies of a man killed in battle tried to drag his corpse away, strip it of its armour, mutilate and dishonour it.[62] His friends fought to save it and give it proper burial; for if it was dishonoured, they themselves were dishonoured.[63] This is a manifestation of the network of dependence and obligations between the living and the dead which sustained Greek mentality about burial for many centuries, surviving the changes in the attitudes towards death: the dead depend on the living (especially their family) for proper burial, and the living have the moral duty to provide it; failure to do so brings dishonour. When Achilles ill-treats Hector's corpse the gods, and Homer, denounce his conduct.[64] This may represent a new, more ethical attitude, a comment on the earlier behaviour described in the inherited epic material.

Another dimension of good death is good death in battle; it involves honour and glory and depends on the ethos of the Dark Age and eighth-century aristocratic warriors.[65] It is less strong than may at first appear, and the idea of 'dying for one's country', though not unknown in the epics[66] is not significantly developed. A peaceful version of good death is that prophesied for Odysseus (*Odyssey* 11. 134-7): an easy death in ripe and prosperous old age, surrounded by his people: death after a 'full portion' of life in the bosom of a happy community, and—another facet of good death, manner—a painless death. This easy death, projected into the utopian past, is presented in terms of the falling asleep image in Hesiod (cf. above p. 19). Suddenness and lack of illness also characterized death in the quasi-utopian island of Syria.[67] Death through illness is the least desirable.[68] The death of young people who have not had their full portion of life is tragic, especially if they have no sons to continue their line. But early death is not in itself a bad death; on the contrary, it can be a glorious one, like that of Achilles.

A good death which brings glory ensures man's 'survival' in memory. Memory-survival is one of the ways in which men could leave their mark on life, continue to 'exist'—other than as ghostly shades in Hades. The other

---

[61] See Ariès, *L'Homme*, pp. 50-2.

[62] *Iliad* 17. 125-7; 18. 170-80.

[63] *Iliad* 16. 492-501; 17. 91-105, 254-5; 18. 170-80.

[64] *Iliad* 24. 39ff.; cf. 24. 133-7. See also *Iliad* 17. 205-6. And a related view expressed by Odysseus: *Odyssey* 22. 412-3.

[65] Warfare then depended primarily on the aristocratic champions, whose pursuit of honour and glory provides the dominant ethos in the epics.

[66] See *Iliad* 15. 494-9; 17. 220-8; see also J. Griffin, 'Homeric pathos and objectivity', *Classical Quarterly* 26 (1976), 186-7.

[67] See above p. 20. In certain societies with comparable familiar attitudes towards death, sudden death is a very bad thing: Ariès, *L'Homme*, pp. 18-20; Vovelle, *Mourir* p. 193 (where a change to a more positive attitude towards sudden death is recorded). There are, of course, fundamental differences between early Greek and medieval eschatology, and, more generally, conception of the nature of man and the relationship between man and god.

[68] *Iliad* 13. 663-72.

was through children, or rather sons who alone were perceived as extensions of the 'self': by plugging oneself into the biological/social stream of the continuity of the generations.[69] Memory-survival, survival of one's social persona in the collective memory of the community, or, through song, of many communities, depends on excellence and is not open to all; in terms of class it is limited to the aristocracy. In *Iliad* 16. 31–2 the notion that one should act in a way that will benefit future generations is found, linked to memory-survival. In a special version of memory-survival, not firmly rooted in the poems and possibly more recent, the memory of a person is focused on, or reinforced by his grave-monument.[70] In a more complex variant (*Iliad* 7. 85–90) one's victim's grave-monument is expected to preserve one's own memory. Dark Age and eighth-century grave-markers (pots or undecorated block-like stones) gave little information about the deceased (cf. below), so the mentality here is that one's memory will survive within the (stable) community with the grave serving as a focus; not that the grave itself will preserve the memory, recording one's life and death as in archaic and classical times when graves became more individualized.[71] There is one instance of a limited individualization of the grave in the epics: Elpenor's shade (*Odyssey* 11. 71–8) asks Odysseus to bury him and fix his oar on the grave-mound: the oar (made of perishable material) gives more individualized information about the dead than just the sex of the Dark Age grave-markers known to us, and the sex and status of some eighth century ones.

The model of collective attitudes towards death proposed here gains confirmation from the archaeological evidence.[72] First I should stress that the choice between cremation and inhumation can be shown to be a matter of fashion, with no significance.[73] Since the means by which the corpse became an inarticulate skeleton, and the length of time it took were matters of indifference, it follows that no value, positive or negative, was attached to the remains once they were buried. What mattered was the burial ceremony, culminating in the 'sealing off' of these remains. The burial customs of the different regions show great diversity in the Dark Ages and the eighth century, and the evidence is patchy. But there are some common trends in the main categories of thought determining burial behaviour. One

---

[69] In *Odyssey* 11. 458–60, 492–537 Agamemnon and Achilles who are in Hades are concerned about their sons' fate and fame; Agamemnon also had daughters, but he does not enquire after them. For a comparable attitude, a man's survival through his sons, see E. E. Evans-Pritchard, *Nuer Religion* (Oxford 1956), pp. 162–3.

[70] See, for example *Iliad* 11. 371–2; *Odyssey* 11. 71–8.

[71] However, the monument is sometimes dislocated in the epics, so that it appears outside one's community: cf. *Odyssey* 4. 584.

[72] On Dark Age and eighth-century burial customs see Snodgrass, *Dark Age*, pp. 140–201; R. Hägg, *Die Gräber der Argolis in sybmykenischer, protogeometrischer und geometrischer Zeit* 1 (Uppsala, 1974); Kurtz and Boardman, pp. 31–67, 170–99 *passim*; Coldstream, op. cit. (n.1) *passim*.

[73] See Snodgrass, *Dark Age*, pp. 143–7.

such concerns the dimensional distinctions recognized in the burial practices.[74] Age is the dimension of the social persona of the deceased most significantly differentiated: the distinction between children and adults. Small children have no social persona, and hardly any social relationships outside the family—except in stratified societies where position is inherited. Hence their death affects only the close family. When the regular death-ritual is a community affair, this produces a sharp differentiation between child- and adult-burials, the former being unobtrusive and private where the latter are obtrusive and public.[75] This is the case in most Dark Age Greek communities, though the manner of differentiation varied from area to area. This differential burial is another sign of the community-participation and normality-disruption of early Greek adult burials. The well-documented case of Attica provides further confirmation for our model. Through the Dark Ages and until *c.* 760, almost all Athenian children were inhumed intramurally, sometimes under a house-floor (in the family's life-space), while adults were cremated or inhumed, depending on the fashion, and mostly buried in extramural cemeteries (where child burials are extremely rare). From *c.* 760 intramural burials of children no longer predominate over the intramural burials of adults, and children's burials in the extramural cemeteries become common.[76] Some differentiation in children's burials continues (in the type of grave, the lesser care lavished, sometimes in a differential location within the cemetery). This change seems to coincide chronologically with the appearance of the tendency, all over Greece, to incorporate single graves into groups, family-plots.[77] Both phenomena, I suggest, reflect the fact that community involvement in each death began to become looser in the eighth century and correspondingly family involvement became stronger. For aristocratic families—who could call upon others to provide a supportive framework—there were additional pressures to emphasize the family element in the death-ritual and express it symbolically in the cemeteries. These families, who came together in the context of the new city-states, had to define themselves as a 'class', and define the criteria for power-holding in the new socio-political framework. In Athens the criterion for office was membership in one of the aristocratic families or 'clans' making up the nobility (*Eupatridai*).[78] This process of definition entailed the reinforcement of the hereditary principle and the definition and assertion of membership in the family

---

[74] On dimensional distinctions see L. R. Binford, 'Mortuary Practices: Their Study and their Potential' in L. R. Binford, *Archaeological Perspective* (New York and London, 1972), pp. 225–39.

[75] See Binford, op. cit., pp. 232–4.

[76] See Snodgrass, *Dark Ages,* pp. 149–50, 198 n.4; Kurtz and Boardman, p. 55.

[77] Snodgrass, *Dark Ages,* pp. 194–5; Kurtz and Boardman, p. 56; see also J. M. Geroulanos, *Athenische Mitteilungen* 88 (1973), 1; C. K. Williams ii and J. E. Fisher, *Hesperia* 42 (1973), 2.

[78] See Forrest pp. 145–6; Murray p. 177; and on clans (*gene*) in general: S. C. Humphreys, *Anthropology and the Greeks* (London, 1978) pp. 194–7.

group; the family graves were used as a symbolic focus in the process.[79] Put more generally, it is those dimensions of the social persona which are socially significant that are given differential recognition in the burial practices of a society, so the indication of family-group affiliation in eighth-century burials suggests that this has now become important. The trend was probably set by the aristocracy and spread to other strata because of the *de facto* growing importance of the family in the funerary rituals of the new city-states. All these developments inevitably affected the perception of death as a collective phenomenon which was to come under increasing pressure as time went on. In the circumstances described, the small children of the aristocracy acquired a significant social persona as members of an aristocratic family, reflected in their burial in the main cemeteries—now a symbolic focus for aristocratic self-definition. Again the aristocracy probably set the trend for burying children in the main cemeteries, and others followed because the diminishing community involvement in funerals had altered the earlier realities and the distinctions that went with them. In the succeeding, archaic and classical periods child-burials became progressively less differentiated at the same time as community involvement in funerals progressively diminished, except probably for the aristocracy, and was eventually forbidden to all by law.

The use of monumental painted pots as grave-markers signalling status in eighth-century Athens[80] is another manifestation of the aristocratic self-definition and its symbolism. Status was also differentiated through the grave furnishings, as before, in the Dark Ages. Sex was differentiated through grave-goods, ash-urns, and apparently, at least sometimes, grave-markers.[81] This multi-faceted sex-differentiation may reflect the importance of the male-female opposition in Greek society, mentality and funerary ritual.

The last significant facet of Dark Age and eighth-century Greek burial behaviour is indifference to intramural burials, not only of children, but also of adults.[82] While in the fifth century intramural burial outside Sparta and her colony Taras is almost totally unknown (except for children and people like city-founders),[83] in the Dark Ages intramural and extramural burial are practised side by side. In the eighth century, with growing urbanization and the development of the city-state, extramural burial begins to become the norm, and this tendency is strengthened in the archaic period, when

[79] See also Snodgrass, *Dark Age,* p. 195.
[80] See Coldstream p. 137.
[81] Kurtz and Boardman, pp. 37, 53, 58.
[82] For an excellent discussion on the question of intramural and extramural burial in the Dark Ages and the eighth century: Hägg, pp. 87–91. See also: Kurtz and Boardman, pp. 70, 188–9; R. S. Young, 'Sepulturae intra urbem', *Hesperia* 20 (1951), 67–134; Snodgrass, *Dark Age* pp. 147, 150, 152, 154; Williams and Fisher, pp. 2–4; Burkert, p. 295.
[83] See R. Martin, *Recherches sur l'Agora grecque. Etude d'histoire et d'architecture urbaines* (Paris, 1951), pp. 194–201; see also C. Bérard, *Eretria. Fouilles et recherches* iii. *L'héroon à la porte de l'ouest* (Bern 1970) *passim* and esp. Chapters 5 and 6. See also L. H. Jeffery, *Archaic Greece* (London and Tonbridge, 1976), p. 65.

apparently burial within the settlement was eventually forbidden by legislation. Shortage of space inside the city is too simplistic an explanation for
the disappearance of intramural burial, which must be connected with the
receding familiarity in the attitudes towards death and the dead apparent
in other aspects of archaic death-related behaviour.[84] The growing fear and
revulsion generated by death expressed itself through the—inherited but
flexible—concept of pollution, a conceptual and ritual mechanism for articulating boundaries. Much of the earlier trend towards greater use of extramural cemeteries was probably urbanistically inspired. But the diminished
physical contact with, and proximity to the dead which ensued contributed
to the shift from the familiar model of death, and so fuelled the tendency to
remove burials outside the city, which again reinforced the recession of
familiarity, and so on. There is evidence that early Greek mentality perceived
a link between intramural burial on the one hand, and familiarity with death
and diminished death-avoidance on the other. A law attributed to the
legendary Spartan legislator Lycurgus permits intramural burial in order
to familiarize young men with death, so that they do not shrink from it
fearing that whoever touches a corpse or treads on a grave becomes polluted.[85]
We do not know which part of this report was incorporated in the law,
reflecting seventh-century B.C. mentality,[86] and which was Plutarch's elaboration, but archaeological and other evidence shows that intramural burial
was indeed customary in archaic and classical Sparta.[87] Lycurgan legislation
aimed at transforming the Spartan citizens into elite warriors; to achieve
this it had taken elements from an older social system, adapted them, and
used them to serve new purposes.[88] In this instance, the legislation aims at
restoring to citizens who have to be above all warriors the attitude of
familiarity towards death which had characterized the earlier society, and
so stem the incipient death-avoidance. That earlier attitude was felt to have
been connected with the physical familiarity with, and proximity to the dead
resulting from intramural burial. So the legislator set out to reconstruct the
earlier physical circumstances as a means of recreating the old mentality. If
this is right, we have a valuable testimony for the connection between
intramural burial and the familiar attitude to death and its perception by
Greek mentality, and support for the suggestion that the accelerating trend
towards extramural burial in the archaic period is another manifestation of
the change in the collective attitude to death. Returning briefly to the earlier

[84] For the suspension of intramural burial in Western Europe caused by a change in the
collective attitudes to death masquerading as a concern for hygiene see Ariès, *L'Homme*, pp.
468–93; ibid., *Arch. sc. soc. des rel.* 39 (1975), 10, 12.
[85] Plutarch, *Lycurgus* xxvii.
[86] For the date see Forrest, pp. 123–42; Murray, pp. 59–72.
[87] See P. Cartledge, *Sparta and Lakonia. A Regional History 1300–362 B.C.* (London, 1979),
p. 174, see also p. 106; Jeffery p. 132. n.9; Pausanias iii. 14. 1–3.
[88] See Murray, pp. 170–2; also M. I. Finley, 'Sparta' in J.-P. Vernant (ed.) *Problèmes de la
guerre en Grèce ancienne* (Paris, The Hague 1968), pp. 143–60.

period, we conclude that the indifference to intramural burials is indeed another aspect of the familiar and 'accepting' early Greek attitudes towards death.

The shift in social attitudes to death in the archaic period was a very complex process, and any attempt to summarize it inevitably entails distortion. I must stress that what happened was not a drastic change, but a partial shift in the collective representations. The earlier model did not disappear: in some places and circles it became modified in ways I will sketch below, in others it lived on. Its 'survival' was two-fold: first as a living reality—sometimes perhaps slightly altered—in certain areas, circles and individuals (cf.n.6); and second as a consciously held and propagated intellectual position, derived from Homer and adapted to serve an emerging ideology of patriotism which glorifies death in the service of the city-state (cf. the poets Callinus and Tyrtaeus).[89] I will deal briefly with the shift, starting with its manifestations, the changes in funerary ideology and death-related behaviour which indicate it. But first let us consider a schematic summary of the main aspects of this shift as we detect it from these manifestations. The most important aspect is a more individual perception of death, the affirmation of one's individuality in death which now appears primarily as the end of one's person and one's life, rather than an episode in the history of the community and the life-cycle: the feeling of one's personal identity to which death appears to put an end is stronger than the feeling of death as a collective phenomenon through which the life-cycle operates. With this goes a certain recession in the easy acceptance of one's end, and a greater anxiety about it and concern for survival in memory and hope for a happy after-life, and finally a certain loss of familiarity with, and distancing from death. The most radical changes are in eschatology. First, the belief that 'everybody dies' is much weakened: more and more heroes are believed to have escaped Hades and to live in some kind of paradise. As for Heracles, he not only does not die, but he now becomes a god after his death. Second, the concept of the collective destiny of the shades in Hades recedes, and new beliefs appear, involving individual salvation, a happy afterlife depending on individual initiation to Mysteries or sects[90] and/or moral behaviour, and a judgement of the dead, followed by rewards and punishments in Hades for one's conduct in life. The influence of intellectual/philosophical thought on archaic eschatology is strong, and it is in these circles that the theory of reincarnation was born at this time. A third change took deep root in the collective representations: the shades no longer have to face the journey to Hades alone; two divine psychopompic figures have developed, Hermes Chthonius and Charon the ferryman of the dead, whose function is two-fold. First to guide the shades in the (awesome) transition from life to death, and so provide reassurance to the individual;

[89] See Murray, pp. 130–1.
[90] See Burkert, pp. 305, 413–51.

the 'automatic' Homeric transition to Hades is expanded and articulated in explicit and familiar, and so reassuring, terms: journey, payment of fee to the ferryman, etc. Second, Hermes and Charon serve as divine guarantors of the margins between the Upper World and Hades, life and death. This development suggests a greater anxiety about one's own death seen now as an individual experience, and a greater concern with separating firmly, and securing the margins between life and death, that is, ensuring that death is kept securely away. But the other side of this is that now that the two worlds have been more sharply and securely distinguished, controlled access of the dead to the Upper World on fixed occasions can be, and is tolerated—so that the descent into Hades has lost some of its unequivocal finality.

We saw that the termination of intramural burials in the archaic period indicated loss of familiarity with death and a trend towards a certain death-avoidance; and that these tendencies were expressed in conceptual/ritual terms through the idea of pollution which provides the means for expanding and articulating boundaries. In the archaic period pollution beliefs hardened[91] due to this increased fear and revulsion. Moreover, from the early sixth century B.C. onwards, in Athens and elsewhere, death's encroachment on life and the community is firmly restricted by funerary legislation[92] determined by a mentality aiming at pushing death away, limiting the disruption and lowering the emotional tone of the death-ritual and restricting the number of mourners, especially of women.

The new individual perception of death also manifests itself in the new individualization of the grave through inscriptions[93] recording the fact of one's life and death, and so preserving one's individual memory—and so personal identity—and through grave-monuments, especially grave-statues (though not actual portraits, the Greeks did not develop those until later) and grave-stones (grave-stelai) decorated with a representation of the deceased (again a type rather than a portrait).[94] Space prevents me from discussing the views expressed by some poets and philosophers, which

---

[91] See Burkert, p. 310; purification of Delos from graves: Thucydides iii. 104; gods no longer come in contact with death: Euripides, *Alcestis* 20–3; ibid., *Hippolytos* 1437–9.

[92] On funerary legislation see Burkert, p. 299; Alexiou (n.43), pp. 17–23; see also Snodgrass, *Archaic Greece*, p. 146.

[93] On grave-inscriptions see C. W. Clairmont, *Gravestone and Epigram. Greek Memorials from the Archaic and Classical Period* (Mainz, 1970); Kurtz and Boardman, pp. 260ff.; M. B. Wallace, 'Notes on Early Greek Grave Epigrams', *Phoenix* 24 (1970) 95–105. It is simplistic to attribute the new individualization of the grave through inscriptions (beginning in the early seventh century) to the greater spread of the alphabet, independently from a change in mentality. The alphabet had been in use since at least 750 B.C., and if the 'need' for grave-inscriptions had arisen earlier it would have been used earlier for that purpose. For there is always interaction between needs and means, especially when it is a matter of diffusion rather than invention.

[94] The bibliography on archaic grave-sculptures and grave-monuments is vast. See a summary in Kurtz and Boardman, pp. 79–90, 219ff; see also J. Boardman, *Greek Sculpture. The Archaic Period* (London, 1978), pp. 22, 86, 162ff; B. S. Ridgway, *The Archaic Style in Greek Sculpture* (Princeton, 1977), pp. 149–77.

manifest these new attitudes towards death, and especially one's own death, and life. One example will suffice to illustrate not so much the new tendencies, though it does illustrate one aspect of them, but especially how far from the traditional model of death some individuals had travelled: a fragment of Heraclitus (fr.96 Diels) says: 'for corpses are more worth throwing out than excrement'.

These changes, we saw, originated ultimately in the revolution of circumstances in the eighth century, enhanced by the continuing fluidity of the archaic period. These circumstances affected collective attitudes to death through four main channels (each interacting with the others, and with the death-attitudes, and generating feedbacks). Firstly, through the break-up of the earlier small tightly-knit communities, with all that entailed;[95] secondly, through the emergence of individualism which affected directly the perception of, and feelings about one's death; thirdly, through the intellectual developments which occurred in the archaic period, and especially philosophical speculation of an eschatological and ethical nature; and fourthly through the general mental tone of insecurity and fear of disorder resulting from the upheavals involved in the dramatic expansion of horizons, the drastic and rapid socio-economic and political changes, and the continuing unrest within the cities. Finally, I should note that the new eschatological beliefs and representations were mostly first articulated in intellectual circles and spread from there; and that the tendency to individualize the grave is, at this time, primarily an aristocratic phenomenon.

The similarities between the social attitudes to death of early Greece and those of medieval Europe, as regards both the earlier model of familiar acceptance and the shift away from it, are considerable. There are also considerable differences, which is natural, given the different circumstances, but also the different eschatology and overall religious ideology and conception of man and the universe involved. The similarities, especially that in the basic mentality, in the 'elementary syntax' of the model, suggest that certain (general) types of attitude towards death depend on a certain nexus of demographic, socio-economic, political and 'intellectual' conditions, and so characterize certain general types of society. But the more complex the society, and the more developed its intellectual thought, the more individual and less 'typical' its collective representations of and attitudes to death are likely to be.

[95] See above and also D. E. Stannard, *The Puritan Way of Death* (Oxford, New York, Toronto, Melbourne, 1977), pp. 132 and 220 n.79 with bibliography.

II

Sacred Corpse, Profane Carrion: Social Ideals and Death Rituals in the Later Middle Ages

R. C. FINUCANE

Saint Augustine, whose writings profoundly influenced the western medieval Church, anticipated modern social scientists by more than 1,500 years when he observed that burial services were really for the living rather than the dead. In a way, archaeologists and anthropologists have for many years unwittingly acknowledged this Augustinian aside in assuming that death rites and beliefs about the dead reflect the social realities and ideals of the living. A funeral, they tell us, is not simply a matter of 'religion'.

In the past two decades an avalanche of books and articles on the subject especially from a sociological and psychological viewpoint has developed into something called the 'death awareness movement'. In 1977, for example, the American *Annual Review of Psychology* began for the first time critically to survey recently published studies of this topic.[1] Historians too have been showing greater interest. Boase, McC. Gatch and Ariès, for instance, survey the theme of death in the Middle Ages.[2] Interesting and suggestive as such studies are, however, there is still a great deal to assimilate from medievalists investigating particular aspects of the problem. This was evident from the papers presented in Strasbourg in 1975, and in other works concerning death iconography and monuments, commemorations of the dead, folklore, sermons and vision-literature, theological aspects of death and the hereafter, the Black Death and other catastrophes (supposedly leading to a deeper sense of 'morbidity'), and liturgical studies.[3]

The present essay merely restates an anthropological axiom, that the

[1] R. Kastenbaum and P. Coates, 'Psychological Perspectives on Death', *Ann. Rev. Psych.* 28 (1977), 225–49; cf. *Death: A Bibliographical Guide* (London, 1977), A. Miller and M. Acri.

[2] T. S. R. Boase, *Death in the Middle Ages* (London, 1972); M. McC. Gatch, *Death: Meaning and Mortality in Christian Thought and Contemporary Culture* (New York, 1969); P. Ariès, *Western Attitudes toward Death from the Middle Ages to the Present* (Baltimore, 1974) and subsequent general essays.

[3] *La Mort au moyen âge*, Colloque des Médiévistes françaises, Publ. de la Soc. Savante, Sér. Recherches et Doc., Tome xxv (Strasbourg, 1977); for recent work in other fields cf. besides Panofsky's classic *Tomb Sculpture* K. Cohen's *Metamorphosis of a Death Symbol* (London, 1973); J. Rosenthal, *The Purchase of Paradise* (Toronto, 1972); P. Dinzelbacher, 'Die Visionen des Mittelalters. Ein geschichtlicher Umriss', *Zeitsch. für Relig.- und Geistesg.*, Bd. xxx (1978), 116–28; Jean-Noël Biraben, *Les hommes et la peste*, 2 vols. (Paris, 1975–6); G. Rowell, *The Liturgy of Christian Burial* (London, 1977).

manner of disposing of the dead reflects social or cultural norms and ideals. In the Middle Ages as in other epochs, death ritual was not so much a question of dealing with a corpse as of reaffirming the secular and spiritual order by means of a corpse. In order to illustrate this, we shall examine the treatment allotted to four quite different 'types' within medieval society as they approach and then pass through death. These will be kings, criminals and traitors, saints, and those who opted out of the Church or never had the chance to join it, such as heretics and stillborn infants. In each of these four groups the maintenance of social ideals through their death rites will be obvious. But there are other facets which bear further examination. Society, for example, can use a corpse to emphasize an accepted ideal, but in addition the deliberate manipulation of the dead can lead to social engineering and the creation of new social attitudes. Such possibilities will be considered in due course. Before examining the four models taken from the 'extremes' of ecclesiastical and lay society, however, we begin with some general observations about death among the ordinary laity and clergy. In a way they were equidistant from the four extremes, and so provide a means of gaining perspective.

Unfortunately little is known about the actual behaviour of ordinary medieval people when they became ill. There is evidence to suggest that they often overstated the seriousness of the case and claimed to see Death's messengers lurking at the foot of the bed even in mild, transient illnesses. Given contemporary levels of hygiene, diet and medical ignorance, this was not entirely just hypochondriac anxiety. Many people (or their families) believing themselves 'sick unto death', *usque ad mortem* as the catchphrase was, frantically sought help anywhere it could be found: magical charms, a talisman, the village wise woman and her nasty potions, holy relics or water, little rituals like bending coins over the patient or measuring him with thread to incorporate into a candle (later offered in church), sending wax images of the sick person or his limbs to a shrine, making vows of pilgrimage, even—when they had the money—calling in doctors. The ignorance which misled them about their illnesses also created uncertainty when deciding whether someone was actually dead.

Centuries earlier Plato had suggested that burials should be held up until the third day after 'death'. Anyone in trance, he assumed, would have recovered by then. In the later Middle Ages a three-day delay was the norm at least for VIPs. Claims of miraculous resuscitations from the dead were made repeatedly throughout the medieval centuries; a Canterbury monk nonchalantly observed that returns from death after two or three days were not uncommon, though after seven days rather unusual. On one occasion an argument took place above the inert form of France's King Louis IX as to whether or not he was still living (which he was, and continued to do for years), and out in the East Anglian fens a man was headed for premature burial when his friends decided to wait a few days, just to be certain that he had died (which he had not).[4] There are many examples of this, which has even led to the suggestion that medieval funerals tended to be long-drawn-out affairs because (besides other obvious reasons) of uncertainty about the moment of death and a—perhaps unconscious—fear of live burial.[5] The 'religious' custom of holding a candle near the mouth of those near death may be linked to this.[6] It is not surprising that some people revived after receiving the last rites. In fact it became necessary for the clergy to inform their flocks that in such cases the sacrament of Extreme Unction *could* be repeated (given certain conditions). Apparently many laymen also believed that the last sacrament conferred a kind of sanctity on the recipient. Anyone, they claimed, who carried on living after Extreme Unction was supposed to behave in a very special—not to say peculiar—fashion: he must not have sexual intercourse, go about barefoot, or eat meat. The clergy condemned such ideas.[7]

Regardless of false alarms the time came when an illness was indeed terminal and all the remedies useless; the rites of separation and transition began. Most Christians hoped to end up in hallowed ground. Of course there were conflicts between monks, mendicants and secular priests over burial rights which sometimes degenerated into unseemly scrambles for corpses, and so on. But in the midst of this the ideal remained fixed. The churchyard, consecrated by a bishop, was a holy place, as was the church itself; the spilling of the life-giving magical fluids, blood and semen, polluted the churchyard as it polluted a church, and ritual reconciliation must follow. Pollution also resulted when excommunicates or Jews or heretics or suicides or any number of proscribed categories were buried in the sacred space.

Burials in cemeteries and all else associated with death followed hallowed patterns. After a night of prayer over the corpse this final act took place after Requiem Mass next day. During a break in the services the priest went into the cemetery with a spade to draw a cross on the ground where the grave was then dug. The body was carried from the church by those of the same social rank as the dead, the seven penitential psalms and other prayers being offered along the way. Women were not to carry the bier, suggested a twelfth-century writer, in case men's limbs were accidentally exposed during the process. Presumably this would excite unfunereal reactions among the females. On the other hand in a popular medieval tale only

---

[4] J. Robertson (ed.) *Materials for the history of Thomas Becket* (RS 67, London, 1875–85), I. 444; R. Finucane, *Miracles and Pilgrims*, Chap. 4 *passim* (London, 1977); Joinville, *Life of St. Louis*, M. Shaw (tr.) (1963), p. 191; A. Jessopp and M. R. James, *Life and Miracles of St. William of Norwich* (Cambridge, 1896), p. 68.
[5] H. Philippeau, 'Textes et rubriques des *Agenda Mortuorum*', *Archiv für Liturg.* IV (1955), 52–72, at p. 63.
[6] E. Friestedt, 'Altchristliche Totengedächtnistage und ihre Beziehung zur Jenseitsglauben und Totenkultus der Antike', Liturg. Quellen und Forsch., xxiv (1928), 40.
[7] W. Maskell, *Monumenta Ritualia Ecclesiae Anglicanae*, 2nd. edn., 3 vols. (Oxford, 1882), I. cclxxxvii; F. Powicke and C. Cheney, *Councils and Synods* (1964), pp. 707, 995-6.

priests' harlots were able to lift the remains of a defunct clerical concubine.[8] At the grave further prayers were offered while the corpse was aspersed with holy water to ward off demons. Before placing the body in the grave the priest might throw in bits of incense, charcoal, sprigs of ivy or laurel (a pagan custom Christianized from at least the fourth century), as well as more holy water.[9] Just as many pagan graves were aligned with the rising sun, Christian corpses were placed with feet to the east in anticipation of resurrection; the dead would rise facing their Maker, who was to appear in the east—in some cases shoes were left on the feet specifically to facilitate this Judgment Day exercise. This orientation was a serious matter, as suggested for instance by the Winchester Cathedral excavations. Archaeologists found that the Norman builders who had disturbed earlier Christian Saxon burials carefully replaced the skulls to the west, leaving all the other bones in a jumbled heap to the east. They could sort themselves out at the resurrection.

If the cemetery was the proper resting-place for the average Christian, then the church itself was considered appropriate to the élite. From at least the sixth century various councils prohibited burial within churches, but such interments went on anyway. Social distinctions among the dead were acknowledged by churchmen themselves as early as the ninth century, when a council decreed that no-one should be buried in churches *except* certain ecclesiastics and important laymen. As far as clerical burials were concerned, there was less objection in any case; it was the encroachment of the laity that caused distress. In the ninth century one prelate grumbled that churches, cluttered with memorials and graves, had turned into cemeteries and in 1200 an English bishop mentioned the physical inconvenience caused by the scatter of tombs in churches.[10] Yet it was difficult to resist the claims of laymen since one reason for the laity to found or patronize a church was to receive burial there. Gregory of Tours in the sixth century provides several examples of Merovingian rulers buried in churches, and Bede in the early eighth century writes of church burial for Anglo-Saxon kings and queens. The canons of the Fourth Lateran Council (1215) acknowledged it as old custom. Even so, some churchmen—like a thirteenth-century bishop of Chichester—went on trying to curtail lay burials in churches.[11] By the thirteenth century burial in church was a mark of social and spiritual elevation. There were additional refinements. Generally speaking burial in the 'holier' section of the church, from the choir eastward, was reserved to

[8] J. Beleth, *Explicatio Divinorum Officiorum*, cap. CLXI (Naples, 1859), p. 844; F. Tubach, *Index Exemplorum* (Helsinki, 1969), no. 1265.

[9] W. Durand, *Rationale Divinorum Officiorum*, Lib. VII, cap. 35 (Naples, 1859), pp. 705–7. The charcoal signified that the land was henceforth withdrawn from normal usage. D. Hinton, *Alfred's Kingdom* (1977), p. 99, mentions Saxon burials over charcoal.

[10] E. Martène, *De Antiquis Ecclesiae Ritibus*, 2 vols. (1788), I. p. 371; *Magna Vita Sancti Hugonis*, H. Farmer and D. Douie, 2 vols. (London, 1961–2), II p. 192.

[11] Powicke and Cheney, *Councils and Synods* II, p. 1117.

the greater figures only (though there were exceptions). A bishop, for example, could expect such honourable interment, preceded by an elaborate procession to the cathedral. The cortège might stop along the way at some of the parish churches owing allegiance to the bishop, a final show of episcopal authority. Upon entering the city there was usually a crowd of clergy and noblemen to greet the dead prelate, and sometimes heated competition for the privilege of carrying the corpse into the cathedral.

Prelates and priests were buried in the vestments, and with the trappings, of their office. Bishops, some with freshly-trimmed nails and beard, tonsure renewed postmortem, were entombed in their consecration garments. Their episcopal ring, mitre and crosier—or a wand-like substitute—also accompanied them to the grave. A chalice and paten (usually of base metal), sometimes with the unconsecrated elements, were placed at the clerical shoulder or breast. Other ecclesiastics were buried with appropriate apparel, such as the chancellor of Hereford cathedral who died at the end of the thirteenth century. His corpse, hands in an attitude of prayer, had been dressed in silk and gold lace, a chalice and paten at his right shoulder. There was a square of silk on the paten and in the chalice a stain left by evaporated wine.[12] Some prelates ordered even more explicit tokens of faith to be buried with them. A cautious twelfth-century bishop of Paris went to his grave with a note pinned to his chest: 'I believe that . . . on the last day of the world I shall be resurrected.'[13]

There was little essential difference in the form of burial used in monasteries, although the spiritual milieu was of course quite distinctive. In fact death and burial rituals of the later Middle Ages, though their distant origins may be scattered across prechristian—even prehistoric—time and space, acquired a great deal of their form and matter in medieval monasteries. Yet to speak of a dying monk is something of a tautology, for in theory monks were already dead to the world. They had begun that disengagement from transient, temporal society which culminated with death and entrance into the real, eternal world. Unlike people living on the outside they no longer bothered 'to fatten and fondle a putrid corpse destined undoubtedly to be erelong the food for worms', as St. Bernard so indelicately put it. The monk was reborn into a place of protected transition, the monastery. That he had died and was reborn was made clear in the blessing over a new monk: he was *mundo huic mortuus*, 'dead to this world', and God was called upon to 'take up this thy servant, whom you have plucked from the shipwrecks and dangers of this world'.[14] (Part of an English service *for the dead* included a prayer to God to 'take up the soul of thy servant, whom you have thought worthy to call from the prison of this world'.[15]) For three days and nights

[12] F. Havergal, *Fasti Herefordenses* (Hereford, 1869), p. 198, Plate 23.
[13] Martène, *De Antiq.*, I. p. 368.
[14] Ibid., I. p. 162.
[15] Maskell, *Monumenta*, I. p. 136.

the would-be monk must wear his hood up and speak to no-one. On the third day the abbot lowered the hood and the new monk, *quasi resuscitatus,* was resurrected and rebaptized into a new existence.[16] Medieval English lawyers argued that since he was socially dead he would be unable to inherit anything. Furthermore, any last will that he himself had made in his 'mundane' state took effect at once as if he had actually died.[17] A thirteenth-century sermon collection included a story of a man who asked a favour of his own brother, a monk, but was plainly told, *'Et ego mortuus sum,* I am dead and will give you nothing'.[18]

When physical death followed ritual death the monk, in the bosom of his surrogate extended family, was assisted with all of the commendatory powers at their disposal. In addition, other religious houses subscribed their prayers for his soul on a roll of parchment carried from one monastery to another. Commemoration went on every day for thirty days after death, when his soul was in greatest need, and every anniversary thereafter. He was buried in the monastic cemetery or possibly within the church itself. Wherever the precise place, he would lie within that magic circuit which marked off a very special world from the other, profane world. No wonder that many pious or anxious laymen on the point of death 'took the cowl', took on the monk's habit and vows hoping to be buried in the midst of so much prayer which, they hoped, would lighten their purgatorial pains.

In contrast to the rites associated with the death and burial of ordinary laymen, prelates and monks, the death rituals of kings, the first of our four medieval 'types', were as complex and as evolutionary as the ideal of kingship itself. Put quite simply, by the end of the Middle Ages the practical and theoretical foundations of monarchical power in western Europe were far stronger, and an aura (though generally not yet the reality) of absolutism surrounded kings and princes. Consequently the public, birth-to-death ceremonial associated with such figures had become encrusted with symbols of power and respect. By the later medieval period the royal or noble burial was an occasion not only of formalized mourning but also of great ceremonial triumph, a final public 'appearance'. Even in the so-called Dark Ages special ceremony accompanied royal burials. This ceremonial developed along with the sacral character and political powers of kings until, by the fourteenth and fifteenth centuries, the greatest pomp attended royal deaths and funerals.

Naturally the deathbed was a focus of activity, the higher clergy in constant attendance, the great ones of the realm paying final visits. Kings were expected to die with special dignity and composure even in Bede's day. In later centuries the routine was well established: a will was made describing

---

[16] Martène, I. pp. 163, 165; cf. pp. 171–2. Mass for the Dead said over one about to become anchorite, I. p. 178.

[17] F. Pollock and F. Maitland, *History of English Law before the time of Edward I,* 2 vols. (1898) reissued with new biblio. (Cambridge, 1968), I. 434–5.

[18] Jacques de Vitry, *Exempla,* T. Crane (ed.) (London, 1890), p. 54.

inter alia the disposition of his remains; as the end neared he forgave his enemies, received the *viaticum* or communion along with Extreme Unction, and died—preferably with pious exclamations upon his lips. When death occurred some distance from the place traditionally or specifically designated for burial the body must be protected from decay. The intestines, heart and sometimes brain and eyes were removed by doctors or by monks with some medical knowledge, even occasionally by butchers and cooks.[19] The innards were given local burial, although in the later Middle Ages many followed the growing custom of burying the heart at a favourite church or shrine. The rest of the corpse, soaked in vinegar or wine or treated with salt and aromatics—balsam was popular—was wrapped in animal hides for transport. One of the earliest recorded attempts to embalm a medieval king involved Charles the Bald, who died in 877. The operation was not a success and the horrible stench made life extremely unpleasant for the cortège. England's Henry I (d. 1135) provides yet another example of the failure of primitive preservation techniques, with particularly revolting results.[20]

An alternative to embalming seems to have been tried perhaps as early as the tenth century in Imperial territory. The *mos teutonicus* or 'German method' consisted of cutting up the body and boiling the pieces in wine or water until fat and flesh separated from bone. Then the skeleton was packed up and sent off for burial, while whatever happened to be left over was given decent interment. It was employed by the French in the thirteenth century (used for example on St. Louis) but only occasionally by the English. Not a royal prerogative, it could be applied to anyone important enough to warrant the bother, like the noble bishop of Hereford who died in Italy in 1282. At the end of the thirteenth century Pope Boniface VIII condemned the practice, sometimes carried out in the side-chapels of churches, whereas some churchmen such as William Durand defended it. In any case, it was not difficult to obtain licences for the process even from the papacy itself.

There were other alternatives for royal ministers faced with the problem of transporting dead kings. It seems that Henry II of England set or restored a fashion in not only being buried dressed in royal vestments and insignia—the Carolingians had done that—but by being exposed to view, carried to church on an open bier as if to show that 'même mort, le corps du roi continuait à posséder ce caractère spécial que lui avait donné l'onction'.[21] This was copied in France for Philip II (d. 1223), whose body

---

[19] R. Giesey, *The Royal Funeral Ceremony in Renaissance France* (Geneva, 1960), pp. 19–22; W. H. St. John Hope, 'On the Funeral Effigies of the Kings and Queens of England', *Archaeologia* lx (1907), 521; A. Erlande-Brandenburg, *Le Roi est Mort* (Geneva, 1975), pp. 27–30. For further discussions of royal burials see C. Beaune, 'Mourir noblement à la fin du moyen âge' in *La Mort au moyen âge*, p. 125, and E. Brown's article on the funeral of Philip V in *Speculum* 55, 2 (Apr. 1980), 266–93.

[20] *Henrici archid. Huntendunensis hist. Anglorum,* ed. T. Arnold, RS 74 (London, 1879), pp. 256–8; St. John Hope, 'Effigies', p. 521.

[21] A. Erlande-Brandenburg, op. cit., p. 17.

was regally dressed, sceptred and crowned. The Emperors too followed the fashion, for example Otto IV in 1218. This public exhibition after death could only occur, however, when the site of burial was nearby and there was little probability that decay would become obvious in the interim. Naturally, this could not always be arranged since kings seldom planned their own deaths for administrative convenience. The effigy solved the problem. Apparently this was first mentioned in England at the funeral of Edward II (d. 1327), on whose coffin a wooden likeness of the king was placed, *quamdam ymaginem de ligno ad similitudinem dicti domini E.*, wearing a copper crown.[22] The first (fully documented) French effigy was made for Charles VI (d. 1422). This was to become customary for kings, queens and then the nobility, some of whose effigies even reproduced the wounds which had caused death. At first the effigy was merely a stand-in for the dead king but eventually, especially in France, it very nearly developed a life of its own. This royal dummy also greatly extended the time available for ritual embellishments, since the rotting corpse was safely sealed up in its coffin. The effigy itself wore state or coronation robes, whereas the corpse was dressed in the simpler and skimpier garments actually used at the moment of coronation anointing—as in the case of bishops, who were buried in their original consecration vestments.

Further rites emphasized the continued symbolic existence of the king such as the public display of the effigy on a 'bed', slightly inclined so that more visitors could view and pay their respects to the replica. A 'herse' (or hearse), a large wooden framework, was built over and around the effigy and coffin beneath it (though the coffin might even be kept in another room). The hearse had various functions. It advertised the nobility of the king through the little shields and other heraldic devices attached to it. It served a 'religious' purpose, supporting images or statues of angels and saints, with perhaps a representation of the Last Judgment on the underside of the canopy for the effigy's perusal. It was also a giant candelabrum. There were about 700 candles on the hearse of the Earl of Flanders (d. 1385), each weighing one pound. As this last point demonstrates, the hearse was not only for kingly obsequies but in simpler form had been used for lesser beings, clerical and lay, from the central Middle Ages.

A ceremonial meal accompanied later medieval royal funerals, an empty place at table reserved for the dead king. This may have stemmed from a monastic custom in which the food that would have supported a recently-deceased monk was given to the poor for the sake of his soul, for thirty days after his death. In a similar way the poor (and mourners and other attendants) benefited from the royal funeral meal. So did the king's reputation as a source of largesse—even from the grave.

---

[22] St. John Hope, op. cit., citing PRO Exchequer KR 383/3. He suggests that Henry III had an effigy, pp. 526–7, but Giesey, op. cit., pp. 81–2, disagrees.

The next stage was the move into church in grand procession. Each social rank had a place, though argument sometimes developed on precisely which place. Normally the clergy preceded the coffin, the kin and chief mourners accompanied and followed it. Only the highest ranks were allowed near the bier as it moved along crowded streets. To bear the coffin or hold the edges of the pall draped over it was a great honour, the right to approach royalty which only the few enjoyed whether the king be alive or dead. There were even further social differentiations: mantles worn by chief mourners, for example, were longer than those of ordinary mourners. Somewhere in the procession too were the paupers hired for the occasion, often wearing the livery of the dead, usually carrying torches, whose main function was to pray for the deceased. Their numbers varied. Some noblemen went to extravagant lengths to make sure that they were featured in as many prayers as possible immediately after death.

At the church the effigy/coffin were placed within yet another hearse blazing with candles. On occasion the heat and fumes were overpowering and doors had to be opened, glass removed from windows.[23] Even so, the funeral party held candles during parts of the service, heavier ones given to people of greater social importance.[24] The most important moment in royal and noble ceremonies came during the Requiem Mass when at the Offertory the 'achievements' or sword, helm, shield, etc., even the battle-horse of the deceased were offered. By the late fifteenth century this ceremony followed rigid protocol under heralds' supervision. Only certain people participated, in specific order. Once again this emphasized the special status and function of the king *as well as* his noblemen and their relationships to each other in contemporary society. For example, during the funeral of Edward IV (d. 1483) 'ther was a question whether the son and heir of an erle should go above a viscount, etc.' in presenting offerings.[25] Apart from these offerings the sermon was especially important. In addition to the usual pious sentiments, the worldly fortunes and great deeds of the dead and his predecessors were extolled—in the case of one sixteenth-century sermon occupying ten out of fourteen pages.[26]

The church ceremonial ended with the burial of the king although (in France anyway) the effigy might be stored away for the more important commemoration services. Naturally, ample provision had been made for these memorials, like the chantry established in 1363 by the Black Prince thirteen years before his death. There are many such examples. Wills reflect this common desire for postmortem prayer, but sometimes in an uncommon

---

[23] Beaune, op. cit., p. 137; Rock, D., *The Church of our Fathers* (London, 1849–53), II. pp. 500–01, where two panes of glass had to be taken out at John Paston's funeral to 'lete owte the reke of the torches'.

[24] D. Dendy, *The Use of Lights in Christian Worship* (London, 1959), p. 106, actually a cardinal's funeral.

[25] *Archaeologia* vol. 1 (1770), 353, 354.

[26] Beaune, op. cit., p. 140

way: in 1395 Lady Alice West of Hampshire—to take an often-cited testament—provided £8 10s. for 4,400 Masses to be said (no doubt very rapidly) within fourteen nights of death. As for royal tombs themselves, by the thirteenth century some were practically objects of veneration. At the end of the medieval era it was customary for the royal and the noble to be buried beyond the choir near the altar, in the sacred eastern sanctuary. When the King of Kings appeared, they would be among the first to greet him—a matter of spiritual protocol.

The elaborate rites surrounding the death and burial of kings emphasized their special position within medieval secular society. But if the king represented law and authority, then in the lay world the opposite extreme would be the criminal who flaunted the law and even more so the traitor who rejected that authority. We descend, then, from the world of kings to that of vagabonds and outlaws, from pampered effigies to decomposing bodies on gibbets and rotting heads impaled at city gates.

Hanging was a common way to deal with the troublesome malefactor. This certainly cut him off from temporal, but not necessarily from spiritual society. If he had confessed and asked for or received the viaticum he merited church burial, Masses and offerings for his soul.[27] On the other hand he could be 'punished' if wrongly given Christian burial. A collection of popular tales includes the story of a Kentish man, about to be hanged, who refused to do penance for his sins. Even so his body was buried in a churchyard by well-meaning neighbours. Afterwards one of them saw it in a dream: it was stripped of its skin, horrible and stinking. The woman who had this nightmare remembered it for the rest of her life.[28] Whether destined for a churchyard or not, before removing an executed person the consent of the civil authority was usually required. It was then normally handed over to friends or relatives.

The people who had most to gain by being taken to holy ground after being hanged were those who actually recovered. If they revived while in sanctuary they would be free at least temporarily from further harassment by the authorities. Recovery may have been due to the crude manner of medieval hanging, which caused slow strangulation. The victim might be cut down inadvertently or intentionally while still semi-conscious. Or the rope might break, a matter easily arranged by sympathetic or corruptible executioners. In England in the later Middle Ages a royal pardon was

[27] Even a substitute for the host would do as viaticum, such as a bit of earth: cf. *Meier Helmbrecht*, ed. J. Pilz (1962), p. 125, 'ein Bauer/hob ein Stück vom Grund/und steckt es Helmbrecht in den Mund/dass es der Seele Schutz gewährt'. In 1527 the megalomaniac Cellini reported that as he lay stunned after being struck 'some stupid young soldiers had stuffed my mouth with earth in the belief that they were giving me communion. . . . I had a job to recover and the earth did me more harm than the blow I received'. *Autobiography of Benvenuto Cellini* (tr. G. Bull, 1956), p. 73.

[28] J. Welter, ed., *Speculum Laicorum* (Paris, 1914), p. 102, no. 524, corpse *excoriatum, ita fetens et horridum;* cf. Greg. the Great, *Dialogues,* IV. 53–6.

customary for survivors of hanging, though this was not granted in every case.[29] Characteristically, survivors often attributed their good luck to the miraculous intervention of a saint, a standard hagiographical motif.[30]

A striking illustration comes from Wales in the later thirteenth century. A hanged man's face was described as blackish and swollen, eyes bloody and bulging, neck, throat, nose and mouth bloody, his black, swollen tongue protruding and gashed by his teeth. He had fouled himself 'as was usual' when the hanged were in their death agony. One eyewitness said he was 'stone dead' (*tanta vita . . . quanta in lapide*). Even so he recovered, reputedly as a result of saintly assistance. During the investigation into this event the possibility of fraud was brought up. It was declared that in that part of the country hanged men died at once because the noose was knotted so as to secure immediate suffocation, *ita quod statim suffocantur.* If because of trickery a criminal did not die, however, the executioner was himself hanged.[31]

By whatever means, the Welsh brigand managed to survive his ordeal. Traitors were usually not so lucky. By the later Middle Ages treason was considered in some circles to be a crime worse than any other. Even in King Alfred's day the betrayal of one's lord was the greatest evil, like the sin of Judas. As the theory and practice of kingship developed in the later medieval period crimes against the highest authority called for correspondingly harsher punishments. Treason deserved the mightiest torments and most horrible deaths that could be devised. The execution sometimes began by dragging the guilty one through the streets at a horse's tail, and even the dead bodies of traitors were subjected to such treatment. Drawn to the place of execution, one of the killers of the Count of Flanders was hanged without his breeches and a dog's intestines were then wrapped round his neck. Afterwards his corpse was tied to a wheel with another dead traitor, their arms twisted into a macabre embrace.[32] All of this happened in the twelfth century.

By the thirteenth century hanging was but the mildest of punishments for treason. After Simon de Montfort was killed at Evesham in 1265 his limbs were cut off and sent to various parts of the kingdom, his head—and testicles—to the wife of one of his enemies.[33] Traitors were also subjected to

[29] N. Hurnard, *The King's Pardon for Homicide before AD 1307* (Oxford, 1969), pp. 43–4, 176, 246–7; Langland, *Piers the Ploughman* (trans. J. Goodridge, 1959), p. 266 and n. 38; E. Magnusson, ed., *Thómas Saga Erkibyskups*, 2 vols. (RS 65, 1875–83), II. p. 115.

[30] B. de Gaiffier, *Études Critiques d'hagiographie et d'iconologie* (Brussels, 1967), 'Un thème hagiographique: le pendu miraculeusement sauvé'; cf. Caesarius of Heisterbach, *Dialogus Miraculorum*, IX. 49.

[31] MS *Vatican Lat. 4015*. f. 8ʳ–13ᵛ and 219ᵛ–227ᵛ; a less coherent version in *Acta Sanct.* (1765), I Oct., 633–37, 676.

[32] J. Ross, tr., Galbert of Bruges, *The Murder of Charles the Good, Count of Flanders* (New York, 1967), pp. 211–13, cf. p. 175.

[33] J. Halliwell, ed., *The Chronicle of Wm. de Rishanger of the Barons' Wars*, Camden Soc. vol. 15 (1840), xxxi–xxxii.

evisceration.[34] The rebel William Wallace got the full treatment in 1305. He was drawn through London's streets at the tail of a horse to the place of execution where he was hanged, but taken down still living. His innards were cut out and burned. The body was then quartered and decapitated, the limbs sent into Scotland, the head mounted at London Bridge. As he had committed many crimes, so he suffered in numerous ways. By the end of the thirteenth century 'high treason demands a cumulation of deaths' as the highest crime.[35] It should be noted, however, that even these arch-criminals might receive church burial. In 1406 the relatives of an executed traitor petitioned the Paris *Parlement* for permission to bury his body in a chapel he had founded. They were graciously allowed to collect the pieces.[36]

Considering these two extremes—king and traitor—disparate attitudes toward them were clearly 'realized' in distinctive rites of death. The same is true within the ecclesiastical world. If the king, hedged in his divinity, was the apex of lay society his counterpart within the Church was the saint. But this medieval 'type' is of a very different world, or rather worlds: saints were supposed to belong as much to the eternal as to the mundane. By the central Middle Ages primitive ideals of sainthood were buried under accretions of ritual, art, legend and belief. Saints' shrines continued to attract pilgrims for many different reasons, including the perennial human craving for 'miracles'.

It was believed at least in the earlier Middle Ages that as such people neared death they could see over the boundary separating the worlds. Their deaths were transitions to another, higher and therefore more powerful state. This state could be anticipated: they could foresee their own deaths and other secrets of the future.[37] Their statements were especially valued because in a sense they came from beyond the grave. It was a privilege to be present at their deaths and only 'worthy' auditors should hear their last words. Conversely, it came to be expected that the dying holy man or woman would, even should, bequeath his special knowledge to intimates.[38] In addition, since he would soon be in God's presence, those gathered in the death-chamber might use him as their personal go-between with the Almighty. When Bishop Hugh of Lincoln was a few moments from death his companion-

---

[34] K. v. Amira, 'Die germanischen Todesstrafen', *Abhandl. der Bayer. Akad. der Wissenschaften. Philos.-philol. und hist. Klasse*, XXI, Bd. 3 (Munich, 1922), 132, 143, cites the pulling apart by horses as a very primitive, quasi-religious method, and sees *evisceratio* as peculiarly Anglo-Norman.

[35] Pollock and Maitland, *English Law*, II. pp. 501, 511.

[36] A. Bernard, *La Sépulture en droit canonique* (Paris, 1933), p. 115 n. 2.

[37] M. McC. Gatch, *Preaching and Theology*, p. 46, Guibert de Nogent in the version called *Self and Society in Medieval France*, ed. J. Benton (New York 1970), pp. 142-3; D. Gutmann, 'Dying to Power: Death and the Search for Self-Esteem' in H. Feifel, *New Meanings of Death* (New York, 1977), esp. pp. 340-1.

[38] Greg. the Great, *Dialogues*, IV. 20, 26, 27, 36, 40; Bede, *Hist. Eccl.* III. 8, IV. 23; Felix's *Life of St. Guthlac*, ed. Colgrave (Cambridge, 1956), p. 155; *Memorials of St. Dunstan*, ed. W. Stubbs (RS 63, 1874), p. 320.

biographer said to him three times before receiving a reply, ' "Ask the Lord to provide a good pastor for your Church" '.[39]

At death the usual procedures were followed, washing, dressing and arranging the limbs. In some cases the corpse became a miraculous attraction from this very moment. Before burial in Lincoln cathedral Bishop Hugh performed a miracle by curing a blind woman, which proved 'that he was alive and present'.[40] Another Englishman, Archbishop Edmund Rich of Canterbury, died in France in 1240. Along the route to his final resting place in the austere Cistercian abbey of Pontigny rustics left their yoked oxen in the fields, villagers poured from their hovels to shout 'where is the holy body? Where is the body?' clamouring to touch it, kiss it, or merely to look at it. At one point a group of enthusiasts took the corpse into their church, but the abbot's men forcibly recovered their treasure. The abbot realized that if Edmund performed any miracles along the way the crowds would be aflame with uncontrollable fervour. He therefore admonished the corpse not to do anything spectacular until they reached Pontigny, *nullum facias signum antequam pervenias ad . . . Pontiniacum.* Edmund obligingly performed no major miracles *en route*.[41]

These two saints remind one of Augustine's words about his own mother: 'She was neither unhappy in her death, nor altogether dead', *nec omnino moriebatur.* Saints were not 'altogether' dead. This is certainly the impression gleaned from the visions and dreams of ordinary people. In some of these the dead saints still suffer the physical irritations and discomforts of living beings. One saint wanted to have a cross placed where he could see it from his tomb 'without the pain of turning my head'. Another complained that he could work no miracles since the earth pinned his arms and hands to his sides. A third expressed disgust at latrines he could smell from his tomb.[42] Just as in their waking hours pilgrims knew that saints somehow inhabited their shrines, in their dreams they saw them raise the lids of their tombs, step out and perform miracles.[43] Saints were very 'human' in yet another way. Although usually benign healers of soul and body the saints, who could be in many places at once, also brought recrimination, even injury and death to doubters and the disrespectful.

Saints hovered near the ultimate source of all power, the throne of God; they could be dangerous or beneficent, like God himself. Their movement nearer to God was symbolically expressed in a ritual reburial called *translatio,* or translation (which could be repeated). The overt function of a translation

[39] *Magna Vita Hugonis,* ed. Farmer and Douie, II. p. 197.
[40] Ibid., II. pp. 218, 220, 229, 231.
[41] C. Lawrence, *St. Edmund of Abingdon* (Oxford, 1960), pp. 220, 275–6.
[42] Jessopp and James, *William of Norwich,* p. 214; St. Edmund Rich in E. Martène and U. Durand, *Thesaurus Novus Anecdotorum,* III. 1820; J. Raine, ed., *Libellus de vita et miraculis S. Godrici,* Surtees Soc. 20 (1847), p. 339.
[43] *Vita Godrici,* pp. 389–91, 417–8, 455; *Acta Sanct.* (1765) I. Oct. 668 (Cantilupe); R. Darlington, ed., *Vita Wulfstani,* Camden Soc. 3d ser. vol. 40 (1928), p. 142.

was the movement of a saint's bones to a holier, more honourable position, usually in the eastern end of the church. Sometimes saints already buried there were moved into a more elevated shrine in more or less the same place. Among the best-known English examples is Beckets's translation in 1220. The bones were brought up the steps from the undercroft where they had lain since 1170 and placed in a new shrine built over the original tomb one 'storey' below. The height of a shrine was an important matter since this was commonly taken as an indication of the spiritual elevation of the deceased.[44]

As early as Bede's day certain traditions had grown up around the ritual of translation. In several cases it was said that a sweet odour was detected when the tomb was opened and that the body was found to be uncorrupt, even after many years. Strange lights were also associated with the movement or discovery (called—in many cases appropriately—*inventio*) of holy bones. By the central and later Middle Ages translations usually occurred only after official—papal—canonization. The opening of the original tomb was preceded by a three-day fast since the clergy who were to carry out the ceremony required abundant spiritual protection for the awesome task ahead. Sometimes as part of the preliminaries the tomb was privately opened the night before the translation, the bones (and flesh if any) were inspected and the old rotten garments replaced by new wrappings. Occasionally the washing and re-dressing of the bones was accompanied by a truncated funeral service. The remains were put back until the next day when, amidst a gathering of prelates, nobles and other important figures the saint was ceremoniously taken (again) from the old tomb. Usually the bones were kissed by the principal clergy and guests and carried about the church, even to an outside platform for public viewing. After a sermon extolling the virtues of the saint the remains were deposited in a new shrine.

The exposure of a saint's body during a translation offered privileged bystanders perhaps the only chance they would ever have actually to *touch* such a being. It is not surprising that some made the most of the occasion. The tomb of St. Edmund at Bury was opened one night in 1198 and the linen- and silk-wrapped form of the saint exposed. The abbot approached and after begging the saint to forgive his presumption

> he proceeded to touch the eyes and the nose ... and afterwards he touched the breast and arms and, raising the left hand, he touched the fingers and placed his fingers between the fingers of the saint; and going further ... touched the toes of the feet and counted them as he touched them.

Afterwards they re-entombed the saint, along with a written statement that on that date the abbot 'saw and touched' (*vidit et tetigit*) the body of St.

---

[44] Cf. the quarrel in Jessopp and James, *William of Norwich*, pp. 123–7; also Bede, *Hist. Eccl.* IV. 30; Life of St. Frideswide in *Acta Sanct.* (1853) VIII Oct. 569; J. Raine, ed., *Historians of the Church of York* (RS 71, 1879–94), II. pp. 546–550, referring to Wm. of York, died 1154, translated in 1284 *ab imo in altum, a communi loco in chorum.*

Edmund in the presence of eighteen monk-witnesses.[45] The archbishop of Sens, kissing the breast of the three-month-old corpse of Edmund Rich at Pontigny, 'perceived a wondrous odour'. When the body was translated an English participant enjoyed a great honour:

> we have touched his holy body; his head, with its hair lying thick and uninjured, with a comb we have carefully and reverently, and even joyfully, combed and arranged.[46]

Though saints enjoyed such extravagant caresses quite the opposite happened to many unfortunates who were denied burial not only in churches but even in churchyards. These constitute the final 'type' to be examined. If the saint is the positive ecclesiastical ideal these are the negative, the most extreme example being the unrepentant heretic. For obvious reasons refusal of Christian burial could cause considerable anxiety—even terror—in medieval society. A key idea, later developed by canon lawyers, appears in a letter of Pope Leo I (d. 461): If we may not associate with someone in life, then we must not associate with him in death. This became one of the theoretical bases for a blanket denial of Christian burial to whole categories such as excommunicates, pagans and Jews. Unbaptized infants made up another proscribed group. They were not buried in Christian cemeteries just as their souls, tainted by Original Sin, were never allowed into heaven. This Augustinian concept was widely accepted by theologians in the later Middle Ages, when such children were imagined to be in a 'limbo'. This was usually described as the uppermost region of hell where their only suffering was a denial of the Beatific Vision of God; but it was eternal deprivation, nevertheless. As this pitiless doctrine took shape in the later medieval centuries some bereaved parents, in their urgent desire to get round it, turned to saints who specialized in aiding infants. In fifteenth-century France parents rushed their dead babies to certain shrines were they claimed that the children were miraculously revived. Then they were baptized by laymen, sometimes priests. Afterwards the child died 'again' but now its soul went to heaven, its body could receive Christian burial. In spite of the Council of Langres (1452) which denounced abuses concerning fallacious resurrections of stillborn infants, the *angoisse inventive* of desperate parents brushed such decrees aside.[47]

Unbaptized infants were normally buried outside the circuit of the cemetery, and if inadvertently placed within this magic boundary were dug up and buried elsewhere. In the fifteenth century at Marseilles Jaumette and William were told to exhume their stillborn son and bury him in unconsecrated ground, if the corpse could be found; it had lain in its grave for more

---

[45] H. Butler, ed., *The Chronicle of Jocelin of Brakelond* (London, 1949), pp. 114, 115; a similar expression at Godric's death, *videre et contingere, Vita Godrici*, p. 327.

[46] B. Ward, *St. Edmund* (London, 1903), pp. 174–6, 195–6.

[47] P. Paravy, 'Angoisse collective et miracles au seuil de la mort', *La mort au moyen âge*, pp. 87–102.

than a year.[48] In the case of a pregnant woman dying, there were two schools of thought, the tough-minded and the tender. Proponents of the first would prefer to cut the foetus from its mother's corpse and bury it outside the cemetery (*aperiri et foetus extrahi et extra coemeterium sepeliri*). The tender approach allowed dead mother and foetus to share the same grave.[49] The problem arises in one of Boccaccio's tales. Because the woman 'had not been pregnant sufficiently long for the unborn creature to be perfectly formed they troubled themselves no further on that score' and buried her 'just as she was' (i.e., without a postmortem Caesarian).[50] Finally, another clerical opinion along these lines held that a woman who died in childbirth should not be brought into a church for funeral services since any blood falling from her body would pollute the sacred building. Some (more humane) ecclesiastics criticized this as wholly unjust.[51]

Another category prohibited burial in cemeteries is somewhat unusual since the exclusion was due to 'leprosy', which in the Middle Ages could mean anything from teenagers' acne to elephantiasis. It is true that the clergy managed to find some connection between sin and leprosy, an Old Testament idea; yet the social treatment of lepers—which amounted to far more than ostracism—is a peculiarity of medieval society deserving greater study. Lepers were isolated even after their deaths, for they were not to be buried with non-lepers. Some of the rites of separation of living lepers from society were none other than quasi-funerals, though some Church authorities strongly objected to what they considered a misuse of the liturgy. In such rites the priest led the leper (his face covered) to church chanting the seven penitential psalms of the ordinary funeral service. In church the leper knelt down under a black cloth spread between two trestles *ac si mortuus esset*, as if he were dead; candles stood by this makeshift bier. After a Mass of the Dead the leper confessed his sins and took Communion. Commendations for his soul were recited over him just as they were recited over a corpse. The priest then led him into the cemetery, where he threw a spadeful of earth at his body or feet. Finally he was led to the place he must inhabit for the rest of his life, near which he must eventually be buried.[52]

Exclusion or ejection from the churchyard was also the fate of excommunicates of all sorts by the central Middle Ages. It affected anyone who did not take communion at least once a year, to priests' concubines who refused to desert their mates, to those who were killed in tournaments to public usurers, to anyone dying during or just after committing a serious offence, for example—as one commentator theorized—while going home

[48] Bernard, *La Sépulture*, pp. 134–5.
[49] Ibid., p. 117 n. 3
[50] *Decameron*, day ten, story four, tr. G. McWilliam (1972), p. 750.
[51] Wm. Durand, op. cit., p. 38, and J. Beleth, op. cit., p. 841 (Naples, 1859).
[52] Martène, I. p. 361, *ordo* IV. Other *ordines* specifically prohibiting these rites are *ordo* I and II on pp. 358–60. An English translation of a similar *ordo* in R. Clay, *The Mediaeval Hospitals of England* (London, 1909), pp. 273–76.

from a brothel. The men who killed the Count of Flanders in the church of St. Donatian at Bruges committed sacrilege as well as murder, polluting the church with blood. They were therefore excommunicated and after their executions buried 'outside the cemetery, at the crossroads and in the country'.[53] Burial could be refused to laymen who did not pay tithes, to those dying intestate, to suicides. Even monks dying possessed of illicit property were excluded. In the early twelfth century Guibert of Nogent was retelling a story at least 500 years old when describing how a dead monk found to have a money-bag hidden on his person was buried in the fields. Another group falling under the ban were debtors. Creditors could demand that church burial be refused them, even have them exhumed from sacred ground. A dead bishop of Bayeux excommunicated for debt had to wait eighty years for church burial, that is until the debt was paid off by one of his successors, in 1440.[54] There were objections to burial exclusion because of debt from the more reasonable—or less avaricious—clergy. These theoretically harsh regulations were enforced or ignored depending upon the wishes and weight of authority of local ecclesiastical or lay Establishments. There was also room for discussion. Among suicides, for instance, those who deliberately killed themselves had been excluded from at least 563. But those who did so while mentally deranged were allowed burial and their property was not confiscated by the authorities. In the fifteenth century a widow who hanged herself was buried in a Devonshire churchyard. The local priest had second thoughts about the question of pollution, but the bishop of Exeter settled things by pointing out that she had committed suicide while insane; the churchyard had not been polluted.[55]

In the earlier medieval centuries major excommunication was a dreadful separation from society, a rupture which damned the body to a dog's burial and the soul to eternal fellowship with the devil. The excommunicate, though physically alive, was socially dead: no-one was to associate with him. He was also, of course, spiritually dead. In one of the rituals of absolution *from* excommunication the person concerned was commanded to 'rise from the dead'. In another service he must first lie on the floor while the seven penitential psalms of the funeral rites were sung over him.[56] As clerical powers grew during the central Middle Ages excommunications were levied for a growing variety of—sometimes trivial—offences, in an increasingly complex society. There was, however, one class for whom Christian burial was out of the question not only because of the prohibitions of canon law, but also because in some cases there was no body to bury: the relapsed or unrepentant heretic.

Along with the growth of individualism, personal piety and canonical

[53] Galbert of Bruges, *Murder of Charles the Good,* pp. 254–5.
[54] Bernard, *Sépulture,* p. 128 n. 6.
[55] Register of Edmund Lacy (Exon.) in *Canterb. and York Soc.* vol. cxxix (1960–61), I. 13–14.
[56] Martène, I. pp. 323–6.

orderliness, heresy became an increasingly visible part of the religious scene from the eleventh century. Early responses to heresy included uncontrolled violence, often by zealous mobs but sometimes with the approval of local authorities. Some heretics were burnt to death by the crowds. It was only during the twelfth century, however, when heretical movements began to create problems on a wider scale, that there was a corresponding acceleration of action by prelates, kings and papacy. Inquisitorial procedures were set in motion under papal authority, canonists like Sicard of Cremona (d. 1215) were advocating the death penalty as part of Church policy, and heretics were rigidly excluded from church burial. Meanwhile some secular authorities declared themselves in favour of burning relapsed or impenitent heretics. This became a widely-accepted civil policy with Frederick II's 1224 decrees, which Pope Gregory IX adopted for the Church.

In the mid-thirteenth century Pope Alexander IV not only excommunicated anyone who knowingly buried heretics in consecrated ground but ordered them publicly to dig them up with their own hands and throw them out of the cemetery. This was already carried out on local ecclesiastical authority. A well-known case of posthumous ejection (and punishment) for heresy involved John Wyclif, whose ideas lay behind England's only indigenous heretical movement, Lollardy. Wyclif died at his parish church of Lutterworth (Lincoln diocese) in 1384. Since he was not (yet) a 'heretic' he was given church burial. In 1415 his works were found to be heretical and an exhumation order was issued. This was ignored by the bishop of Lincoln but—after another papal order in December 1427—the next bishop had to act. In the spring of 1428 he disinterred what were assumed to be Wyclif's bones and burned them, casting the ashes into a nearby stream.

Execution by burning was hardly a medieval innovation. It is found, for example, in the Twelve Tables as the appropriate penalty for arson. In about 296 Emperor Diocletian decreed that Manichaeans were to be burned, a law repeated in Justinian's sixth-century imperial code. This in turn may have influenced the canonists and civil lawyers of the eleventh and twelfth centuries. Burning was also a common punishment in early Germanic law for sorcery, adultery, arson, poisoning and theft.[57]

Heresy, like these occult felonies, assaulted society secretly, from within. But in addition it attacked those spiritual values which were believed to be essential to individual and collective salvation. On the other hand heretics, like Jews, were sometimes condemned for more 'practical' reasons as well. But condemned they were, and if executed even their ashes were ritually ejected from society and dispersed by the blind and guiltless forces of nature.[58]

---

[57] J. Reinhard, 'Burning at the Stake in Medieval Law and Literature', *Speculum* 16 (1941), 186–7; Amira, *Die germanisch. Todesstrafen*, pp. 195–6.

[58] Reinhard, op. cit., 190–91. Amira, op. cit., p. 220, views the process as a kind of offering, 'das Lebendigverbrennen von Menschen als Opfer'. For natural dispersal 'in den Wind gestreut oder in fliessendes Wasser geschüttet werden' see p. 161, with medieval refs.

They were not only denied burial in holy ground, but were refused any kind of posthumous existence whatsoever. In addition burning was appropriate in some cases since total destruction left nothing for misguided followers to venerate. Finally, the destruction of the body was a symbol of the destruction of the soul and of the chance for resurrection. It is undoubtedly true that medieval theologians easily explained how God could reconstitute disintegrated bodies, make them ready for Judgment Day. But ordinary mortals are not theologians. Even among theologians and apologists there is enough discussion of the matter to suggest that not all medieval Christians were at ease with their explanations. The state of the body at resurrection had been worrying Christians long before the days of Justin Martyr and Athenagoras. As St. Augustine put it, the question Christians were 'accustomed to discuss among themselves [was] when and in what manner will we be resurrected'. The *manner* of resurrection also interested Aquinas, who composed a treatise on the subject. The continuing questions and doubts of ordinary laymen may perhaps have prompted some of these scholastic discussions of the state of the hair and fingernails at resurrection or the nature of the intestinal contents.[59] Perhaps many believed that heretics were receiving a foretaste of punishment from which not even the resurrection would momentarily rescue them, in spite of what theologians claimed.

*   *   *

Obviously, as our four extremes demonstrate, fundamental social assumptions were hallowed in death rites, but sometimes a corpse was deliberately used to achieve a limited, specific end. Though it is not always easy or, fortunately, necessary to distinguish between tampering with and observing tradition, there are many cases of overt manipulation for particular purposes. This took place on several planes. At its most basic, literal level, a corpse might be 'compelled' to perform various acts: Pope Formosus was dug up, dressed, condemned by a synod and dumped into the Tiber; Patriarch Arsenius, dead some forty years, freed his enemies from anathema by means of the bull of absolution thrust into his hands. Related to these posthumous antics but only slightly less theatrical were the trials held over the bodies of suicides and traitors, like the purported trial of Thomas Becket, a victim of Tudor propagandists.[60]

On a less bizarre level the reputations as well as the bodies of the dead were manipulated by particular groups for their own ends. Norwich cathedral needed a saint, Norwich citizens owed money to Jews, so a little apprentice

---

[59] Augustine's sermon 361 in J. Mourant, tr., *Augustine on Immortality* (Villanova Univ., 1969), p. 52; Aquinas, *Summa Theol.*, Supp to Pt. III, Q. 80, Art. 1, Obj. 2. Odo of Ourschamp considered similar problems in the twelfth century in *Quaestiones* ed. J. Pitra, *Anal. Novissima* (1888) II. 40-41.

[60] J-C. Schmitt, 'Le suicide au moyen âge', *Annales, ESC,* vol. 31 (1976), 11–12, 25, notes 54, 57; A. Cohen, 'Political Symbolism' in *Annual Rev. of Anthropology,* vol. 8 (1979), 92–94, discusses modern manipulation for political ends.

discovered buried in the woods became 'Saint' William, killed 'by the Jews'. After Simon de Montfort's death his political supporters discovered that he was a saint—though excommunicated by a papal legate.[61] Still in the political realm, the canonization of a king, especially after the twelfth century when papal controls tightened, was a dynastic as well as a spiritual coup.

The fact that kings can become saints raises the question of the relationship between these two medieval archetypes. There is, for instance, the assimilation of their antitheses, heretics and traitors, by the eminent decretist Huguccio and his student Pope Innocent III. In the thirteenth-century *Mirror of Justice* heresy is a treason against the divine majesty. At the other end of the spectrum saints were princes in the spiritual realm, like mundane kings both feared and honoured. The rituals which blossomed around saints may have influenced royal cults. It has been suggested that Corpus Christi processions in the later Middle Ages made some impact on the form of royal funerals.[62] Perhaps there were further borrowings: uncorrupted saintly bodies and royal effigies which never decayed; multiple burial sites for the 'relics' of kings and the nobility especially from the twelfth century. In addition, it is probably more than coincidental that thaumaturgy—miracle-working—became a royal attribute in the later Middle Ages.[63] All such developments point toward the sanctification of kingship, the absorption of ecclesiastical ideals and powers by an increasingly dominant secular force. When Becket's brains and blood splashed across the floor of Canterbury cathedral in 1170 the common folk smeared bits of cloth with the gore, to treasure as miracle-working relics. When Charles I was beheaded in 1649 it was said that people rushed to dip their handkerchiefs in royal blood. Death and funeral rites in the later Middle Ages played their part in guiding and illustrating this transfer of magic and inversion of values, as they influenced and elucidated so much else in medieval society.

To sum up, the death-rites of our four principal types reinforced medieval ideals on both a literal and a metaphorical level.[64] The first aspect is most clearly seen in the secular examples, the second in the ecclesiastical. At the most basic level the wealth and ceremony of royal funerals emphasized the grandeur of kingship. In addition, however, the carrying out of elaborate ceremonial re-established precise relationships between king, kin and nobility. Perhaps this clarification and re-affirmation of ranking within the nobility was even more important than emphasis upon the dead king. Ideals of a different order were expressed, at least in France, when the effigy came to represent kingship itself. In stark contrast, while kings' effigies were symbols of the unified and undying nature of their powers the ritually

---

[61] For William and Simon see Finucane, op. cit., chap. 7, 8.

[62] Beaune, op. cit., pp. 132–3.

[63] For a recent revision see F. Barlow, 'The King's Evil', *English Hist. Rev.* vol. xcv (1980), 1–27.

[64] Cf. R. Huntington and P. Metcalf, *Celebrations of Death: The Anthropology of Mortuary Ritual* (Cambridge, 1979), pp. 61–7, 159–72.

divided body of the traitor, his limbs scattered across the realm, was a literal as well as symbolic demonstration of the effects of that power.

The function of the body as symbol for the soul is most evident in rites associated with saints. The uncorrupted, sweet-smelling and light-emitting corpse of a holy man 'represents' the soul of the saint, which enjoys the eternally uncorrupted sweetness and light of heaven. In addition these attributes negated death itself, its rot, stench and darkness. A saint's corpse represented his soul even more clearly in rites of translation. As in secondary burials described by anthropologists in many cultures today, translation marked the culmination of the dead man's journey to final, complete spiritual development. The corpse moved to the holiest, highest position within the church, for the soul had 'arrived', moved near to the centre and highest source of all holiness.

The fate of the soul was linked to that of the corpse in all classes, not just among saints. The same spatial relationships are evident. The 'holy' were entombed within the church, the holiest at the east end; but the common folk, most of whom supposedly began their otherworldly existence in purgatory, were buried outside in the churchyard. Excommunicates lay beyond the holy bounds of the cemetery altogether, their souls banished to hell. They had chosen to cut themselves off from Christian society. Pagans, Jews and unbaptized infants were also excluded because they never joined it. Consequently they too were banished to the wilderness of unconsecrated ground. Finally we have seen that the active rejection of the Church by the relapsed or impenitent heretic was punished by denial of burial whether inside or outside consecrated ground: far from being preserved in an aura of holiness, he was literally cast to the winds. The rich symbolism of these distinctive death-rites expresses *inter alia* the violent contrasts found within later medieval society. There is much to explore. As one of Lucian's characters said, 'Truly, it is well worth while to observe what most people do and say at funerals.'

I wish to thank J. C. Dickinson and the Editor for their helpful suggestions about particular points raised in this chapter.

III

From 'Public' to 'Private':
the Royal Funerals in England, 1500–1830*

PAUL S. FRITZ

Historians or royal biographers who have written on ceremonial at the time of a royal death in England have generally misunderstood the nature of the proceedings, not only in their details but their broader significance as well. Two of the most recent royal biographies[1] have failed to grasp the basic distinction that existed by the late seventeenth century in England between the terms 'public' and 'private' as they related to royal funeral ceremonial. To be sure, both the funeral of Charles II (1685) and Queen Anne (1714) were designated as private funerals, but this did not mean they were of a secret nature. An examination of royal funeral ceremonial over a broad chronological sweep from the beginning of the Tudor until the end of the Georgian eras will demonstrate that the distinction is an heraldic one, referring primarily to the 'degree' of ceremony to be used. This was first pointed out several years ago by Sir Anthony Wagner in his monumental study, *Heralds of England*.[2] An understanding of royal funeral ceremony in this wider context of time reveals not only the complexity involved in arranging such ceremonies, but demonstrates that between these dates such ceremony underwent a profound change. By the year 1830 the spectacle of the great public funeral—with its enormous procession, numbering a cast of well over a thousand, with its magnificent chariot bearing the coffin with its life-like effigy of the deceased monarch, with the hearse or mausoleum beneath which the body was placed for the funeral service itself—had gone. All this had given way to a much simpler and greatly scaled down form of earlier ceremonial. The public funeral under the direction of the Earl

* Research for this was carried out as part of a Leave Fellowship held in 1979–80. I wish to thank the Social Sciences and Humanities Research Council of Canada for their financial support. I should also like to thank the Chapter of the College of Arms for permission to quote from manuscripts in their possession and in particular Mr. F. S. Andrus, Lancaster Herald of Arms, and Mr. Robert Yorke, Archivist and Librarian of the College, for their help.
   The following abbreviations are used to refer to manuscript collections: CA (College of Arms); BL (British Library); LC (Lord Chamberlain's Papers); PC (Privy Council Registers); PRO (Public Record Office); SP (State Papers Domestic).
[1] Antonia Fraser, *King Charles II* (London, 1979), pp. 458–60; Edward Gregg, *Queen Anne* (London, 1980), pp. 397–8.
[2] Sir Anthony Wagner, *Heralds of England. A History of the Office and College of Arms* (London, 1967), p. 340. (Hereafter, Wagner.)

Marshal all but disappeared. The only symbol of sovereignty that remained as part of the procedure was the use on top of the coffin of either the real crown or a replica of it. The great heraldic public funeral was, by the end of the seventeenth century, retained only for the funerals of prominent military and political heroes such as the Duke of Marlborough (1722), the Earl of Chatham (1778), Lord Nelson (1806), and the Duke of Wellington (1852). In this change from 'public' to 'private', while the Officers of the College of Arms argued for the maintenance of the appropriate precedents, it was a wide range of personal, political, and economic considerations that determined the final form for any particular royal funeral.

I

On 21 April 1509, Henry VII died at Richmond Palace.[3] Following a period of masses and dirges held in the Great Chamber of the Hall, on 9 May his body was placed in a chariot for the first of a two-part funeral procession from Richmond to St. Paul's and from there to its final resting place in Westminster Abbey. The Chariot, covered with black cloth of gold, was drawn by five great horses draped with black velvet garnished with escutcheons of gold. On the coffin, which contained the embalmed remains, rested a life-like effigy 'apparelled in rich robes, with the crown on the head, and sceptre and ball in the hands, lay'd on cushions of gold'.[4] A vast number of prelates and king's servants in full mourning preceded the chariot and 600 others followed with lighted torches. When the procession reached St. George's Fields near Southwark it was met 'by the religious of all sorts in or about the city' who, together with the Mayor, Aldermen and other city dignitaries swelled the procession as it reached St. Paul's. Here the King's body was placed in the choir beneath 'a stately hearse of wax' and a solemn mass and sermon was preached by the Bishop of Rochester. The next day the body was brought to Westminster where it rested beneath a second great hearse 'full of lights' and the King's effigy, made especially for the occasion, rested on a pall of cloth of gold. For the ceremony the next day, the mourners sat within the first rail of the hearse, the Knights with the banners within the second rail, and the officers of arms who marshalled the ceremony beyond them. Three masses were solemnly sung and then the achievements—the

---

[3] The best printed source for this funeral is F. Sandford, *Geneological History of the Kings and Queens of England, and Monarchs of Great Britain from the Conquest, Anno 1066 to the Year 1707.* (Hereafter, Sandford.) The main manuscript sources are CA, *Briscoe* vol. 2 fos. 311–12; BL, *Add. MSS., 45, 131* (The Wriothesley Heraldic Collections), vol. II; *Egerton 2642* (The Booke of Heraldrye and Other Things . . .); PRO, *LC 2/1*—Funeral of Henry VII.

[4] For the effigy see Sir William St. John Hope, 'On the Funeral Effigies of the Kings and Queen's of England', *Archaeologia*, LX (1907), 539. The face modelled from the death mask still exists in the exhibition of Royal and other effigies in the museum in the Norman undercroft at Westminster Abbey.

bannerols, coat of arms, sword, target, helmet, etc.—were offered.[5] Immediately following the interment, the Lord Treasurer, the Steward, the Chamberlain of the Household, and the Comptroller broke their staves of office and threw them into the open grave and Garter King of Arms cried—'Vive le Roy, Henry Huitième, Roy d'Angleterre et de France.' Thus ended the first of the heraldic funerals for a sovereign for which a detailed account survives[6] and with it were established those features—the huge procession, the chariot, the life-like effigy, the hearse—that were to characterize, with but one exception (the funeral of Charles II), subsequent royal funerals until the end of the seventeenth century.

Not until thirty-seven years later did the next funeral for a sovereign occur with the death of Henry VIII in 1547.[7] As with his father, three hearses were used. The first for the Chapel at Whitehall Palace was:

> a sumptuous hearse of Virgins wax ... with six goodly pillars, weighing by estimation 2000 pounds under which hearse was a canopy of rich cloth of gold, whose vallance was half gold and half black silk, into which the corpse was conveyed, covered with a pall of cloth of tissue.[8]

Beneath this elaborate structure, which in turn was railed about with timber and covered with black cloth, the body rested from 2 to 14 February, when, at about 10 a.m., it was removed for the start of the procession towards Windsor and the final burial in St. George's Chapel. For this the body was drawn in a 'stately' chariot and on top of the coffin rested the effigy:

> with the true Imperial Crown on the head, and under it a night cap of black satin, set full of precious stones, and apparelled with robes of crimson and velvet, furnished with miniver, powdered with ermine, and collar of the Garter, with the order of St. George about the neck, a crimson satin doublet embroidered with gold, two bracelets of gold about the wrists, set with stones and pearls, a fair arming sword by the side, and sceptre in the right hand and the ball in the left, a pair of scarlet hose, crimson velvet shoes, gloves on the hands, and several diamond rings on the fingers.[9]

This spectacle formed the focal point in a procession estimated to be some four miles long. At its first resting place—Syon House—the body was received by the Bishops of London, Bristol and Gloucester and placed beneath a second hearse. The following morning the procession reformed at 6 a.m. and reached Windsor, by 1 o'clock where the body was met by the Bishops of Winchester, London, and Ely and conveyed into the Chapel. Here a third hearse had been prepared, estimated to weigh some 4,000 lb and to include some thirteen pillars.

[5] CA, *Briscoe,* vol. 2, fol. 311.
[6] For the evidence on earlier royal funerals see Sir William St. John Hope, 'On the Funeral Effigies . . .', *Archaeologia,* LX (1907).
[7] Sandford, pp. 492–4; LC 2/2 (1547); CA *Press 62/Shelf C/Briscoe,* vol. II, pp. 313–14.
[8] CA, *Press 62/Shelf C/Briscoe,* vol. II.
[9] Ibid.

The next day, 16 February, the final ceremony took place which included the customary offering of the King's banners, hatchments, bannerols, etc.[10] The service concluded with the breaking of the staves of office by the Lord Chamberlain, the Lord Great Master, the Treasurer, the Comptroller, and the Serjeant Porter 'upon their heads in three parts'. Then, as with the ceremonial for Henry VII, Garter proclaimed the state and name of the new King, Edward VI, and, to the sound of trumpets, the ceremony ended.

With the funeral of Edward VI, one notable change occurred in the nature of the trophies used in the procession.[11] As the first Protestant funeral for an English sovereign, the four great banners were not of Saints, as had been previously used, but were of the Order of the Garter, the Red Cross, Edward VI's mother's arms, and the Queen Dowager's arms. With the ceremonial for Mary Tudor, five years later, for the last time in English royal funeral ceremonial, the four great religious banners—the Trinity, Our Lady, St. George, Mary Magdalene—were displayed. The hearse prepared for the Abbey service for Mary was adorned with wax angels and the valance fringed with escutcheons of England and France. As with Henry VII and Henry VIII, three hearses were used.[12]

For the funeral of Mary's successor, Elizabeth I, we have the first full pictorial portrayal of the funeral procession of a sovereign that has survived.[13] In it, the main features of the heraldic funeral are well illustrated, especially the chariot with its coffin drawn by four horses. On the coffin covered with purple velvet lies the life-like effigy of the Queen. Six knights bear the canopy and twelve noblemen carry the banners with the arms of the Queen's royal ancestors (*plate* III. 1).

The detailed accounts among the Lord Chamberlain's papers for the funeral of her successor, James I, in 1625 clearly indicate something of the magnitude of the operation necessary for staging one of these great public spectacles.[14] Some twenty-one tailors were employed full time to cut, fit, and hang the vast quantities of black material required to prepare the various rooms for mourning at Denmark House and the Abbey. In addition they had to turn some 1,320 yards of black cloth into the 325 gowns that were to be worn by the poor men who were to walk in the funeral procession. Joiners and carpenters provided not only the necessary seating for the Abbey but built the requisite number of hearses. They also constructed for the Abbey seven chairs of state, thirty-one high stools, thirty-two black chairs, five foot stools and one folding table with a desk. A host of other tradesmen supplied the remaining necessaries—buckram, damask, velvet, and leather

[10] This ceremony was known as the offering of the 'achievements'. For a description of this see: Wagner, p. 107.

[11] CA, *Press 62/Shelf C/Briscoe,* vol. II, p. 314.

[12] Ibid., pp. 314–15; Sandford, pp. 506–7.

[13] BL, *Cotton MS. Faustina E. i* (The Funeral Procession (1603) of Queen Elizabeth I).

[14] Sandford, p. 580; CA, *Press 20F/Royal Funerals 1618–1738 (Nayler);* PRO, *LC 2/6* (1625–James I).

for the chariot horses and the horse of estate; gilt spurs, a gilt sword, ceremonial bits, bearing the arms of Great Britain, France and Ireland, for the horses' mouths. The royal feather dresser, William Audley, provided enormous numbers of purple, crimson and black feathers, while the joiner, Richard Brigham, constructed the two chariots; the College of Arms and their painters supplied the numerous banners; Maximillian Colt modelled the two life-like effigies. The one for the Abbey was provided with 'several joints in the arms and legs and body' and the face and hands were moulded by him from a death mask. Daniel Parkes supplied the periwigs and eyebrows for both effigies.

The massive funeral procession occurred in two stages—from Theobald's to Denmark House where a lying-in-state took place and from there to Westminster Abbey for the funeral service. For the first part, the body was placed on a chariot of black velvet drawn by six black horses draped in black with festoons of black feathers on their heads. At Smithfield, the funeral procession was joined by the City dignitaries.

For the lying-in-state at Denmark House, six large silver candlesticks (that had been bought by Charles I in Spain) stood about the body and great wax tapers burned throughout the night. Upon the pall covering the coffin rested the effigy in its robes of estate.[15] A sumptuous hearse or mausoleum was prepared for Westminster Abbey (*plate* III. 2).

On the day of the funeral the Knight Marshal on horseback and several footmen cleared the streets and the procession wound its way towards the Abbey. Prominently displayed as part of the procession were the standards, banners, bannerols, etc., all carefully provided by the officers of arms. In addition to the elaborate chariot, there was (as with previous funerals) the horse of estate draped in black.[16]

Seventy years later, on 5 March 1695 there took place the last of the great public or heraldic funerals for a sovereign with the death of Queen Mary. Both the circumstances of her death (she died at the age of thirty-one of smallpox) as well as personal and political considerations account for the massive scale of the ceremonial that marked her death. Not since the death of James I was so much time, energy, and expense devoted to the ordering of a royal funeral. By contrast, the preparations for her predecessor, Charles II, seem paltry. An examination of the arrangements made for this funeral gives considerable insight into the nature of the decision-making at such a time and the wide complex of factors that resulted in the final form for the ceremony.[17]

On the day of her death—28 December 1694—twenty-four members of the Privy Council met at Whitehall and from this initial meeting the first

---

[15] These robes were usually borrowed from the Wardrobe and then returned after the ceremony.
[16] PRO, *LC 2/6* (1625—James I).
[17] Sandford, pp. 720–1; PRO, *LC 2/11(2)*; PRO, *PC 1/13/48; PC 2/76; CA/S.M.L./30/ Ceremonials; CA Press 20F/Funerals 1684–1714.*

orders-in-council were issued. These related to, among other things, the removal of the body from Whitehall, the preparation of the necessary hearses, the burial of the bowels in the Abbey, and the preparation of the coffin.

Once these preliminary details were settled the Privy Council turned its attention to the funeral ceremonial. Towards this end, the Earl Marshal, the Duke of Norfolk, sent an express to Henry St. John, the Garter King of Arms, requesting that he and several other officers of arms attend the next council meeting 'to give an account in writing ... of what had been done on like occasions with expedition and without any great expense'.[18] In compliance with his request the officers presented Council with an elaborate scheme for both the lying-in-state and the funeral ceremony. As could have been predicted they drew as precedent on the funeral of James I. They proposed that four rooms at Whitehall be hung with mourning—the Council Chamber, the Presence Chamber, the Privy Chamber, and the chamber where the body would lie in state. In the latter room they suggested that Council require a hearse and a bed of state. On the latter, the officers of arms proposed the placing of 'an effigy of her majesty in wax apparelled in her royal coronation robes with an imperial crown on her head and her sceptres in her hands, the head resting on a purple velvet cushion fringed and tasselled with gold'.[19]

Immediately following their presentation they were ordered to withdraw and, after extensive debate in Council, they were recalled and ordered to draw up a second scheme for the lying-in-state that would add two additional mourning rooms, but would leave out the elaborate hearse and the effigy. As had been done for Charles II it was decided that no life-like effigy would be used for the ceremonial. Instead, it was resolved initially (as with Charles II) to place on the coffin 'a purple velvet cushion with fringe and tassells, and thereon an imperial crown gilt'.[20] Instead of the hearse, so characteristic a feature of previous lyings-in-state, there was to be displayed at the foot of the coffin the Great Banner and the banner of the Union painted on satin and on the sides were to be the four lesser banners of the four Kingdoms and twelve bannerols of their majesties' descent. There were also to be twelve black stands with large white tapers.

Further details were worked out by a special committee of the Privy Council with the full council to give its final approval. During the course of six subsequent meetings, the special committee consulted the officers of arms on such matters as the type of hearse that would be appropriate for the Abbey and the heraldic honours that had been carried at the funerals of Mary Tudor and Elizabeth. Finally, on 8 January 1695 they presented their carefully worked out scheme to Council, who approved it. The final arrangements included provision for the erection of special galleries in the Abbey

---

[18] CA, *Press 20F/Royal Funerals 1694–1772*, p. 23.
[19] CA, *Press 20F/Royal Funerals 1694–1772*.
[20] Ibid.

for the House of Commons and the House of Lords and for 'ladies of quality and foreign ministers'; for the hanging of the choir of the chapel from top to bottom with black cloth; and for the building of an elaborate hearse and chariot on the basis of plans drawn up by Sir Christopher Wren (*plate* III. 3). That political considerations played a large part in their deliberations is indicated by their decision to depart from all previous ceremonial in one central aspect. Whereas the funerals for Charles II and previous sovereigns had been held by torchlight at night, Queen Mary's was to take place in the daytime and was to begin at 10 a.m. In this way maximum benefit could be gained from the public viewing of the event.[21]

Throughout the month of January further details were settled. Specific instructions provided for fitting out the chariot to carry the body and, for the first time, it was decided to use purple instead of black velvet throughout—on the chariot, on the hearse, and on the canopy that was to be carried over the body for the procession from the chariot to its placement beneath the hearse in Henry VII's chapel. Also, the full heraldic achievements (helm, crest, target, banners, etc) would be used in the procession. The most significant alteration in ceremonial occurred, however, with the substitution of the real crown for the replica together with other items of the coronation regalia—the orb and sceptres. These would be used for the lying-in-state that was to last from 21 February until the day of the funeral 5 March and for the funeral procession, where care would be taken to see that they were 'well fastened to the cushion'.[22]

Narcissus Luttrell described the lying-in-state:

> This afternoon (21 February) the queen began to lye in state in the bed chamber, all the officers of her household attending, according to their offices under the direction of the Marquess of Winchester, her chamberlain; and the ladies of honour also attended, four of whom stand about the corpse, and are relieved by others every half hour; upon her head lyes the crown, and over it a fine canopy; at her feet lies the sword of state, the helmet and her arms upon a cushion, the banners and escucheons hanging round; the state is very great, and more magnificent than can be exprest: all persons are admitted without distinction.[23]

By early March the final order for the ceremonial was printed by order of the Earl Marshal and on 5 March the public witnessed the largest funeral procession ever held in England for a sovereign, with the size of the procession greatly swelled out by the inclusion of both houses of parliament in mourning cloaks. Certainly nothing of this scale had been observed within living memory, not even the grand spectacle that had in 1670 accompanied

---

[21] It is not certain when the ceremony actually got under way. Sandford in his published account says 3 p.m. but in a minute of 12 January 1695 the council indicated that it was to begin at 10 a.m. (PRO, *PC2/76*).

[22] PRO, *PC 2/76*.

[23] N. Luttrell, *A Brief Historical Relation of State Affairs from September 1678 to April 1714* (Oxford, 1857), III, p. 442.

the ceremonial for the Duke of Albemarle's funeral.[24] As Evelyn remarked: 'Never so universal a mourning, all the parliament had cloaks given them, 400 poor women, all the streets hung, and the middle of the streets boarded and covered with black cloth; there was also the nobility, mayor, and aldermen, judges etc.'[25]

This was by far the most expensive royal funeral to date. The largest item figuring in the accounts presented to the Lord Chamberlain's department for collection was for the thousands of yards of black cloth—5,510 yards for the Presence Chamber; 1,370 yards for the Chapels at Whitehall and St. James's; 2,970 yards for the King's Presence Chamber; 3,132 yards for the House of Commons; 9,927 yards for Henry VII's Chapel, etc. Bills from joiners, mercers, tailors, coachmakers, feather dressers, herald painters, upholsterers, merchants and a host of others steadily flowed into the department for collection as a result of the 168 separate warrants issued in connection with these funeral preparations.[26] Although at the outset the council had expressed a strong wish to cut the expense such did not happen. A total of well over £50,000 was ultimately required to stage this elaborate pageant of death.[27]

II

Although the funeral of Queen Mary was the last of the great 'public' or heraldic funerals for an English sovereign, the change to what may be called the first of the 'private' funerals for a sovereign had occurred a decade earlier with the arrangements made for Charles II in 1685.[28] Not only was the idea of the vast funeral procession put to one side, but the three central features that had marked the great public funeral—the chariot, the effigy, and the hearse—were omitted.

Final decisions respecting the disposal of the sovereign's body rested with the successor, but by 1685 the details relating to the disposal of the body, the form and order of the procession, and the nature of the religious ceremony were worked out by the Privy Council. Between 1685 and 1830 the Council approved funeral ceremonial for seven sovereigns—Charles II, Mary, William III, Anne, George II, III, and IV. As on previous occasions, the Council met immediately after the death of each sovereign to decide the course of action to follow and usually requested advice from the officers of arms. The first of their tasks was the disposal of the body and, with but one exception,

---

[24] F. Sandford, *The Order of Ceremonies Used For and At the Solemn Interment of George Duke of Albemarle* (1670?).
[25] A. E. S. de Beer (ed.), *The Diary of John Evelyn*, V, p. 203.
[26] PRO, *LC 2/11(2)* 1695-Funeral of Queen Mary.
[27] Ibid.
[28] PRO, *PC 2/71*; PRO, *PC 1/13/49*; BL, *Add. MSS. 38, 141*; CA, *Chapter Book, L. 3*; CA, *I Series/Vol. 4 (Funerals)*; CA, *A.W.W.*; CA, *Briscoe*, vol. I.

the practice adopted in 1685 did not vary.[29] The first orders issued requested that the physicians who had attended at the sovereign's death conduct an autopsy and present a full written and signed report to Council. In the case of Charles II, his body was opened and examined 'in the sight of all his majesties physicians and several others that had been called in to consult in the time of his said sickness'.[30] The report was then presented to Council in the presence of James II. Following the precedent set for James I, the next step was the embalming of the body. By this time, the process required a separate burial of the entrails, a practice that dated back at least to the death of Henry I in 1135.[31] From the late seventeenth century, until at least the end of the Georgian period, a separate ceremony was devoted to the transporting of the entrails in separate urns for immediate burial. Once embalmed, the body was then wrapped in cere cloth, covered tightly with lead, soldered up and enclosed within one or more coffins. The explanation for this latter elaborate procedure lies in the fact that great care had to be taken to avoid any unpleasant consequences, since a long gap separated the moment of death from the final funeral ceremonial. After these immediate concerns were provided for, Council could turn to consider the other arrangements: the nature of the orders for court and general mourning and the style of the depositum to be affixed to the exterior coffin.[32] The form and order of the actual ceremony occupied most of their time and here a wide number of factors influenced their final decisions. Although it has often been assumed that custom and precedent were the primary factors determining the final form of royal funeral ceremonial, planning for Charles II's, and subsequent funerals, reveals clearly a much wider range of factors.

Charles II died at Whitehall on 6 February 1685, and after the first matters were dealt with—the autopsy, embalming, etc.—the Privy Council considered on 10 February what order and form of ceremonial would be appropriate for the first English sovereign's funeral since James I's in 1625.[33] The officers of arms were required to attend the meeting and it was obvious that they would place before the council the scheme used at James I's funeral. They suggested, therefore, a full heraldic funeral. Their scheme was, however, rejected as a model for Charles II's, after close consultation with the new King, James II. Instead, council decided that the funeral would not be after the manner of the previous ones but would be greatly scaled down to what Stephen Martin Leake, Garter King of Arms, was to refer to

---

[29] The exception was George III who left specific instructions that no autopsy was to be performed.

[30] BL, *Add.MSS., 38, 141*, vol. II, fo. 62.

[31] Ralph E. Giesey, *The Royal Funeral Ceremony in Renaissance France* (Geneva, 1960), p. 20.

[32] Over the years court and general mourning varied in both form and length. The latter could last as long as two years as happened for Queen Mary in 1695 or the period could be as short as six months. See my 'Trade in Death: The Royal Funerals in England 1695–1830'.

[33] PRO, *PC 2/71*.

later as a funeral after 'the private manner'.[34] Bearing this in mind the officers of arms were requested to return the next day and place before the committee the precedents for the funeral ceremonial for Charles II's brother, the Duke of Gloucester, that had been used in 1660.[35] On this basis, and with this precedent in mind, the council worked out the final form. Although the officers of arms expressed their reluctance to sanction such a form for a sovereign's funeral by indicating to council that they did not have among their records a precise account of the ceremonial used for that funeral, council responded by admonishing them to be 'more diligent and careful in the performance of their duties'.[36]

At this second meeting orders were issued for the preparation of a canopy of black velvet lined with taffeta, and for a cushion of purple velvet with fringe and tassels of gold. This latter order was a significant one, for on this cushion was to rest 'an imperial crown of tin gilt with a cap of crimson velvet turned up with ermine'.[37] Although the most recent account of Charles II's funeral by his biographer[38] claims that the Lord Chamberlain ordered the preparation of a wax effigy 'dressed in robes of crimson velvet trimmed with ermine, and surmounted with an imperial crown of tin gilt' and that this was used in the funeral ceremonial, the final plans for the ceremonial excluded the use of the effigy.[39] Although at one stage in their deliberations Mr. Coling, secretary to the Lord Chamberlain, had been instructed to discuss the question of taking effigies, no action was taken.[40] At both the lying-in-state and the funeral itself only the replica of the crown on the purple velvet cushion adorned the coffin and in the Abbey procession Norroy King of Arms carried it before the coffin.

On Friday, 13 February, the final form of the ceremonial was settled at a full council in the presence of James II and the funeral took place the next day starting at 7 o'clock in the evening from the Painted Chamber. When the funeral procession reached the Abbey, it was joined by the Dean and Prebends attended by the choir who fell into the procession just before Norroy King of Arms.

Within the space of nine days, therefore, the funeral plans and the actual ceremony had been completed. Certainly the ceremony lacked all of the pomp, grandeur and spectacle associated with previous ones. Had precedent alone determined the form, many more heraldic devices would have been used. The major factor in determining the scale of this particular ceremonial was the wish of Charles's successor, James II, and it was publicly stated

---

[34] CA, *S.M.L.* 65, p. 91.
[35] PRO, *PC 1/13/49.*
[36] PRO, *PC 2/71*, fol. 11.
[37] PRO, *PC 1/13/49; PC 2/71;* CA, *Press 20F/Royal Funerals 1618–1738.*
[38] Antonia Fraser, *Charles II,* p. 458.
[39] Ibid.
[40] PRO, *PC 1/13/49,* fo. 2.

that he wished it to be done with as 'little charge and expense as possible'.[41] When the final form was agreed upon, it was announced that the king was to be 'privately interred (respect being had to his dignity)'.[42] It is not improbable that James wished to spare himself and his deceased brother the full pageantry of a royal funeral particularly in view of his brother's death-bed conversion to Roman Catholicism. As it was, James himself stayed away from the funeral. Had precedent been followed in this particular, then he would, as Charles I had done at James I's funeral, have gone in the procession as chief mourner. Instead this role was delegated to Prince George of Denmark.

An understanding of the arrangements made for the funeral of Charles II is important for it was this format that established the 'degree' of ceremony for those that followed.

William III died on 8 March 1702, and a committee of the Privy Council was appointed immediately to 'take care of the disposal of the King's body'. When it came to settle the form of ceremonial the committee had before them, for the first time, the late King's own wish that he was to be 'interr'd by his Queen without any pomp' and following discussions with the officers of arms, it was decided to follow the form used for Charles II.[43] The ceremony itself took place, however, much later at night (11 p.m.) and, unlike the funeral of Charles II, did include a 'public' feature. By far the most moving sight must have been the great chariot covered in purple cloth that bore the body from Kensington to Westminster together with the 300 persons carrying lighted torches. Prior to the funeral ceremony the lying-in-state took place at Kensington Palace where several rooms had been hung with mourning. As with Charles II, the final forms were approved in the presence of the sovereign. In a comment in his memorial written some years later, Stephen Martin Leake, Garter King of Arms, pointed out that William III's funeral had been 'a private funeral after the manner of a publick one'.[44] What he meant was that whereas the two previous sovereigns, Charles II and Mary, had been conveyed from the palace where they had died in a 'private' manner (i.e. without undue ceremony) William III's body had been brought in great state in an open chariot to the Princes Chamber.

On the death of Queen Anne on 1 August 1714, as on prior occasions, a committee of the Privy Council was appointed to draw up a plan, but, in this case, they acted only with the advice of the Lords Justices.[45] Orders were immediately provided for the examination of the body, the embalming of it, and the presentation of a full report to committee. In this latter respect,

[41] CA, *Ceremonials/A.A.W.*, p. 9.
[42] PRO, *PC 1/13/49*, fo. 3.
[43] N. Luttrell, *A Brief Historical Relation* ..., V, p. 150.
[44] CA, *S.M.L. 30/Ceremonials*, p. 357.
[45] The Regency Act continued the existing Privy Council for six months following the death of Queen Anne. Until the arrival of her successor, George I, interim control was vested in the Lord Justices.

Queen Anne had left specific instructions. The examination and embalming were to be carried out not only by her physicians in ordinary but also 'by the Serjeant and Surgeon and Mr. Blundele who usually attended Her Majesty in her illness'.[46] On 3 August Dr. Lawrence reported their findings in writing to the committee.[47]

For the funeral itself the committee of the Privy Council decided initially to follow the scheme for William III's and, with this in mind, had proceeded. The discovery, however, in the Queen's closet of two drafts of her will altered this. In her last will (unsigned) the Queen left specific instructions that:

> my body shall be buryed within the Chappel of our Royal Ancestor King Henry the Seventh in the colegiate Church of St. Peter in Westminster, in the same vault with, and near unto the body of my Dear Husband the Prince of Denmark deceased, and that my Funeral with the proceeding thereunto, the mourning and all other matters concerning the same be performed in the same manner and forme and with the same solemnities as were used or appointed upon the decease of my said Dear Husband.[48]

In the light of this the Lords Justices directed that the arrangements be altered. The burial, therefore, would not be from Kensington but from Westminster.[49] In drawing up a new scheme, however, it was clear that the late Queen's wishes could not be fully adhered to in view of her status as a sovereign and the resulting plan combined, therefore, elements from the ceremonial used for both the funeral of William III and Prince George of Denmark. On 14 August the revised plan was presented to the Privy Council and the Lords Justices agreed to it on 17 August and set 22 August as the day of the funeral. Also certain features relating to earlier ceremonial would not be observed, most significantly the practice of breaking the staves of office at the conclusion of the ceremony, since a statute of parliament had continued the officers in their place.[50]

As with the funeral of William III, the Surveyor General, Christopher Wren, was instructed to provide a chariot to convey the body from Kensington to Westminster but this was later changed to a simpler vehicle—the hearse.[51]

Although George I died *en route* to Hanover in June 1727 and it was anticipated that his body would be returned to England for burial, the funeral and burial actually took place in Hanover.[52] With the death of

[46] PRO, *PC 1/2/247*; PRO, *LC 2/18*.

[47] PRO, *PC 1/2/245*.

[48] PRO, *SP 44/116*.

[49] This account differs in several important respects from that given by the most recent biography of her by E. Gregg.

[50] PRO, *SP 35/1*.

[51] The 'chariot' was associated with the full public funeral and was last used for the funeral of William III. The idea of the 'chariot' or 'funeral carriage' was revived for both the funerals of Lord Nelson (1806) and the Duke of Wellington (1852).

[52] George I had left specific instructions in his will that his body should not be opened or embalmed. I am indebted to Professor R. M. Hatton for this information.

George II on 25 October 1760, there occurred the last funeral for a sovereign in Westminster Abbey and in the organization of this ceremonial[53] a significant departure from previous procedure took place. As already indicated, the officers of arms had been ordered by council to attend meetings and to outline what they felt the appropriate procedure should be. For the funeral of George II, however, John Anstis, Garter King of Arms, was summoned before the committee of the Privy Council and was presented by the Lord Chamberlain with a fully drawn scheme for the ceremonial and Anstis was asked only for comment. 'The Duke of Devonshire, Lord Chamberlain, directed the whole ceremony, by authority of the council, which more properly belonged to the Earl Marshal,' wrote Stephen Martin Leake in his memorial.[54] The power of the officers of arms to control ceremonial was even further eroded in the course of the plans made for the funerals of the next two Hanoverian monarchs—George III and George IV.[55] Among other things, the entire ceremonial achieved an even more 'private' character when the two main ceremonies connected with the funerals—the lying-in-state and the funeral service—took place at Windsor. Although the printed version of the ceremony for George III omitted the word 'private',[56] the degree of ceremony was greatly reduced. For the first time, however, two symbols of sovereignty were used for both the lying-in-state and the ceremonial procession: the Royal Crown of Hanover and the Imperial Crown of the United Kingdom. The same practice was followed a decade later for the funeral of George IV except that the lying-in-state took place not in the Audience Chamber (as with George III) but in the Great Drawing Room (*plate* III. 4).[57]

III

By 1830, therefore, the public ceremony so characteristic of early funeral ceremony for the sovereign had ended and had been replaced by one that lacked almost all of the pageantry of the previous ones. The 'public' royal funeral had given way, in heraldic terms, to the 'private' one. What explains this change? Certainly it cannot be argued that there was a decreasing interest in ceremonial in general after 1685 for pomp and pageantry continued throughout the eighteenth century to play a significant role in the social and political life of the nation at all levels. The coronation ceremony, for example, came to be staged with even greater and greater displays of pomp and glamour. That for George IV rivalled all others, concluding as it did with the impressive ritual banquet in Westminster Hall.[58] The coronation

---

[53] PRO, *LC2/28.*
[54] CA, *S.M.L./65*, p. 271.
[55] PRO, *LC 2/45, 46, 47, 57.*
[56] PRO, *LC 2/46.*
[57] PRO, *LC 2/57.*
[58] Sir George Nayler, *The Coronation of George IV* (1824).

ceremony remained a popular event and both it and the Garter Ceremony became set theatre pieces. As the German visitor, D'Archenholz, remarked: 'All the great events that occur to the nation are dramatised and represented on the stage; for example the coronation of the present King; the Prince of Wales receiving the Order of the Garter; the grand review at Portsmouth in 1774.'[59] Referred to as 'afterpieces' or 'Entertainments', the coronation ceremony of George III was but one of the many pageants along with Garrick's presentation of *The Institution of the Knights of the Garter* (a ceremony revived by Charles II) that continued to attract and enthral theatre audiences. Such rituals were still viewed by the authorities as essential to reinforcing the special status of the monarchy.

What was happening by the end of the seventeenth century, however, was that certain royal ceremonies—baptisms, christenings, weddings and funerals—were being removed from the control of the Earl Marshal's Office and were increasingly carried out under the direction of the Lord Chamberlain's department. In this sense these former 'public' royal ceremonies had become 'private' ones. The explanation for this change lies in an understanding that these particular ceremonies, especially the funeral ceremony, no longer served their intended purposes. This was particularly true of one of the central features that had come to characterize the 'public' funeral—the effigy.

By the last half of the seventeenth century the effigy had outlived its symbolic function. As already observed, from Henry VII to James I (1509–1625), a life-like effigy of the sovereign had been used at various stages in the ceremony—for the processions, the lying-in-state, and the final religious ceremony an effigy (also called a 'picture', a 'representation', and an 'image') had dominated.[60] This practice, predating the Tudor period, began at least as early as 1327 when a wooden effigy of Edward II, arrayed in coronation robes and fitted out with the royal regalia, was placed on the coffin for the funeral procession and for the final burial service in the Abbey of St. Peter at Gloucester. From this date, when circumstances allowed, an effigy had been used as part of the proceedings.

The reasons for the use of the effigy are complex. Initially it would seem that it had no ritual significance at all but served instead a practical function. Given the primitive nature of embalming procedures it was a substitute for the corpse and allowed for a greatly protracted funeral preparation and ceremonial. As time went on, however, the effigy came to play a crucial symbolic role.[61] This was particularly true in France where, as the authority

---

[59] Quoted in Cecil Price, *Theatre in the Age of Garrick* (Oxford, 1973), p. 77.

[60] For the effigy see: Sir William St. John Hope, 'On the Funeral Effigies . . .', *Archaeologia*, LX (1907), 517–70.

[61] The symbolic significance and the role of ritual significance generally in royal funeral ceremony has long been recognized by the anthropologist. For a survey of recent work in this area see Richard Huntington and Peter Metcalf, *Celebrations of Death. The Anthropology of Mortuary Ritual* (Cambridge, 1979).

on Renaissance funeral ceremony has remarked, it played a vital part in 'the attempt to resolve the dilemma of two competing traditions of Kingship'.[62] While the symbolic role of the effigy seemed to be less pronounced in England, the use of it was, nevertheless, of considerable importance. Ernst Kantorowicz in his *The King's Two Bodies: A Study in Medieval Political Theology* (Princeton, 1957) has argued that the entire funeral ceremony and in particular the concluding part when the stewards break their staves and the slogan 'The King is dead! Long live the King!' is cried aloud, 'powerfully demonstrate the perpetuity of kingship'.[63] More specifically, he argued that the effigy in the English context served a quasi-legal purpose closely linked with the theory of the king's two bodies.[64]

The life-like wooden or wax effigy ceased to be used for the funeral of a sovereign after 1625. The ensuing decades of political chaos that culminated with the restoration of the monarchy in 1660 and the acceptance by the end of the century of constitutional monarchy meant that the theory linked with the use of the effigy no longer applied. Although the effigy continued to be made for later sovereigns—Charles II, William III, Mary, Anne—they played no part in the ceremonial, but were employed solely for commercial purposes.[65] As already noted only the Crown—a replica or the real one—and, in certain cases, other symbols of sovereignty were utilized. The 'fashion' too was changing. The discontinuance of the effigy in England closely corresponds with the end of the tradition in France where the last recorded use of the effigy for a French monarch was for Louis XIII in 1643.[66]

The most important factor in explaining the shift in England away from the great heraldic funeral was, however, the decline in the influence of the College of Arms and, in particular, the steady erosion of its central role in marshalling not only royal, but all funeral ceremonial in England. According to Sir Anthony Wagner, the heralds first participated in marshalling a funeral ceremony in 1462-63 for Richard Neville, Earl of Salisbury, and his son, Sir Thomas, and by the the sixteenth century had come to control this ceremony.[67] By 1547 with the ordering of Henry VIII's funeral, they were claiming a fee of £40. They also derived a substantial part of their income, as time went on, from the supply of the vast number of painted banners, bannerols, pencils, coats of arms, crests, escutcheons, etc. that were used for the procession and after the ceremonies, claimed as their 'perks'

---

[62] Giesey, *The Royal Funeral Ceremony*, p. 82.

[63] Ibid, p. 412.

[64] He describes the symbolic role of the effigy as follows: 'Enclosed in the coffin of lead, which itself was encased in a casket of wood there rested the corpse of the King, his mortal and normally visible—though now invisible—body natural, whereas his normally invisible body politic was on this occasion visibly displayed by the effigy in its pompous regalia: a *persona ficta*—the effigy—impersonating a *persona ficta*—the *Dignitas*' (p. 421).

[65] Lawrence E. Tanner, *The Royal and Other Effigies* (n.d.).

[66] Ernst Benkard, *Undying Faces. A Collection of Death Masks* (translated from German by Margaret Green) (London, 1929), p. 24.

[67] Wagner, pp. 106-7.

75

several items, including the hearse and its cloth coverings.[68] They had a vested interest, therefore, in not only perpetuating these ceremonies but in keeping them as elaborate as possible. Also, during the course of the sixteenth century an increasingly elaborate set of rules was established to govern funeral procedure at all levels of society. One of these was entitled *The manner of the ordering of the setting forth of a corpse of what estate that he be of and how every shall go in order after the estate and degree that he be of.*[69] Among other things, the exact number of mourners was indicated for each rank in society: an Emperor (fifteen), a King (thirteen), a Duke (eleven), an Earl (nine), a Viscount or Baron (seven), Knight baronet or bachelor (five), and esquire or gentleman (three). The central role played by the officers of the College of Arms had been at the instigation of the Tudor monarchy, especially Henry VIII, and it is quite clear that heraldic regulation of funeral ceremony, as in other areas, was for the part it played in maintaining stability and social order.[70] Not only was the size of the funeral procession rigidly regulated, but also the scale of the funeral accoutrements, especially the size of the hearse. Clearly the most elaborate hearse (and often more than one) was reserved for the sovereign and by the end of the sixteenth century Augustine Vincent[71] in his *Book of Presidents* had carefully set down precise measurements for the hearse that could be used for all ranks of society from monarch to citizen.[72] Obviously the procession and its various parts were to mirror one's rank in society.

The instability and political turmoil already referred to in the course of the seventeenth century challenged and weakened the capacity of the officers of arms to perpetuate this system and by the end of the century the officers found that their monopoly was being invaded when the Company of Painter Stainers of London began to take on the painting of arms for funerals. By the late 1680s one of the members of this company, William Russell, presented the college with the most serious threat of all when he established a new trade—coffin maker—and offered to supply as part of his services all of the necessary accoutrements for the funeral ceremony.[73] As the very first of a new breed—the undertaker—he and his successors were to cut sharply into the herald's role in marshalling funeral ceremonial. By the year 1700 so serious had this challenge become that the heralds were planning to take legal action against such interference. At this time they formally declared that it was their undisputed right, and had been for over 200 years, to marshal all 'publick' funerals and that they were opposed to 'the undertakers'

---

[68] This whole area was to lead to endless disputes between the College of Arms and the Dean and Chapter of the Collegiate Church of St. Peter's, Westminster. Wagner, pp. 113–14, 236.

[69] CA, *S.M.L./28/Ceremonial.*

[70] Roy Strong, *The Cult of Elizabeth. Elizabethan Portraiture and Pageantry* (London, 1977).

[71] Rouge Croix (1621), Windsor (1624).

[72] CA, *Vincent, 151.*

[73] Wagner, p. 237.

encroaching on these since it was 'contrary to the laws of Arms and the Common Laws of Great Britain'.[74] Stephen Martin Leake referred to them as 'cold cooks' who 'intermeddled' with the proper conduct of funerals.[75] He was especially upset to learn that for the funeral of the Duchess of Buckingham large numbers of 'painters' not of the College and 'undertakers' had been employed.[76] In 1735 the College of Arms issued an order against 'undertakers, painters and others', who have frequently 'presumed to marshall and direct the proceedings of solemn funerals without regard to the rights of arms and likewise employ mean persons to carry trophys of Honour at such funerals'. Since this was, they argued, their indispensable right it was agreed in Chapter that: 'if hereafter any person or persons shall presume to carry any such Trophy's of honour or shall marshall or direct the proceedings of any such funeral, such person or persons shall be prosecuted with the utmost severity according to the law.'[77] It was clear, however, that their control in this area had been steadily eroded by this new group. Although initially undertakers did not seriously affect the marshalling of royal funeral ceremonial, by the mid-years of the eighteenth century their influence was being felt here as well. If one can accept the evidence of Stephen Martin Leake, they were responsible by mid-century for at least one vital change in royal funeral ceremony—the use of women in a capacity other than that of mourner at a funeral. In the arrangements for the funeral of Princess Louise in 1768, when it was announced that women were to be used as supporters of the pall at the funeral, Garter King of Arms immediately informed the Lord Chamberlain 'that women had never gone in a funeral procession but as mourners, or attendant upon the chief mourner'.[78] The idea that they were now to be used in a very different capacity, he argued, could only be in imitation of what was being done elsewhere 'at funerals directed by undertakers'. In the end, however, four baronesses supported the pall.

Although the officers of arms tried many obstructionist tactics to preserve their position, such as attempting to prevent the Upholders Company with whom the undertakers were increasingly identified from obtaining a new charter, they were fighting a losing battle. By the last half of the century the undertakers occupied a central role. From the large list of tradesmen who supplied the Lord Chamberlain's Office with the necessaries for the funeral, the Upholders (Upholsterers) accounts were an increasingly large part of the total expenditure. By the early nineteenth century one firm in particular, Messrs. France and Banting of Pall Mall had established themselves as the Royal Undertakers and managed the greater part of the funerals of both

[74] CA, *Herald's College Papers*, fo. 14.
[75] CA, *S.M.L./65*, p. 19.
[76] The Duchess of Buckingham died in 1743 and at her funeral an effigy of her dressed in her Coronation robes was used for the last time in England.
[77] CA, *S.M.L./65*, p. 84.
[78] Ibid, p. 25.

George III and George IV.[79] Out of a total cost to the wardrobe of £25,994 6s. 5d. for George III's funeral, France and Banting submitted bills to the total of £7,434 9s.6d.[80] and, for George IV's funeral, they claimed fees of £6,375 2s. 3d. out of a total cost to the wardrobe of £22,491 2s. 4d.[81] They also came to draw more and more of the operation within their own grasp. The use of outside tailors was soon dispensed with when France and Banting hired their own. So, too, were mercers and other suppliers of materials bypassed when they furnished their own cloth for fitting out rooms, etc. When queried by the Lord Chamberlain about this, they remarked that now that they were 'employed by the most noble families in the Kingdom' they had become their own manufacturers of black goods and were convinced that they could sell as low, if not lower, than any draper could.[82] By 1830, the business of marshalling a royal funeral had largely passed from the control of the heralds and into the Lord Chamberlain's Department where he was assisted by the undertakers.

The Privy Council, too, in its arrangement for a royal funeral came increasingly to support this change—of playing down the pageantry and of placing more and more emphasis on the private nature of the ceremony. Ironically, even the officers of the arms used less in the way of ceremonial for their own members. In 1792 Peter Le Neve, Norroy King of Arms, died and directed in his will that he was to have as small a funeral as possible—'a hearse and one coach, no mourning—no rings—no room hung with black'.[83] Upon the death of Stephen Martin Leake's father in 1736, several of the officers offered their services in the hopes that it might serve as a means of 'reviving the publick funeral' but the offer was declined.[84] As already observed the Privy Council in the course of the eighteenth century did not rely heavily on the advice of the officers, and it would seem that they did so with some justification. So 'evasive' had the officers been about possible arrangements for Queen Caroline's funeral in 1737 that they served only to 'perplex the Council'. Indeed, so badly was the final ceremonial ordered that the council could only marvel at the officers' incompetence. In 1757 they excluded them altogether from participating in the planning of Princess Caroline's funeral. When the Lord Chamberlain was asked why the Earl Marshal had not been summoned at this time it was pointed out that since this was 'a private funeral in the Household' the Lord Chamberlain alone would have the direction of it. When the officers were finally consulted on this occasion they

[79] According to the *London Directories* for these years a firm of Upholders, France and Banting, were located at 101 St. Martin's Lane in 1780. William France was Upholder to the King by the year 1806 and went into partnership with Banting in 1812. France and Banting continued in Pall Mall until at least 1825. I am indebted to Mr. Bernard France, the Director of the present firm, for this information.

[80] PRO, *LC 2/47*.

[81] PRO, *LC 2/57*.

[82] PRO, *LC 2/42*.

[83] CA, *S.M.L./65*, p. 129.

[84] Ibid., p. 85.

were asked only to supply information on 'the most private funeral that could be made for a daughter of the Crown'. Three years later (1760) the officers were once again bypassed when plans were made for the funeral of George II. Much to the dismay of the heralds of the Lord Chamberlain, the Duke of Devonshire, 'directed the whole ceremony by authority of Council'.[85]

Although they were no longer in charge of marshalling royal funeral ceremony, up to and including the funeral of the Duke of York in 1827, and for the subsequent funerals of sovereigns, all the officers of arms, when possible, attended the ceremony. For all other funerals only Garter King of Arms was present.[86] With the exception of the marshalling of the funerals of three peers,[87] their role was limited in the ensuing years to planning the 'state' funerals that were held at public expense: the Earl of Chatham's (1778); Lord Nelson's (1806); William Pitt's (1806); the Duke of Wellington's (1852); William Ewart Gladstone's (1898); Earl Roberts's (1914); Viscount Alanbrooke's (1963); Sir Winston Churchill's (1965). These represented the last of the great heraldic funerals that had been so characteristic a feature of not only the funerals of royalty and aristocracy but of knights and citizens in the sixteenth century. By the end of that century, however, they were already in decline due in part to a change in mental attitude and a desire to economize when, as one historian has argued, 'the cost incurred was out of all proportion to the prestige earned'.[88] A century later the heraldic funeral for royalty had all but disappeared, when it was revived, largely for political purposes, for the funeral of Queen Mary in 1695.[89] As has been argued, a complex of factors of a personal, political and economic nature, together with a steady erosion of the herald's monopoly by, among others, 'the undertakers', explains the change from the 'public' to the 'private' royal funeral in England.

[85] Ibid, pp. 91, 237, 257.
[86] Wagner, p. 113.
[87] Earl of Bridgewater (1700); Duke of Buckingham (1721); Duke of Kingston (1773).
[88] Lawrence Stone, *Crisis of the Aristocracy 1558-1641* (Oxford, 1965), p. 578.
[89] It is interesting to note that Oliver Cromwell's funeral was conducted by his own heralds with the full use of all the devices including replicas of the crown. (See Wagner, p. 114.)

IV

Symbolism for the Survivors: The Disposal of the Dead in Hamburg in the Late Seventeenth and Eighteenth Centuries*

JOACHIM WHALEY

In 1841 the Reverend Johannes Geffcken wrote 'We will perhaps all agree that our funerals are in many ways unsatisfactory and deficient, that the homely element is wholly absent. In earlier days, people paid more attention to the dead, ... now one often sets them outside the door without any ceremony at all, and callously places them in the hands of uncaring professionals.'[1] He was thus pinpointing a long-term change in attitudes to death which has increasingly attracted the attention of historians and sociologists.[2] But what concerned Geffcken was not the ritual of the death bed, but rather the symbolism of the funeral. Like many of his predecessors in Hamburg he saw the ritual to which the corpse was subjected before interment, neither as a personal, nor a family matter, but as a public event.

Death was not only the tragic and inevitable end to life, a perennial incursion into the existence of families and groups of friends, but a matter for government. For city councils concerned to enforce social distinctions; for churches determined to reinforce orthodoxy in an increasingly heterodox world; for communities bent on reflecting in death the success or failure of a life—the structure of the funeral was of paramount importance for them all. Funerals and the legislation which governed them also become an acute economic issue for all those professional 'impresarios of death' who emerged to provide the service. The scholarly study of death and the art of dying bulks large in our understanding of grief in the past; but to contemporaries, the problems it created for government and the maintenance of social order were equally important.

The social and political significance of funeral symbolism has been largely ignored by recent scholars. The quantification of mortality, the study of mentalities, and sometimes the study of both of these together have produced

---

* Abbreviations used in footnotes: CBH (Commerzbibliothek, Hamburg); SUB Hbg (Staats- und Universitätsbibliothek, Hamburg); LKA (Landeskirchenarchiv, Hamburg); StAH (Staatsarchiv der Freien und Hansestadt Hamburg).
[1] Johannes Geffcken, 'Die Leichenbegängnisse im siebenzehnten Jahrhundert', *Zeitschrift des Vereins für hamburgische Geschichte,* i (1841), 497–522, at p. 498.
[2] See Philippe Ariès, *Western Attitudes to Death* (Baltimore, 1974); Philippe Ariès, *L'Homme devant la mort* (Paris, 1977); G. Vernon, *The Sociology of Death* (New York, 1960); H. Feifel (ed.), *The Meaning of Death* (New York, 1959); David E. Stannard (ed.), *Death in America* (University of Pennsylvania Press, 1975); see also Introduction above pp. 4–14.

an image which would have been virtually unrecognizable in the early modern period.[3] That mortality was high in an age of primitive medicine and dearth cannot be doubted. The expression of grief was both profound and channelled into socially acceptable forms. But the study of long-term changes spanning the life of civilizations, rather than the more malleable traditions of limited communities, has resulted in too generalized a perspective.[4] While it encompasses the universality of emotion, it cannot reflect the rapidly changing demands of economic, social and political reality. Ariès has claimed that: 'Throughout the seventeenth century people were buried in exactly the same fashion (with variations in the liturgy, of course) in Pepys' England, in the Holland of those genre painters who specialized in church interiors, and in French and Italian churches. The mental attitudes were the same.'[5] But the study of English and French habits reveals not only differences in liturgy, but varied social and political motives too.[6] Ceremonies everywhere were marked by survivals from a remote past and also by profanities resulting from local circumstances.[7] In the towns, such usages became an inextricable part of the process whereby new groups, like Jews or dissenters, were assimilated by and legitimized within a traditionally more fluid social organism. Ariès again argues that the great watershed in attitudes to death in the late eighteenth century must be read as yet another chapter in the history of man's emotions; but there were other, more material, motives for the shift. A new concept of town planning, derived partly from an improved understanding of the mechanics of infection and disease, combined with traditional arguments against luxury and conspicuous consumption to reinforce or perhaps even to create new attitudes.[8]

Funerals were a necessary piece of social ritual which impinged on many other areas of life like politics and economics. Louis XIV was well aware of the emblematic effects of his action when he began his campaign against

[3] Ariès, *Western Attitudes*; Michel Vovelle, *Piété baroque et déchristianisation en Provence au XVIIIe siècle* (Paris, 1973); François Lebrun, *Les Hommes devant la mort à Anjou au XVIIe et XVIIIe siècles* (Paris, 1971).

[4] This is particularly true in such studies as Edgar Morin, *L'Homme et la mort* (Paris, 1951).

[5] Ariès, *Western Attitudes*, p. 80; similarly Ariès, *La Mort,* pp. 293–4, 299–301. This judgement must be contrasted with contemporary views such as those expressed by P. Muret, *Rites of Funeral Ancient and Modern in Use Throughout the Known World* (London, 1683, trans. P. Lorrain), esp p. 243ff.

[6] For England see the excellent survey by C. Lucas and P. Cunnington, *Costumes for Births, Marriages and Deaths* (London, 1972); for France, the works cited above (fn. 3) alone show significant variations in local customs and usages.

[7] For Germany the literature is positively overwhelming. See among many others: E. R. Lange, *Sterben und Begräbnis im Volksglauben zwischen Weichsel und Memel* (Würzburg, 1955); G. Buschan, *Das deutsche Volk in Sitte und Brauch* (Stuttgart, 1920); J. Lippert, *Christentum, Volksglaube und Volksbrauch* (Berlin, 1882); E. Semter, *Geburt, Hochzeit und Tod* (Leipzig and Berlin, 1911); W. Sonntag, *Die Totenbestattung* (Halle, 1878).

[8] Ariès, *Western Attitudes,* pp. 69–72 and Lebrun, op. cit., p. 480ff; for a discussion of a specific example see O. and C. Hannaway, 'La Fermeture du Cimetière des Innocents', *Dix-Huitième Siècle,* ix (1977), 181–91.

the Huguenots with a decree restricting their funerals to the ignominy of the dead of night.[9] The *Encyclopédie,* declared bleakly: *'Les Funérailles sont les derniers devoirs que l'on rend à ceux qui sont morts, ou pour mieux dire, c'est un appareil de la vanité et de la misère humaine.'*[10] Few, however, challenged their necessity, though many questioned the morality of their ostentation.[11] Even Voltaire, whose view of Church liturgy and human ritual was nothing if not secular, declared to La Harpe after his last confession, that he had taken his decision *'à fin d'être enterré en terre sainte, et d'avoir un service aux Cordeliers'.*[12] It is precisely the implication of Voltaire's statement which will concern this article: not the transition from life to death, the *Ars Moriendi,* but the disposal of the corpse.[13]

I

In Germany, the form of the early modern funeral was set in most areas by the Reformation. It produced not only a redefinition of dogmatic principles, but also allowed the state to play a greater role in many areas of religious life.[14]

The medieval funeral, which originated in the monasteries, was founded on the twin belief in the resurrection of the dead and the Last Judgment.[15] The priest had a duty to provide an honest burial for his parishioners. Even the poor were not excluded: they were interred gratuitously as one of the seven works of mercy. Only schismatics, heretics and excommunicates were ostracized, and also those who died through bloodshed for it was feared that their bodies might desecrate the sacred ground of the church.[16]

The rich could hire more mourners or young scholars to swell the final

[9] W. J. Stankiewicz, *Politics and Religion in Seventeenth Century France* (Berkeley, 1960), p. 188.

[10] *Encyclopédie, ou Dictionnaire raisonné des Sciences, des Arts et des Métiers par une Société des Gens des Lettres . . . Mis en Ordre et publié par M. Diderot,* 17 vols. (Paris, Neuchatel, 1751–65), vii, p. 368.

[11] The discussion of the morality of lavish funeral expenditure reached even the furthest corners of Europe in the period around 1700. In May 1706, for example, Professor Jakob Wilde delivered a dissertation in the University of Dorpat entitled *Templa non Templa* which concluded with an agonized discussion of this issue: Georg von Rauch, *Die Universität Dorpat und das Eindringen der frühen Aufklärung in Livland 1690–1710* (Essen, 1943), pp. 233–4.

[12] Quoted by John McManners, *Reflections on the Deathbed of Voltaire. The Art of Dying in Eighteenth Century France* (Inaugural Lecture, Oxford, 1975), p. 31.

[13] On the *Ars Moriendi* see most recently: J. Kröll, 'Ars Moriendi. Bayreuther Leichenbegängnisse um die Mitte des 17. Jahrhunderts', *Archiv für die Geschichte von Oberfranken,* i (1972), 365–91.

[14] J. H. Zedler, *Grosses vollständiges Universal-Lexikon* 64 vols (Leipzig and Halle, 1735–50), xliv, *sub Trauer;* also H. Möller, *Die kleinbürgerliche Familie im achtzehnten Jahrhundert. Verhalten und Gruppenkultur* (Berlin, 1969), pp. 189–96.

[15] The most detailed analysis of the medieval funeral is still: H. Grün, 'Das kirchliche Begräbniswesen im ausgehenden Mittelalter', *Theologische Studien und Kritiken,* cii (1930), pp. 341–81. The following summary draws heavily on this article.

[16] Ibid, p. 343. Women who died in childbirth were also included in this category.

chorus at the grave, or might have more bells rung. But the basic formula remained the prerogative of all: extreme unction before death, followed by an all-night vigil over the corpse, a communal procession led by the priest to the church, the progress to the grave accompanied by friends and neighbours, and the remembrance services thereafter. The Church as the embodiment of the community held the centre of the stage. The significance of the requiem mass and the subsequent services arose from the uncertainty about the length of the deceased's stay in purgatory. Individual prayer alone could not effect the transition from the *ecclesia militans* on earth to the *ecclesia triumphans* of eternity. The Church united the *communio sanctorum* of both worlds and held the key to eternal life: prayers *pro vivis et defunctis* underlined the solidarity of the living with the dead as members of one community.[17]

Luther's main concern was to reduce the symbolic functions of the clergy. The priest now became a major-domo rather than the arbiter of the individual's fate in eternity. Above all, Luther stressed the role of the secular community in the burial process. He destroyed the dogmatic foundation of the requiem mass and sought to underline the meaning of death for the living. The funeral sermon was now paramount, rather than the celebration of the mass for the souls of the departed.[18] The corpse was important not as a symbol of life to come, but as an object of contemplation for the living, a true symbol of the religious and social aspirations of the survivors.

The new Lutheran church constitutions thus created a ritual of burial in which the major role of the clergy ended after the ministration of the last sacraments.[19] The community was notified by the tolling of bells; services were held at specified times to enable as many as possible to participate without disrupting the working day. The presence of friends, neighbours and compatriots in faith was the most important aspect of the Lutheran funeral.

The ceremony itself remained elaborate and marked by the public ritual of commemoration rather than by a private concern about life in the world to come. It was the size and nature of the procession which reflected the deceased's station in life and his standing in the memory of the survivors; for many sought to express their social aspirations in ostentatious funerals. This idea was reinforced by the prominence given to the sermon in the short

[17] See also Keith Thomas, *Religion and the Decline of Magic. Studies in Popular Beliefs in Sixteenth and Seventeenth-century England* (Harmondsworth, 1973), pp. 719–21.

[18] H. Grün, 'Die kirchliche Beerdigung im 16. Jahrhundert', *Theologische Studien und Kritiken,* cv (1933), pp. 138–214; on the function of the funeral sermon see: H. Grün, 'Die Leichenrede im Rahmen der kirchlichen Beerdigung im 16. Jahrhundert', *Theologische Studien und Kritiken,* xcvi (1925), pp. 289–312; more recently also the studies by E. Winkler, *Die Leichenpredigt im deutschen Luthertum bis Spener* (Munich, 1967) and R. Mohr, *Protestantische Theologie und Frömmigkeit im Angesicht des Todes während des Barockzeitalters* (Marburg, 1964).

[19] The following information, unless otherwise stated, is derived from H. Grün, 'Die kirchliche Beerdigung' and Möller, op. cit., pp. 189–96.

service which followed the public procession. Mourners of differing grades wore clothes corresponding not only to their own status, but also to their relationship with the departed. All men, with only a few clearly defined exceptions, had a right to these ceremonies.

If the churches thus created the framework, the secular governments felt obliged to address the problems of social distinctions and of public order arising from the elaborate ritual. The legal and social differences which divided men in life were mirrored in death. From the so-called 'Donkey's burial' accorded to criminals, to the state burial of the great, the art of interment expressed a whole range of public social judgements.[20] Most areas knew several legally defined classes of funeral: in Ansbach eleven distinct categories existed.[21] Similar considerations were also important in the formulation of police and sumptuary laws. Unlimited expenditure was frowned upon as much as the evasion of a socially appropriate funeral. The former was the more usual object of legislation, but in 1675 the City of Brunswick felt obliged to ban the increasingly common custom of 'silent funerals' which by-passed the complex provisions of the church constitution.[22] Similarly, many rulers promoted funeral societies to provide rudimentary insurance against the potentially ruinous consequences of an untimely death in the family. While approving of the fundamental social importance of public funerals, they wished to limit conspicuous expenditure.[23]

II

Hamburg was unusual since neither Bugenhagen's church constitution of 1529 nor the revision of 1556 mentioned funerals.[24] But in other ways the city demonstrated in graphic form the ritual surrounding the disposal of the corpse. Visitors after 1700 repeatedly remarked upon the extravagance of the ceremonies. In 1729 'The German Spy' commented on the size of processions and on the practice of paying Senators and other dignitaries to attend. Similarly von Uffenbach noted drily that, in view of the exorbitant medical fees charged in the city, this was definitely not a good place in which

---

[20] The 'Donkey's Burial' is described in Otto Beneke, *Von unehrlichen Leuten* (Hamburg, 1863), pp. 240–2. It rested on the Biblical foundation of Jer. 22, 18–21.
[21] J. B. Fischer, *Geschichte und ausführliche Beschreibung der Markgräflichen Stadt Anspach* (Ansbach, 1786), pp. 174–6. Similar variations are cited in Möller, *kleinbürgerliche Familie*, pp. 186–96.
[22] H. Bodemeyer, *Hannoversche Rechtsalterthümer. Erster Beitrag: Die Luxus- und Sittengesetze* (Göttingen, 1857), p. 173. For similar problems in Jena and Weimar see F. Schmidt, *Sitten und Gebräuche bei Hochzeiten, Taufen und Begräbnissen in Thüringen* (Weimar, 1863), p. 96ff.
[23] There is no good study of burial fraternities which were founded in large numbers after 1700. Many later critics commented that they were rarely effective. See: Anon., *Ueber die Zeit, die Art und den Ort der Beerdigung* (Hamburg, 1790), p. 59.
[24] Printed in E. Sehling, *Die evangelischen Kirchenordnungen des XVI Jahrhunderts* (Leipzig, 1913), v, pp. 487–540, 543–56. Neither mentions the funeral ceremony. Only the *Ordnung* of 1544 for the *Amt* of Ritzebüttel is concluded by a short section headed *Von begreffnisse der verstorven* (ibid, pp. 561–2).

to die. About 1750 Thomas Nugent declared that: 'Their weddings and christenings are most sumptuous, and even their funerals, where human vanity ought naturally to terminate, . . . partake of the same extravagance.'[25] Bernard Picart, that most diligent observer of religious customs, wrote that 'At Hamburg . . . these Funeral Solemnities are degenerated from their first laudable institution into Extravagances and ridiculous Superfluities . . .'.[26]

Such excess had not always existed: as late as 1657 one commentator noted how ordinary the customs of Hamburg were—a simple procession attended only by men, without funeral sermons. But by the 1680s a veritable funeral mania had developed. In 1682 the Chronicler Sperling claimed that school-teachers kept a tally of funerals and, for a fee of 1 *Reichsthaler per annum,* would notify 'enthusiasts' in good time 'so that they might know who has died and whose corpse they should follow'.[27] This was no cult of the dead in Ariès' sense of the term: it was an intensely time-consuming and often profitable piece of social ritual. Vast in size and expensive, the funeral cortège proved no less immovable than the execution as a form of public entertainment.[28]

The profound social and political significance of funerals is illustrated by the disputes between Senate and Church over the burial of non-Lutheran aliens. As a rapidly expanding commercial and diplomatic centre after 1600, Hamburg naturally attracted settlers of all religious denominations. The Spanish and Portuguese expulsions in the late sixteenth century and the Dutch upheavals led to the growth of substantial Jewish and Calvinist communities. Both groups were accepted by the Senate; their position was defined by Contracts in 1605 with the Dutch and 1612 with the Jews. The latter (a more obviously alien sect) were easier to deal with: they were to behave quietly and abstain from the practice of their faith; their dead were to buried in Altona or 'elsewhere'. A similar clause was inserted into the revised contract of 1698. The arrangement worked well. Few complaints were made about Jewish burials and the tightly knit 'Portuguese' community appeared content to accept this public sign of their alien status.[29]

---

[25] Thomas Lediard, *The German Spy* (London, 1738), pp. 173, 265–6; Z. C. von Uffenbach, *Merkwürdige Reisen durch Niedersachsen, Holland und Engelland,* 3 vols (Ulm and Memmingen, 1753), ii, pp. 77–8; Thomas Nugent, *The Grand Tour, or, a Journey through the Netherlands, Germany, Italy and France. To which is now added the European Itinerary,* 2nd edn., 4 vols (London, 1756), i, pp. 60–1.

[26] Bernard Picart, *The Religious Ceremonies and Customs of the Several Nations of the Known World,* 6 vols. (London, 1731–7), v, p. 444.

[27] Ernst Finder, *Hamburgisches Bürgertum in der Vergangenheit* (Hamburg, 1929), pp. 85–9, 99.

[28] The Hamburg funeral is satirized in *Der Patriot. Nach der Originalausgabe Hamburg 1724–26 in drei Textbänden und einem Kommentarband kritisch hrsg. von Wolfgang Martens,* 3 vols so far published (Berlin, 1969–), i, pp. 221–9.

[29] Hermann Kellenbenz, *Sephardim an der Unteren Elbe. Ihre wirtschaftliche und politische Bedeutung vom Ende des 16. bis zum Beginn des 18. Jahrhunderts* = Beihefte der Vierteljahresschrift für Sozial- und Wirtschaftsgeschichte Band 40 (Wiesbaden, 1958), pp. 25–57.

The Calvinists raised more thorny problems. Related at least in spirit to the Lutherans, their claim to Christian burial was less easy to deny. Their economic importance enjoined caution on those anxious for the city's prosperity.[30] On the one hand, the Church insisted on the preservation and reinforcement of orthodoxy; on the other hand, the Senate, aware as always that trade did not necessarily follow the true cross, supported the Calvinists. It attended their funerals and on several occasions bluntly informed the Ministry that matters of religious conscience could not be allowed to prevail against political prudence (an argument which never failed to elicit characteristically dogmatic reactions from the clergy). The dispute began in 1599 and was never resolved.[31] By the end of the seventeenth century the Lutheran church in Hamburg had become infamous throughout north-west Europe for its intolerance on this issue.[32]

Ultimately an uneasy compromise emerged. Calvinists were buried either outside the city or in the old Cathedral (which stood on neutral ground belonging to the Duchy of Bremen). If such aliens must be granted the right to bury their dead in public, then at least it should not occur on truly public territory in any of the five city parishes.[33] Only the English merchants were exempted from this rule: a treaty of 1611 granted them free public burials with full ceremonies.[34]

It did not however prove easy to maintain strict discrimination. In the first plague year of 1713, the city of Altona closed its gates to all funeral processions. The Senate, pressurized by the King of Prussia, was forced to concede a Calvinist burial ground outside the walls which was not closed after the epidemic. While unwilling to grant more than *de facto* terms of toleration, the Senate, moved by explicitly political and commercial considerations, habitually gave way to the pressures exerted by the Dutch and Prussian Residents.[35]

[30] They never went to the extent of actually threatening to leave the city *en bloc* as the Jews did on several occasions: Ibid, pp. 52-7.

[31] Christian Ziegra, *Sammlung von Urkunden zur Hamburgischen Kirchenhistorie,* 4 vols. (Hamburg, 1764-70), iv, pp. 469-74; see also StAH Senat: Cl.VII Lit.Hf No.1 Vol.2a.

[32] StAH Ministerium: III A1h, p. 52ff—complaints made by the clergy against an offensive article in the *Leyden Courante* 1702; references to all cases concerning Calvinist burials may be found in StAH Bestandsverzeichnis 511-1, Band 2 and Band 4 under the heading *Calvinistische Leiche.*

[33] See the discussions over the burial of a Calvinist child in August 1706 in StAH Ministerium: II 5, pp. 62, 78, 95, 125 and III A1i, pp. 377-7a; and StAH Senat: Cl.VII Lit.Hb Vol.3, fols. 48-9. On the neutrality of the Cathedral see also F. Otto, *Die rechtlichen Verhältnisse des Domstiftes zu Hamburg von 1719 bis 1802* (Hamburg, 1962), *passim.*

[34] H. Hitzigrath, *Die Kompagnie der Merchant Adventurers und die englische Kirchengemeinde in Hamburg 1611-1835* (Hamburg, 1904), pp. 2-4, 73-8. Most Englishmen were buried in the Cathedral.

[35] StAH Senate: Cl.VII Lit.Hf No.1 Vol.2b(a)—12 September 1713, King of Prussia to Senate. See also Johannes Klefeker, *Sammlung der Hamburgischen Gesetze und Verfassungen in Bürger- und Kirchlichen, auch Cammer-, Handlungs- und übrigen Policey-Angelegenheiten und Geschäften samt historischen Einleitungen* 12 vols. (Hamburg, 1765-73), viii, pp. 777-82. Subsequent discussions are in StAH Senat: Cl.VII Lit.Hf No.1 Vol.2b(b) and Cl.VII Lit.Hf No.3 Vol.13(1).

Equally significant were the problems connected with those citizens of Hamburg who were denied a public burial by virtue either of their way of life or their mode of death. The former fell into two groups: those who rejected or scorned the church and those who belonged to a whole series of conditions which were described by the term *Unehrlichkeit*.[36] They included suicides, duellists and others, like criminals, whose corpses were handed over to the public executioner to be interred quietly in an ignominious grave outside the walls.[37]

The strictures placed on suicides were in many ways less rigid. Although most were buried quietly at night, they were interred in sacred ground in the churchyard of St. Annen, a subsidiary chapel in the parish of St. Catherine's.[38] The parish administrators did not always concur in this practice. In July 1711, the deacons wrote to the Senate protesting against the interment of the suicide Hinrich Schmidt. They declared that they found it increasingly burdensome and embarrassing to have this churchyard used as a burial place for the deviant elements of the city.[39]

In other cases more specifically social pressures were manifest. The death of executioners continually raised problems, the result of deep-rooted superstitions connected with the profession. In September 1653 the assistant executioner Juergen Garmers was buried without a procession in front of the tower doors of St. Peter's. A similar procedure was adopted in the case of the excutioner Ishmael Asthusen in 1664; and when in 1674 another assistant, Hans Burstabs, died, his widow decided to avoid all awkward problems by transporting him to Glückstadt where he was given a Christian burial without further discussion.[40]

III

The importance of such strictures is only placed in perspective if the sheer amount of time and money lavished on funerals is considered. Between 1650 and 1764, the Senate issued 28 separate statutes and ordinances on the

---

[36] This concept is discussed with reference to Hamburg in Beneke, *unehrliche Leute, passim* and Klefeker, *Verfassungen*, iv, pp. 189–216 and viii, pp. 774–7.

[37] J. F. Blank, *Sammlung der von E. Hochedlen Rathe der Stadt Hamburg so wol zur Handhabung der Gesetze und Verfassungen als bey besonderen Eräugnissen in Bürger- und Kirchlichen, als auch Cammer, Handlungs- und übrigen Policey-Angelegenheiten und Geschäften vom Anfange des siebzehnten Jahrhunderts bis auf die itzige Zeit ausgegangenen Mandate, bestimmten Befehle und Bescheide, auch beliebten Aufträge und verkündigten Anordnungen*, 6 vols (Hamburg, 1763–74), ii. pp. 969–77 (December 1720); Klefeker, *Verfassungen*, viii, p. 776.

[38] Geffcken, 'Leichenbegängnisse', p. 504; see also the account of the suicide of Johann Meintz (1695) in Otto Beneke, *Hamburgische Geschichten und Sagen*, 3rd edn., 2 vols. (Berlin, 1886), i, pp. 328–32.

[39] StAH Senat: Cl.VII Lit.Hc No.5 Vol.6—letter dated 8 July 1711; Beneke, *Geschichten und Sagen*, ii, pp. 286–90.

[40] StAH Handschriftensammlung No. 493a—'Arnold Amsincks hamburgische Chronica bis 1679' (n.p.) entries for 1653, 1664, 1674.

subject.[41] In the latter part of the seventeenth century women were employed to count the mourners so that a proper record might be kept.[42] Processions of several thousands of people were not uncommon: some 4,000 followed the corpse of the *Bürgermeister* Schulte in 1692—the coffin had been in the church for two hours before the procession ended.[43]

Few days passed without at least one funeral. In June 1669, in a sermon which subsequently caused much acrid debate,[44] the young cleric Marnikenius bitterly attacked the time-wasting occupation of walking behind corpses. The introduction of the afternoon sermon in 1674 was opposed by many clergy who, as one pastor declared, wished only to walk round after the dead—though he himself complained bitterly when a procession started without him so that he lost his fee.[45] The frequency of the ritual was not always conducive to the maintenance of due propriety. Senatorial decrees complained sharply about unruly and unseemly behaviour in processions; but for many the funeral remained primarily a social event rather than a religious celebration.[46]

The cost of funerals was above all inflated by their size. The practice of paying what amounted to high class mourners in the form of Senators, clergy and graduates imposed a considerable burden in addition to the fees and charges ordinarily incurred. For they were not only paid a gratuity for their attendance; the most elevated received gold coins to place in the poor box on entering the church.[47] The Hamburg *Patriot* noted in connection with the imaginary will of a rich and status-hungry citizen, that the deceased 'Herr Eitelhard Bookesbeutel', the epitome of ostentatious financial investment in tradition, had specifically asked for large numbers of learned men to be hired—primarily because their dress added a variety not provided by the Senators and the clergy whose ceremonial costumes were similar. Many graduates, lawyers and minor clergy were more than willing to oblige since funerals formed a significant, and for some the most important, source of income.[48]

---

[41] Listed in Blank, *Mandate*, v (index) under the heading *Leiche*. Not all of them were startling innovations: some reiterated previous laws, while others contained only minor amendments or instructions.

[42] Finder, *Hamburgisches Bürgertum*, p. 101.

[43] Geffcken, 'Leichenbegängnisse', p. 515. Such processions are astonishingly large compared with those of the English aristocracy around 1600: Lawrence Stone, *The Crisis of the Aristocracy* (Oxford, 1965), pp. 573–5.

[44] Geffcken, 'Leichenbegängnisse', p. 513.

[45] LKA: Handschrift OA1—'Abschrift eines Tagebuches des Hauptpastors Georg Haccius' pt. II, p. 32ff.

[46] See the Comments made in the diary of Senior Schultz: StAH Senat: Cl.VII Lit.Hb No.3 Vol.2b.

[47] Ziegra claimed that the custom of paying Senators originated in the late sixteenth-century efforts by the Calvinists to protect their burials from disruption by the intolerant mob (Ziegra, *Sammlung*, iv, pp. 469–70).

[48] *Der Patriot*, pp. ii, 225–6, 245–6.

The preparations for the procession reflect these concerns. Plans for the interment began with the leasing of a church grave, generally for the individual and his family with a specified number of 'years of rest' after the last burial. This was an action of the greatest importance among the wealthy: the grave purchase books of St. Maria Magdalena reveal many young children as owners of graves; the dating of purchases suggests that many were given as a Christmas gift.[49]

The ceremony itself was organized immediately after death by the *Sorgemann* or chief mourner, usually a prominent member of the family or a close friend.[50] He invited the guests and decided who should be asked into the house and who should join the main procession. He also acted as majordomo throughout the ceremony. The burial was announced by either of two professional bodies: normally the *Leichen- und Hochzeitsbitter*. More elevated families hired the *Reitendiener* (servants on horse-back of the Senate) whose magnificent habit and long daggers made a greater show than the sombrely and simply-clad *Leichenbitter*.[51] They visited the invited guests; but the whole city was informed by a placard hung outside the Exchange—which invited general participation in the ceremony as an act of Christian duty which the bereaved family promised to reciprocate.[52] Similarly Pastors were commissioned to deliver funeral orations in the house before the procession; funeral poems were also produced for distribution among the guests as they arrived. In the late seventeenth century the practice arose of minting a commemorative medal for deceased *Bürgermeister*.[53]

At the funeral the *Sorgemann* acted as host in the bereaved household; he received the invited (i.e. paid) guests while the main body of mourners gathered outside. Church bells were rung an hour before the start. The number depended on the wealth and status of the deceased. High ranking families paid for peals in all the main churches, others used only those of their local parish. Many middling families who could not afford burial in the exclusive church of St. Peter had bells rung there all the same. The bell-

---

[49] Otto Beneke, 'Die Gräber zu St. Marien Magdalenen', *Zeitschrift des Vereins für hamburgsiche Geschichte* v (1866), pp. 592–615.

[50] Michael Richey, *Idiotikon Hamburgense,* enlarged edn. (Hamburg, 1755), p. 280; J. F. Schütze, *Holsteinisches Idiotikon, ein Beitrag zur Volkssittengeschichte,* 4 vols (Hamburg and Altona, 1800–06), iv, pp. 159–60.

[51] Karl Koppmann, 'Die Leichenbegängnisse im 18. Jahrhundert', in Karl Koppmann (ed.) *Aus Hamburgs Vergangenheit,* 2 vols. (Hamburg, 1885), i, pp. 255–77; on the *Reitendiener* see J. F. L. Meyer, *Skizzen zu einem Gemälde von Hamburg* (Erstes Heft, Hamburg, 1800), p. 99 and C. F. Gaedechens, 'Der Herrenstall und die Reitendiener', *Zeitschrift des Vereins für hamburgsiche Geschichte* ix (1894), pp. 517–56.

[52] For examples see CBH: S/256—until about 1750 such notices were generally handwritten on vellum.

[53] F. G. Buek, *Genealogische und biographische Notizen über die seit der Reformation verstorbenen hamburgischen Bürgermeister* (Hamburg, 1840), pp. vii–viii; J. P. Langermann, *Hamburgisches Münz- und Medaillen-Vergnügen, oder Abbildung und Beschreibung hamburgischer Münzen und Medaillen* (Hamburg, 1753), pp. 577–80. The first such medal was minted in 1676.

ringing accounts reveal that this practice became increasingly popular in the late seventeenth century.[54]

The tolling of bells marked the commencement of the ceremony. The guests assembled and the scholars arrived with their choirmaster to accompany the corpse to the grave. As each guest arrived, the *Sorgemann* received condolences on behalf of the family; refreshments were generally taken, though a decree of 1654 attempted to curtail this practice which added little to the sobriety of the occasion.[55]

When all were assembled, the *Sorgemann,* alerted by an announcer, gave the signal to begin. The procession was headed by choirboys with their master, after whom the corpse was carried.[56] The *Sorgemann* followed together with four privileged guests wearing long cloaks. After them came the other invited guests and the rest of the procession in strict order of ranks: first came the Bürgermeister, the Doctors of Theology, Law and Medicine, the clergy and the other Senators, all in ceremonial dress; the graduates and licentiates of law and members of the civil colleges followed together with anyone else who wished to join the throng. The size of the crowd depended largely on the status and popularity of the deceased, but on less predictable factors too. One chronicler remarked in 1694: 'Many people came to the funeral for the weather was good.'[57]

The long-winded orations delivered in the house before the procession and the interminable walk marked the climax of the occasion. The public function of the guests ended as they placed their gold coins in the poor box. The ensuing service was short. Funeral orations were rare and sermons brief. They were in any case the prerogative of the five major pastors, a circumstance which effectively limited them to the rich. Only the most elevated received a musical commemoration—men like *Bürgermeister* Schulte or the Commandant von Dallwig. Even the higher clergy were not considered worthy of this honour.[58] The interment itself was an anti-climax, a hurried end to a remarkably elaborate and lengthy ritual.

There were other differences in the form of burial. The most splendid was that of the *Bürgermeister.* J. F. L. Mayer wrote in 1800 that 'the preparations in the house beforehand, the lying in state of the corpse in full regalia, the velvet covered coffin decorated with tresses and drapes, the military guard of honour etc. cost large sums of money even today . . . even in most recent times . . . the funeral of a *Bürgermeister* and his wife who

---

[54] StAH St. Petri: A IX No.1a (Läutebuch 1649–86) and No.1b (Läutebuch 1686–1815).

[55] Blank, *Mandate,* i, p. 135.

[56] Ibid, p. 132–5—this law of 1654 gives a good impression of the procedure adopted at funerals. On the order of ranks at burials see Finder, *Hamburgisches Bürgertum,* p. 100, and Geffcken, 'Leichenbegängnisse', p. 514.

[57] Quoted by Finder, *Hamburgisches Bürgertum,* p. 106.

[58] Geffcken, 'Leichenbegängnisse', p. 520; A. Aust, *Der Ohlsdorfer Friedhof* (Hamburg, 1953), p. 85; see also the mandate concerning the length of memorial prayers (1731) in Blank, *Mandate,* iii, pp. 1189–97.

died about the same time ... cost 26,000 marks'.[59] Such grandeur was extraordinary even in Hamburg. But the evidence suggests that the elaborate ritual was not confined to the most wealthy classes alone.

Children, admittedly, received short shrift—much to the chagrin of the *Leichenbitter* who complained that the decline of their income was due partly to the fact that children were buried quietly without ceremony. But they were at least publicly interred in Hamburg: many German states attempted to ban mourning for children outright.[60]

The really indigent were also excluded from this costly social ritual: the 'Nose-squeezer', a plain cramped box, deposited without ceremony in a communal grave, marked the end of many a miserable life on the margins of subsistence. But the emphasis was on real indigence rather than mere poverty. The *Leichenbitter* often boasted that they provided their services free to the poorer sort.[61]

When in 1681 the caretaker of St. Catherine's died suddenly (leaving an estate of only 24 *mark* 10 *schilling*) the deacons decided to subsidize his funeral expenses of 33 *mark* 12 *schilling*. The account reflects the ceremony of the rich in microcosm. The *Leichenbitter* received 3 *mark*, the corpse bearers 6 *mark*; black cloth cost 1 *mark* 8 *schilling*. The *Sorgemann* placed 10 *schilling* in the poor box; those who accompanied him received 7 *schilling* in all. The bells cost 4 *mark* 8 *schilling* and the choir was paid 3 *mark*. Finally 10 *mark* 12 *schilling* (the largest item) was given for beer distributed among the mourners. If not magnificent, the ceremony was both elaborate and appropriate for one of whom it was written—'My conception: shame and futility; my birth: pain and sorrow; my life: labour and toil; my death: happiness and bliss.'[62]

The funerals of merchants, of academics and of shopkeepers were far more expensive. In 1779 the merchant Martens paid 2,694 *mark* 14 *schilling* for the burial of his wife. The wife of a small shopkeeper in 1789 received a burial which cost 754 *mark*.[63] In 1736 the funeral of the classicist and professor at the Gymnasium, Johann Albert Fabricius, cost 3,453 *mark* 4

[59] Meyer, *Skizzen*, p. 96. For the burial of soldiers see C. F. Gaedechens, 'Das hamburgische Militär bis zum Jahre 1811', *Zeitschrift des Vereins für hamburgische Geschichte*, viii (1889), pp. 421–600 (esp. 490–501).

[60] StAH Senat: Cl.VII Lit.Lb No.4 Vol.3 (1720). The Burial of children is mentioned in Blank, *Mandate*, iii, pp. 1197, 1561. A typical law banning mourning and elaborate burials for children was that published in Sachsen-Hildenburghausen in 1754: *Fürstliche Sachsen-Hildenburghäusische provisional Verordnung wegen Einschränkung der übermässigen Kosten bey Trauer und Begräbnissen* (in British Library).

[61] K. J. B. Wolters, 'Die Leichenbegängnisse der vorigen Jahrhunderte in Hamburg', *Zeitschrift für die evangelisch-lutherische Kirche in Hamburg*, ix (1903), pp. 87–106 (esp. 103); see also Finder, *Hamburgisches Bürgertum*, p. 95. On the *Leichenbitter* see letters in StAH Senat: Cl.VII Lit.Lb No.4 Vol.1(II).

[62] StAH St. Katharinen: II, Einzelakte BIc1.

[63] Koppman, 'Leichenbegängnisse', pp. 266–76.

schilling; his wife's burial in the same year cost 1,715 *mark*.[64] These totals include a multitude of minor expenses ranging from the cost of the coffin to the fee paid for cleaning the streets before the procession.

It is difficult to measure the real cost of such events. Fabricius and the merchant Martens were not poor, but they were not part of the wealthiest class. Fabricius belonged to the established *Gelehrtenrepublik* rather than the commercial plutocracy.[65] At all events the costs were high. Later critics of the funeral ritual, who denounced the practice of paying mourners, claimed that many had been ruined by this form of 'death duty' exacted by society.[66]

Few rebelled against tradition. The cleric Johann Riemer (d. 1714) expressly stated that no bells should be rung at his funeral, and that no 'screeching choirboys' should be present.[67] In 1743 the death of Senator Anderson caused a minor crisis of state when it emerged that he had decided to forego the privilege of an official funeral.[68] But until the end of the century the tyranny of social pressures ruled unchallenged.

It proved difficult to limit expenditure. For Hamburg was one of the few areas which had no table of ranks, or legally defined class structure. Differing forms of burial did exist: statesmen received special treatment, similarly the higher clergy; the guilds and brotherhoods developed their own rituals. Children and spinsters were buried in different ways too.[69] But this diversity resulted from fashion and local customs and not from specific legislation. In contrast with other German rulers, the Hamburg Senate experienced diffi-culty in imposing limitations on individual groups and thus merely attempted to place a general curb on excessive expenditure. As Klefeker wrote: 'How would it have been possible to distinguish between the clothes to be worn by academics and merchants who are not divided by law? And how difficult also to draw the line between large and small merchants? There remain then the artisans and the poor . . . But these know themselves what they can and must do . . . if they do not restrict themselves . . . then poverty and misery . . . provide the punishment.'[70]

The *Policeyordnung* of 1634 envisaged a tripartite division of society; while both wedding and funerals laws speak of large, middling and small

---

[64] From account sheets in SUB Hbg: Nachlass Reimarus (Hereafter: NR) II c 1 and II c 2: 'Geschäftspapiere' (unsorted).

[65] H. Schröder (ed.), *Lexikon der hamburgischen Schriftsteller bis zur Gegenwart*, 8 vols. (Hamburg, 1851–83), ii, pp. 238–59.

[66] For example: Meyer, *Skizzen*, pp. 96–7.

[67] Schröder, *Lexikon*, vi, p. 283. This evidence for Hamburg must be contrasted with Ariès' comments on the rise of a general desire for more modest funerals at this time (Ariès, *L'Homme devant la mort*, pp. 317–19).

[68] See the relevant documents in StAH Senat: Cl.VII Lit.Ab No.1i.

[69] On spinsters see Finder, *Hamburgisches Bürgertum*, p. 102 and Klefeker, *Verfassungen*, xii, p. 504. The guilds and brotherhoods had their own form of burial too and were exempt from the compulsory payments: Blank, *Mandate*, iv, pp. 1825–6

[70] Klefeker, *Verfassungen*, xii, p. 498.

ceremonies.[71] But even in the eighteenth century the *Bürgerschaft* resisted any attempt to formulate a more precise legal distinction between classes or *Stände*.[72] Social standing as expressed in the funeral depended on what individuals could afford, or what they thought essential, regardless of the cost. Even so, Hamburg was not a classless society: the fluid social structure of the seventeenth century became more solid thereafter as a relatively small governing patriciate emerged.[73] The impact of economic growth on the Lutheran community was corrosive—a trend reflected in changing funeral fashions as the ceremony became more elaborate and more of a spectator sport.[74]

IV

The ritual of burial and the nuances of social position expressed in it are best illustrated by the case of the bookseller Gottfried Schultze in 1686. A list of expenses, copies of invitations, guest lists and notes on the ceremony drawn up by his brother Johannes Schultze, *Rektor* of the Johanneum school, provide a clear picture.[75]

Schultze was born in 1643 of 'genteel parents' in Gardelegen. He learnt the rudiments of Latin and was then apprenticed to the book-trade. He migrated to Hamburg and became a relatively prosperous burgher with business interests extending to Schleswig, Leipzig and Frankfurt; he also owned his own press.[76] But he was not a wealthy man. Bookselling and publishing were not big business in late seventeenth-century Hamburg. Even so, the sum of 314 *mark* 4 *schilling* paid for the funeral represented about one tenth of his total estate.[77]

It was Johannes Schultze who acted as *Sorgemann* following the death of his brother on 1 March 1686. He drew up the invitation to the funeral held on Monday, 8th March, in the church of St. Peter. It was addressed to all 'burghers, inhabitants and others' in the name of the widow and of Johannes Schultze.[78] The *Proto-Scholarch,* head of the school administration board, received a separate Latin invitation requesting him to lend yet more dignity to the occasion by his worthy presence.[79]

---

[71] StAH Senat: Cl.VII Lit.La No.3 Vol.4b, fols. 777–8.

[72] Blank, *Mandate,* i, pp. 113–14.

[73] For a brief discussion of this issue see Franklin Kopitzsch, 'Lessing und Hamburg. Aspekte und Aufgaben der Forschung', *Wolfenbütteler Studien zur Aufklärung,* ii (1975), pp. 47–120 (esp. 51–3).

[74] Cf. Ariès, *L'Homme devant la mort,* pp. 317–35.

[75] SUB Hbg: NR I c: Johann Schultze.

[76] SUB Hbg: NR I c 3(Sch); see also R. Naumann, 'Sortimentskataloge des hamburgischen Buchhändlers, Gottfried Schultze, 1668–1683', *Serapeum. Zeitschrift für Bibliothekwissenschaft, Handschriftenkunde und ältere Literatur,* Nr. 16 (1865), 241–50.

[77] No will has survived. This estimate is based on documents in SUB Hbg: NR a 13–15(Sch).

[78] SUB Hbg: NR I c 2(Sch), r.

[79] SUB Hbg: NR I c 2(Sch), v.

Two days before the funeral, the more prominent guests and family friends were sent personal invitations conveyed by the *Leichenbitter*.[80] The husbands of female family friends were also requested to attend. On the day before the funeral the entire community was informed of the time and place by a public notice in the Exchange. Efforts were made to find a Senator, a friend or acquaintance of the household, who was requested '*nostro nomine*' to invite the attendance of his colleagues; a similar procedure was adopted regarding the *Oberalten*, the council of parish administrators.

Two or three pairs of Doctors of Law, and the same number of Doctors of Medicine and clerics were invited to walk by the Sorgemann in front of the coffin as 'friends of the house'—'the others remain behind the corpse'. The four *Bürgermeister* were to walk together: but if one accompanied the Sorgemann, the others would select the Deacon of the Cathedral or a *Syndicus* to make up their party. Furthermore Schultze noted that the *Ratsherren* and *Licentiati* could enter the house of mourning without restriction as they wished. Finally he listed how much each was paid: a *Bürgermeister* received 1 *Ducat*, a *Syndicus* 4 *mark*, the Doctors 2 *mark* each, the *Licentiati* 1 *mark* 8 *schilling* (as did the pastors and those deacons invited as special guests). Deacons who merely followed the corpse received either 1 *mark* or 12 *schilling*. This was the minimum rate—'below these rates, few will accept; but above them one may pay as much as one wants'.

The complexity of the arrangements and the concern to maintain social prestige are reflected in the account sheet drawn up by Johannes Schultze (see Table 1). His brother's standing is measured against the expenses paid for the burial of Frantz von Bremen, a 'distinguished old burgher'. Each item is meticulously listed: on the right Schultze's expenses appear; on the left, for comparison, those of the von Bremen family.

Some items cost the same at both ceremonies. But the von Bremen funeral was much grander: his coffin was decorated with pewter; a poetic obituary was published; more bells were rung at more churches; and the guests were given more money to place in the poor box. These distinctions clearly reveal a difference in social standing.

But this does not account for all discrepancies. Virtually the largest expense on the von Bremen account is the payment made to invited guests (235 *mark* 8 *schilling*). The Schultzes paid only 33 *mark*. Although they did not invite as many guests as the von Bremens, Schultze's account of the procession indicates that many more attended than were actually paid. His position as *Rektor* of the Johanneum brought him into frequent contact with the urban elite and many guests granted their services without payment on account of this.[81]

---

[80] SUB Hbg: NR I c 2(Sch), r.

[81] On the practice of attending funerals without payment as a sign of honour see: *Briefe des hamburgischen Bürgermeisters Johann Schulte Lt. an seinen in Lissabon etablirten Sohn Johann Schulte geschrieben in den Jahren 1680–1685* (Hamburg, 1856), pp. 50, 71, 179–80.

Before the funeral two lists were drawn up: one of those invited into the house, another of those who would place money in the poor box. The first included the presiding *Bürgermeister* Schulte and Franciscus von Bremen who walked with the *Sorgemann*. They were followed by four Doctors of Law and four Doctors of Medicine; then came four clergymen; lastly four Senators and eight licentiates—26 individuals in all. Some of these were included in the second list of those who received money for the poor—seventeen names including the *Sorgemann*, his two acolytes and other close family friends.[82]

They all took prominent place in the procession which began at half past five in the evening.[83] The *Sorgemann* led the way preceded by the choir; he was followed by '*4 Doctores juris, 4 Doctores medicina, 2 Pastores und 2 Diaconi*' together with several licentiates, five pairs of friends (all in long coats) and 'many other neighbours and good friends'. The procession circled the streets around the church of St. Peter where the grave lay. The main body of mourners followed the corpse: 20 Doctors, 20 preachers, 10 Senators, 32 licentiates, the professors of the Gymnasium and the teachers of the Johanneum, 6 Oberalten 'and a whole procession of people wearing long cloaks, and distinguished people, so long that, as the *Sorgemann* entered the church, the procession was still making its way around the church and stretched back into the *Piltzer-* and *Schmiederstrasse*'. For the graduates were followed by 121 pairs of mourners wearing long cloaks and 30 pairs wearing short cloaks—apart from those who simply followed the procession. The service itself was simple: Schultze merely notes that three hymns were sung.

The documentation of the case of Gottfried Schultze is unusual. But from other evidence we know that his funeral was not exceptional by the standards prevalent in Hamburg in the late seventeenth and eighteenth centuries. The scale of expenditure varied enormously from the destitute, whose burials were paid for by the city, to the very rich who could afford the most extravagant funerary rites. But the principle was very similar. For all groups the celebration of the departure from life was the most complex, and for many perhaps the most expensive they encountered during their lifetimes.

V

The ritual of burial was thus both intricate and elaborate at most levels of the social scale. Indeed it was so strongly buttressed by social pressures that the Senate found it impossible to limit expenditure. For if the Church exercised an all-powerful censure on death, the Senate and its sub-department of the *Wedde* was responsible for the regulation and control of the funeral.[84]

[82] SUB Hbg: NR I c 12, 2(Sch), r and v.
[83] SUB Hbg: NR I c 8(Sch).
[84] Klefeker, *Verfassungen*, viii, p. 784 and xii, pp. 412–16.

Table 1

The following burial account is the only surviving list of funeral expenditure in Hamburg from the late seventeenth century. The list was drawn up by Johann Schultze for the funeral of his brother, Gottfried. Each item is listed together with the price paid. On the left hand side of the page the appropriate costs for the funeral of Frantz von Bremen are given for comparison.

Costs of burial Anno 1686

Mk.	Sch.		Mk.	Sch.
Herr Frantz von Bremen — A distinguished old burgher			Herr Godfried Schultze — Bookseller	
6	—	For the thanksgiving to the father confessor	6	—
3	—	For the thanksgiving to the Pastor of St. Petri	3	—
3	—	For the thanksgiving to the Pastor of St. Nicolai	—	—
6	—	For the thanksgiving to Pastor Elmenhorst, as a relative	—	—
48	—	For the coffin	48	—
3	2	To bring the same into the house, and lay the body in it	2	—
2	—	To close the same	—	12
3	—	To paint the coffin	—	—
18	—	To decorate the coffin	16	8
1	8	For those who held vigil by the coffin	—	—
1	8	To bring the bier into the house	1	8
4	8	To the tin smith for tin on the coffin	2	—
6	—	For the burial notice	3	—
—	8	To hang the same in the exchange	—	8
2	—	For dressing the corpse	—	—
18	—	3 *Leichenbitter* at 6 mk.	12	—
1	8	For the man who announces the *Sorgemann*	—	—
6	—	Another *Reitendiener* who invites the graduates and Senators	6	—
3	—	For the same to follow the *Sorgemann*	3	—
6	—	For a woman or female *Leichenbitter*	6	—
4	—	For another woman to serve in the house	—	—
9	6	To print one sheet of poems, one sheet of rice paper in all	—	—
10	6	For the cloth and wreath on the coffin, with beer money	8	6
—	8	To put up the lights and take them down again	—	8
—	6	For mourning cloth around the lights	—	12
1	—	For wax in the lights	—	9
12	—	To the *Leichenbitter* for food and drink, and mourning cloth at 3 mk. each	9	—
1	8	To the *Leichenbitterin* for food	1	8
3	—	Fee to the Church for registration of the burial	3	—
6	—	For the grave digger—to the same for stones to close the grave	9	2
4	2	For diverse mourning coats (1 for the *Sorgemann* at 2 mk.)	1	8
1	10	For the street sweeper	2	—
66	—	Into the basin for the poor *summa* (for the *Sorgemann* and friends)	37	8
1	8	To open and smoke out the grave in the church	1	8
—	6	For him who announces the procession in the name of the Senate	—	6
18	—	To the school, namely 6 teachers at 3 mk.—at 2 mk.	12	—
18	—	To the school, 72 pairs of scholars at 4 sch—at 1 sch.	9	—
—	12	To the school, extra for the procession	—	—
3	—	For the bell ringer at St. Nicolai in the evening	—	—
3	—	For the bell ringer at St. Petri	3	—
15	—	For those who count the procession 7 hats of sugar (the same for the corpse bearers)	4	—
—	12	Sugar cakes at 12 sch. per hundred	1	2
14	—	4 barrels of wine at 3½ mk. after the procession	3	8

Mk.	Sch.		Mk.	Sch.
3	8	Sugar biscuits	—	12
1	8	To the stable boy to alert the *Reitendiener*	—	—
30	—	10 *Reitendiener* as corpse bearers at 3 mk.	—	—
—	—	10 Students as corpse bearers at 3 mk.	30	—
		For the procession:		
24	—	to the *Bürgermeister* at 6 mk.	6	—
6	—	to the *Syndicis* at 3 mk.	—	—
22	8	15 Senators at 1 mk. 8 sch.	—	—
6	—	*Secretarÿs* at 1 mk. 8 sch.	—	—
12	—	Pastors as friends into the house at 2 mk./at 1 mk. 8 sch.	6	—
8	—	the same, but not as friends	6	—
22	8	Deacons, 15 at 1 mk. 8 sch./at 1 mk.	15	—
24	—	*Doctoribus* at 2 mk.	—	—
52	—	The same, behind the corpse, but not into the house	—	—
55	8	*Licentiatis* at 1 mk. 8 sch.	—	—
3	—	Professoriby, Rectori & Conrectori at 1 mk. 8 sch.	—	—
13	—	For bells at St. Petri	13	—
3	12	For him who gives the sign for bells to be rung, or beer money	2	12
16	12	For bells at St. Nicolai, together with beer money	—	—
—	—	For bells in the Cathedral, with beer money	15	12
2	6	For bells in St. Mariae Magdal., with beer money	—	—
2	6	For bells in St. Johannis, *item*	—	—
3	—	For bells in the prison	—	—
648	10		314	4

Notes

Currency: 1 *Mark* = 16 *Schilling*.

Sugar cakes: a form of sweet traditionally handed out to the public at funeral processions ('hats of sugar' were larger, cone-shaped masses of sugar).

Source

Staats- und Universitätsbibliothek Hamburg: Nachlass Reimarus, II, c, 1: *Geschäftspapiere*

Two concerns emerge from the legislation produced by the authorities. The first was that of imposing limits on expenditure (a part of the broader structure of sumptuary legislation) and an attempt to curb the danger of disorder and unruly behaviour. The second concerned the problem of mediating between vested interests, and of fixing prices for their services. The whole issue was infinitely complicated by an important long-term change in funeral fashion: the transition from day to evening burials after 1700.

Until that time, day funerals were more usual, although evening burials were mentioned already in 1664. The clergy had advocated their introduction in 1650 believing that they might bring a desirable reduction in funeral expenditure. But the mandate of 1664 attempted to ban them outright.[85] Gradually, however, the custom grew and, far from curbing extravagance,

[85] StAH Ministerium: II 2, pp. 32, 35; Blank, *Mandate,* i, p. 345.

the new mode of burial encouraged it. Some expenses were saved: the choirs became superfluous and fewer guests were invited; hence the *Leichenbitter* were no longer necessary (nor indeed the corpse bearers, since the coffin was now transported on a horse-drawn hearse). But more was spent on torches and torchbearers, on ornately decorated coaches and on festive meals after the ceremony.

Funerals did not become more modest after 1750: only their outward form changed.[86] In most cases the evening burial meant the decline of the communal element: the use of carriages implied the exclusion of the general public, now relegated to the role of passive observers rather than active participants. The paid high class mourner alone remained.

But the exclusion of the community did not entail a rejection of the social meaning with which the burial ritual had always been imbued. On the contrary, the development of the more theatrical and exclusive evening funeral must be seen as part of that dynamic long-term socio-economic process which transformed Hamburg from a limited Lutheran community into an expanding heterodox society dominated from the early eighteenth century by an urban patriciate with almost aristocratic pretensions. This placed a premium upon obvious material success in a society which lacked legal definitions of class and status. The funeral remained as central to the public sphere of the new society as it had been to that of the old.

The guilds and the clergy complained that less was being spent on funerals, but in reality expenditure was merely channelled into other pockets. Already in 1692 the Senate had attempted to legislate against excessive pomp at evening funerals. But after 1700 the practice became even more prominent.[87] By the 1770s yet another change had occurred, since the Senate now allowed the use of carriages in the afternoons.[88] The important factor was thus the decline of the procession on foot: the funeral became more exclusive, and more spectacular.

The problem of restricting pomp and ceremony was, however, perennial. The *Policeyordnung* of 1634 sought to limit all funerals by placing a ceiling on expenditure on mourning clothes. The first printed mandate in 1650 was even more explicit. It decreed that processions were to be punctual, laid down a code of behaviour for the scholars, *Leichenbitter* and *Reitendiener* and drew up an approved list of prices. 'All other expenditures', it concluded, '. . . are abolished by the publication of this law . . .; he who transgresses the law, and pays more than is allowed . . ., must pay . . . a fine of 5 *Reichsthaler*'. Other laws banned the provision of wine before or after the funeral; and

---

[86] See Wolters, 'Leichenbegängnisse', *passim*; Aust, *Ohlsdorfer Friedhof*, pp. 76–85; H. J. Bonhage, 'Tod in Hamburg', *Merian. Das Monatsheft der Städte und Landschaften*, Heft 9/XXV, pp. 129–32. All stress the persistence of tradition in Hamburg's burial customs.

[87] Blank, *Mandate*, ii, pp. 863–5; the preachers of the four minor churches clearly saw the plague years (1713–15) as crucial in the transition from day to night funerals: StAH Senat: Cl.VII Lit.Lb No.4 Vol.4a(2)—letter dated 1751.

[88] Klefeker, *Verfassungen*, xii, p. 506.

also prohibited the use of long mourning cloaks since they were not only expensive, but cumbersome as they trailed along the ground in the streets.[89]

The *Mandat Wegen der Abendleichen* of 1729 marked the apogee of this form of sumptuary legislation. The fines imposed were greater than ever before—an indication that the evening burial was popular especially among the wealthy. Bell-ringing at night was to be punished by a fine of 100 *Reichsthaler;* anyone who used more than four coaches was to pay 20 *Reichsthaler* for the first, 40 for the second and for each subsequent coach a similar doubled sum. A limit of 24 torches was specified with a fine of 10 *Reichsthaler* for each additional light.[90] These were indeed heavy fines. But many merely incorporated the fines into the normal costs of a burial.[91]

Similarly, efforts were made to control behaviour at funerals. A law of 1660 protested against unnecessary detours on the way to the Church.[92] Nor was the conduct of the participants always exemplary. In 1743 a warning was issued to those who behaved in a 'disgusting and unchristian' manner at interments: the warning was reissued three times in the next two decades.[93] At evening ceremonies the use of naked torches posed a grave fire risk too.[94]

Despite its all-embracing character, the legislation was ineffective. The *Wedde* accounts register frequent sums paid for wearing cloaks which were too long, for illegal luxury and illicit bell-ringing at night. In 1759 such fines, ranging from 2 to 100 *mark*, amounted to 2,642 *mark*.[95] Many complicatons arose from the vagueness of successive mandates which were open to gross and often wilful misinterpretation. The rage of funeral fashion knew no bounds. Senatorial reports before 1729 frequently mention inordinate numbers of coaches and torch bearers.[96] New problems constantly emerged. When in 1729 nocturnal bell-ringing was prohibited, trumpets were blown from the church towers.[97] Law enforcement was difficult for the Senate employed only a single man as a *Köstenkieker* to attend both weddings and funerals.[98] *Post facto* action thus merely tended to express mild disapproval rather than impose an outright prohibition.

Far more intricate and time-consuming was the difficulty experienced by the Senate in mediating between vested interests. Indeed, it was partly the nature of these problems which frustrated any sumptuary legislation for

[89] Blank, *Mandate,* i, pp. 90–4, 132–5, 217–19.
[90] Ibid., iii, pp. 1419–22 (renewed 1743).
[91] Klefeker, *Verfassungen,* xii, p. 505.
[92] Blank, *Mandate,* i, pp. 167–9. The law of 1729 made a similar point. (Ibid., iii, p. 1422).
[93] Ibid., iii, pp. 1698–9, 2153, 2298; v, p. 2561.
[94] Ibid., ii, pp 796–7.
[95] Finder, *Hamburgisches Bürgertum,* p. 109.
[96] StAH Senat: Cl.VII Lit.Lb No.4 Vol. 4b; see also the earlier dispute over the interpretation of luxury laws (1716) in StAH Senat: Cl.VII Lit.Cc No.13 Vol.8 Fasc.2.
[97] StAH Senat: Cl.VII Lit.Lb No.4 Vol. 7a.
[98] Literally 'one who looks at feasts'—see Schütze, *Holsteinisches Idiotikon,* ii, p. 333. The office was sold for the first time in 1707 for 700 *Mark:* J. L. von Hess, *Topographisch-politisch-, historische Beschreibung der Stadt Hamburg,* 3 vols. (Hamburg, 1787–92), ii, p. 334.

burial. The rise of the evening funeral (which represented a saving on traditional expenses accompanied by a plunge into new extravagances) created economic issues which were never resolved.

Several groups drew their livelihood from the elaborate burial ritual. The *Reitendiener,* the personal guard of honour of the Senate, acted as undertakers at more exclusive funerals. The *Hochzeits-und Leichenbitter* emerged as a recognized guild about 1650. Students and unbeneficed clerics organized themselves into a brotherhood of corpse bearers after 1700. The *Marstallkutscher,* keeper of the city stables, provided coaches and *chaises* for evening burials; and in the 1720s the office of *Leuchtenpächter* was sold to supply torches and torchbearers. Scholars, teachers and the minor clergy all derived considerable income from funerals, an income which was increasingly eroded by the popularity of the evening ceremony.

Early laws had specified the payment they were to receive. But there was no obligation to employ them.[99] The situation was, however, complicated by the sale of city offices in 1686. The municipality now derived substantial revenue from these groups (often heavily in debt as a result of their purchase of office), and the Senate was thus morally obliged to ensure them a steady income. The obligation was constantly pointed out by those concerned—much to the embarrassment of an administration eager to curb funeral expenditure.[100]

Some suffered less than others. The *Marstallkutscher* profited from the popularity of evening funerals; the *Leuchtenpächter* prospered too.[101] The *studiosi* were also easily dealt with: they were in any case only a semi-professional body of students and unbeneficed clerics who acted as undertakers at the burials of clerical families. Their income also declined after 1720, but they remained outsiders in the harsh battle for revenue from funerals.[102]

The guilds together with the preachers and schoolteachers posed more thorny problems. It was their persistence, the desperation and bitterness of their struggle for survival which forced the Senate to impose a system of payments, compulsory even where the services of professional bodies were not used. Each phase of the debate produced new regulations, culminating in the monumental *Hochzeits- und Leichenordnung und Schragen* of 1746, complemented by the *Marstallkutscher Ordnung und Schragen* of 1754.[103]

The *Leichenbitter* not only suffered from the prominence of evening funerals after 1700, but were also rivalled by the more prestigious *Reiten-*

---

[99] This principle was established in 1674: J. H. Bartels, *Nachtrag zum Neuen Abdrucke der vier Haupt-Grundgesetze der hamburgischen Verfassung* (Hamburg, 1825), p. 200.
[100] J. F. Voigt, *Beiträge zur hamburgischen Verwaltungsgeschichte,* 3 vols. (Hamburg, 1917–18), ii, *passim.* See also StAH Senat: Cl.VII Lit.Lb No.4 Vol.1(II)—'Extractus Protocolli', 23 January 1722.
[101] On the office of *Leuchtenpächter* see StAH Senat: Cl.VII Lit.Lb No.4 Vol.4d.–1–3.
[102] StAH Senat: Cl-VII Lit.Lb No.4 Vol.2, *passim.*
[103] Blank, *Mandate,* iii, pp. 1553–71; iv, pp. 1984–6.

diener. In 1706 they renewed their guild laws in an attempt to counteract the decline: membership was limited to a maximum of 32, and a detailed code of professional conduct was drafted. But new regulations alone could not improve their lot. Letters to the Senate after 1709 talk of unbearable debts and of the general degradation of their colleagues. They even claimed to have difficulty in recruiting new labour.[104]

Their complaints were plausible. Their offices were expensive and they paid local taxes too; yet the Senate seemed unwilling to guarantee them a steady income. But the violence with which they pursued their rights was not always conducive to their cause: in November 1739, they invaded a private house and confiscated goods equivalent to the sum of their fee. The injured party rightly protested that he owed them nothing since he had not even employed the guild at the funeral of his child. But similar cases recurred, until at last the law of 1746 recognized the Senate's obligation to support those to whom it had sold offices.[105]

The position of the *Reitendiener* was less desperate. Their brightly coloured robes and daggers made them more desirable as corpse bearers, escorts and announcers than the *Leichenbitter*. Their efforts to restrict the role of the latter merely to inviting guests were successful—as the complaints of that body indicate.[106]

But they too inevitably shared in the general loss of income from burials. In 1731, they claimed that they had not been to a single funeral in two weeks, notwithstanding the mandate of 1729 which implied that they were to be used exclusively at evening ceremonies.[107] They also complained that their functions were being usurped by the military garrison which officiated at state and aristocratic funerals after 1736.[108]

Negotiations between the Senate and the schoolmasters and the minor clergy reveal similar difficulties. The schoolmasters' position was regulated in 1736 when it was decreed that those who preferred an evening funeral should pay them a minimum of 8 *Schilling* compensation.[109] The minor clergy were affected not only because they were no longer called to processions. A report by the *Oberalten* of 1725 noted the decline in sales of candles since the introduction of torches at evening funerals: hence the law of 1729 stipulated that no more than four torch bearers should enter the church.[110] But such minor emendations did little to improve the situation. In 1751 the preachers complained that their income from funerals had declined from 400 *thaler* per annum before 1713 to a miserable 10 *thaler* in 1749. Their

[104] StAH Senat: Cl.VII Lit.Lb No.4 Vol.1(II).
[105] This case and others in StAH Senat: Cl.VII Lit.Lb No.4 Vol.1(III).
[106] StAH Senat: Cl.VII Lit.Cc No.7 Vol.5h—28 July 1728, *Leichenbitter* to Senate.
[107] StAH Senat: Cl.VII Lit.Cc No.7 Vol.6d—9 April 1731, *Leichenbitter* to Senate.
[108] Ibid., 17 August 1736, *Leichenbitter* to Senate. See also StAH Senat: Cl.VII Lit.Ab No.1a and Klefeker, *Verfassungen,* xii, pp. 508–9.
[109] StAH Senat: Cl.VII Lit.Lb No.4 Vol.4a.1.
[110] StAH Senat: Cl.VII Lit.Lb No.4 Vol.4b; Blank, *Mandate,* iii, p. 1421.

plea proved effective. In March 1751, a mandate appeared which decreed that those who used coaches for evening ceremonies were to pay the four minor preachers 2 *thaler* each.[111]

The Senate was placed in a paradoxical position by these intricate and troublesome disputes. It agreed that conspicuous expenditure should be limited. But it was obliged to support vested interests by enforcing payments which would otherwise have been avoided. The elaborate funeral ritual was thus made more complex not only by changes in burial fashion, but also by the unsavoury squabbles of groups whose livelihood depended on the perpetuation of the old system. Fashion conflicted with tradition. Money was invested in both. The Senate was forced to attempt the unenviable task of mediating between the two without the ability, or perhaps even the inclination, to deny the demands of either.

VI

Despite the complexity and confusion of the issue, there is little evidence to suggest that burials became more modest. Klefeker wrote that *Bürgermeister* Anderson's precedent of avoiding the excess of a public funeral in 1743 provided a salutary example.[112] But the voices in favour of a more simple form of interment were drowned by the chorus of tradition and fashion. Even *Der Patriot,* which mocked the whimsy of 'Herr Eitelhard Bookesbeutel', concluded that a mean should be found between old and new: 'For it is easy to move from one extreme of stupidity to another, and in avoiding the Bookesbeutel, to become a slave of inconstancy and new fashions. Both are equally laughable. . . .' Tradition must be respected, though new customs should not be rejected out of hand.[113]

Some believed that the transition to evening funerals represented an outright rejection of the formal public interment of the past. In 1748 the moral weekly, *Der Hamburger,* declared that any respectable patriarch should be buried by day, accompanied by 16 *Reitendiener*: 'That one simply puts people away by night is surely a crying shame.'[114] It is true that the day time procession, the expression of corporate civic mourning in the post-Reformation community, had lost its monopoly by 1760. But the new form of burial by night with coaches and torches was no less magnificent, nor any less public.

The debate over the morality of expensive funerals continued for some decades. Klefeker was convinced that the female section of the community was responsible for the stubbornness of tradition: 'The Bookesbeutel is a

[111] StAH Senat: Cl.VII Lit.Lb No.4 Vol.4a.2; Blank, *Mandate,* iv, p. 1789.
[112] Klefeker, *Verfassungen,* xii, pp. 507–8.
[113] *Der Patriot,* i, pp. 228–9.
[114] *Der Hamburger. Das erste Blatt. Dienstags den 10 December 1748* n.p. (in StAH Z900/29).
[115] Klefeker, *Verfassungen,* xii, p. 502.

law imposed not by the authorities, but by the fair sex . . . for they have long since dominated the men in this respect, and have regulated customs and proprieties in matters of clothing, entertainment, weddings and funerals.'[115] Even enlightened observers were often in two minds: von Griesheim who in many respects regarded Hamburg as a model well-governed community, clearly approved of the elaborate form of public mourning, which could be justified if it contributed to the livelihood of the crafts and guilds which serviced it.[116]

That great revolution of sentiment and emotion identified by Ariès in the mid eighteenth century seems to have been absent in Hamburg. The cult of funerals remained ostentatiously public. Even the most bitter critics of the ritual, who ridiculed the *Reitendiener* and the other 'impresarios of death', harboured doubts about a complete reform. J. F. L. Meyer, for example, thought the sound of bells and trumpets at burials rather pleasing—a custom he wished to retain.[117] Meyer realized that the age-old arguments against extravagance, the repeated Senatorial decrees, had achieved nothing. He noted that it was only in 1794 that the distinguished *Syndic* Matsen consciously broke the custom of having a hired procession: 'The public voice, the voice of the fatherland itself, appeared to have called forth these mourners. The loving spirit of his fellow burghers shed tears at his grave.'[118] Many despaired of ever seeing change: 'Where is our Enlightenment?', asked one writer in 1790, 'What purpose has it served, if it cannot destroy such gross and harmful abuses which were mocked by the heathens more than a thousand years ago?'[119]

The most vitriolic attack on the pomp and ceremony of the Hamburg funeral appeared as late as 1800. 'Why', the author asked, 'do you want to march ostentatiously round the alley ways in pomp with your honoured and beloved dead and then, . . . complain . . . that it has cost you so much?' Only the extremes of human vanity could persuade one to invest so much money in a dead and useless corpse: it would be better employed in promoting the 'living arts and manufactures'. All human beings must die; and in death all are equal—so why should one strive to prolong the social differences between men on the way to the grave? Dressed up corpses are grotesque, he declared; the ceremony to which they are subjected obscene.[120]

The winds of change blew from a different direction. The efforts of the late eighteenth-century moral reformers did not destroy the ritual of the early modern funeral, nor did the eminent examples of men like Anderson

[116] C. L. von Griesheim, *Vermehrte und verbesserte Auflage des Tractats. Die Stadt Hamburg in ihrem politischen, ökonomischen und sittlichen Zustande* (Hamburg, 1760), pp. 292–4, 309.

[117] Meyer, *Skizzen*, pp. 100–1.

[118] Ibid., p. 95.

[119] Anon., *Ueber die Zeit, die Art und den Ort der Beerdigung* (Hamburg, 1790), p. 63.

[120] Anon. *Wahrheit und Licht ueber Leichengepränge und luxuöse Einkleidung der Todten in Hamburg* (Hamburg, 1800), p. 3.

or Matsen. It was the removal of the cemeteries from the city, and in particular from the churches, which ultimately effected a change in custom.[121] This was not a new concept. Luther himself had written that 'My advice would be to place the graves outside the city'. In Hamburg too one late sixteenth-century physician had argued that graves inside the churches posed a serious threat of infection and disease.[122] But the church had its own material interests to bear in mind: the sale of graves was a vital source of income for the parish.[123]

By the eighteenth century, however, the issue could no longer be ignored. The rapid expansion in population, the disastrous experience of plague in the years 1713–15 and again in 1735, the putrefying stench in the churches of the accumulated corpses of several centuries, the open graves of the poor in the churchyards—all these factors provided a new incentive to attack the problem at its roots. In 1765 J. P. Willebrand declared that it should be one of the foremost principles of good policy to remove graves from the city centres.[124] In 1779 the plague corpses of 1713–15 were disinterred and placed in a new cemetery outside the city walls.[125] In 1786 the Patriotic Society offered a prize for the best proposal for new cemetery regulations.[126]

It was the parish administrator of St. Jacobi, Heinrich Kühl (probably also the instigator of the Patriotic Society project and the author of a pamphlet on this issue in 1786), who made the first effective move.[127] In 1793 he purchased a plot of land outside the *Steintor* to be used as a cemetery for his parish. His action proved seminal as the other parishes followed suit during the next two decades. As Meyer wrote in 1800: 'We owe the salutary beginning of this reform since 1793 to an enlightened parish administrator who . . . achieved more in one year than legislation had done in decades.'[128]

The last burial held inside a city church was that of Frau Senatorin Jänisch on 31 December 1812. For in October 1812 the French occupation Mairie had issued a decree with effect from 1 January 1813 prohibiting interments within city limits. It was to be one of the few French innovations which survived the Restoration and constitutional retrenchment after 1815.[129]

A similar process had occurred in many other areas. France led the way

---

[121] Cf. Ariès, *Western Attitudes*, pp. 69–73; Hannaway, 'La Fermeture', *passim*; Lebrun, *Les Hommes devant la mort*, pp. 480–6.

[122] Both quoted by Finder, *Hamburgisches Bürgertum*, pp. 90, 93.

[123] This source of income became particularly important after about 1690. See notes in StAH St. Jakobi: A III 3.

[124] J. P. Willebrandt, *Abrégé de la police, accompagné de reflexions sur l'accroissement des villes*, 2 vols. (Hamburg, 1765), ii, p. 16.

[125] Finder, *Hamburgisches Bürgertum*, p. 95.

[126] *Verhandlungen und Schriften der hamburgischen Gesellschaft zur Beförderung der nützlichen Künste und Gewerbe* (Hamburg, 1792ff), i, p. 79.

[127] Anon., *Gründe der Wahrheit, den Christen zu bewegen, die Gräber für Verstorbene von Kirch und Stadt zu entfernen. Begleitet mit Vorschlägen, wie die Verlegung, ohne die Einkünfte der Kirchen zu schmälern, vollzogen werden kann* (Hamburg, 1786).

[128] Meyer, *Skizzen*, p. 101.

with a royal decree of 1775; Joseph II issued a similar law in 1782.[130] In Bavaria, a decree of 1803 forbade burials in the cities.[131] In all cases the consequences were not confined merely to new standards of civic hygiene. The ritual of the funeral was also profoundly affected. The corpse was moved from the centre of the community to the chapel of rest. The cult of the cemetery and the art of the gravestone replaced the living symbolism for the survivors which had been the hallmark of the early modern funeral.[132]

[129] Geffcken, 'Leichenbegängnisse', p. 500; and N. A. Westphalen, *Hamburgs Verfassung und Verwaltung in ihrer allmähligen Entwicklung bis auf die neueste Zeit,* 2 vols. (Hamburg, 1846), ii, p. 178.

[130] Lebrun, *Les Hommes devant la mort,* pp. 480–6; for Austria see A. Huber (ed), *Sammlung der K. K. Landesfürstlichen Gesetze und Verordnungen in Publico Ecclesiasticis vom Jahre 1776 bis Ende 1782* (Vienna, 1782), pp. 181–2; L. Ruland, *Die Geschichte der kirchlichen Leichenfeier* (Regensburg, 1901), p. 208; for a more general discussion see C. Bär, *Mozart, Krankheit—Tod—Begräbnis* (Salzburg, 1966), *passim,* esp. pp. 125–6.

[131] Ruland, *Geschichte,* p. 208. Cf. H. Wesemann, 'Dörfliches Brauchtum um Tod und Begräbnis im Mindener Land', *Mitteilungen des Mindener Geschichts- und Heimatvereins,* xli (1969), 121–35.

[132] On the cult of cemeteries see Ariès, *L'Homme devant la mort,* pp. 517–23; S. French, 'The Cemetery as a Cultural Institution: The Establishment of Mount Auburn and the "Rural Cemetery" Movement', in Stannard, *Death in America,* pp. 69–91. The change in custom did not please all critics of the old form of burial: by 1800 J. F. L. Meyer was already decrying the grotesque tombstones and mausoleums found in the new rural cemeteries. He advocated a return to the ancient practice of cremation, but thought that this would not be acceptable to most people. (Meyer, *Skizzen,* pp. 102–8.)

V

Death and the French Historians*

JOHN McMANNERS

In 1944, German troops captured 'Colonel Berger' of the Alsace-Lorraine group of the French Resistance. Expecting to be handed over to the Gestapo and to perish cruelly, the 'Colonel' asked for a Bible, and read the Gospel according to St. John. In his *Antimémoires*, André Malraux, *alias* Colonel Berger, tells of his feelings. 'Alone and facing death, my heart went out towards that age-old Presence that had swept away the despair of so many helpless souls, just as the Last Judgement would roll away their sepulchres. "Lord, help us in the hour of our death." But faith needs belief. I admired the Christian story that had been preached in all the earth—in some corner of which, no doubt, I should soon be laid to rest—but I did not believe it.'[1] *Lord, help us in the hour of our death.* For even the most sophisticated agnostic, at the last moment there is only one direction in which consolation may be sought: Malraux did not find it and turned sadly away. But that sadness could easily become anger. In his novel, *La Voie royale,* published fourteen years earlier, he had described how Claude looked on helplessly as Perken died, and in striving by look and gesture to express his despairing friendship, 'remembered with hatred the phrase from his childhood, "Lord help us in the hour of our death".'[2] This onrush of bitterness is significant. For those who face death without hope, it is impossible not to envy others who retain the comfort of their illusions.

From the eighteenth century in France,[3] the question of human destiny which every man must ponder in his secret, lonely thoughts, had become a matter of ill-natured public dispute and the occasion for recurrent skirmishes in the guerrilla warfare between clericals and anticlericals—encounters marked by sanctimonious manoeuvering on the one side and macabre gamesmanship on the other. The theologians had their terrifying scenario of the after-life: the individual judgment immediately after death and the recapitulative Last Judgement, the Great Assize which proclaimed the victory

---

*By kind permission of the Editor, I have been allowed to incorporate in this chapter most of my article 'The History of Death' in *The Times Literary Supplement,* 14 December 1979.

[1] *Antimémoires* (Gallimard, 1967), I, p. 230.

[2] *La Voie Royale: roman* (1930), *ad. fin.* 'Claude se souvint, haineusement, de la phrase de son enfance, *Seigneur, assistez-nous dans notre agonie.*'

[3] See my forthcoming *Death and the Enlightenment* (Oxford Univ. Press).

106

of Christ and the doom of the wicked, for whom the eternal fires of Hell were waiting. Everything depended on a man's dispositions in his last hour. With true repentance (however difficult or improbable this might be) even the most hardened sinner would be saved, while a last-minute divergence from habitual austerity and piety could consign a noble soul to irremediable destruction. How important then was the assiduous, life-long preparation for the end, and the presence of the clergy at the death-bed, of confession and absolution, of the anointings and the viaticum—the furnishing of the passport, the staff and the nourishment for the final journey! Against these Catholic ceremonies of dying there was a rising tide of criticism in the age of the Enlightenment: from Protestants who denied the doctrines of Purgatory and the confessional, from deists rejecting eternal punishment as unworthy of a God of love, from atheists and agnostics who regarded Hell as ridiculous and judgement as a fable, and from anticlericals of every shade of belief (including Catholicism), who resented the public parade, *l'appareil,* of the Church's ministry to the dying, and the way in which the clergy achieved their moment of supreme influence when human resistance was at its lowest—'le moment ... favorable pour les prêtres, toujours forts dans ce cas-là'.[4] Hence, a whole series of tragi-comic anecdotes about death-bed scenes, when the clergy were defied or ridiculed, outwitted or evaded. The Revolution, with its wars and anticlerical vandalism did much to destroy the routines of conformity and deference, but the death-bed remained the decisive battleground between the clergy and their opponents. At this moment of his life, if at no other time, a man was constrained to reveal his allegiance; this was the point at which, as it were, everyone had to lie down to be counted. There was no neutrality: to do nothing meant joining the goats rather than the sheep. From churchmen came pictures of the quiet hope and confidence that was the prerogative of the Christian, and the contrasting despair of the unbeliever; Hell was reaffirmed as a (literally burning) reality, and continual warnings were given of the imminence of death and of its paralysing terrors. 'C'est la mort qui rôde autour de nous. Quelle assiégeante infatigable! Quelles ruses! Quelles surprises! Quels détours savants!'[5] Unbelievers replied with

---

[4] Cit. J. McManners, *Reflexions at the Death Bed of Voltaire* (1975), p. 27.

[5] Henri Perreyve, *La Journée des malades* (approved by the archbishop of Paris, 1860; 2nd edn. 1864. B. Nat. D47424). The preaching of the grim old theology of judgement and Hell went on, with the worm and the fire taken literally, and Matthew 25:46 proving everything. (see e.g. Mgr. de Ségur, *Instructions familières et lectures du soir* (2 vols. 1864. B. Nat. D51965) I, pp. 13, 50, 117, 174, 237; also *Sermons de Mgr. Gay* (2 vols. 1894. B. Nat. D83921) I, pp. 308-9, 337-8, 379. By contrast, however, there was a good deal of consolation, addressed to the sincere Christian, which spoke essentially of forgiveness, hope and the joys of heaven. See, e.g., Mgr. Gaume, *Histoire du bon larron, dédiée au XIXᵉ siècle* (1868. B. Nat. H. 14634) and *La Vie n'est pas la vie, ou la grande erreur du XIXᵉ siècle* (1869. B. Nat. D59437), pp. 172, 176-7, 225. Also B. Gassiat, *Le Dogme de la mort, ses splendeurs, ses délices* (1879. B. Nat. D65971), pp. 12, 27-8. There is a clear example, in the case of bishop Gay, of one work full of the terrors of Hell (see above) and another full of consolation (*De l'Espérance chrétienne* (1891, B. Nat D. 82486 pp. 105, 145, 151, 212, 218)). The nineteenth century seems to differ from the eighteenth in distinguishing sharply between the

selections from the definitive corpus of the arguments against Hell which had been compiled in the eighteenth century by Voltaire and Diderot, and with praise of the heroes who rejected the gospel of fear and faced death without hope in the future, sustained only by the affection of their families and friends. The story of what had happened at a death-bed could be inferred from the funeral ceremonies—whether the rites of the Church were performed or omitted; and at the funeral the family manifested its religious or irreligious allegiances. Hence, societies of Freethinkers arose in the 1870s to collect funds to buy up the corpses of paupers to give them 'civic burial' as a device of propaganda against the clergy. At Lyon in July 1873 there were 60 lay funerals without benefit of clergy, and the churchman who records this scandal rejoiced in the attitude of the conservative prefect, who compelled those who walked in irreligious funeral processions to do so at 6 in the morning (7 a.m. in the winter).[6] In December 1882, the great anticlerical statesman of the Third Republic, Gambetta, was buried in an unblessed grave with purely lay ceremonies. This was regarded as the decisive victory of the republicans of Government against the clergy. 'Not a priest, not a whisper of a prayer', wrote Camille Pelletan the day afterwards, 'the Catholic Church, yesterday lost something of its power.'[7] In 1887, as part of its war against clericalism, the Government passed a law enabling citizens to make a declaration prescribing a non-religious funeral for themselves, and imposing heavy penalties on heirs and executors who infringed this registered declaration of intention, even if there had been a death-bed conversion.

The role of death in the warfare between churchmen and anticlericals under the Third Republic may be illustrated by two very different novels, one frivolous, but with a serious purpose, the other tense and sombre. In an ironical cameo, Anatole France[8] depicts a funeral scene in a little provincial town in the 1890s. Everyone had turned out for the procession for the obsequies of the aged and devout *premier président* Cassignol, though the bourgeoisie resented the 'proud humility' which had inspired him to leave instructions forbidding all secular and military pomp. Even so, the General and the army officers were there in mufti, and so were all the children of the schools run by religious congregations, ordered in files of black and grey as far as the eye could see. M. Bergeret, M. Formerol the doctor, and M. Mazure the archivist walked together near the coffin, as befitted notables. The doctor entertained his two companions as they proceeded with accounts of the deaths of various local inhabitants at which he had officiated, 'and M.

---

faithful Christians who are trying hard, and the careless men of the world: Hell-fire preaching is for the latter category.

[6] Mgr. Gaume, *Le Cimetière au XIXᵉ siècle, ou le dernier mot des solidaires* (n.d. 1873? B. Nat. D. 62634), pp. 85–92.

[7] J. McManners, *Church and State in France, 1870–1914* (1972), p. 59.

[8] Anatole France, *L'Anneau d'améthyste* (19th edn. 1899), Chap. VIII.

Mazure, who was a free-thinker, was taken—in face of the idea of death—with a great desire to have an immortal soul'. Accordingly, he put forward a theory of a 'thinking principle' which survives the body. M. Bergeret was sceptical, though the doctor thought it was well for most people to believe in a life after death. 'Religious belief', he said, 'is a therapeutic agent'; look at Mme Péchin coming out of the fruiterers with her tomatoes—she wants to be immortal; tell her that she'll endure as long as the galaxies, but not for ever, and all the pleasure of munching her tomato salad will be destroyed. Bergeret pressed Dr. Formerol: did he really expect to rise again himself? 'I've no need to believe in God to be a moral man', said the cautious physician, 'in matters of religion, as a man of learning, I simply do not know, but as a citizen I believe everything. I am an official Catholic. I think religious ideas are essentially moralizing, and that they contribute to give the populace humanitarian sentiments.' As the procession moved into the cemetery, the doctor clinched his argument. 'M. Bergeret, if like me you visited a dozen sick people every morning, you'd understand, as I do, the power of the clergy.' No doubt it was easier, as M. Formerol was insisting, to make sceptical conversation at someone else's funeral than to maintain anticlerical practice as one's own drew near. This was the central tension in Roger Martin du Gard's novel, *Jean Barrois* (finished in May 1913).[9] All through life there is the haunting, inescapable problem—what will a man do in his last hour? The hero's father, a sceptical doctor, confessed and received communion at the end, apologizing to his son for his weakness in face of the final mystery. 'Je me suis confessé hier ... Tu sais, mon petit, on a beau dire ... C'est un x terrible.' After a career of anticlericalism and religious doubt, Jean Barrois breaks down in the same way, and makes his peace between the hands of his old friend the abbé Lévys. 'I am going to die! Tell me. I am going to die? ... Ah save me! Do not let me suffer. You are sure He has pardoned me?' And 'Hell!' is the last word he breathes. Immediately he is dead, Cécile, his estranged and pious wife, finds his atheistical 'testament' in a drawer—a disavowal, before the event, of any weakness he might show at the end. The priest sits by the bedroom fire and does not intervene as she goes to the hearth to burn it.

For so many French families death-beds and funerals have been the points of decisive encounter in the warfare between churchmen and anticlericals which was the central theme of so much of French history from the eighteenth century onwards. Perhaps, this is one of the reasons why French historians have pioneered the study of death—or rather, we should say, of attitudes to death (for in what sense can an historian study an event which has no succeeding events to put it into context?). In England, the story of the scene at the death-bed or the rehearsal of the details of obsequies could be left to the biographer rounding off his volume. The way a man dies may be

---

[9] *Oeuvres complètes de Roger Martin du Gard* (2 vols., Pléiade, 1955), I, pp. 257, 451, 556–9. For another powerful death scene see I, pp. 1259–98 (*Les Thibault: La Mort du père*).

revealing in interpreting his character, and the fashion in which he is buried may illustrate his place among his contemporaries, but death-beds and funerals do not normally have a resounding, public significance. In France, it has been different: death has been an occasion for the testing of political and religious allegiances. Certainly, a good deal of French writing about the history of death turns around the question of the power of the Church and the clergy over men's minds and over the arrangements of the social order. Ariès, for example, describes how in the Middle Ages churchmen annexed death and its terrors as a weapon of domination: 'la colonisation ecclésiastique de la mort.' Vovelle's work on the wills of Provence is directed essentially towards the analysis of the 'de-christianisation' of French life; he is concerned, less with the changing attitudes of Frenchmen to death, than with their changing attitudes to Catholicism and its observances.

Eternal punishment was a proposition difficult to defend, and the penumbra of lurid details which traditionally accompanied it did not make the task of the Catholic apologist easier. Unbelievers concentrated their attacks at this weak point in the doctrinal fortress, where Christian principles themselves could be used as ammunition for the siege engines. In the long-continuing debate, Churchmen—though they did not admit it—learned much. Apocalyptic details were tacitly banished to the sphere of non-essentials, and above all, the harsh mechanical picture of the Divine Judgement ceased to be preached as an isolated phenomenon; the doctrine of the love of God manifested in Christ became the regulator of all beliefs and the key to the interpretation of all the proof texts of the Bible. This had been the fundamental theological principle of Rousseau's deism: it could be argued that, in the long run, Christian spirituality has learned more from Jean-Jacques than from Pascal or Bossuet. For this and, no doubt, for other reasons, the crude appeal to fear became discredited as a device of apologetics. Besides, as a result of improvements in hygiene, food supply and medical science, life became so much more secure and predictable: death was no longer the ever-present shadow over daily existence. By the twentieth century, the massive literature of the seventeenth and eighteenth centuries on preparation for death, on Hell and Judgement, had largely passed out of use and was forgotten. Then, in 1932, Henri Bremond published the ninth volume of his famous *Histoire littéraire du sentiment religieux en France,* in which he studied the 'art of dying' under the *ancien régime.* It was a revelation of a vanished mental universe, and proof that the feelings and emotions of mankind are not a given, unchanging factor in history. In 1953, appealing for the writing of a new kind of history, the history of human sentiments, Lucien Febvre prophesied that the results would be surprising—'Que de surprises à prévoir!' He went on: 'I referred earlier to Death. Open the ninth volume of the *Histoire littéraire du sentiment religieux en France* by Henri Bremond, his study of Christian life under the *ancien régime.* Open it at the Chapter entitled "L'Art de mourir". This was less than three hundred years ago, but what an abyss between the customs and feelings of the men of that time and ours!'[10]

From his youthful days in various noviciates in England to 1904 when he was excluded, the abbé Bremond had been a member of the Jesuit Order, and in broad conception his volumes on Spirituality were an apology for the alliance of religion and culture, as the Jesuits conceived it. Erasmus, he insisted, was 'the precursor of the Jesuit Order'[11] and not the harbinger of the Reformation, a reformer of the Church, whose legitimate proposals were not to be regarded as necessarily linked with the 'pessimistic' heresy of Luther. Similarly, the genius of Pascal and Racine belonged to Catholicism, and only incidentally were these great writers Jansenists—'let us reclaim our heritage'.[12] Readers of Sainte-Beuve might imagine that Port-Royal was the only school of spirituality in seventeenth-century France; readers of Bremond were shown how orthodoxy, sympathetically and closely examined, revealed a vivid pattern of spiritual insights, diverse and original. Yet Bremond was never at ease among the Jesuits (even as he took the major vows, in February 1900, his doubts were overwhelming).[13] A 'liberal', who welcomed Loisy's New Testament speculations as a 'Noah's Ark' where Catholic exegetes could take refuge, who was disciplined by the Church for preaching at Tyrell's funeral, and whose life of Sainte Chantal was put on the Index,[14] he lived always on the margins of strict orthodoxy, and in his *Histoire littéraire* his detachment and independent judgement are evident when he is dealing with individual writers and ideas. And his detachment was a reality in more than this obvious sense, for his eleven volumes recounted in innumerable variants the story of the great encounter of man with God which the writer himself had never experienced. 'How is it that others, at least at one moment in their lives, have been able to meet you, but me, never, never?' 'Lord, how long must I knock at the door . . . I have cried unto you and you have not answered.'[15] Bremond was in his early thirties when he confided these sad reflections to his notebooks, and throughout his life he followed the way of the 'prayer of desolation'. As an historian, he observed the various schools of spirituality from the outside, as one who believed with conviction, but had been denied the emotional experience which certainty might have been expected to bring. In the *Histoire littéraire* he takes his place with those who receive no answer from God yet serve him.

There was, then, more than a hint of critical reserve in Bremond's presentation of the seventeenth-century experts on preparation for death,

[10] L. Febvre, *Combats pour l'histoire* (1953), p. 236.
[11] Bremond's posthumous work, *Autour de l'Humanisme*, cit. F. Hermans, *L'Humanisme religieux de l'abbé Henri Bremond, 1865–1933* (1965), p. 89.
[12] H. Bremond, *Histoire littéraire du sentiment religieux en France*, IV (1920), p. 244.
[13] Père André Blanchet, S. J., *Henri Bremond, 1865–1904* (1967), p. 117.
[14] Blanchet, *Histoire d'une mise à l'Index: la 'Sainte-Chantal' de l'abbé Bremond* (1967).
[15] Ibid. p. 78; Blanchet in *Henri Bremond: Actes du Colloque d'Aix, 1966* (Fac. Lettres Aix-en-Provence 1967), p. 21.

111

with their daily exercises, their periodical retreats and self-examinations, their 'spiritual testaments'[16] and reflections on the corruption of the grave. Their obsession with the end of life in an uncompromising quest for certainty was alien to him. So too was their use of the ceremonies of death as a device of religious propaganda, hence his ironical observations on the clergy who gathered round the dying with exhortations culled from professional hand-books—fifteen pages for hardened sinners and eight for ordinary ones, 'Monsieur' for the respectable and 'Mon frère' for the commonalty.[17] Bre-mond himself was inspired by the humane tradition of the *De Arte bene moriendi* of Erasmus, by Saint François de Sales' doctrine of the 'fine pointe de l'esprit' by which God remains in contact with the soul in spite of all our confusions, and by Fénelon's recommendation of the path of 'pur amour', the willingness to love and serve without hope of reward. Like Erasmus, Bremond accepted the inevitability of fear, but like him too, he seized on the promises of Christ with simple confidence. St. Paul must be our model: 'to depart and be with Christ is better.' By hints and nuances, through his analysis of a strange and sombre literature, Bremond reveals his own attitude to death, so that we find, in reading him, that we both understand the ideas and emotions of the past and recognize their strangeness. By a sad but fitting irony, this master of prose style who had reported to his own generation so many eloquent and pathetic death-bed speeches of an earlier century, lay dying himself for four months without power of speech. 'Il ne pouvait plus parler', said his brother André (another Jesuit), 'mais son geste et son sourire nous donnaient le dernier adieu.'[18]

Bremond insisted on the strict meaning of the title of his book.[19] He was not writing straight history ('l'histoire tout court'), but literary history. Archives, diaries, wills, contracts, records of the foundation of masses he left to others. He had no statistics: he was 'recreating a spiritual atmosphere'. It was not his task to break through from the world of prayer, devotion and theological speculation to evaluate the religious beliefs and allegiances of the majority, or the effect of the propaganda of the élite on the peasants. 'So many men who know Racine by heart have minds that are closed to poetic inspiration'[20]—he was under no illusions about the difficulty of transferring an historical analysis from the books that men read to the motives of their minds.

Reviewing volume IX, Lucien Febvre qualified his admiration by pointing out that the title, 'Christian life under the *ancien régime*' was too wide for

[16] The idea comes from Lalemant, *Testament spirituel* (1666)—make an inventory of beliefs and hopes, keep it up to date, ready for the final confirmation in your last hour.
[17] *Histoire littéraire*, IX (1932), pp. 354–8.
[18] *Henri Bremond et Maurice Blondel: Correspondance*, ed. A. Blanchet (3 vols., 1970–1) III, pp. 462–3.
[19] For this para. see Marc Venard, 'Histoire littéraire et sociologie historique: deux voies pour l'histoire religieuse', *Actes Colloque d'Aix, 1966*, pp. 75–7.
[20] *Hist. littéraire*, IX, p. 379.,

the content. What was missing is evident when we look at the article of Gabriel Le Bras, published the year before, in 1931: 'Statistics and religious history'. It was an exhortation to ecclesiastical historians to use precisely the sources which Bremond ignored. From then onwards the study of religious attitudes was given a statistical basis—how many folk, in what areas and from what social class, made their Easter communion, or sought ordination, entered a monastery, founded masses for their souls, abstained from sexual intercourse in Lent, or gave money to charity?[21] Bremond's literature on the 'art of dying' has now been classified chronologically and geographically (the heyday for original works on death, for example, was in the last quarter of the seventeenth century),[22] and the way has been cleared for a sophisticated study of the affiliations and interlinkages of ideas. Even so, the problem always remains—how to link evidence from conformity, vocation, generosity, spiritual reading or fear, with the motivation of men's actions.

Gabriel Le Bras was adapting, for the ecclesiastical historian, the methods already in use by reforming bishops for evaluating the effectiveness of pastoral work in individual parishes (with the investigations and publications of Canon Boulard, from 1945 onwards,[23] the Church of France was to plan its home missionary strategy on the basis of sociological evidence). It was about 1945 also that a whole new statistical dimension came into the writing of history with the rise of demography as a major scientific discipline. The mathematical study of the patterns of human existence and of the arbitrary workings of death began in the late seventeenth century with the English writers on 'Political Arithmetic', and continued in France in the eighteenth century with government surveys, polemical works on the great population controversy, and in projects for tontines, annuities and other rudimentary forms of insurance. After the publication of pioneering works by Deparcieux (1746), Messance (1760) and 'Moheau' (1778),[24] every educated man knew the expectancy of life at different ages, and the types of terrain, climate, months of the year and occupations that favoured survival. During the nineteenth century, demography established itself as a coherent discipline in

[21] G. Le Bras, 'Statistique et histoire religieuses. Pour un examen détaillé et pour une explication historique de l'état de Catholicisme dans les diverses régions de France', *Revue d'histoire de l'Eglise de France* Oct. 1931, 425–49.
[22] D. Roche, '*La Mémoire de la mort*: recherches sur la place des arts de mourir dans la librairie et la lecture en France au XVIIᵉ et XVIIIᵉ siècles', *Annales* 1976, 76ff; F. Chartier, 'Les Arts de Mourir, 1450–1600', ibid. 55–7; also F. Furet (ed.), *Livre et société dans la France du XVIIIᵉ siècle* (2 vols., 1970).
[23] F. Boulard, *Problèmes missionaires de la France rurale* (2 vols., 1945); *Essor ou déclin du clergé français* (1950); *Premiers itinéraires en sociologie religieuse* (1954).
[24] Deparcieux, *Essai sur les probabilités de la durée de la vie humaine* (1746); Messance, *Recherches sur la population des généralités d'Auvergne, de Lyon, de Rouen ... etc. avec les réflexions sur la valeur de bled tant en France qu'en Angleterre depuis 1674 jusqu'en 1764* (1766); 'Moheau' (prob. the baron de Montyon), *Recherches et considérations sur la population de la France* (1778).

its own right, without, however, making much impact on historical studies.[25] Then, in 1945, the Institut National d'Etudes Démographiques was founded, and in the following year the first number of the review *Population* was published. In the fifties, the methodology of handling parish registers (the 'reconstitution of families' technique) was refined by Louis Henry and Michel Fleury,[26] and in 1958, Gautier and Henry published their famous *La Population de Crulai: paroisse normande*[27], the first of a series of demographical monographs which have given us a new insight into the lives of the mass of the population of France in the eighteenth and nineteenth centuries, and into the workings of death in the process of history.

In the meantime, the idea of taking attitudes to death as a major subject of historical enquiry arose, partly because of the evolution of theories concerning the proper subjects of historical study (and their appropriate methodology) and partly because of the influence of two remarkable books. The first of these volumes was the Dutch historian Huizinga's *The Waning of the Middle Ages,* which was translated into French in 1932.[28] This was a brilliantly evocative picture of the mental and spiritual climate of Western Europe in the fourteenth and fifteenth centuries—portrayed as an age obsessed with transience and mortality. 'No other epoch has laid so much stress . . . on the thought of death.'[29] The mendicant preachers, the crude and vivid woodcuts, the *Ars moriendi* multiplied by the printing presses towards the end of the period, transmitted and intensified the tremors of fear and revulsion; the imagination lingered on the ugliness of old age, the horrors of the entombed and decaying corpse, and the Dance of Death portraying the end of all pleasures and the futility of greatness—a dance which began as a dance of the dead, a sad, reflective warning of our common mortality, but finished dominated by a skeleton that was Death itself personified, grimly presiding over the cavortings of his slaves. Since *The Waning of the Middle Ages* was published, its sombre interpretation of the evidence has come to appear one-sided. Huizinga was a pessimist and an élitist,[30] too prone to infer decadence and decline from artistic and literary evidence, and to ignore the gross vitality of the multitude. On his own showing, the age was also one of highly-strung emotions and thunderous passions, lusting for

[25] Achille Guillard, *Eléments de statistique humaine ou démographie comparée* (1855). (See P. Guillaume and J.-P. Pousson, *Démographie historique* (1970), pp. 23-4).

[26] L. Henry, 'Une richesse démographique en friche: les registres paroissiaux', *Population* 1953 (2), 281-90; M. Fleury and L. Henry, 'Pour connaître la population de la France depuis Louis XIV. Plan de travaux par sondage', *Population* 1958, 663-86.

[27] I. N. E. D. Cahier 33, 1958.

[28] First Dutch version 1919, then an amended version 1924. French translation 1932. Quoted in what follows from the English translation by F. Hopman (Penguin 1955). For a recent commentary on death in this period see S. Lebecq, 'Sur la mort en France et dans les contrées voisines à la fin du Moyen Age', *L'Information historique* 1978, 21-74.

[29] p. 134.

[30] See Pieter Geyl's criticisms in 'Huizinga as Accuser of his Age', cit. G. Steiner in the introd. to Johan Huizinga, *Homo Ludens* (1974).

adventure, revenge and domination, oscillating between asceticism and the frantic search for pleasure, between humility and ostentation, a paradoxical age impregnated with the 'mingled odours of blood and roses'.[31] Philippe Ariès, in his long-ranging comparative studies of attitudes to death, takes the later Middle Ages as a time when men were passionately in love with life and proudly asserting their individuality—and therefore bitterly resenting the grave which brought their strivings to dust; only in this sense were they obsessed with transience and decay. Even so, Huizinga's writing exercised enormous influence in France. Lucien Febvre in 1953 took *The Waning of the Middle Ages* as the best available example of 'how to reconstitute the emotional life of past generations' ('comment reconstituer la vie affective d'autrefois').[32]

The other book, published in 1951, was Edgar Morin's *L'Homme et la mort dans l'histoire*. It is a brilliant essay, argued from Freudian premises as much as from historical evidence; the theme is that the sight of death inspires an affirmation of their own personal individuality in those who witness it, while by contrast, the social group as a whole resorts to rituals and ceremonies which imply the refusal to accept mortality: the collectivity is closing its ranks and insisting that the business of the community must be carried on. Morin's inspiration lies behind the generalizations of so much of the more learned historical writing about death which has followed. But as Lucien Febvre, reviewing in the *Annales*,[33] pointed out, Morin had virtually no serious evidence to draw on once he left the realm of anthropology and the story of primitive peoples. 'Death', said Febvre, 'is now a fashionable subject' ('la mort est à la mode, très à la mode'), but it is sociologists, doctors and psychologists who are monopolizing it; the historians are failing to contribute. A similar complaint had been made in 1931 by Marc Bloch[34] in reviewing Maurice Halbwach's book, *Les Causes du suicide*: the sociologists are handling statistics and posing questions, while the historians, who ought to be devising categories for the analysis of social structure and motivation, are asleep. Febvre was particularly scathing about the failure of the historical establishment to direct research into subjects which will throw light upon our human condition. If a young man proposes to write a thesis on Louis XIV's diplomatic relations with a particular German Elector, he is applauded; he would be laughed at if he wished to offer a comparative study of mourning customs before and after the Reformation.

Marc Bloch and Lucien Febvre were the founders of the brilliant '*Annales* School' of French historians.[35] They stood for a history which utilized the

[31] *The Waning of the Middle Ages*, p. 25.
[32] *Combats pour l'histoire*, pp. 222, 236.
[33] 'La mort dans l'histoire', *Annales* 1952, 223.
[34] 'Les causes du suicide', *Annales d'histoire économique et sociale* 1931, 590–1.
[35] The *Annales d'histoire économique et sociale* 1929–39 became the *Annales d'histoire sociale* 1939–41, then *Mélanges d'histoire sociale* 1942–5, then *Annales Economies— Sociétés—Civilisations* from 1946. On the school see F. Braudel's 'Personal Testimony',

whole range of scientific disciplines which concern man—sociology, demography, economics, psychology, medicine, biology (all relevant, incidentally, to any historical enquiry concerning death). They did not propose to collect curious facts for erudition's sake, but to work from hypotheses and to ask questions of the past which are relevant to the present needs of Humanity.[36] While they would work statistically, their primary interest was the whole man—not a man sliced up into abstract political, economic, social and religious beings plav'.,g a specialized part in separate departments of historical study.[37] V. nat then ought to be the proper theme for research and writing? It is easier to answer this question in the abstract than to constrain the edifying lunacy which seizes the minds of historians when they get loose in the archives. Lucien Febvre's attempt to answer the question was significant. He had graduated himself from local studies to the evaluation of geographical factors in history to psychological investigations of Luther and Rabelais,[38] and he was acutely conscious of the fact that men of past generations lived in their own peculiar moral and intellectual universe. Marriage for love was not a concept understood in the sixteenth century, Rabelais was not a modern freethinker, Lamarck was not a Darwinian before Darwin, the magistrates who burned witches were logical men, not fools. So Febvre proposed to recreate 'la vie affective' of the past, to write 'l'histoire des sentiments'—to recapture the emotions, fears, inspirations, prejudices, affections of vanished generations. 'We have no history of Love' he complained, 'we have no history of Death'—nor of Pity, nor of Cruelty, nor of Joy. He did not ask for such a history to be written covering all ages, a broad sweep handled by a single researcher—he wanted 'a vast collective enquiry into the fundamental sentiments of men and of their modalities'.[39] And he went on to speak of the strange and alien world of the seventeenth-century 'art of dying', as revealed by the abbé Bremond.

Lucien Febvre proposed a professional, collective and cumulative programme of research on (among other human sentiments) attitudes to death. Instead, the subject was annexed by a gifted amateur, who recklessly took the whole sweep of European history for his province. Philippe Ariès' first venture into serious historical writing was his *Histoire des populations françaises et de leurs attitudes devant la vie depuis le XVIIIᵉ siècle* (1948). In his preface he described his method: demography used, not to study contemporary political or economic problems, but to illuminate 'the way men live, the conception they have of themselves . . . their attitude to life'.[40]

Journal of Modern History 44 (1972), pp. 457 ff., and H. Trevor-Roper, in ibid., pp. 468 ff.

[36] 'A nos lecteurs, à nos amis', *Annales* 1946, 2–8; 'Au bout d'un an', ibid. 1947, 1.

[37] M. Bloch, *The Historian's Craft* (E. T. Putnam, 1954), pp. 151–2.

[38] On Febvre generally see Hans-Dieter Mann, *Lucien Febvre: la pensée vivante d'un historien* (Cahiers des Annales, 31).

[39] L. Febvre, *Combats pour l'histoire* (1953), pp. 236–7.

[40] p. 13.

The book was impressionistic and its conclusion—that we have moved from a civilization of instinct towards one of technical manipulation, but have lost our way—was too grandiose for the supporting structure. But twelve years later, with the publication of his *L'Enfant et la vie familiale sous l'ancien régime* (1960), a brilliant pioneering study of the origins of the modern, child-centred nuclear family, Ariès leapt into fame; from henceforward, 'l'histoire des mentalités' was to be a major branch of French historiography. In the meantime, he had been turning to the history of death. In the decade from 1950 to 1960, Ariès tells us,[41] he studied mourning customs in contemporary France, wondering if the sentimental cult of the tomb was an inheritance from distant antiquity. To his surprise, he discovered that it was a creation of the late eighteenth century; before that, the common burial pit with frequent evictions of the bones had been the lot of the majority. He then studied wills and funereal monuments, until a reading of Geoffrey Gorer in 1965[42] made him aware of another, very different modern attitude: the American and N.W. European evasion of the thought of mortality, as if it were an 'obscenity'. Yet by now, the taboo was breaking and the rush by doctors, psychologists, anthropologists and sociologists to publish books on death was under way. With his researches having reached an interesting point of diversification, and with rivals from other disciplines in the field, Ariès decided to leave the 'semi-clandestinity' of his 'solitary adventure' and to join the chorus of the 'thanatologues'. In defiance of the procedures of professional historians, he proceeded to take a full two thousand years as his chronological field, and in diverse evidence unsystematically studied, to seek to define the major epochs of change in 'une sensibilité collective'.

After publishing numerous articles over a period of fifteen years, Philippe Ariès has finally (1977) consolidated and expanded his adventurous essays into a major volume.[43] Before the ordinary processes of research by thesis and monograph has produced much in the way of definitive work on any one century or aspect, he has provided a general picture of the changes in human attitudes to death manifested in all of them. The common-sense view, it might be supposed, would be that the blow by blow establishment of the truth concerning individual details in the various generations of past history, is the necessary prelude to comprehensive generalization. M. Ariès has argued that this is not necessarily so. Without accepting his theories about the rôle of the 'collective unconscious' in history, one can see that the search for the *assumptions* of one century as compared with another, conducted by reference to literary and artistic evidence, might well succeed and, indeed, produce a useful cadre within which the writers of specialist monographs

---

[41] *Essais sur l'histoire de la mort en Occident du moyen âge à nos jours* (1975), pp. 9–12. The 25 pages on 'Les techniques de la mort' in the *Histoire des populations françaises* of 1948 had been chiefly interesting for observations on old age and on medical progress.

[42] G. Gorer, *Death, Grief and Mourning in Contemporary Britain* (1965).

[43] Philippe Ariès, *L'Homme devant la mort* (641 pp., Paris, Editions du Seuil 1977).

would be able to operate. Certainly, he has proved the point in practice. Free from the professional misgivings which so often confine historians to limited periods of time and restricted geographical areas, ignoring their carefully devised boundaries and the clichés of periodization and theme, and refusing to bother about the problem of how many examples are needed to prove a trend or justify a general assertion, and dipping recklessly into the mass of disparate evidence thrown up by liturgies, art and literature, he has glimpsed, vividly, some sharply contrasting patterns of human reactions. And these patterns extend over no less than the past two thousand years of European history. To have sketched, over the whole duration of Christian Europe, the changing attitudes of men to the one certain, inescapable and tragic event which comes equally to us all and makes us all equal when it comes, is an astonishing achievement.

In presenting an account of this panoramic survey, it is probably best to use as little as possible the half-dozen emotive titles which the author has invented to catalogue various reactions towards death. They are too idiosyncratic, and there is a danger that they will be too closely identified with particular epochs of West European history. It is fairer to M. Ariès' methodology to regard them as describing continuing attitudes, sometimes in the forefront of the mind, sometimes in the subconscious. 'La mort apprivoisée', the first attitude chronologically speaking, sums up the model in which the dying man accepts his fate calmly and acts out his death-bed scene with the collectivity supporting him. This is exemplified, not only in the archaic military society of the *Chanson de Roland,* but also in the nineteenth-century peasant communities of Tolstoy: it is the universal, uncensored, natural reaction. This naïve and uncomplicated pattern of conduct gains force from the early Christian concept of death; the faithful accept it as the entry into their long sleep, and they end their lives full of confidence in the final resurrection. From the fifth century onwards, the bodies of the Christian dead were buried in or near to the church buildings. If this was the beginning of fear, it was also the expression of the comforting solidarity of the whole community of believers.

The great change in mental attitude comes in the twelfth century, among the intellectual and spiritual élite. Men begin to realize their individuality, to insist on their personal and lonely destiny. Freedom and independence involve judgement and the possibility of damnation. The tableaux of the Second Coming in stone or fresco, become representations of the Last Judgement; 'Judex' is added to the halo of Christ, and the terrifying assize of Matthew Chapter 25 ousts the Gospel of love. Since the Church has conquered the World—meaning that the World has infiltrated the Church—everyone is nominally Christian, so there must be a Purgatory to take care of the fate of the majority, and masses for the dead so that the living can show their affection and strive to aid them. The whole development is logical, and is presided over by the clergy, who find in it an enhancement of their power, a guarantee of their indispensability. This ecclesiastical take-over is subsequently seen in the elaboration of the system of indulgences, in the evolution of the liturgy to the point where the requiem mass completely overshadows the graveside ceremonies, and in the priest becoming the presiding figure at the death-bed, administering extreme unction and the viaticum. In one sense (though Ariès does not draw out this contrast) the priest is representing the collectivity; in another, he is replacing it—he is the supernatural agent helping the lonely individual. As such, he is forwarding the interest of his caste; we see, says Ariès, 'la colonisation ecclésiastique de la mort'.

From the thirteenth to the fifteenth century, the growing sense of individuality is seen in the addition of biographical details to the epitaph, in the evolution of funereal sculpture towards realistic portraiture, and in the arrival of the praying figure on the tomb instead of the recumbent one. In rituals and prayers, in stone and brass, the relatives and friends of the dead man are affirming his individuality and, looking ahead to their own inevitable end, affirming their own. The obsession of the later Middle Ages with the macabre, with worms, corruption and the half-decayed corpse, Ariès interprets, not as the decadent or haunted revulsion of an age worn out with plague and rapine, but as the fierce resentful expression of a frantic lust for life, an angry repudiation of the crude natural processes which bring us to a repulsive end.

The next development is complex. By the seventeenth century, the epitaph has become, not only a biographical document, but a monument to family piety. For the few, the claim to be remembered may be derived from their saintliness or heroism; for the many, it is based on family sentiment—'Son père a fait poser ce marbre'. The affirmation of individuality now goes forward within the tightening bonds of the small nuclear family, which takes over the role of mourning from the collectivity, and mourns with introverted intensity. Beginning with the Christian élite in search of the virtue of humility, and spreading to the intellectual and social élite for reasons of decorum, the eighteenth century sees the acceptance of the ideal of the simplified funeral ceremony (this is true only of the *ideal*; baroque funeral splendours were probably more common than ever, because more people could afford them). The old custom of prescribing the details of funeral ceremonies in the last will and testament declines, a fact which Ariès ascribes to the intensification of family affections, which inclined testators to leave these matters of posthumous pomp or, even, of prayers, to the generosity of their heirs and executors. Hygienic reformers force the removal of cemeteries outside city boundaries just at the time when family affection begins to insist on the visit to the tomb as a necessary gesture of solemn remembrance. And so to the nineteenth-century cult of death, which Ariès describes in two of his arcane phrases: 'La mort de toi' and 'Le temps des belles morts'. Romanticism makes the death-bed a scene of haunting beauty, the tomb becomes a last resting place to be revered in perpetuity, and visits to the cemetery are of the essence of family piety.

But as medical science develops, men become less accustomed to the sight of death. The population explosion and the Industrial Revolution (one assumes that these must be the explanations) break the old cadres within which the collectivity gave psychological support to mourners. By the twentieth century,[44] the small nuclear family faces the death of one of its members as an unexpected tragedy, a paralysing disaster, more intensely felt because, outside the home circle, it is unnoticed, in a vast technological complex in which no one is indispensable. Whether unfamiliarity breeds unwillingness to face reality, or whether grief so introverted is unbearable (the author does not ask these questions), in the urbanized, industrialized society of the twentieth century there comes an entirely new way of dying, 'la mort inversée'. The end comes privately, in a hospital, under the supervision of professionals: no warning that death is near, no goodbyes. The funeral is a reticent affair—young children are not taken to it. There is, however, a North-American variant: the death-bed remains under the control of the hospital machine, but 'le vieux courant romantique', the spirit of 'la mort de toi' takes over the mourning observances, with embalming, the 'casket', the 'funeral parlour', 'grief therapy', the green lawns of the 'garden of remembrance' and all the mellow glow of nostalgic pseudo-happiness that 'morticians' can devise. We may infer what M. Ariès wishes us to do about all this. We should try to get back to the naturalness of 'la mort apprivoisée', so that we can face death in the spirit of Charlemagne's paladins or Russian peasants. Once again the collectivity should support the mourners of the small nuclear family. The dying and their relatives should be told that the end is near, so that all can play their parts in the last scene of a lifetime. We should get out of the grip of medical technology and stop organizing people for their own good. Père Dainville, the Jesuit historian, complained in an intensive care unit, 'on me frustre de ma mort', 'I am being deprived of my death'; we should remedy that complaint. To life, liberty and the pursuit of happiness, Ariès would add a further right of man, the right to die. Here, I confess to being out of sympathy with him and the enlightened medical and sociological experts he is quoting. I would wish to depart as painlessly as possible, and with a minimum of fuss. Dying is a grim business and significant,[45] but for those who believe in the Christian God it is a landmark

---

[44] Interesting comments on our own day by L. V. Thomas in *La Mort aujourd'hui* (Centre Universitaire de recherche sociologique d'Amiens, 7, 1977), ed. L. V. Thomas and Trink van Thao.

[45] There is a debate among theologians. Does the spirit take wings as the body declines? Is death the great opportunity for the believer to make his self offering to God? Are we to think of total annihilation—a powerful reminder that we have no hope save in the risen Christ? Should we even speak of 'the darkness of death', unrelieved and opaque? (These ideas, successively in R. Troisfontaines, *I Do Not Die* (1963), Ladislas Boros, S.J., *The Mystery of Death* (1965), Rahner, *On the Theology of Death* (1965), are discussed by B. J.

on the journey, something to keep your eye on for directional purposes, but becoming less important as it draws nearer and the mind moves towards further horizons.

This summary makes M. Ariès' argument appear clearer than it is, while failing to do justice to the complexity of his erudition and the force of his originality. His book is packed with digressions, picturesque fragments of information and flashes of insight. There are striking excurses on the tombs of the kings of Spain in the Escorial and on the humble cemetery of Marville (department of the Meuse), on the 'heraldry of death' as a prelude to the eighteenth-century cult of melancholy, and on the Victoria and Albert Museum's collection of funeral jewellery, on the Bronte family and their writings and *La Sorcière* of Michelet. Two such digressions, interesting in inverse proportion to their relevance to the main argument, are the reflections on the advent of the artistic concept of 'still life' from the fourteenth century onwards, and the alliance of Eros and Thanatos in the writings of the marquis de Sade whom—alas!—in the modern fashion, Ariès takes seriously.

Criticism of such a pioneering, impressionistic survey should be limited to broad issues. Ariès is clearly right to emphasize the significance of the rise of the self-conscious individual with his passion for living; without appearing to have studied the medievalists who insist on the importance of the twelfth century in this respect, he has unerringly chosen the decisive date. And having already written a masterly book on family relationships, what he says about the impact of family affections can be confidently accepted. Three recent writers on aspects of the mortuary theme in history agree, but they also suggest additional possibilities of explanation. Dr. Stannard[46] would wish to turn to the structure and ethos of society. In his attempt to account for the change in seventeenth-century New England from austere mourning to diversified ritual, he resorts to the formula of V. Gordon Childe: as societies become culturally and materially more stable, their funeral customs become less elaborate and, conversely, as they lose stability, elaboration comes again. The Puritans, seeing their ideals eclipsed by commercialism and indifference, and thinking God's treaty with them was coming to an end, attempted to compensate for their 'tribal vulnerability' by ceremonies. In fairness to Dr. Stannard, one hastens to add that this far from convincing explanation is an uneasy flourish added to a powerful and moving study of New England Puritanism. God's predestination is unfathomable, extending to 'some who never sought Him'. 'Will my Saviour accept me?' There is no certain answer. Death is the time of maximum temptation. 'Every frog will be croaking towards the evening', says the author of *The Sting of Death* (1680), 'every puddle will send up a stinking vapour ... all the several

Collopy, S. J., in 'Theology and the Darkness of Death', *Theological Studies* 39 (1), March 1978, 22–54).

[46] David E. Stannard, *The Puritan Way of Death: a Study in Religion, Culture and Social Change* (Oxford Univ. Press, New York, 1977).

shallows . . . will concert to compleat the misery of the poor sinner'. Children must be reminded of Death and Hell: 'Tis not likely that you will all live to grow up'.

> 'Xerxes the great did die,
> So must you and I'

Yet, these stern believers loved their children desperately, accepted personal responsibility for the fate of these 'innocent vipers', and hoped that, at the very worst 'the easiest room' in Hell would be given to them. And, maybe, there could be 'indicators' of salvation; perhaps even (how they tortured themselves!), the surest sign was to be unsure. In the eighteenth century this sombre attitude to death changed rapidly to something very near to nine-teenth-century Romanticism—to die in rapture and confidence, to thank God for taking away one's children to a better world, to talk of reunion beyond the grave. 'Self indulgence' and 'sentimentality', Stannard calls it, and so it is, but here is an example of the rediscovery of the God of love without benefit of Rousseau's glowing Deism or Voltaire's ironies about eternal punishment. Perhaps both Ariès and Stannard have neglected the possibility of an internal evolution of theological ideas under no other pressures than intellectual reflection inspired by a continuing spiritual quest.

As Pierre Chaunu's *La Mort à Paris*[47] has at its basis a massive collection of statistics, he naturally wishes to see Ariès pay more attention to the works of demographers. In the seventeenth century the death rate was something like 35 per thousand, thrice the 'weight' which we bear, and life was precarious (when plague struck, the 'panic threshold' was 50–60 deaths per thousand). In the eighteenth century, however, men lived longer, and they knew it. Hence, the seventeenth century was the age of the art of dying, while the Enlightenment was to be preoccupied with the art of living. I am not sure that correlations can be so straightforward as this: where death is concerned we can neither assume that frequency brings fear nor that familiarity breeds contempt. Even so, one notices how, under the old demography, loneliness was the accepted lot of old age, how remarriage after the death of a partner came swiftly, especially for men, and how affection for small children was held in check until they had reached the age when there was a reasonable chance of survival.

As against Chaunu's demography and Stannard's social change, Michel Vovelle complains that Ariès rejects the intellectual side of history, failing to recognize the 'diffusion des idées forces'.[48] That this reproach comes from an historian of left-wing political inclinations to one who is known to be on the far right is no surprise in the French context, where the history of ideas is being approached by sociological and quantitative methods. Ariès notes how the Roman *Rituel* of 1614 has none of the paschal joy which Chrysostom described as the dominant note of early Christian burial rites (a recent essay

[47] Pierre Chaunu, *La Mort à Paris: 16e, 17e, 18e siècles* (Paris, Librairie Arthème Fayard, 1978).

by Geoffrey Rowell[49] describes this evolution towards gloom, the work of monastic liturgiologists who made the funeral into a meditation upon death for the edification of the survivors, and how the Roman Church and some branches of the Anglican have, in our own century, recaptured the note of paschal triumph). But Vovelle, looking at seventeenth-century Catholicism, sees there more than an inheritance of penitential apprehension, but a deliberate propaganda exercise, the post-Tridentine reform movement seizing on the most emotive available issue and inventing 'the pedagogy of death'. (This corresponds to Chaunu's category of 'la mort baroque . . . une mort prédicateur'). The theme of the eighteenth century, says Vovelle, is the Enlightenment's attack on the Church at this bastion of its propaganda, overthrowing eternal punishment by logical arguments. Then, at the end of the century, the rise of neo-classical reverie and Romantic *sensibilité* began to create the new lay cult of death, a substitute religion of Nature and family affection to console us in the face of our tragic destiny. Both Vovelle and Ariès have concentrated too exclusively on Catholicism. If we turn to the Protestant reformation, we find Luther and Calvin insisting that death has been vanquished. Though there is no logical necessity for believers in Predestination to have a doctrine of assurance, there are wonderful passages of trust and confidence in some of the French Calvinist writers of the seventeenth century: Christ is our eternal friend and it is the law of friendship that friends support one another; Death is God's messenger, and if we force open the fingers of his iron hand we find there the divine message of love.[50] The Anglican liturgy, even after the changes towards severity in 1552, retained the note of confidence. Death, Jeremy Taylor was to say, 'is so harmless a thing, that no good man was ever thought the more miserable for dying, but much the happier'. The radiant death of Rousseau's Julie,[51] the great eighteenth-century manifesto against the contemporary orthodox way of dying, is a Protestant phenomenon as well as an invention of Deism and the Enlightenment.

These disagreements—even the very clear one between Ariès and Vovelle—arise from differences of emphasis, and will be long debated, probably inconclusively. There are subtle connections between changes in social structure, the movement of ideas, demographic pressures, the psychological development of the human personality and the evolution of the family; each of these subjects of historical enquiry leads eventually into the others, and each has special advantages as a starting point, depending on the particular period of the past which is being investigated.

[48] M. Vovelle, 'Les attitudes devant la mort, problèmes de méthode', *Annales* 1976, 127.
[49] G. Rowell, *The Liturgy of Christian Burial* (Alcuin Club, 1977).
[50] Ch. Drelincourt, *Les Consolations de l'âme fidèle contre les frayeurs de la mort* (2 vols., 1760, Berlin), II, p. 6; Pierre du Moulin, *Traité de la paix de l'âme* (1695, The Hague), p. 42.
[51] J.-J. Rousseau, *La Nouvelle Héloïse, Oeuvres* (Pléiade) II, p. 718 ff.

Though Ariès had been a pioneer in the use of demography, the thrust of his work remains impressionistic. In this respect he stands apart from the methodology of contemporary French history writing (more especially from that of the *Annales* school), which demands solid statistics as the starting point of every essay on the 'histoire des mentalités'. Though there have been remarkable demographical studies of the medieval and early modern period (chiefly concerned with the effect of famine and plague and the extinction of families),[52] it is only in the later seventeenth and in the eighteenth centuries that the sources—more especially the parish registers—become complete enough to provide comprehensive evidence about human living and dying.[53] Since Pierre Goubert's *Beauvais et le Beauvaisis de 1600 à 1730* in 1960, some of the most distinguished historical writing in France has been devoted to major theses dealing with a province or other coherent area over a century or so in the modern period, prefaced by exhaustive demographical and economic chapters. In 1971, François Lebrun produced a brilliant variant: a study of the operations of death over the seventeenth and eighteenth centuries in the province of Anjou.[54] The author began with the intention of investigating the assumption—so often made—that the death rate was falling through the eighteenth century. It was not so in Anjou. The years from 1750 to 1765–70 were years of hope, but from 1770–90 was a grim period marked by particularly heavy mortality among babies and children. Against the background of a macabre fresco of plague, war, famine and rampant disease, Lebrun portrays the zealous but humanly speaking not very effective activities of administrators, churchmen and medical practitioners, and the superstitions, hopes, fears and ceremonies which the shadow of mortality engendered. Yet perhaps, the growing effectiveness of social organization was beginning to count for something; the great conjoined crises of famine and epidemic never reached the peaks of devastation of earlier centuries. In that sense, it was possible to catch a glimpse of a hope of a demographic 'take off'. Lebrun's is a masterly thesis, full of vivid detail about all classes of society, though since Anjou, with its stagnant population, remained under the curse of the old demography, there is no scope here to illustrate Chaunu's thesis of an increased expectation of life leading to a concentration on the art of living.

Last wills and testaments, like parish registers, first become a coherent source of statistical information in the eighteenth century (at the beginning

---

[52] Arlette Higounet-Nadel, *Périgueux aux XIVe et XVe siècles: étude de démographie historique* (1978), espec. pp. 297, 339, 341–411; also, *Les Comptes de la taille et les sources de l'histoire démographique de Périgueux au XIVe siècle* (1963), pp. 65–6. For the early modern period, E. Baratier, *La Démographie provençale du XVe au XVIe siècles* (1961).

[53] René Le Mée, *Les Sources de la démographie historique française dans les archives publiques (XVIIe–XVIIIe siècles)* (1967), p. xii; B. Gille, *Les Sources statistiques de l'histoire de France: des enquêtes du XVIIIe siècle à 1870* (1964).

[54] F. Lebrun, *Les hommes et la mort en Anjou au 17e et 18e siècles: essai de démographie et de psychologie historiques* (1971).

The Charrett Drawne by 4 Horses uppo[n] y[e] Charrett stood the Coffin Covered w[i]th purple velvet, & uppo that the representation, The Canopy borne by 6 knights

Gentlemen pensioners.   Gentlemen pensioners.

III.1 ABOVE Hearse and funeral effigy of Elizabeth I. On the chariot or hearse rests the coffin covered with purple velvet and upon that the lifelike effigy of the Queen. The canopy is borne by six knights. Engraving from *Vetusta Monumenta*.

III.2 RIGHT The mausoleum built in Westminster Abbey for the funeral of James I in 1625. Within the mausoleum rests the lifelike effigy of the King. This was the last time the effigy was actually used as part of the funeral ceremony for a British sovereign. Engraving by J. Nutting from F. Sandford, *A Genealogical History of the Kings and Queens of England . . .*, London, 1707.

The MAUSOLEUM in the Abbey Church of S[t] Peter in Westminster at the Funeral Obsequies of JAMES the First King of Great Britain &c.

The MAUSOLEUM *Erected in the Abbey Church of S.t Peter in Westminster, at the* Funeral Obsequies *of* QUEEN MARY II. March *the* 5.th 169⁴⁄₅

III.3 **LEFT** The mausoleum designed by Sir Christopher Wren for Westminster Abbey for the funeral of Queen Mary in 1695. Engraving by J. Sturt from F. Stanford, *A Genealogical History of the Kings and Queens of England . . .*, London, 1707.

III.4 **BELOW** The lying-in-state of George IV at Windsor in 1830. Lithograph by Henry Perry, 1830. *(Public Record Office, London)*

VI.1 Monument to Maurice, Comte de Saxe, by Jean-Baptiste Pigalle, 1752/3–1776, in the Church of Saint Thomas, Strasbourg. *(Caisse Nationale des Monuments Historiques, Paris)*

ERECTED AT THE PUBLIC EXPENSE
TO THE MEMORY OF
VICE-ADMIRAL HORATIO, VISCOUNT NELSON, K.B.
TO RECORD HIS SPLENDID AND UNPARALLELED ACHIEVEMENTS,
DURING A LIFE SPENT IN THE SERVICE OF HIS COUNTRY
AND TERMINATED IN THE MOMENT OF VICTORY BY A GLORIOUS DEATH,
IN THE MEMORABLE ACTION OFF CAPE TRAFALGAR ON THE XXI OF OCTOBER MDCCCV.
LORD NELSON WAS BORN ON THE XXIX OF SEPTEMBER MDCCLVIII.
THE BATTLE OF THE NILE WAS FOUGHT ON THE I OF AUGUST MDCCXCVIII.
THE BATTLE OF COPENHAGEN ON THE II OF APRIL MDCCCI.

VI.2 ABOVE Monument to Vice-Admiral Horatio, Viscount Nelson, by John Flaxman, 1807–18, in St. Paul's Cathedral, London. *(Paul Mellon Centre for Studies in British Art, London)*

VI.3 RIGHT Monument to Pope Alessandro VII, by Gianlorenzo Bernini in St. Peter's, Rome. *(Alinari, Florence)*

SACRED TO THE MEMORY OF HARRIET SUSAN, VISCOUNTESS FITZHARRIS,
DAUGHTER OF FRANCIS BATEMAN DASHWOOD ESQ: OF WELL VALE, IN THE COUNTY OF LINCOLN,
AND WIFE OF JAMES EDWARD VISCOUNT FITZHARRIS, OF HERON COURT IN THIS PARISH,
WHERE SHE DEPARTED THIS LIFE ON MONDAY NIGHT SEPTEMBER THE 1, 1815,
IN THE 32th YEAR OF HER AGE.

FLAXMAN,
R.A.
SCULPTOR:

GIFTED BY NATURE WITH UNCOMMON BEAUTY OF PERSON AND COUNTENANCE,
POSSESSING MANNERS EQUALLY DIGNIFIED AND ENGAGING,
SHE NEVER ALLOWED HERSELF TO BE INFLUENCED BY THE FLATTERIES AND ALLUREMENTS
OF THE WORLD, BUT ENJOYED WITH RATIONAL CHEERFULNESS THOSE HOURS WHICH SHE
COULD SPARE FROM THE PERFORMANCE OF HER DOMESTIC DUTIES.
THE CARE AND EDUCATION OF HER CHILDREN WERE HER DARLING OBJECTS,
ON THEM SHE EQUALLY BESTOWED THE VIGILANT FONDNESS OF A MOTHER, AND THE
SUCCESSFUL EFFORTS OF A WELL CULTIVATED MIND.
WHILE ALL WHO SHARED HER LOVE AND ...... CULTIVATED MIND,
RELATIONS OF ......

JAMES HOWARD HARRIS, BORN MAR...
EDWARD ALFRED JOHN, BORN MAY...
CHARLES AMYAND, BORN AUGUST...

OF THESE BOYS, THE ELDEST, JAM...
EARL OF MALMESBURY, AND IN ...
... OF STATE FOR FORE...

VI.5 ABOVE Monument to Lieutenant-General Sir John Moore, by John Bacon junior, 1810–15, in St Paul's Cathedral, London.
(Warburg Institute, University of London)

VI.4 LEFT Monument to Harriet Susan, Viscountess Fitzharris, by John Flaxman, 1816–17, in Christchurch Priory, Hampshire.
(National Monuments Record, London)

VI.7 and 8 ABOVE Monument to Louis de France, Dauphin, and Marie-Josephe, Dauphine, by Guillaume II Coustou, 1766–77, in the Cathedral, Sens.
The view on the left shows 'Conjugal Love and Time'; the view on the right 'Religion and Immortality'.
(Studio Allix, Sens)

VI.6 LEFT Monument to Vittorio Alfieri, by Antonio Canova, 1806–10, in the Church of Santa Croce, Florence.
(Alinari, Florence)

VI.9 ABOVE Monument to Mrs. Margaret Petrie, by Thomas Banks, 1795, in the Church of St. Mary, Lewisham, Kent.
(National Monuments Record, London)

VI.10 BELOW Antique Roman sarcophagus panel. Engraving from Pietro Santi Bartoli, *Admiranda Romanorum Antiquitatum*, 1693.
(David Irwin)

FOR THINE IS THE KINGDOM

SACRED
TO THE MEMORY OF
FRANCES. AGED 6 YEARS,
AND CHARLES D'OYLY. AGED 5 MONTHS.

VI.11 ABOVE Monument to the Baring Family, by John Flaxman, 1806–*c*. 1810, in the Church of St. Mary, Micheldever, Hampshire. Detail showing the left panel: 'For Thine is the Kingdom'.
(David Irwin)

VI.12 BELOW Monument to Andrea Vaccà Berlinghieri, by Bertel Thorvaldsen, 1828–29, in the Church of Camposanto, Pisa.
(Alinari, Florence)

TANQUAM . CÆLO
HOMINUM . BONO
DEMISSUM
TE . UNIVERSI
SUNT . REVERITI.

LUCTUS ▲ PUBLIC
OBIISTI
DE . TE
NULLAS UNQUA
SITRET . PONTRI

A . Ρ . Ω
ANDREÆ . VACCÀ . BERLINGHIERIO . NOB . PISANO
EQUITI . ORD . S . IOSEPHI
DOCTORI . CHIRURGIÆ . IN . PATRIO . ATHENEO
QUI . SUMMA . ARTIS . PERITIA . ET . MANUS . STRENUITATE . PROFUIT . MULTIS
IISDEMQUE . LAUDIBUS . ET . IN . ENTIS . ET . SCRIPTIS . EDITIS
ADMIRABILIS . FUIT . OMNIBUS
DECESS . VIII . ID . SEPTEMBR . AN . M . DCCC . XXVI . AET . S . LIV . M . VII . D . III
AMICI . UTRO . OPTIMO . ET . EXIMIÆ . BENIGNITATIS . AERE . PROPR . ET . COLLATICIO
PON . CUR

Within the monument, inscribed on the column:

IOH · VOLPATO
ANT · CANOVA
QVO · SIBI · AGENTI · ANN · XXV
CLEMENTIS · XIV · P · M

AMICO · OPTIMO · MNEMOSINON
DE · ARTE · SVA · POS

ANNO · DOMINI · MDCCCVII

VI.13 Monument to Giovanni Volpato, by Antonio Canova, 1804–7, in the Church of Santi Apostoli, Rome.
(Alinari, Florence)

of the sixteenth century 5 per cent of Parisians made a will; at the beginning of the eighteeenth, 18 per cent). By subjecting them to detailed classification, Michel Vovelle has developed the statistical study of religious conformity, which Gabriel Le Bras had advocated, to a unique degree of sophistication. He had earlier analysed the 'de-christianization' movement in the S.E. of France during the French Revolution, using principally the evidence concerning priests who had surrendered their vocation.[55] He then asked whether 'de-christianization' (or 'laicization' or some other term, for there is a controversy here)[56] had already begun, in a less brutal form, before 1789? In a conformist society in which the Church was rich and respected, the figures for Easter communions, ordinations and so on would be weighted by inertia and social convention; Vovelle found that there were more dramatic statistical variations in the study of wills on a large scale.[57] Did the testator use a pious preamble, and if so, what invocations—to God, to the merits of Christ, to Our Lady or particular saints or angels—did he make? How many masses did he commission for his soul, and which religious institutions were given the intercessory tasks? How much was given to the poor, and through what channels? Was there a specification of ceremonies and candles, or was a complete simplicity prescribed? Was there a request to be buried in a particular place—inside a church, near to an altar, in a family tomb? What was the attitude to families and relatives? The answers to these questions had to be sieved through various grilles of enquiry: the sex, the social class, fortune and literacy of the testators provided classifications; so too did geographical areas—city, small town or village (with varying provision of religious establishments in parish or monastery) whether the predominant spirituality was Catholic, Jansenist or Protestant, which diocese was it, and how fervent were its bishops and clergy? There were some clear findings. For example, at the beginning of the century 90 per cent of the wills used the rich baroque terminology, by 1789, 66 per cent used a simple invocation to God and 22 per cent contained no religion at all. The collapse was complete in Marseille, but there was hardly any change in Nice. The number of masses rose to about the year 1750 then fell—in Marseille another collapse of the graph, but in Senez, an actual increase because Jansenism was rooted out in the diocese in the course of the century. Yet these, and many other findings, are ambiguous in their interpretation. Was it a decline

---

[55] Early findings published in *Prêtres abdicataires et déchristianisation en Provence sous la Révolution française,* Actes du Congrès des Sociétés savantes de Lyon, 1964 (1965); full-scale treatment in *Religion et Révolution: la déchristianisation de l'an II* (1976).

[56] See Vovelle's discussion in his introduction, also R. Rémond, 'The Problem of Dechristianisation: the present position and some recent French Studies', *Concilium* VII (1), 1965, 77. For the whole question of methodology see Vovelle's 'Etude quantitative de la déchristianisation au 18e siècle', *Dix-huitième Siècle,* 1973, 170 ff. His own study of the evidence from iconography is found in 'La mort et l'au delà en Provence d'après les autels des âmes du Purgatoire', *Cahiers des Annales* 29 (1970).

[57] *Piété baroque et déchristianisation en Provence au XVIIIe siècle: les attitudes devant la mort d'après les clauses des testaments* (Paris, Plon, 1973).

in Christian sentiment or a refinement of piety (or the influence of Prot-
estantism and Jansenism) that reduced the number of masses, abandoned
complex pious phraseology, turned away from baroque display at funerals
and burials in churches? M. Vovelle faces all the difficulties and complexities
and leaves us to make up our minds, though his own view is that there is
such a strong convergence of evidence that we can infer 'a major mutation
of collective feeling', evidence of a creeping 'de-christianization' working in
society for two generations before the spectacular attacks on religion during
the Terror.

Vovelle's book, a remarkable break-through to a new method of handling
old evidence, has provided a model technique which Pierre Chaunu (with
the aid of the theses of more than fifty research students) has applied to
8,000 of the wills of Paris between 1550 and 1800.[58] In Paris, the erosion
of the rich old religious formulae in wills was more rapid, even, than in
Marseille, which in turn was far ahead of the rest of Provence. And in the
capital, a refinement within the trend can be detected, since the appeal to
the merits of Christ, which had come in powerfully at the end of the sixteenth
century, began to go out in the eighteenth, and the appelation 'the Son of
God' became rare. Pressure by churchmen ensured that fewer people
neglected the business of making a will until their last illness came upon
them (28 per cent of the wills of the sixteenth century were made by healthy
folk, but the figure had risen to 42 per cent in the second half of the
eighteenth century). On the other hand, requests for funeral display or for
a specific place of burial decline rapidly after 1740; so too does the demand
for masses, though there were more masses for the dead between 1700 and
1750 than ever before, because the lower average number specified was
counterbalanced by the larger number of people asking for them. These
findings are paralleled by statistical evaluations of the production of books
on preparation for dying, and of engravings of death-bed scenes, and by the
findings of demographers—we see the slowing down of the Parisian death
rate after 1743 and the loneliness of the inhabitants (20 to 30 per cent of the
dying had no relatives, and there are large numbers of widows and unmarried
girls). One could go on for long cataloguing the information which Chaunu's
vast enquiry has furnished. It is an odd, unusual volume from the pen of an
amazingly prolific historian, who averages more than a book a year on
subjects ranging from theology to currents of maritime trade. The first
hundred pages are a sweeping account of attitudes to death in recorded
history; the ensuing 400 pages are the statistical tabulation of the wills of
two and a half centuries. What is remarkable here is Chaunu's skill at
detecting the manifold possibilities of interpretation which lie behind the
evidence. Whether the issue is 'de-christianization' or anything else it is clear
that statistics, even if they cannot lie, can always be ambiguous.

[58] Chaunu, op. cit.

Chaunu's book has 'Death' on its title page, and what could be more concerned with dying than a series of last wills and testaments? Yet most of what he says is about life, which is as it should be for, no doubt, we study attitudes to death to support ourselves—or maybe merely to distract ourselves—as we get on with the business of living. Similarly, Jacqueline Thibaut-Payen's *Les Morts, l'Eglise et l'Etat*,[59] a study of burial arrangements in France in the seventeenth and eighteenth centuries, is essentially a collection of essays on legal and administrative history, an account of the jurisprudence and executive interventions of the Parlement of Paris. We learn of burial litigation setting families against their local clergy, parish against parish, parish priests against monasteries; of the refusal of sepulchre to Jansenists, suicides, stage players and unbelievers; of the sad and stealthy arrangements to which Jews and Protestants had to resort; and above all, of the dismay and thrifty recalcitrance of the parishes when the Royal Edict of 1776 ordered the removal of the cemeteries away from habitations. The *procureur général* of the Parlement, Joly de Fleury, is seen to be astonishingly active in interpreting and enforcing the royal legislation: it is a pity that there is no index to facilitate our study of the full range of his interventions.

The vast archive of the Joly de Fleury family has provided Mme Thibaut-Payen with curious anecdotes—a bonus that frequently comes the way of researchers who brave the aridities of legal documentation. But one might be forgiven for overlooking the possibility that the picturesque side of history would be well represented in Box D 4 U1 7 of the Archives de la Seine, a collection of *procès-verbaux* concerning corpses fished out of the river, or picked up in the streets or on the quayside in the *quartier* of Paris around the old Châtelet, between October 1795 and mid-September 1801. Fortunately, it was Richard Cobb who found it.[60] The dead (404 of them) were poor, for richer folk were quickly recognized and taken away to be buried at the expense of their families. The *juge de paix* and his two assistants entered up every detail of clothing and possessions; witnesses came forward to identify the bodies, reminiscing about games of cards or dominoes in *cafés* and visits to the bakers; old women testified to what they had noticed from their chairs in the street, and urchins, vastly mobile, what they had seen in their wanderings (there is a typical speculation by Professor Cobb about how a height of four feet might be a better observation platform than the five foot six inches of the average male pedestrian). Though the author is the scourge of statistical historians, he shows he can play the game with the best of them, witness his chapter on the 274 suicides. Two-thirds of them were unmarried or had lost their partner; only one-third had been born in Paris or nearby; men tended to kill themselves on Mondays or Fridays, women on Saturdays or Wednesdays; no less than 249 had drowned them-

---

[59] Jacqueline Thibaut-Payen, *Les Morts, l'Eglise et l'Etat dans le ressort du parlement de Paris au XVIIe et XVIIIe siècles* (Paris, Editions Fernand Lanore, 1977).
[60] R. Cobb, *Death in Paris, 1795–1801* (Oxford Univ. Press, 1978).

selves, and of these three-quarters lived within a few minutes of the river—it was only in spring or summer that they threw themselves in, and generally between 9 a.m. and noon; there were no prostitutes or domestic servants among the women, and women never shot themselves. There is analysis of this kind throughout the book, but it is not obtrusive; it is tucked away in the dramatic convolutions of the sweeping baroque narrative that carries us through streets and alleyways, lodging houses, tenements and work-shops—through the real life of Paris flowing darkly under the surface foam of political *coups*, revolutionary committees and orations, fanfares for victories and the roll of drums for executions. The clothing of the world of this poor majority came down to it at second hand: from the family wardrobe in the provinces; from the cast-offs of the rich—those bottle-green *redingotes* worse for wear, canary waistcoats and check handkerchiefs; by desertion and theft from the armies on the frontier—jackets with braid shoulder straps or golden frogging, or the blue tunics with high red necks of the old National Guard. 'It was probably one of the few advantages of war and conquest to have redounded to the male population as a whole'. No one wore a cockade. These political and patriotic emblems were for the middle class demagogues; 'The motley armies of the dead are not those of the [Republic] one and indivisible.' The masterly evocation of this down-at-heel and colourful world of marginal survival by the use of discoveries in the archives, the exercise of a sympathetic imagination and the march of a brilliant and reckless prose style will strike a familiar chord with the readers of Richard Cobb's earlier volumes in English. Hardened professionals will note, however, that without insistence and in throw-away observations, the author is compelling a re-assessment of some established generalizations. The supposed 'uprootedness' of the isolated individuals who had poured into the capital from the provinces fades before the deftly sketched evocations of the ties of sociability and neighbourhood among the poor, and the 'anarchic' Paris of the Directory is seen to have had few murders, and these very obvious and explicable ones. And once again, we see how little ordinary people cared about the glories of the Revolution and the exhortations of those who found in it a fulfilment of their ideals and an enhancement of their careers.

With Robert Favre's thesis[61] we move to a consideration of attitudes to death among the intelligent and literate minority. It could be that Favre embarked on the mortuary quest almost as early as Philippe Ariès, for his study of death in the literature and thought of eighteenth-century France must have been many years in preparation. It is a massive thesis like two other major studies in the history of ideas in the same century, Robert Mauzi's on the idea of 'Bonheur' (1960) and Jean Ehrard's on the concept

---

[61] R. Favre, *La Mort dans la littérature et la pensée françaises au siècle des lumières* (Lyon, Presses Universitaires de Lyon, 1978). The original, fuller version of the thesis was published in 1978 in two vols., by the Ateliers reprographiques de l'Université de Lille, under the title of *La Mort dans la pensée et la littérature françaises au 18e siècle*.

of 'Nature' (1963). All three are based on a virtually exhaustive reading of everything in the French eighteenth century which has pretensions to constitute literature or serious argument, and are informed by subtlety of thought and lucidity of style. Favre's thesis in particular is fascinating reading, though it is in the detail of illustration and critical comment rather than in generalization that its chief attraction lies. One of its major themes concerns the Catholic Church's way of dying—the shadow of judgement, the severe discipline of preparation, the clergy presiding over the death-bed—and the attempts of *philosophes* and deists to find an alternative. Eternal punishment is unethical, the virtuous pagans cannot be damned; death is 'natural' and fear is unworthy; a good man can find consolation in the thought that he will be remembered by posterity. Yet the question remained—is there a life after death? Another major theme is the population controversy, bound up with the arguments about celibacy, duelling, war and the evils of large cities, and with the debates concerning public hygiene and the attempts to make medicine into a science. Many a by-way of eighteenth-century controversy is explored—the transmigration of souls, the possibility of indefinite progress, scientific models for the way the world will end, the short-lived scare over the Lisbon earthquake and the long-continuing unease about being buried alive, the motivation of suicides, deaths from a broken heart, the advisability of inoculation for smallpox. There is one clear contribution to the broad pattern-weaving of Ariès. Favre ascribes to eighteenth-century France, and more particularly to its sentimental novelists, the invention of a new way of dying—death, not as a public event with the whole community involved, not as a religious event with all the faithful sharing in its hopes and fears, but 'la mort bourgeoise, individuelle et familiale'. (For my part, I would ascribe the phenomenon to the strengthening of the ties of affection between husband and wife, parents and children, which took place in certain favoured middling groups in society, and I have argued that the historian need not try too hard to explain this affection—it was there all the time, only awaiting the improvement of economic and social conditions to break through and manifest itself, redoubling its intensity by the very process of self-expression).[62]

Brooding over the scores of tragedies recorded in Favre's pages, one begins to feel unease about the conviction that the historian can catalogue and periodize changing human attitudes to death. Voltaire afraid but preaching a doctrine of work and mutual consolation (and, in my view, courageously stage-managing his end); Chamfort's agnosticism overthrown by the death of his mistress; Louis XV's notorious callousness broken as he stood on the freezing balcony while Mme de Pompadour's coffin left Versailles; Piron's verses of comic nonchalance; the pious Mme de Custine in her last hours,

---

[62] 'Living and Loving: Changing attitudes to Sexual Relationships in 18th Century France', *British Society for Eighteenth-Century Studies* 12 (June 1977), 9–11.

'calm, gentle, silent . . . fit to serve as a model for a painting by Raphael or Poussin'; 'philosophical' deaths of defiant unbelievers; terrifying last agonies of criminals broken on the wheel; sentimental deaths of those haunted by the *sensibilité* of pre-Romanticism and the cult of melancholy; religious deaths solemnly recorded in edifying manuals—what can we say of the whole catalogue of courage and cowardice, hope and despair? Dying is the loneliest, and therefore the most highly individual thing we do. It is also the moment when we are least likely to be able to reveal our true sentiments, whether through weakness or, if we are strong, through respect for the conventions that make the event bearable for others. The historian's tricks of using converging beams of evidence to infer human secrets, and of interpreting each event in the light of what came after it, cannot operate here. What we really discover about attitudes to death are the longer-term views that the living discussed with others who lived, or set down in reflections for those who would live afterwards to find. Of human attitudes at the last moment, we know so little. The historian has mountains of evidence about the arrangements society makes about the deaths of its members, arrangements that are significant pointers to the nature of the social order, its hierarchies and communal aspirations. But this evidence, though death is the occasion for its existence, is only obliquely revealing about human attitudes to death. Sculptors, painters, poets, musicians, liturgiologists, preachers, undertakers are (in no cynical sense of the words) putting on their performance, operating within the current conventions of their discipline, seeking enlightened applause. Through them, society is affirming itself, the family is expressing its coherence, the Church is exemplifying its beliefs. Demographical evidence, paradoxically, gets us nearer to ordinary grief. We know the burden of mortality which lay so heavily on the past, its incidence, and how the pattern changed and improved; we can see connections between this information and changing attitudes to women, children, the family, old age, the pace at which life is lived, medical science, war, suicide, the death penalty. But almost always, we are investigating, not dying, but living—how people's attitudes to life were affected by their expectations and apprehensions of mortality.

Lucien Febvre asked for a history of 'Death'. His proposal is ambiguous. We can contrive graphs and maps of the fluctuations of death's empire over humankind; we can assess how men's attitudes to life were affected by their knowledge of its ending; we can assess the role of this knowledge in religious beliefs and convictions. Yet La Rochefoucauld's famous observation: that it is impossible to look directly at the sun or at death applies, in a different sense to its original meaning, to the historian, who when he writes about death always turns out to be writing about something else.[63] As he is concerned only with life—like Marc Bloch's ogre who scents immediately the smell of flesh and blood—it could hardly be otherwise.

[63] Cf, 'Or le fait de mourir n'appartient pas à la mort, mais à la vie. Il ne s'oppose pas à elle; il ne la nie pas, il l'achève.' (Raymond Polin, *Du Laid, du Mal et du Faux* (1948), p. 78.

VI

Sentiment and Antiquity: European Tombs 1750–1830

DAVID IRWIN

When Diderot saw a model for the monument to France's great eighteenth-century soldier, the Maréchal de Saxe, he protested against the sculptor's 'half-historical, half-allegorical jumble' of images, saying that he would have preferred a memorial that was 'simpler' and 'newer' in its design (*plate* VI. 1). According to Diderot it would have been far more appropriate to show the marshal reclining in his last hour, accompanied by only two soldiers, instead of a skeleton of Death, a Hercules and a personification of France.[1] Diderot's comments, made when he saw the model exhibited at the Paris Salon of 1767, highlighted the changes that were beginning to take place in contemporary European taste with regard to funerary works. This fundamental change from one generation to the next can be seen if one compares the Saxe monument with a later one to another hero, Lord Nelson (*plate* VI. 2). The Saxe monument looks backwards in its design, whereas that of Nelson represents in many ways a newer outlook.

The designs of these tombs, like that of many others, embody contemporary attitudes to death, and are therefore important visualizations of a range of ideas to be found in theology and literature, as well as in other art forms such as painting. The best museums of European sculpture are the countless cathedrals and churches which provide a wealth of visual historical evidence on many topics, most notably that of death.

Tombs across Europe about 1800 reflect in their designs no religious differences from one country to the next. In an age of Neoclassicism, when the arts of ancient Greece and Rome were the dominant influences on modern art, the common strands of Christianity and paganism were intertwined, producing a universal style and iconography. Variations reflect artists' and patrons' tastes and temperaments, rather than nationalities and religious beliefs. Theological differences persisted of course, but one could not illustrate from tombs, for instance, the different attitudes to death-bed ceremonies in an eighteenth-century French Catholic household and an English Protestant one. Examples for this article have been chosen only from

---

[1] Diderot, *Salons,* III, ed. Jean Seznec and Jean Adhémar (Oxford, 1963), p. 326: 'cela est plus beau, plus simple, plus énergique et plus neuf que tout votre fatras moitié histoire, moitié allégorie'.

France, Italy and England partly to clarify the general discussion, but also because these countries possess some particularly good monuments.

Although in some ways new, the compositions of both the Saxe and Nelson monuments continue a type of tomb that had become firmly established in the seventeenth century, seen most notably in the large-scale papal monuments in St. Peter's in Rome (*plate* VI. 3). This type was so influential that it continued right through into the nineteenth century. Even artists like John Flaxman who normally hated the extravagant rhetoric of the Baroque style, were nevertheless willing to retain the basic forms of such monuments for important commissions. Whilst in Rome in the early 1790s Flaxman made rough sketches of some of these papal tombs which were to influence the design on which he was working at the time for his first major monument, to the Earl of Mansfield, Lord Chief Justice, which was to be erected in Westminster Abbey in 1801. The same Baroque tombs only a few years later were to influence the composition for the monument to Nelson. Flaxman's generation recognized, just as their predecessors had done, that Bernini and his contemporaries had perfected a type of monument, deriving from the Renaissance, which was ideally suited to the glorification of a major figure. A lifesize, full-length portrait of the deceased is placed high above the spectator, and is flanked at a lower level by allegorical figures. Further allusions to the deceased's virtues and achievements could be incorporated in relief panels and inscriptions carved on the numerous surfaces provided by the usual elements of pedestal, sarcophagus and base which constituted the tiers of the composition. Many permutations were possible within the overall scheme, and this flexibility assured the continuation of this type of monument through several generations which witnessed changes in taste from Baroque to Rococo to Neoclassical.

Both the Saxe and the Nelson monuments are by leading sculptors of their day, Jean-Baptiste Pigalle and John Flaxman. Both were official commissions, from Louis XV and from a government committee respectively. The Saxe monument would have been sited in France's national shrine of St. Denis, where Turenne for example was already buried, if Saxe had not been a Protestant. He was therefore ineligible for burial in that church, and the capital of Protestant Alsace was finally chosen as a suitable site, in spite of the artist's attempts to have a Parisian location selected, even if it meant a secular one such as the École Militaire. The Nelson monument is prominently housed in St. Paul's Cathedral, which became the British national shrine for Napoleonic War heroes, chosen as a suitably empty church since Westminster Abbey had become, by the late eighteenth century, too full of tombs.

Saxe's undoubtedly great military achievements in France's wars in the 1730s and 1740s merited commemoration on a grand scale. He had died in 1750, and by the following year Louis XV was discussing a possible monument. The commission was given to Pigalle, as a result of the influence of Madame de Pompadour, some time between the end of 1752 and the beginning of 1753, but the completed marble was not finally erected until after many delays in 1776. Once installed, it was inaugurated with much pomp.

The completed marble conformed in nearly every detail to the model which the king had selected in 1753. The artist's first, rejected, project had consisted of a weeping figure of France holding in her arms the dying marshal, but the king had preferred another idea.[2] On the monument a proud and confident Saxe, still apparently in command at the moment of death, is walking down towards an open coffin that awaits him, yet he had not died on the field of battle but in his bed at his chateau of Chambord. France intercedes on his behalf with a skeletal figure of Death, clutching his customary hour-glass, whilst a genius of Death holding an inverted torch, symbolising the extinction of life, stands weeping. Saxe's military career is shown by the flags to the right, and the lion, leopard and eagle to the left, representing victories over Britain, the Netherlands and Prussia, including his brilliant success against the Allies at Fontenoy in 1745. The strength of France's military power is further emphasized by the unusual presence on a church monument of the figure of Hercules. A prominent inscription (not shown in the photograph reproduced here) recording Saxe's military exploits is written across the background pyramid, an architectural form that traditionally symbolized immortality. The allegory of the Saxe monument, although very literary, is readily comprehensible, but to avoid any possible confusion the programme was described in detail by the sculptor himself in a memorandum he prepared for the benefit of Strasbourg officials soon after the erection of the monument.[3]

The literary nature of the Saxe monument led some contemporaries later in the century to believe that Pigalle had not actually worked out the iconography himself. At the time of the Revolution (when the Saxe monument was safely hidden from any anti-religious mob by strawbales), Alexandre Lenoir, creator of the temporary Musée des Monuments Français, claimed that the engraver Nicolas Cochin had actually designed the monument. As Cochin was a friend, and certainly had a hand in designing a monument for another sculptor (to be discussed shortly), the assertion is not improbable. It cannot, however, be proved conclusively, just as the contemporary suggestion that another friend, the Abbé Gougenot, helped design the Saxe tomb must also remain inconclusive.[4]

Fighting to defend Britain against her enemies during the Napoleonic Wars, Nelson was just as successful on behalf of his country as Maurice de

[2] Louis Réau, *J.-B. Pigalle* (Paris, 1950), p. 87.

[3] The manuscript in the Strasbourg archives was first published in Samuel Rocheblave, *Le Mausolée du Maréchal de Saxe* (Paris, 1901).

[4] Réau, op. cit., pp. 89–91. For the funeral itself, see Victor Beyer, 'Le Recueil Werner-Boudhors et la Pompe funèbre du Maréchal de Saxe', *Bulletin de la Société de l'Histoire de l'Art Français, Année 1976* (Paris, 1978), 219–25

Saxe had been for France. The half century between their two deaths, however, resulted in different styles of monuments, although fundamentally they are similar in type.

Like Saxe, Nelson is shown still actively in command, not at the moment of the fatal wound on his flagship nor on his death-bed in his cabin: these moments would not have been glorious enough. The President of the Royal Academy at the time, Benjamin West, was doubtless expressing a widely felt conviction that the commemoration of a contemporary event of such magnitude as a hero's death should 'excite awe and veneration'. Just as the death of General Wolfe when represented in art, argued West, should not be depicted like that of 'a common soldier under a bush, neither should Nelson be represented dying in the gloomy hold of a ship, like a sick man in a prison hole. To move the mind there should be a spectacle presented to raise and warm the mind, and all should be proportioned to the highest idea conceived of the hero. No boy would be animated by a representation of Nelson dying like an ordinary man, his feelings must be roused and his mind inflamed by a scene great and extraordinary. A mere matter of fact will never produce this effect'.[5] Pigalle and Flaxman would certainly have agreed with West. Neither sculptor depicted a 'mere matter of fact', but combined their naturalism of detail with a high degree of allegory.

Whereas the Saxe monument is very rhetorical in style, the one to Nelson is calm and restrained. Anguish and tears are held in check; no figure of Death threatens with his hour-glass. Naval victories are symbolized in the low relief carvings on the pedestal of classical river gods, one of whom leans on an Egyptian sphinx, and the names of Nelson's three main battles are spelt out prominently above the head of each god. Classical allegory is continued in the lefthand figure, who is not Britannia as perhaps one might expect, but Minerva, as a generalized symbol of war. She is drawing the attention of two young midshipmen to Nelson's achievements. Britain itself is represented by the usual symbolic lion on the right. The inscription on the base records no Christian message, but is an entirely secular one referring to Nelson's 'splendid and unparalleled achievements, during a life spent in the service of his country, and terminated in the moment of victory by a glorious death'.

Nelson's funeral carriage and coffin had also combined classical allegory with contemporary realism in their decoration, and since Flaxman lived in London it is highly likely he saw the procession at some point in its progress from Greenwich to St. Paul's Cathedral. He could also have seen the prints that were very rapidly published after the event, and would have known that the car was carved to resemble the prow and stern of Nelson's *Victory*,

---

[5] West's remarks were made in the course of a conversation on Arthur William Devis's painting of the death of Nelson, recorded in Joseph Farington, *Diary*, ed. James Greig, (London, 1922–28), IV, p. 151, 10 June 1807. The painting is in the National Maritime Museum, Greenwich.

with four palm trees supporting a classical canopy, ornamented with the Greek honeysuckle pattern. The velvet covering of the coffin was decorated by the printseller Rudolph Ackermann with figures of Britannia, Neptune, a classically inspired Grief, a sphinx, a crocodile and other images, as well as a proposed monument. The description of this last ornament, as it appears on Ackermann's print, is worth quoting in full as an indication of the fairly stock range of images available to Flaxman, and the extent to which he was to deviate from them. The monument was 'supported by eagles, the emblems of Victory, with the portrait of the deceased hero in basso-relievo, surmounted by an urn containing his ashes, over which reclines the figure of Grief. At the base are seen the British Lion, with one of his paws laid on the Gallic Cock, sphinxes and other trophies, intended to commemorate the memorable victory, which the gallant Admiral obtained on the shores off Egypt, and to indicate that he might fairly claim the Sovereignty of the ocean'.[6] Flaxman transcended the banality of this proposed design, although incorporating some similar images. One crucial difference is that Nelson's portrait was not relegated to a relief panel, but became a lifesize figure.

Some of Flaxman's friends expressed alarm that the important Nelson commission might even be given to a foreigner, the Italian Antonio Canova, whose sculptures found many influential British admirers and collectors. For patriotic reasons alone the suggestion of employing Canova was strongly opposed by contemporary British critics, but the architect Charles Robert Cockerell, one of Flaxman's friends, recorded his dismay at Canova's design on artistic grounds as well as patriotic ones. Canova proposed a freestanding square sarcophagus ornamented on all sides with low basreliefs: 'May our sense and taste defend us from it', wrote Cockerell in his diary. He particularly disliked the proposed subject on the reliefs, 'representing a dead Roman borne from a galley to Britannia in the dress of a theatrical priestess'. The surviving plaster model for the monument in the Gipsoteca at Possagno, in Northern Italy, shows that Cockerell's description is no partisan exaggeration. He continued: 'What is the English tar to say when he sees his beloved Nelson in a Roman petticoat, why, he will say, are British sailors to imitate a Roman dress, are we not original, as great a people as ever ruled the waves and influenced the world!'[7]

Like Pigalle's image of the Maréchal de Saxe, Flaxman sided with fellow artists who believed that modern dress was more appropriate than ancient for the commemoration of a contemporary hero. The problem of ancient versus modern attire was much discussed in the course of the eighteenth century, and both schools of thought were still active about 1800. Canova's

---

[6] For another imaginary Nelson monument with a bas-relief portrait, decorating a sarcophagus, see James Stanier Clarke and John McArthur, *Life of Admiral Lord Nelson* (London, 1809), II, p. 470.

[7] Quoted in David Watkin, *The Life and Work of C. R. Cockerell* (London, 1974), p. 20. For an interesting discussion of Canova's *Nelson*, see Pietro Verrua, *Orazio Nelson nel Pensiero e nell'Arte del Foscolo e del Canova* (Padua, 1919).

Nelson would have been dressed like a Roman warrior, and Benjamin West's Nelson on the pediment he designed in 1810 for Greenwich Hospital is half naked, dying in the lap of Britannia, surrounded by a clutter of allegorical figures. In St. Paul's Cathedral, some sculptors preferred contemporary portraits, whilst others stripped their heroes almost naked, even if the modern warrior was standing beside a contemporary cannon, as in the case of Banks's monument to Captain Rundell Burgess (1802). The results of such an abandonment of modern dress could on occasions be ludicrous. Robert Southey would have found many sympathizers for his strictures about war monuments when he wrote in his *Letters from England of Don Alvarez Espriella* (1807): 'The artists know not what to do with their villainous costume, and, to avoid uniforms in marble, make their unhappy statues half naked.'[8] Flaxman knew Southey's book, and it is not improbable that its caustic comments contributed to the choice of modern dress.

As far as the eighteenth century was concerned, the most important step forward in this discussion was taken in 1771 by the young Benjamin West when he exhibited his version of the *Death of Wolfe* at the Royal Academy. Sir Joshua Reynolds, as President of the Academy, apparently felt obliged to visit the painter in his studio and dissuade him from taking such a drastic step as to portray Wolfe in his modern army uniform. Reynolds argued that 'the inherent greatness' of the event being portrayed merited the use of ancient dress, but West disagreed, arguing that the event on the Heights of Abraham had not taken place in ancient Greek or Roman times.[9] Undeterred, Reynolds reverted to the theme of dress in sculpture, in his tenth discourse, delivered at the Royal Academy in 1780, when he told his audience: 'The desire for transmitting to posterity the shape of modern dress must be acknowledged to be purchased at a prodigious price, even the price of everything that is valuable in art.'[10] Although West himself seems to have been ambivalent about the problem, as his Greenwich pediment shows, his painting of Wolfe was an important landmark, specifically mentioned for its influence on heroes' dress in at least one magazine article published at the time the discussions were going on about the war memorials in St. Paul's Cathedral.[11]

The English tar would have had no difficulty in recognizing Flaxman's image of Nelson in his contemporary naval uniform. But in spite of its apparent realism, enhanced by the anchor and coil of rope which add verisimilitude to an admiral alive and in command on a ship's deck, we know from one of Flaxman's letters that he was worried about Nelson's physical defects even before he received the commission for the monument.

[8] 1807 edition, I, p. 311.
[9] John Galt, *The Life, Studies and Works of Benjamin West* (London, 1820), II, pp. 47–9.
[10] Reynolds, *Discourses*, ed. R. R. Wark (San Marino, 1959), p. 187.
[11] In *La Belle Assemblée* (London, 1808), IV, Supplement, p. 9. Several versions of West's painting exist, including ones in the National Gallery of Canada, Ottawa and the Royal Collection in London, usually hung in Kensington Palace.

136

'Although Lord Nelson had nearly or quite lost the sight of one eye', he wrote, 'that was no apparent defect in his face, and in the execution of a statue the loss of his arm might so be indicated yet obscured that it would not injure the general effect of the work, or he might be represented as you observe in his perfect figure.'[12] When he came to designing the actual monument in the following year, Flaxman conceived the face without any noticeable defect in one eye, and allowed the cloak to hang in such a way that it concealed the loss of one arm. He therefore succeeded in creating a portrait of Nelson that was both recognizably naturalistic, and at the same time had been idealized, ultimately in the spirit of that classical idealization that he admired so much in the art of ancient Greece and Rome.

The suggestion on Ackermann's print that a figure of Grief should mourn over an urn became in Flaxman's monument a quite different, and more original, image in the figure of Minerva with two midshipmen. Instead of grieving they are gaining inspiration and encouragement: the group has become a homily on patriotism. This element of the composition might well have been suggested to Flaxman from another source, amongst the innumerable commemorative verses on Nelson's death. One of these poems,[13] presumably bearing Ackermann's print in mind since it refers to an urn, contains the lines:

> '. . . when autumn brings the shadowy year,
> Thy circled urn shall drink her warmest tear:
> The mother there shall lead her child to con
> The deeds engraven on thy sculptur'd stone!
> The boy shall turn a hero from the pile,
> And rise the future Nelson of the isle!'

Flaxman's preliminary sketches for the monument (in the British Museum and York City Art Gallery) show only a motherly Britannia pointing out to two boys the glories of the navy, which are inscribed on a panel behind them. As the elaborate composition of the final marble was to emerge at a later stage, this group is obviously central to Flaxman's concept of his commemoration of a national hero. Although partially classical in the inspiration of the dress of the female figure, the group's most important characteristic is its unmistakably contemporary sentiment. The mood, if not the details, of this group was to be echoed a few years later in a Flaxman monument of a quite different kind, to Viscountess Fitzharris, shown as a mother instructing her sons from the Bible (*plate* VI. 4). There had been a possible and slight concession to the growing importance of sentiment in contemporary taste in both art and literature in the Saxe monument, by the sculptor's late alteration of the original helmeted Genius of war into the

---

[12] British Library, Add. MSS. 39790, f. 19, Flaxman to Revd. William Gunn, London, February 1806. Quoted in David Irwin, *English Neoclassical Art* (London and Greenwich, Conn., 1966), p. 67.

[13] Anonymous, in *Luctus Nelsoniani. Poems on the Death of Lord Nelson, in Latin and English, written for the Turtonian Medals* (London, 1807), p. 147.

present figure of a weeping Genius of death, looking more like a cupid or putto who could have strayed from a painting by Boucher. But sentiment is only a marginal and formalized element in the Saxe monument, and arguably perhaps not even present at all. But a genuinely felt sentiment is crucial in the design of the Nelson monument, reflecting the widespread importance of sensibility in the visual arts, not just funerary sculpture, by the turn of the eighteenth and nineteenth centuries.

The theme of the mother and child, and the tender relationship established between them, was a favourite subject in Flaxman's work, and its dominant role in the Nelson monument was singled out by a German critic when visiting St. Paul's Cathedral a few years after the monument had been erected: 'Full of inner motherly love and also respect for the hero, this tall woman seems to lead the boys, and this double feeling is expressed as much in her face as in her very noble bearing. This single figure was sufficient for me to acknowledge the respected artist, whose mind and soul strike through the most difficult and reluctant material and captivate the observer'.[14]

Flaxman 'struck through' with a mixture of sentiment, naturalism, and classical allegory, producing—like his fellow sculptors in St. Paul's—a patriotic and pagan, rather than a Christian, memorial to a Napoleonic War hero.[15] Flaxman successfully overcame the difficulties that such a commission inevitably created for a sculptor. As an anonymous correspondent had written to the *Monthly Magazine* in 1806, on the subject of Napoleonic monuments, a sculptor can be 'embarrassed with costume, restrained with portrait, and betrayed into the frigid wilds of allegory'. The writer then proceeded to offer his unsolicited advice: 'It is natural to expect in the first place, to find the effigies of the hero; gratitude loves to perpetuate the traits of the countenance, as well as the actions of the life and the character of the mind. But a single figure is not sufficient; we require a group to give mass and dignity to the monument; symbols to explain the motives of its erection, the profession, and the action, of the object: besides that, a portrait statue is an ungrateful subject to the artist. The allegory should be clear and simple; a fable which strikes at a glance, not an enigma to be deciphered; uniting the figures in one consistent action, and concentrating the interest around the hero.'[16] At the end of his letter, the writer expressed concern about the kind of monument that would be erected to Nelson, and his advice could easily have been read by Flaxman since his memorial conforms to the list of recommendations.

Some of the other Napoleonic monuments in St. Paul's represent the moment of death or burial. The most impressive example of this theme is the younger John Bacon's monument to Lieutenant-General Sir John Moore (*plate* VI. 5), which provides a striking contrast to Flaxman's Nelson. In the

---

[14] Ludwig Schorn, 'Besuch bei Flaxman in 1826', *Kunst-Blatt*, 1827, p. 114.
[15] For a rival design for a Nelson monument in St. Paul's, by James Paine the Younger, see John Physick, *Designs for English Sculpture 1680–1860* (London, 1969), fig. 127.
[16] *Monthly Magazine*, no. 137, 1 January 1906, p. 497.

year that Bacon was awarded the commission in 1810, Robert Southey published in the *Edinburgh Annual Register* part of his history of Europe, concluding with the recent events of the Peninsular War. He wrote of Moore's burial:

> He had often said that, if he was killed in battle, he wished to be buried where he fell. The body was removed at midnight to the citadel of Corunna. A grave was dug for him on the rampart there, by a party of the 9th Regiment, the aides-de-camp attending by turns. No coffin could be procured, and the officers of his staff wrapped the body, dressed as it was, in a military cloak and blankets. The interment was hastened; for, about eight in the morning, some firing was heard, and the officers feared that, if a serious attack were made, they should be ordered away, and not suffered to pay him their last duty. The officers of his family bore him to the grave; the funeral service was read by the chaplain; and the corpse was covered with earth.

John Bacon must have known this account, since his design is so obviously based on the facts of the actual burial. Moore's body is shown being lowered 'dressed as it was' but without the cloak and blankets, straight into the grave. This central part of the design is realistic *reportage,* but it is flanked by classical allegory, including a winged Victory kneeling to assist with the burial. The 'mere matter of fact' to which Benjamin West had been objecting, in a different context, is here used with great visual success because the sculptor has removed the scene from an arena of humdrum reality by incorporating the unreality of allegory. The simplicity of Bacon's design—at least relatively simple when compared to other Napoleonic monuments—is paralleled by the straightforward inscription on the base, which is a list of the main facts of his life, without any eulogy beyond the bald statement that 'He fought for his country'. The simple poignancy of the burial was shortly to become the basis for the widely read poem by Charles Wolfe, 'The Burial of Sir John Moore', first published in 1817 and hailed by Byron as a great work. The poem opens with the well known lines:

> Not a drum was heard, not a funeral note,
> As his corpse to the ramparts we hurried;
> Not a soldier discharged his farewell shot
> O'er the grave where our hero was buried.

Attacks on tyranny, the defence of political liberty and the encouragement of a sense of nationalism were virtues that were also being commemorated in funerary art elsewhere in Europe at the same time. In the church of Santa Croce in Florence, a personification of Italy comes to mourn at the sarcophagus of Vittorio Alfieri (*plate* VI. 6), commissioned by the wife of the Jacobite pretender Charles Edward Stuart, the Countess of Albany, with whom Alfieri had been in love·for many years. The great Italian writer, seen later as a precursor of the Risorgimento, is commemorated by a fine tomb designed by Canova, sited in a church which is as important as a shrine to the country's great men as are St. Denis, Westminster Abbey and St. Paul's. Like the heroic monuments that have just been discussed, Canova

139

too combines patriotism with sentiment, deriving much of his imagery from the art of classical antiquity. When inaugurated in 1810, the monument was enthusiastically received, especially the figure of Italy which was appreciated both as a beautiful piece of sculpture and as a fine statement of patriotism.

By giving his figure of Italy such a major role in his composition, far more prominent than that of the portrait of the poet himself, Canova was undoubtedly stressing the importance of Alfieri's contribution to the growing cause of Italian nationalism. Canova's Italy is paralleled exactly by Flaxman's first ideas for his Nelson monument, which concentrated on the figure of Britannia, and even excluded a portrait of the admiral. Like Flaxman's Britannia-Minerva figure, Canova's Italy is a source of encouragement to present and future generations: although she mourns it is not only for Alfieri's death but also probably for the currently French-occupied Italy, plundered of many of its art treasures which had been taken away to Paris. Alfieri had often strolled in Santa Croce for inspiration, and this habit is mentioned by Ugo Foscolo in his long and famous poem *I Sepolcri,* published in 1807, only a year after Canova had started to work on the Alfieri design. Foscolo used the present tense as if Alfieri was still alive and still visiting the church:

> ... E a questi marmi
> venne spesso Vittorio ad inspirarsi. ...
> Con questi grandi abita eterno, e l'ossa
> fremono amor di patria. ...   (lines 189–90, 196–7).

In the second half of the poem, Foscolo's major theme is the patriotic role of tombs to the famous, as through their tombs they can inspire future generations to strive for the cause of nationalism: a message presumably shared by Canova, otherwise the dominant role of his Italy on the Alfieri tomb would be inexplicable. The sculptor in his monument seems to have epitomized the aspirations of leading nationalists of his own generation, so that the tomb is more than a memorial to an important dramatist and poet. It is also a celebration of the ideas for which Alfieri stood.

The overt nationalism of the Alfieri monument can be substantiated from further sources, close to Canova himself. Some evidence is provided by a sonnet on the figure of Italy written by his friend and future biographer, Melchiore Missirini, in which he shares Foscolo's belief that Alfieri is really still alive, his verses inspiring those around him. Another source is the early analysis of the tomb by the Countess Albrizzi in her book on Canova, in which she described the figure of Italy, 'weeping for a son whose lofty and energetic strains have awakened the love of virtue and patriotism in the breasts of his countrymen, and called forth a race of men animated only by the desire of greatness'.[17]

---

[17] Missirini's poem is included in his collection *Sui Marmi di Antonio Canova* (Venice, 1817). Countess Albrizzi, *The Works of Antonio Canova,* English translation (London, 1828), III, not paginated, 'Model of a Monument for Victor Alfieri'. Her book was first published in Florence, 1809, with a new edition in Pisa, 1821–24.

Behind the contemporary patriotic message of the Alfieri monument lies Canova's deep knowledge of classical art, both in the basic forms of his composition and in the details, which he has combined in ways that have no antique precedents, so that they are not in any sense mere pastiches. The monument shows a fine understanding of classical art, primarily Roman, which Canova has recreated in the spirit of his own time. Italy herself is most probably based on a weeping Andromache or Agrippina, substituting a sarcophagus for the traditional urn. The expression of Italy's face, however, is not classical, having been imbued with as much contemporary sentiment as Flaxman's Minerva and midshipmen. Both female figures are also introspective, calmly unaware of the spectator, unlike the very extroverted figure of France on the Saxe monument, which represents the tail-end of Baroque emotion stretching out into the surrounding space. The spectator or worshipper is now involved in a calmer piety, pulled into the monument by Italy who seems to have stepped up onto the plinth from the aisle of the church, just as Minerva and the midshipmen also look as if they have just climbed up onto the base of the Nelson monument, with the midshipmen casually and naturally even resting their feet on part of the monument.

The piety and sentiment expressed in figures on monuments such as the ones to Alfieri and Nelson reflect the new mood that had been growing from the 1760s onwards, and had been shown in Diderot's comments on the monument to the Maréchal de Saxe. Although some of the iconography in the second half of the century is not new, the mood is a fresh one, clearly revealed in the almost total absence of skeletons of Death and of the deceased on tombs in the second half of the eighteenth century onwards. The macabre element in 'Gothic' novels, and the increasing interest in embalming both within and outside freemasonry, are aspects of eighteenth-century ideas that remain quite separate from tomb design and had no influence. The event of death in a Christian context, which is the one directly relevant to funerary art, was no longer generally regarded with horror, and consequently any suggestion of the macabre is very rarely seen. There are no macabre elements in the design of either the Nelson or Alfieri monuments, and Diderot clearly showed the new spirit when he had hoped to banish the skeletal figure of Death from the monument to Saxe.

The disappearance of skeletons can only be partially explained in terms of theology. An equally important reason lies in the new assessments of ancient art within the Neoclassical period. The 1760s was an important decade in setting the pattern for the rest of the century. Flaxman, Canova and their generation inherited ideas already current, and they would have found a theoretical basis for some of their ideas about funerary designs in two important publications that had appeared in that decade.

Late in life, the influential German antiquarian, Johann Joachim Winckelmann, had published his *Versuch einer Allegorie* (1766), a sort of dictionary of iconography, attempting to bring allegories more up-to-date than the reader could find in the standard work in this field, by Cesare Ripa, whose *Iconologia* had first been published as long ago as 1593, and gone through many editions. Winckelmann's article on death is quite different to Ripa's, stressing in his *Allegorie* that skeletons of Death, as far as ancient art was concerned, were unimportant. He noted that 'skeletons appear on only two old monuments and marble urns in Rome', and with difficulty he could quote few examples published by other antiquarians. Winckelmann's article was therefore largely devoted to alternative images of death, associated with classical myths of Apollo, Aurora and other figures.

Winckelmann's book was published in the same year as Lessing's *Laokoon*, which contains passing references to the absence of skeletons of death in ancient art, a subject to which he was to return in more detail in his long essay published in 1769, *Wie die Alten den Tod gebildet*. In these pages Lessing attacks other scholars, including Winckelmann, arguing that even the scanty evidence on skeletons had been incorrectly interpreted. The ancients did not portray Death as a skeleton, wrote Lessing, but as a twin brother to Sleep, as described in Homer's *Iliad* (xvi, lines 681-2), when recounting the death of Sarpedon. In ancient art, Lessing and the artists of the Neoclassical age found ample justification for a rejection of medieval skeletons of Death; the antique image of a Genius with an inverted torch was infinitely preferable. Lessing's use of archaeological evidence may be unsound in terms of today's scholarship, but in the context of the 1760s he produced an important contribution to the fight against the Baroque, in particular some of its iconography. One of the most theatrical and threatening images of seventeenth-century sculpture is surely the skeletal figure of Death half-hidden under the heavy marble draperies on Bernini's tomb to Pope Alessandro VII in St. Peter's, its arm outstretched, holding an hourglass just below the seated figure of the praying Pope (*plate* VI. 3). This portrayal of Alessandro VII epitomises all that the Neoclassical generation hated so much in the Baroque, and which seemed to them so contrary to the serenity of ancient art which Lessing, Winckelmann and their generation, and followers, regarded as the main characteristics of the arts of Greece and Rome. In his first important essay published in 1755, *Gedanken über die Nachahmung der griechischen Werke in der Mahlerey und Bildhauerkunst*, Winckelmann had already produced one of the most often-quoted of Neoclassical sentences: 'The last and most eminent characteristic of the Greek works is a noble simplicity and sedate grandeur in gesture and expression'. Simplicity and sedateness were two of the most important characteristics of Neoclassical art, and much of the sculpture and painting of the latter part of the eighteenth century, and the early years of the nineteenth, can be described in words similar to those used by Winckelmann of ancient art. The writings of Winckelmann, Lessing and Diderot reflected in their different ways the major changes in taste that were taking place in the middle years of the century. The banishment of images of skeletons of Death is only one element, but nevertheless a significant one, in a widespread art movement.

Diderot was able to translate theory into practice at the same time as he was finding fault with the Saxe monument, since he influenced the design of the tomb commissioned by Louis XVI to commemorate the Dauphin. He had died in 1765, and had specified in his will that his monument should be erected in the Cathedral at Sens, for which he had a special affection since his tutor had been Archbishop there. The Dauphine was to die only two years later in 1767, and the tomb therefore became a joint one (*plates VI. 7 and 8*). The marble was carved by the youngest of the Coustou family, Guillaume II, but behind the marble lie the ideas of Diderot and his friend Cochin. Early in 1766 Diderot was already writing in a letter about the royal commission for the Dauphin's monument, telling his correspondent that the artists had turned to him for ideas, and he proceeds to give precise details about three different designs he had planned. A few weeks later he wrote a further letter giving ideas for a fourth and fifth project, saying that Cochin had reported that the Court would be unsympathetic to his earlier ideas as they were too elaborate.[18]

Elsewhere in his writings in 1766, in a short essay entitled 'L'Éloge du Dauphin par Thomas', Diderot argued that in praising the Dauphin one should concentrate on his private life, on the happiness of his marriage, his tenderness towards his family and attachment towards friends.[19] This theme of conjugal love was to form an important part of the design of the monument finally erected in Sens. The Dauphine was still alive when the monument was commissioned, and in response to Cochin's suggestion that the design should refer to the future reunion of husband and wife, Diderot produced his fourth project:

Erect a tomb. Place on it two urns, one closed and the other open. Seat eternal Justice between the two urns, who poses with the everlasting crown and palm in one hand on the closed urn, and who holds on her knee, with the other hand, the everlasting crown and palm with which one day she will cover the open urn. That is what the ancients would have called a monument.

Imagine near this monument a standing Religion, trampling underfoot Death and Time. Death, wrapped in her long draperies and with her face turned away from the ground; Time, in an opposite pose, angered by a monument erected in our day to Conjugal Love, and striking it with his scythe which breaks into pieces.

Religion shows the urns to Conjugal Love and says: *There rests his ashes; there one day yours ought to rest, and the same honours which he has received are destined for you.*

Conjugal Love, desolate, has her face hidden in the bosom of Religion. She has let fall to her feet the two torches, one of which is extinguished and the other still

---

[18] Both letters are to Sophie Volland, 3 and 20 February 1766. In Georges Roth's edition of the Diderot *Correspondance,* letters 381 and 385 in vol. 6 (Paris, 1961).

[19] Diderot, *Oeuvres Complètes,* ed. J. Assézat, (Paris, 1875), VI, pp. 347–50.

burns. A beautiful, large and completely naked child, symbol of the family, has seized one of her arms to which he has pressed his mouth.

Of the four [designs] this is the one which pleases Cochin the most. The idea of the urns seems to him noble and ingenious. This Death trampled underfoot by Religion, and this Time incensed by the monument, two speaking figures; and this large, beautiful and quite naked child, with the two figures, [form] a most interesting group.

Cochin agreed with most of the ideas proposed in Diderot's fourth project, retaining the two urns, allegorical figures of Time, Religion and Conjugal Love, and a naked child, even using poses that Diderot suggested. However, Cochin made some improvements, the most significant being the division of the composition into two separate, but interlocking, parts. When originally sited, the monument was in the middle of the choir, so that on entering the cathedral the spectator first saw the figures of Conjugal Love and Time; only when he walked round the far side of the monument nearest the altar would he see Religion and Immortality. The more secular aspect of the monument was turned away from the altar, but by so doing its visual impact was greatly increased. In its present position in a side chapel, where the monument was subsequently re-sited, the original intention is lost.

Diderot and Cochin seem to have been determined in this important commission to establish a new type of funerary monument, owing little to the immediate past, and incorporating classical details in a novel way. The most striking feature of the final design is the absence of any images of the deceased, unlike Diderot's first ideas which included a death-bed scene with the Dauphin asleep. The commemoration is conceived entirely in terms of allegorical figures, half Christian and half pagan, who belong as much to the generalized concept of religion that one associates with the Enlightenment as to a long tradition of Christian iconography. The drapery of the figures and the shapes of the urns derive from ancient Rome, that pagan source of inspiration that was to be so important for several generations of Neoclassical artists, on to Flaxman and Canova, and beyond. Coustou's marble group in Sens Cathedral was one of the first major Neoclassical monuments in France.

The composition of the figures has been arranged to create a feeling of quiet and pious introspection. There is no extroverted posturing; the group is self-contained in its grief. The melancholy is calm and dignified, with emotion controlled, qualities which contemporaries so much admired in such famous antique groups as those of Laocoon and his sons, and Niobe and her family. The pathos of the monument at Sens is therefore essentially classical, yet the tearfulness is sentimental and modern.

Diderot's suggestion that the Dauphin's family life should form the basis of an evaluation of his achievement, is not only typical of Diderot's *sensibilité*, but also of an increasing interest in the family in literature and art, in particular the relationship between a mother and child. Flaxman's monument to Viscountess Fitzharris epitomizes the importance of the theme of maternal affection in the late eighteenth and early nineteenth centuries (*plate* VI. 4).

She is presented as a serene image, a mother still alive, reading from the Bible to her three sons. A memorial to the dead has become a contemporary genre scene imbued with sentiment and piety.

In order to make sure that the group was as natural as possible, Flaxman made detailed portrait drawings of the childrens' heads from life, and also got them to pose in the way they would appear on the final monument. At the same time he made drawings of a wife of a friend together with two of her young sons, with the older one helping the younger one onto his mother's knee. This charmingly intimate group has many details in common with the Fitzharris monument, and it seems highly likely that Flaxman persuaded her to pose because of the commission for the monument.[20] The drawings leading up to the Fitzharris tombs are some of the best documents we have concerning Flaxman's working method, laying a firm foundation for the Romantic naturalism of the figures in marble. The result is an intimate group, as convincingly realistic in its execution as the absence of colouring will permit. The youngest son has curled up contentedly on his mother's lap, whilst she holds him gently with an arm round him. The two other boys, the older with an arm around the younger, stand resting against their mother's knees, gazing in rapt attention at her. Lady Fitzharris's devotion to her children is amongst the many virtues described in the lengthy inscription on the base, which refers to her 'domestic duties', and the 'care and education of her children' which were 'her darling objects, on them she equally bestowed the vigilant fondness of a mother, and the successful efforts of a well cultivated mind'. The inscription also refers to Lady Fitzharris's 'feelings and confidence of a true Christian'.

Underlying the naturalism of the delightful Fitzharris genre scene, however, are well established, but not overtly used, iconographic traditions of the figure of Charity with a group of children, as well as that of the Virgin and Child. On this monument Flaxman has secularized a religious theme, which itself is a basic human relationship. For most of his life, a mother and child and also Charity figures were important subjects in Flaxman's sculptures and drawings, and he often used a Charity group on his monuments. The basis for this aspect of his art was laid not only in his profound convictions as a practising Christian (well known at the time for his almsgiving in London streets), but also in his study of Italian Renaissance art. Both whilst in Italy between 1787 and 1794, and subsequently when lecturing at the Royal Academy in London after his appointment as the first Professor of Sculpture there (in 1810), Flaxman singled out for special attention altarpieces depicting the Virgin and Child. The earliest example he selected whilst in Italy was the *Rucellai Madonna* by Duccio, then still in Santa Maria Novella in Florence (but nowadays in the Uffizi), dating

---

[20] One of the drawings of the Fitzharris sons, together with one of the other drawings, of Mrs. Charles Augustus Tulk, are reproduced in David Irwin, *John Flaxman: Sculptor, Illustrator, Designer* (London, 1979 and New York, 1980), plates 198 and 199.

from the late thirteenth century.[21] Later altarpieces included Correggio's famous *Virgin of St. Jerome (Il Giorno)* in S. Antonio (now in the Galleria in Parma), which he already knew before he went abroad because he possessed a good engraving of it. The painting consists of a particularly charming, and intimate, family group which Flaxman praised for its originality. He returned to the subject of the Renaissance in his lectures, drawing a clear distinction between the subject-matter of ancient and modern art. Much as he admired the classical art of Greece and Rome, he found an important theme insufficiently treated in it, namely 'parental affection, and domestic charities, being cherished in the Christian dispensation much more powerfully than in the Grecian codes: to these graces of benevolence we owe those lovely groups—the Holy Families of Raphael and Correggio, and the Charity of Michelangelo, unequalled in any ancient composition of mother and children, and one of the finest groups in existence'.[22] The *Charity* by Michelangelo to which Flaxman refers forms part of the fresco decoration of the Sistine Chapel, a playfully affectionate family group included amongst the ancestors of Christ, which is nowadays identified as Joram with three of her children. Another work by Michelangelo which Flaxman particularly admired in the same lecture was the marble of the *Madonna and Child,* on the altar of the Medici Chapel in Florence. Maternal affection is not necessarily the theme in Michelangelo's art that would first come to one's mind, and it is interesting to see Flaxman selecting specific aspects of the art of this great Renaissance artist that are directly relevant to his own art, so absorbing what he has seen that it emerges in due course as a subtle and indirect influence on monuments such as the one to Lady Fitzharris.[23]

The Fitzharris monument is a particularly good example of a tomb at the turn of the eighteenth and nineteenth centuries which belongs to the same world as Rousseau's *Émile* and Blake's early lyrical poetry: a world that found much to praise in the virtues of family life, and in particular the affectionate and instructive relationship of a mother to her child. Some artists expressed this new theme in the form of paintings with titles such as the *Age of Innocence.* Other artists found outlets in tombs and other religious works, including a controversial *Charity* by Flaxman's younger Italian contemporary Lorenzo Bartolini. Commissioned between 1817 and 1822, Bartolini's statue was intended to be one of a series of the Christian virtues, executed by a variety of artists, for the Grand Duke of Tuscany's Chapel of the Assumption at Poggio Imperiale. When completed, the *Charity* was regarded

---

[21] For comments on Duccio, as well as on later Italian artists, in Flaxman's Italian unpublished journals, see D. Irwin, *Flaxman,* pp. 33 ff.

[22] Flaxman's tenth lecture, in his *Lectures on Sculpture* (London, 1829), with a second edition in 1838.

[23] Amongst the rare instances of the theme of a seated mother with her children on an ancient Roman monument, Flaxman would have known the example on plate 72 in Vol. V. of Bernard de Montfaucon, *L'Antiquité expliquée* (Paris, 1719). But the Renaissance prototypes are of more immediate relevance to the Fitzharris monument.

as inappropriate for its religious setting because it was too naturalistic, an ironic decision since the sculptor had gone to great pains with many life studies to make the group as realistic as possible. Only a secular setting was thought adequate by the Duke's officials, and today Bartolini's *Charity* resides in the Palazzo Pitti in Florence, a reminder that new ideas in art can be too far ahead of those of a patron. Flaxman was more fortunate in the same period with his Fitzharris monument, which is no less naturalistic than Bartolini's *Charity*.

Maternal tenderness was a dominant subject in art at the turn of the eighteenth and nineteenth centuries, which in the context of church monuments shared its leading role with the subject of domestic affliction, epitomized in the scene of the death-bed. Religious treatises and contemporary novels regarded the death-bed as important both as a means for propounding Christian doctrine and as an expression of what Samuel Richardson called the 'happy exit', a phrase he used when describing Clarissa Harlowe's death. Death was now no longer to be feared. It was accepted with humble piety and gentle melancholy of the kind that the eighteenth century would have called 'white' rather than 'black', and the mood of the scene when represented might also be tinged with sentimental charm.

James Hervey's *Meditations among the Tombs* was the most widely read of all the many volumes of melancholia. First published in 1748, it was frequently reprinted, and together with Edward Young's *Night Thoughts* (1742) and Thomas Gray's *Elegy written in a Country Churchyard* (1751), exerted a considerable influence on the literature of death both in Britain and on the Continent, where their ideas are reflected in such poems as Jacques Delille's *L'Imagination* and Ippolito Pindemonte's *I Sepolcri*. Hervey's *Meditations* included a very typical death-bed scene:

> The soul, just going to abandon the tottering clay, collects all her forces, and exerts her last efforts. The good man raises himself on his pillow; extends a kind hand to his servants, which is bathed in tears; takes an affecting farewell to his friends; clasps his wife in a feeble embrace; kisses the dear pledges of their mutual love; and then pours all that remains of life and of strength, in the following words: 'I die, my dear children: but God, the everlasting God, will be with you. Though you lose an earthly parent, you have a Father in Heaven, who lives for evermore. Nothing, nothing, but an unbelieving heart, and irreligious life, can ever separate you, from the regards of his providence, from the endearments of His love.

Such descriptions were paralleled by a vast body of devotional manuals, of which one of the most widely circulated was by the evangelical divine Henry Venn. His *Complete Duty of Man* (first published in 1763, and often reprinted into the middle of the next century) included a whole chapter on various methods of instructing children. On the subject of death-beds, Venn wrote: 'It is of great benefit early to teach your children also that life and death, as well as sickness and pain, are at the supreme disposal of God. The

147

proper season to rivet this instruction, is when a servant, a friend, or neighbour known to your children, is just expired, and the awful report is brought to their ears. Then the circumstances of the deceased immediately before death, the medicines used, the help of physicians, the sorrows, sighs and tears of friends and relations, are to be urged as sensible proofs that it is God that taketh away our breath in infancy, youth, or riper years, just as he sees fit, and that none can deliver out of his hand.' The tone of this type of instruction was echoed in many other volumes. A short-lived annual in the 1820s entitled *The Children's Friend*, for instance, was full of moralizing tales, especially about death in both Britain and abroad, with a typical story entitled 'The Life and Death of a Sunday Scholar', illustrated by a crude woodcut of weeping children at his bedside.[24]

The same theme was taken up in many funeral sermons at the time, regardless of the church or chapel in which the service was being held. One vicar told his congregation in a Yorkshire town: 'The peaceful death of a saint of God is a very instructive scene', whilst a minister in a dissenting chapel further south, in a Devon village, declared: 'There is a peculiar solemnity in the death-bed of the Christian, which no words can describe. He feels a deep and impressive interest in the blessed hope of a resurrection from the grave, to which he is soon to be conveyed.'[25]

Tomb sculpture in Britain and on the Continent reflected this concern with the death-bed, often influenced either by the type derived from Etruscan art in which the deceased is shown reclining on top of the tomb, or by the type of bas-relief panels on Roman sarcophagi. A good example of this second kind can be seen in a parish church near London, the tomb to Mrs. Margaret Petrie, sculpted by Thomas Banks in 1795 (*plate* VI. 9). The lady had been the widow of the Reverend Robert Petrie, and the monument was commissioned by the son, so that unlike most of the monuments discussed so far, it was not a grand, aristocratic or wealthy commission. Mrs. Petrie is shown lying in bed, humble and pious, attended by the Christian virtues of Religion, Hope and Faith. On the left, separated by a cippus, sits the weeping figure of the devoted son. The composition shows the elements usually employed by sculptors in their designs for this type of monument, the variations normally involving different numbers of mourners, who need not be allegorical but could all be members of the family. Usually all the figures surround the bed, without a separate division of the kind used on the Petrie monument. Sometimes mourners kneel close to the head of the dying person, and occasionally angels minister at the beside or hover overhead.

[24] Rev. W. Carus Wilson, *The Children's Friend: For the Year 1826* (Kirkby Lonsdale, 1826), pp. 49–56.

[25] Rev. William Steadman, *A Sermon preached at Hebden Bridge, near Halifax, August 10, 1817, on the occasion of the decease of the Rev. John Fawcett* (Halifax, 1817), p. 16; and Rev. Thomas Jervis, *A Sermon preached at the Dissenting Chapel, Lympstone, on Sunday, March XXVI, MDCCCXX, on the death of Mrs. Howorth* (Exeter, 1820), p. 24.

In his monument to Mrs. Petrie, Banks relied heavily on the classical past for both the general arrangement of his composition and for the details of dress and furnishings, so that the marble comes close to—but is not an actual copy of—several of the plates in one of the best known compendia of sarcophagi and other relief panels, namely Pietro Santi Bartoli's *Admiranda Romanorum Antiquitatum,* first published in 1685 (*plate* VI. 10). Banks has chosen a setting in the classical past, excluding any association that might remind one of a contemporary event. At the same time, however, the facial expressions, especially those of Mrs. Petrie and of Religion, are unmistakably modern in their sentiment.

When Banks exhibited the marble for this monument at the Royal Academy he concealed the identity of the deceased—as was customary in the catalogue—by using another title. He chose *The Death of Eloisa,* an interesting interpretation of the scene which would suit contemporary sentiment well, with its evocation of one of the most famous of all love stories. The new title only fits the panel, however, if one assumes that as an elderly Heloïse dies in her nunnery she remembers a youthful Abelard, which is presumably how one is supposed to transpose the mourning son on the left. In choosing his exhibition title (for which he does not give the source in the catalogue), it is quite likely that Banks had in mind Alexander Pope's poem 'Eloisa to Abelard', which was much admired in the eighteenth century for Pope's treatment of sensibility. Lines from the poem fit Banks's composition fairly closely:

> O Grace serene! oh Virtue heav'nly fair!
> Divine Oblivion of low-thoughted Care!
> Fresh blooming Hope, gay Daughter of the Sky!
> And Faith, our early Immortality!
> Enter, each mild, each amicable Guest;
> Receive, and wrap me in eternal Rest!
>   See in her Cell sad Eloïsa spread,
> Propt on some Tomb, a Neighbour of the Dead!

At the time of Banks's death in 1805 the most obvious fellow Academician to deliver a funerary oration was John Flaxman. He used the occasion to expound his views on seventeenth- and eighteenth-century sculpture in general, making many references to tombs, and when discussing Banks's achievement singled out the Petrie monument for special attention.[26] As a Christian and as a partially classically-orientated artist, Flaxman found much to admire in this tomb which he knew well, especially as he had himself designed two monuments in the same church, one of which was to Mrs. Petrie's husband. Flaxman said that he could find no other contemporary monument in either France or Italy to equal that by Banks, and he would even place the tomb to Mrs. Petrie amongst the ranks of classical

---

[26] Flaxman's address on Banks is printed in the second edition of his *Lectures,* pp. 271 ff.

antiquity, the highest praise that any writer of his generation could bestow on a work of art. The most important part of Flaxman's comments, however, is devoted to the Christian message conveyed by such pieces of sculpture. 'As the situation represented is the most important to humanity', Flaxman told his audience, 'so the expression is most powerfully penetrating, the dying woman is piously resigned, and the theological virtues which surround the bed, are such as you might expect to see,—the departed good, eminent for those qualities in a better state of existence: the son is an admirable human figure absorbed in grief'.

The Petrie monument depicts both the present grief of someone close to the deceased and Christian hope for the future. The pose of the son on this monument, and the piety which he expresses, find parallels in many other tombs of the period, often represented in the form of a female, cloaked figure of Resignation. The mood of such figures echoes the piety found in such a well-known, new collection as that of *The Olney Hymns*, to which William Cowper's contribution had included 'Submission':

> O Lord, my best desire fulfill,
>   And help me to resign
> Life, health and comfort to thy will,
>   And make thy pleasure mine.
>
> Why should I shrink at thy command,
>   Whose love forbids my fears?
> Or tremble at the gracious hand
>   That wipes away my tears? . . .

The figure of Resignation became interchangeable, in Flaxman's work at least, with the words from the Lord's Prayer, 'Thy will be done'. Flaxman used this line, together with two others from the same prayer, as the subjects of the three panels which constitute his monument to members of the Baring family in their local church in Hampshire. The chancel, where the panels are sited, was unfortunately remodelled later in the nineteenth century so that the sculptor's reason for employing three separate panels has been removed. The present plain wall was originally divided up by arcading, with the central and larger space filled by the theme of 'Thy will be done', flanked in the two smaller spaces by relief panels illustrating 'Deliver us from evil' and 'For thine is the Kingdom' (*plate* VI. 11).

In sculptures of this kind Flaxman created his most overtly Christian works. His frequent use of the spirit of the deceased rising to heaven became one of his best known images, which was to have a strong influence on subsequent tomb design, although Flaxman should not be credited with the exclusive use of this image since it was employed by other sculptors both in Britain and abroad at the same time, as well as by painters when depicting a variety of apotheoses. Flaxman's concept of the rising spirit was, however, familiar to contemporaries through his entries at Royal Academy exhibitions, contemporary engravings of the Baring monument issued in 1812, and the

150

posthumous publication as a small volume of lithographs of Flaxman's designs for the Lord's Prayer (published in 1835).[27]

One of Flaxman's most important uses of this kind of imagery was undoubtedly on the Baring monument. It was originally commissioned as a memorial to his wife by the wealthy Sir Francis Baring, financier and Chairman of the East India Company. Four years later, in 1810, Sir Francis himself died, and the monument then evolved into a tripartite one to commemorate not only the husband and wife, but also two grand-children. Sir Francis's son, Thomas, eventually paid the sculptor the enormous sum of £1,387, a particularly large figure for a private monument, which indicates the importance of this particular work in Flaxman's oeuvre. He used the opportunity to make one of his profoundly Christian statements in marble, with no references back to a classical, and pagan, antiquity. The Baring monument is a strong reminder that the Age of Reason had also been an age of Christian revival: the influence of both trends was to continue into the early years of the nineteenth century.

An alternative way of using a relief panel to express a specifically Christian content is provided by a type of monument depicting the virtues or the profession of the deceased not by an incident in his own life but by a related Biblical story or parable, such as that of the good Samaritan. A particularly interesting example of this kind of memorial is the one erected to Andrea Vaccà Berlinghieri in the cloisters of the Camposanto in Pisa, designed by the Danish sculptor Bertel Thorvaldsen (*plate* VI. 12), as eminent in his day as Flaxman and Canova. On the monument Berlinghieri himself has been relegated to a roundel at the top of the monument, leaving the space below for a large panel depicting Tobias in the act of curing his father's blindness, a direct allusion to Berlinghieri's reputation as a famous ophthalmologist. Further references to his medical profession are included in the main inscription, and also in the two snakes placed on either side of the medallion, symbolizing the power to heal.

Thorvaldsen chose a very classical type of tomb, the stele, which is particularly appropriate in this instance since the Camposanto's collection of Roman sarcophagi is displayed under the same arcading. The style of Thorvaldsen's tomb has much in common with that of such sarcophagi, and the impact of his story-telling panel is certainly more effective than if he had used an alternative idea which was, according to an early biographer, an urn decorated by the Tobias relief, surmounted by a portrait.[28] But although heavily influenced by his study of classical relief sculptures, Thorvaldsen has employed on the Berlinghieri monument a greater naturalism in his details, such as the faithful dog of Tobias's travels, the feathers of the

[27] Engravings of the Baring monument appeared in John Britton's *Fine Arts of the English School* (London, 1812).

[28] Melchiore Missirini, *Intera Collezione di tutte le opere ... Thorwaldsen* (Rome, 1831), II, text to plate 115.

151

Archangel Raphael's wings, and the basket on the ground. In the expression on the angel's face Thorvaldsen has employed a kind of sentiment that in the mid-1820s was still an essentially eighteenth-century one. The sensitive cutting of the marble is the result of the sculptor executing all the carving himself, and not delegating it to studio assistants, extremely successful and busy though his practice in Rome was at the time.[29] Thorvaldsen must therefore have regarded the Berlinghieri commission with particular affection. The combination in the design of the antique with sentiment and with naturalism epitomizes the dominant characteristics of the funerary arts of both his own and the previous generation.

The stele had become one of the most characteristic of the new types of church monument in Europe as well as in Britain by the end of the eighteenth century, showing the Neoclassical style at its most pure. The stele was the only form of classical monument to be copied in its entirety, with the exception of sarcophagi. Monuments were costly and church space increasingly limited, so that a stele which could be mounted on a wall had many practical advantages. At a time when classical taste was so very dominant, the entire concept of a stele could easily and economically be recreated. A whole sarcophagus, on the other hand, demanded more space. Complete neoclassical sarcophagi, such as Canova's project for his Nelson monument, are rare.

Monuments in the form of stele about 1800 are sometimes very close in both composition and style to their prototypes, completely pagan except perhaps for a Christian reference in the inscription. One of the best, and most beautiful, examples of this type of Neoclassical stele is the one erected in the atrium of Santi Apostoli in Rome, commemorating Giovanni Volpato (*plate* VI. 13). For this engraver and close friend, Canova produced a very sensitive design which he repeated, with alterations, in other commissions. Volpato's portrait, a recognizably realistic image, is presented as a large, Roman Imperial bust. It is mounted on a pedestal on which the sculptor has recorded his gratitude for Volpato's part in obtaining for him the important commission for the monument to Pope Clement XIV which is inside the same church, and which had firmly established Canova's reputation two decades earlier as the leading designer of tombs in Italy. That Canova should have chosen the form of a stele for the monument to a man who played such an influential part in his own life (and whose ashes are actually buried in another church), is indicative of the important role that Canova allotted to this new type of monument. In front of the bust sits a weeping figure of Friendship, whose dress, hairstyle and sandals are all correctly classical in their detailing, as are the stool and the architectural motifs of the pediment. Friendship's pose of languid grief, similar in mood to that of Italy on the

[29] Dyveke Helsted, 'Thorvaldsens Arbeitsmethode', in Gerhard Bott, *Bertel Thorvaldsen* (Cologne, 1977), p. 13, quotes a letter by the architect F. F. Friis in 1829, which says that the sculptor worked on this monument himself 'Vom ersten bis zum letzten Meissel'.

Alfieri monument (on which Canova was working at the same time), caused one sympathetic contemporary critic to write of her attitude that it was so full of 'such tender and devoted regret, that she seems to say, "Here will I remain with thee for ever" ': an interpretation both pious and sentimental.[30]

The next generation, especially from the 1840s, was to attack this importation of classical imagery into Christian churches, advocating its replacement by a return to the Christian art of Gothic Europe. In a typically peremptory passage, one such writer penned: 'The urn and sarcophagus—strange ornaments in a Christian Temple!'[31] The new taste which Diderot had been reflecting back in the 1760s was finally on the wane, to be replaced by a stylistically much more complex scene by the middle of the nineteenth century.[32]

[30] Countess Albrizzi, op. cit., II, not paginated, 'Monument of Giovanni Volpato'.
[31] J. H. Markland, *Remarks on English Churches* (Oxford, 1840), p. 10.
[32] The author would like to thank the Carnegie Trust for the Universities of Scotland for awarding a grant which helped towards the cost of research for some of this article.

153

VII

From Ritual to Ceremony:
Death Ritual and Society in Hindu North India
since 1600*

C. A. BAYLY

Hindu India never developed a rich mortuary art like that of the ancient cultures of China and Egypt. The most famous mausoleum in the subcontinent, the Taj Mahal, is a Muslim monument; and if Indians were asked to single out any group for the intrinsic interest of their funerary rites, they would probably choose the Zoroastrian Parsis who exposed their dead in the famous 'Towers of Silence'. Yet the funeral services and rites for ancestors of the orthodox Hindus embody beliefs central to their whole philosophy and provide a dramatic display of the essential features of the still-tenacious caste system. The rites themselves are also remarkably ancient. They were recorded as early as the *Laws of Manu* in the second or third century B.C.[1] They appear in elaborate and often gruesome exegesis in the later books called the *Purānas,* especially the *Markandeya Purāna (circa* A.D. 400–800);[2] and the practice of the orthodox remains outwardly similar today, even though attitudes to the rituals and their institutional context have changed over recent generations.[3]

It is perhaps this appearance of continuity which has discouraged historians of medieval and modern India from taking much interest in death rituals, or indeed in rituals of any kind. This is a curious omission in a society which has given over so much of its time and its disposable income to ritual, and where funerals are so much part of the fabric of daily life. Anthropologists have, of course, used the form of funerals to elucidate their theories of social,[4]

*I have been unusually dependent on the ideas and insights of others in writing this essay. Professor J. C. Heesterman of the University of Leiden has been particularly indulgent to my stumblings in a field where he has much greater expertise. Mr. J. B. Harrison of the School of Oriental and African Studies, London, and Professor Eric Stokes, Dr. C. J. Baker, Rev. Dr. Ian Clark of Cambridge, Dr. S. B. Kaufmann and Professor Walter Hauser of the University of Virginia have all been very helpful.

[1] *Manu. The Laws,* trans. G. Buhler (Oxford, 1886), III, 123–6.

[2] *Markandeya Purāna,* trans. F. E. Pargiter (Calcutta, 1904), pp. 66–8, canto X.

[3] For recent ethnographic discussions see, D. Pocock, *Kanbi and Patidar. A Study of the Patidar Community of Gujarat* (Oxford, 1972), pp. 119–25; J. Parry, *Caste and Kinship in Kangra* (London, 1979), pp. 64–6; A. C. Mayer, *Caste and Kinship in Central India* (London, 1960), pp. 87–9.

[4] H. Orenstein, 'Death and Kinship in Hinduism. Structural and Functional Interpretations', *American Anthropologist,* LXXII, 1970, 1357–77; for an earlier analysis E. Bendann, *Death Customs. An Analytical Study of Burial Rites* (New York, 1930).

and more recently mental structure.[5] But no periodization of the institutions or of the attitudes to death comparable to that of Ariès or Stannard has been attempted.

This essay begins to trace some lines of historical change in three elements of the funeral practice and ideology of high-caste north Indians. The first is the cremation itself and the customs associated with it. The second is the series of rites called *shrāddha* or *parvana shrāddha,* roughly translated as 'pious oblations for the dead', which take place among high castes between ten and twelve days after cremation and thereafter on the monthly and annual anniversaries of death. Third, there are the irregular oblations which richer and more religious people continue to make to the spirits of the ancestors for up to three generations after death at the most holy pilgrimage places of Hinduism. These *shrāddha* rites were traditionally thought to aid in the transformation of the spirit of the dead (*prēta*) into a hallowed and beneficent ancestor (*pitr,* cognate with the Latin *pater,* father).

The essay shows that no abrupt and widespread changes in attitudes to or institutions of death occurred in Hindu India over the last three centuries or so, but that there were significant changes of emphasis. These changes reflect and elucidate modifications in the ideology and inner institutions of Hinduism as it emerged from the period of Muslim rule, faced the influx of Christian missionary teaching, and came to terms with western rationalism and intrusive government. Yet the word 'reflect' is inadequate, for until the last few generations the ritual arena has not simply been a passive mirror of social changes outside; ritual has been an active force in the creation of the Indian social order, a realm of conflict and danger where new statuses can be asserted or destroyed.

To understand the changes of emphasis in death rituals in recent centuries, it is necessary to grasp that Hindu funerary institutions and ideologies were never entirely consistent, even in the ancient culture.[6] There was a hidden contradiction between what might be called the 'tribal' side of the ritual and the philosophies and devotional ideas which gave it meaning. The tribal aspect was concerned with succouring the dead spirits and 'making' ancestors. Its aim was to get the soul of the deceased rapidly into heaven through prayer and oblation, and to confirm the unity and moral continuity of the extended family group. An ulterior but related motive was often to exalt the genealogy of the bereaved family through the conspicuous gifting of priests and by lavish donations at the holy places. But in the eyes of the devotional and philosophical movements which derived from the same corpus of literature and tradition, death rites were at most an act of commemoration and

---

[5] e.g., Meena Kaushik, 'The Symbolic Representation of Death'. *Contributions to Indian Sociology, New Series,* X, 2, 1976, 265–92.

[6] I am indebted to Prof. Heesterman for clarifying this point; for the wider context see his 'India and the Inner Conflict of Tradition', *Daedalus,* winter 1973, 97–113.

an opportunity for rededication by the living, with little influence on the ultimate fate of the dead.

This contradiction in attitudes to the meaning of ritual becomes clear if we consider philosophy. It was the doctrine of transmigration of souls and *karma* which was the spinal cord of the mature Hindu cosmological system.[7] *Karma* implies that the moral and physical status of beings in this world reflects the cumulative energy of their actions for evil or good in past incarnations. They can only attain salvation (*moksha*) by the progressive enhancement of their spirituality over countless rebirths. Now clearly, the notion of this austere and impersonal moral calculus working over aeons of time is not easy to fit with the belief that the dead man's relatives can intervene by appropriate rituals to secure him a quick place in a personal heaven. 'The law of karma is inexorable and impossible of evasion. There is thus hardly any need for God to interfere', states Gandhi.[8] But even those Hindus who put more faith in devotion to a direct personal God were often inclined to reduce the rituals of cremation and *shrāddha* to a mere ceremony of commemoration. Originally the divergent elements of funerary ideology must have arisen from the amalgamation of ancient Vedic rites with the later philosophical schemes of *karma* and transmigration.[9] But in more recent times this ambiguity of ideology meant that within a single local society there could simultaneously exist pressures to elaborate funerary rites for tribal or genealogical purposes, and movements which wished to reduce them to simple acts of commemoration. This ambiguity has persisted to the present, but the essay argues that the intervention of the missionaries and the colonial state has tended indirectly to strengthen the austere, philosophical element at the expense of the 'tribal'. Foreign influence therefore acted not to create a new mentality but to begin to resolve a contradiction within the traditional ideology.

Before passing on to the rituals themselves, two further points must be made. The first is negative and relates to the problem of generalization. The practices and ideas discussed here were those of high caste and urban people in north India. But much of the tribal and lower caste population had only tenuous links with the religion of the Brahmin. Amongst them death rituals continued to have a strong undertone of propitiation, even of exorcism: malevolent spirits of all sorts were conjured to be still. There is, for instance, the famous story of the mischievous spirit of the English conqueror of a south Indian district which could only be stilled by regular offerings of

---

[7] For references see 'srāddha' in M. and J. Stutely, *A Dictionary of Hinduism* (London, 1977); A. C. Lyall, *Asiatic Studies* (London, 1907), p. 46; K. Walli, *Theory of Karman in Indian Thought* (Varanasi, 1977), pp. 127–204.

[8] M. K. Gandhi, *An Autobiography or the Story of my Experiments with Truth* (6th edn., Ahmedabad, 1956) p. 242.

[9] A. B. Keith, *The Religion of the Veda and Upanishads* (Cambridge, Mass., 1925), p. 416; D. R. Shastri, *Origin and Development of the Rituals of Ancestor Worship in India* (Calcutta, 1963), p. 6.

brandy and cigars.[10] Even amongst the high caste, though, practice differs markedly from district to district: less than four hundred miles from Benares there were Brahmins who buried their dead as late as the nineteenth century. Nevertheless, the importance of the orthodox rituals of the high castes cannot be underestimated. The pattern for the last two thousand years at least has been for Brahmanic rituals to come to serve as a reference point for the lower castes and tribal peoples.[11] The growth of settled agriculture, the development of towns and of larger political units have everywhere provided the context for the slow assimilation of priestly to popular religion.

Secondly, the meaning of ritual and the direction of change is closely related to the caste system itself. Caste, of course, is the subject of acute scholarly debate, but most modern writers are agreed on one thing: that caste was and is much more flexible and 'negotiable' than was commonly thought in the nineteenth century.[12] Obviously, the ideal ranking of Brahmin Priest, Warrior, Merchant and Labourer was static, and in modern times it has proved difficult for individuals or families to secure recognition of a change in their caste status in a single generation. But the key unit within Indian society is the larger circle of families which, recognizing themselves to be of the same 'generic substance', marry and eat together (the *jati*). In India there are hundreds of thousands of 'caste' groups in this sense, and their rank within the wider system has often been uncertain or capable of improvement through appropriate transactions with other groups. The most usual manner of edging upwards the status of one's own group has been to adopt the ritual customs and life-style of another group of unimpeachable caste status. The thinking behind this is quite simple. While caste appears in practice as a set of hereditary occupational groupings, its underlying rationale is as a hierarchy of purity and pollution.[13] Association with pure people and pure practices will therefore raise status, while association with the impure will degrade it.

So ritual can be seen as a dramatic embodiment of caste: as something that perpetuates it, but also at times as an arena in which 'negotiation' for higher status can occur. At the simplest level, the adoption of orthodox funerary patterns and *shrāddhas* for the ancestors could help establish a group's claim to be of clean caste status, since it associated them with Brahmin priests and other monitors who were absent from the rites of the impure. But once on the ladder, caste groups could use the order, duration

---

[10] R. Caldwell, *The Tinnevelly Shanars. A Sketch of their Religion and their Moral Condition and Characteristics* (London, 1850), p. 43.

[11] The classic statement of this process of 'sanskritization' was by M. N. Srinivas, *Caste in Modern India and other Essays* (London, 1962).

[12] See, e.g., McKim Marriot, 'Multiple Reference in Indian Caste Systems' in J. Silverberg (ed.) *Social Mobility in the Caste System in India* (1968), pp. 103–4; see also Marriot and R. Inden, 'Caste Systems', *New Encyclopaedia Britannica*, III (New York, 1974), 985–95.

[13] L. Dumont, *Homo Hierarchicus. The Caste System and its Implications,* translated by M. Sainsbury (London, 1970); L. Dumont and D. F. Pocock, 'Pure and Impure', *Contributions to Indian Sociology,* Old Series, vol. III, 9–39.

and form of the rites as an implicit claim for higher status yet. Very logically, the lower the caste the longer post-funerary rituals and oblation needed to be. Death was polluting, so Brahmins, being particularly pure, could remove the impurity of death in a shorter time.[14] This was usually deemed to be eleven days of ritual, rather than the fifteen days enjoined on middling caste groups, or the forty days which lower castes were supposed to undergo. Over time, then, many caste groups in an ambiguous position on the ritual ladder have sought to negotiate for higher status by shortening and simplifying their funerary ritual. Even here, though, we often glimpse the contradiction. Prestigious families needed to be seen as more pure, even austere. But at the same time, those which were involved in warfare and the politics of rural society needed to be seen as great and generous feast-giving men with exalted genealogies (the 'tribal' element). Changes in ritual often seemed, then, to be pointing in two directions at the same time.

DEATH, CREMATION AND OBLATION

Death in India was regarded as a process rather than an event. In fact some classes of people such as ascetics were regarded as 'living dead', and had already gone through funeral rites. Life was thought to consist of the conjunction of various elements such as hearing, sight, locomotion and substance which were paradigms of the basic structure of the universe.[15] Hindu physiology was therefore governed by a philosophical system markedly different from that of the post-Renaissance west, and this was to cause conflict in the nineteenth century. There was no notion of the overriding importance of the activity of the heart or brain. Instead, on the approach of death, the elementary parts of being, fifteen in number, unite with their respective origins; their corporeal faculties, such as vision and feeling, return to their original sources, the sun, the air, and so on. The loss of sight, of hearing, or of locomotion was regarded as a stage in physical dissolution rather than as the manifestation of an 'illness' which might terminate in death. So, for instance, a man who put his fingers in his ears and could not hear the usual buzzing was warned of the approach of death. It was a clear sign that the elemental deity Vayu who presided over hearing had left him.[16]

The spiritual and physical composition of the dying person was thought to alter as further signs of dissolution appeared. It was imperative to give

[14] Parry, *Kangra*, pp. 139–40; for caste differences in degrees of pollution the old Indian provincial and district gazetteers are an invaluable source, see e.g., H. C. Conybeare, F. H. Fisher and J. P. Hewett, *Statistical, Descriptive and Historical Account of the North-Western Provinces of India*, VII, (Allahabad, 1884), 75–7; Mayer, *Caste and Kinship*, p. 87.
[15] B. Subbararayappa, 'The Indian Doctrine of the Five Elements', *Indian Journal of the History of Science*, I, 1966, 53; J. C. Ghose, *The English Works of Raja Ram Mohun Roy compiled and published by Eshan Chunder Bose* (Calcutta, 1885), I, 34.
[16] A. M. Stevenson, *The Rites of the Twice Born* (Oxford, 1920), p. 137.

the spirit access to the pure elements and preferably to a sacred river by which it could begin its journey to the realms of Yama, Lord of the Dead. Moving the dying onto the ground, outside the house, or even to a riverside burning place (burning *ghāt*) minimized the pollution of death in the household and also helped ensure that the entrapped spirit did not become a malignant ghost.

After all signs of life had left the body, there began a series of rites which were not generally complete for three generations (by which time the ancestor was deemed to have achieved beatitude), and lasted with great intensity for at least thirteen days. In normal circumstances the body was cremated at a caste burning ground usually near a river; the putative heir lit the pyre. Special funerary priests called *mahabrāhmins* conducted the ceremony of cremation, while monitors of the scavenging Dom caste actually handled the corpse and tended the fire. One consequence of the cremation itself was to perpetuate ranking within the caste system through proximity to the pollution of death. So the position of the Dom scavengers at the bottom of the caste hierarchy was reinforced, while the cremation priests, absorbing the sins and death of the deceased through the 'sacrifice' of the dead body, assured themselves of the most lowly position among Brahmins. The quality of the priests and the length of the rituals also ranked the family and kin of the dead man both in terms of other castes and by degree of relationship to him. The closer the blood tie, the deeper the pollution of death and the more protracted the rituals of purification.

The *shrāddha* oblations proper were not begun until the worst of the pollution of death had been removed. This was usually on the tenth day after the cremation among the highest castes, and proportionately later for others. Numerous offerings were also made on the important eleventh and twelfth days when it was also considered auspicious to lay on feasts for Brahmins and caste-fellows. Thereafter *shrāddha* offerings became less intense except on the monthly and annual commemorations of the death day, and at certain regular festivals. In orthodox households the offerings them-selves consisted of groups of balls of kneaded rice and wheat paste, mixed with various ritual substances such as honey and milk. These *pindas*, as they are known, were thought to form the actual food of the spirit in its first painful transitional phase as a tiny 'vapour body' beginning its hazardous ascent to the status of an ancestor. Later *shrāddhas*, particularly those made at holy places were supposed to consolidate the status of the ancestor as a beneficent influence in the life of the family and to aid its rapid transition to heaven. This was usually deemed to have occurred after three generations when the personal name of the ancestor was no longer used at the *shrāddhas*. But among the pious, wealthy and orthodox, the practice of *shrāddha* at particularly holy places became more and more popular during the first centuries of the Christian era. So at centres such as Benares, Gaya and Hardwar, there emerged a distinct set of *shrāddha* and pilgrimage priests

159

who maintained records and became the hereditary genealogists of particular sets of families.

What we have called the 'tribal' element was prominent in all these rites. The word for 'relation' in Hindi, *sapinda,* is probably derived from the word *pinda,* the rice ball used in oblation. In this interpretation, the 'relations' were those up to the seventh (or sometimes tenth) degree of relationship whose right and duty it was to offer *shrāddha* for the deceased. In the Dayabhaga school of law which became prominent in eastern India after the twelfth century A.D. the claim to heirship was actually considered to proceed from the competence to perform oblations.[17] Thus people such as barren women who were disqualified from doing *shrāddha* were also disqualified from inheritance. More commonly, the claim to heirship seems to have been capable of decision in the ritual arena. So in a Benares law case of 1783 (which had been appealed from a caste council) the identity of the person who lit the funeral pyre was important evidence of inheritance.[18]

As a genealogical event of such significance to the moral and physical continuity of the family,[19] it was natural that funeral rituals would become embellished. Large *shrāddha* feasts at which a maximum number of relatives and priests were present became common. At the holy places, great men and political leaders began consciously to outdo each other in their gifts of money and lands to the *shrāddha* priests, or in the construction of burning and bathing *ghāts.* But as J. C. Heesterman points out,[20] developments such as these were always to a greater or lesser extent at variance with scriptural authority and the high philosophy. *The Laws of Manu,* for instance, enjoin a small company at *shrāddha,* at most three people and preferably only one learned Brahmin.[21] In the next section we go on to show how these contradictory tendencies were worked out in the century immediately preceding colonial rule. The emergence of new ruling dynasties during these years gave added impetus to the tribal and genealogical aspect of *shrāddha* which was especially visible at the holy places. But the strong anti-ritualism of devotional movements continued to represent the opposite philosophical tendency.

FUNERARY POMP AND PILGRIMAGE CENTRES IN THE IMMEDIATE PRE-COLONIAL PERIOD 1600–1800

From an early period particular centres which were associated with sacred rivers and their purifying properties became centres of Hindu pilgrimage.

---

[17] J. D. M. Derrett, *A Critique of Modern Hindu Law* (Delhi, 1970), p. 176; J. C. Ghose, *The Principle of Hindu Law* (Calcutta, 1903), p. 32.
[18] Proceedings of the Resident of Benares, 6 January 1792, 'Case of Bedamo *v.* Bhowanny Singh', Central Record Office, Allahabad.
[19] See Paul Oltramare, 'Le Rôle du Yajamana dans le Sacrifice Brahminique', *Muséon,* IV, 1903, 7–8.
[20] Personal communication to the author, 1979.
[21] P. V. Kane, *History of Dharmashastra* (Poonah, 1962), V, part II, 930–2.

For 'Just as certain limbs of the body are purer than others, so are certain places on earth more sacred'.[22] In the course of time, a hierarchy of holy places emerged in which the shrines of local godlings and sanctified human spirits were subordinated to a small number of *mahātma tirthas,* or places of special spiritual merit which were venerated in regular cycle by the most orthodox. The pattern was already established by the time of the great corpus of medieval Hindu lore, the *Purānas,* which were compiled from earlier sources between about A.D. 400 and 1000. These places achieved special importance for the performance of *shrāddha* rites because of the relationship between the concept of 'property' and 'competence to perform rites'.[23] It was held that a man could not achieve spiritual benefit from sacrifice on another man's property. The emergence of more sharply defined property rights in early medieval India probably contributed to the import- ance of holy places; since these were sanctified to the gods, anyone could sacrifice there without infringing on the privilege of others. Three such places were the cities of Allahabad, Benares and Gaya which were set on or near the river Ganges in the heartland of orthodox Hinduism. It is with the elaboration of ancestral rites at these three cities that we are concerned here.

First we need to distinguish between some of the types of death rituals which occured at the holy cities. They all saw the normal volume of funerary activity necessary in any large centre of population with its burning grounds adjacent to streams and rivers. But these cities, and especially Benares, also supported large numbers of elderly people who had come specifically to die in the holy places on the Ganges and so achieve immediate salvation. These communities of the moribund were quite large. In Benares between 1880 and 1908, there was an annual surplus of deaths over births of about 24 per cent or 2–3,000 people out of a population of about 180,000,[24] and qualitative evidence suggests that this had long been the case. Allahabad, on the other hand, was held in particular repute as a place to which lepers and others with festering diseases should go to die. A verse in the *Brāhma Purāna* lists the appropriate means of suicide for those about to perish from 'unnatural diseases', 'by fire, starvation . . . by ascending to paradise by a respectful pilgrimage to the Himalaya mountains . . . or by precipitating himself from the sacred Vuta tree at Allahabad, even a great sinner shall meet with supreme bliss in Paradise'.[25] The 'Vuta Tree' was supposed to be located

[22] S. M. Bhardwaj, *Hindu Places of Pilgrimage in India. A Study in Cultural Geography* (Berkeley, 1973), p. 84.
[23] cf. J. D. M. Derrett, *Essays in Classical and Modern Hindu Law* (Leiden, 1975), II, 25, 45.
[24] H. R. Nevill, *District Gazetteers of the United Provinces,* XXVI, *Benares* (Allahabad, 1909), pp. 23–4, Appendices.
[25] cited *Parliamentary Papers* [hereafter *PP*], *1821 Session,* XVIII, 320, 'East India. Widow's Custom of Suttee'.

near the great fort in Allahabad and lepers' suicides were common there until the British authorities forbade them in the 1810s.

The third category of death rituals associated with the holy cities were *shrāddhas* performed by people who came from all over India to honour their ancestors and speed their transition to Paradise. Such pilgrims would, of course, have performed the initial cremation and rites in their home villages, but occasional pilgrimage was considered particularly valuable. Usually these *shrāddhas* were combined with bathing, penance and charitable donation to release the pilgrim himself from his worst sins. It was the city of Gaya in the modern state of Bihar which achieved a particular reputation as an appropriate place for oblations to the ancestors.[26] The proper rites done within the sacred circle of Gaya were supposed to 'procure the immediate admission of [the pilgrim's] ancestors to Heaven'[27] and made further performance of *shrāddha* for them unnecessary. In popular mythology Gaya represented the prone body of a primaeval giant who had obtained by heroic austerities the gift of sending to heaven the souls of sinners who approached him without their passing through the realms of Yama, Lord of the Dead.

These holy places were already established as all-India places of pilgrimage long before A.D. 1200.[28] But it was in a much more recent period that they took on their opulent and elaborate character as ritual complexes. Few buildings in Allahabad or Benares appear to date in their present form from before 1600. The majority of the great bathing and cremation wharves (*ghāts*) on the River Ganges in Benares were constructed in the years 1730 to 1810 and most of the major temples and rest houses for pilgrims and Brahmins which dot the city appear to date from the same period.[29] So, too, many of the most prestigious of the Brahmin teachers and scholars who inhabited the city in the nineteenth century traced their families' arrival there to the sixteenth and seventeenth centuries at the earliest. Though Gaya's rise to ritual pre-eminence can be dated back to the thirteenth century, the majority of its temples were also built between 1700 and 1800.[30] The Vishnu Temple, the most celebrated building here, was erected by the female ruler of the central Indian state of Indore as late as 1770, while the other chief temple, the Gajadhar, appears to have been built about 1700 and modified in the following century. Fragmentary evidence on population and the area of the cities also suggests a very rapid advance between 1650 and

[26] Shastri, *Ancestor Worship,* pp. 255–70; J. D. M. Derrett in A. L. Basham (ed.), *A Cultural History of India* (Oxford, 1975), p. 130.

[27] Montgomery Martin (ed.), *The History, Antiquities, Topography and Statistics of Eastern India,* I, *Behar (Patna City) and Shahabad* (London, 1838), 51.

[28] Bhardwaj, *Places of Pilgrimage,* p. 17.

[29] Interviews by the author Chaukhambha, Dasaswamedh *Ghāt,* Varanasi, 1972–4; Proceedings of the resident of Benares and Duncan Records, 1786–1830, Central Records Office, Allahabad; Moti Chandra, *Kāshi kā Itihāsa* (Bombay, 1962), Part II, Ch. 5; Nevill, *Benares gazetteer,* p. 237.

[30] Martin, *Eastern India,* I, 58–62; cf. Shastri, *Ancestor Worship,* p. 263.

1800. This growth was associated with more general patterns of urbanization in north India. What sorts of changes in contemporary society did it reflect?

First, the growth of the pilgrimage and funerary cities reflected the unity conferred on India through the consolidation of the Moghul Empire, paradoxically a Muslim state. The Moghuls, working from a heartland around Delhi had absorbed into their domain Hindu Bengal to the east, and, before the end of the seventeenth century, large areas of central and western India. The empire was linked together by a network of fortified small towns and military roads which were served by wells, groves and inns (*caravansarais*). At its height before 1720, Moghul rule gave greater security to the long-distance traveller or pilgrim than he had ever before enjoyed. Indeed, the state had a direct interest in promoting easy mobility between the various regions of India as it derived substantial revenues from trade and came to levy a charge on the pilgrims attending the ritual centres. The famous Moghul administrative treatise, the *Ain-i-Akbari*,[31] describes in detail the Hindu holy places and the practices which took place there, for they played a considerable role in the commercial and social fabric of the Empire. At Allahabad, Benares and the more westerly holy places it was the great Hindu servants of the Moghul Empire, and particularly the princes of Rajasthan, who initiated the modern phase of building in the holy cities.

The consolidation of Empire and the expansion of communications stimulated further social changes which diffused the fame of Benares and Gaya. The growth of commerce and the payment of the land-revenue in money tended to absorb into the settled agriculture of the plains tribal, nomadic and warrior communities. Indirectly this process of settlement modified the culture of the fringe communities, often spreading amongst them more orthodox 'sanskritic' or 'brahminical' modes of worship.[32] Many such groups had buried their dead and had not subscribed to belief in transmigration. Their adoption of the classical rituals of cremation and *shrāddha* was, therefore, of great importance, since it registered not only their acceptance of the outward ritual of orthodox Hinduism, but also of the nominal supremacy of the Brahmin and the caste system.

The relationship between orthodox Hinduism and the marginal and low caste communities was extremely complex. It is no longer possible to see the latter moving in a straightforward progression from 'animism' to 'sanskritic Hinduism' as was once thought. Instead, these communities were constantly moving in and out of contact with the Hinduism of the Brahmin, consciously selecting aspects of orthodox ritual which could be accommodated within their universe and rejecting others. Nevertheless, the processes of agricultural expansion and political settlement increased the village and tribal clientele from whom the Brahmins and specialists of the holy places drew support.

[31] Abul Fazl, *Ain-i-Akbari*, trans. H. Blochmann, 2 vols. (Calcutta, 1872, 77).
[32] See, e.g., M. N. Srinivas, *Religion and Society among the Coorgs of South India* (Oxford, 1952).

During the course of the eighteenth and nineteenth centuries, for instance, the Chero and Buiyar tribal populations of central India appear to have adopted *shrāddha* ceremonies.[33] Many lower caste groups in the settled areas too were able to employ wealth accumulated through local trade and service to move nearer to the practice of the higher castes. Funerary orthodoxy was one aspect of this.

Not all the 'new Hindus' of the nineteenth century emerged from tribal, 'animist' or low caste backgrounds. Some were reconverts from Islamic practice. Communities which had been associated with Muslim government service or commerce had sometimes adopted Islamic customs, including burial. Most striking, perhaps, was the case of the Bishnois, a commercial community living in the small Muslim military centres near Delhi. The Bishnois had adopted Muslim names, marriage customs and burial ritual, though they continued to worship Hindu deities. This anomaly was explained by the story that Bishnois once murdered a Muslim judicial officer who had prevented them from burning a Hindu widow along with her husband's corpse, and 'compounded for the offence by pretending to embrace Islam'.[34] But as Muslim power and cultural influence waned all over north India at the end of the eighteenth and beginning of the nineteenth centuries, many of these apostates adopted, or re-adopted, Hindu funerary customs. It was from the elites of these communities also that Allahabad, Gaya and Benares drew their growing numbers of pilgrims.

Weakening Muslim cultural influence was matched in the eighteenth century by the rise of new regional Hindu regimes which inherited the fragmented satrapies of the old empire. It was among the rulers of these new, predominantly Hindu states—the Mahrattas in the west, the Jats near Delhi and the Bhumihar and Rajput rulers of the Gangetic plain itself—that the holy and funerary cities found their most energetic patrons. These ruling dynasties were often themselves drawn from nomadic or peasant communities of relatively low caste status. An essential aspect of the consolidation of their power was a claim to legitimacy which entailed regular association with the cult centres of orthodox Hinduism.[35] By acquiring priests of sufficiently high status to perform ceremonies such as *shrāddha*, these princes could hope to justify their claim to Kshatriya (Warrior) status which was the pride of the older Hindu ruling houses. The repetition and sanctification of the names of ancestors also aided in the creation of genealogical traditions in which their ancestors appeared as semi-divine descendants of the Sun and Moon.

[33] E. A. H. Blunt, *The Caste System of Northern India with special Reference to the United Provinces of Agra and Oudh* (reprint, New Delhi, 1969), p. 289.

[34] *Census of India 1911. The United Provinces of Agra and Oudh*, XV, part I, *Report* (Allahabad, 1912), p. 364.

[35] Satish Chandra, 'Social Background to the Rise of the Mahratta Movement during the Seventeenth Century in India', *The Indian Social and Economic History Review*, X, 3, 1973, 209–18; see also, e.g., Raoji Vasudeva Tullu, 'Mahesvara in Malwa', *The Indian Antiquary*, IV, 1875, 346.

The process of caste elevation was encouraged by the military and official Brahmin families who inhabited the territories of the rising dynasties. It was this simultaneous drive for political power and ritual status which accounts for the rising flood of Mahratta pilgrims to Allahabad, Benares and Gaya during the course of the eighteenth century, and the *ghāt* and temple building of Mahratta lords.[36] By 1820, nearly 8 per cent of the resident population of Benares was Mahratta and the city was regularly visited by armed Mahratta pilgrimages of up to 200,000 men in the more auspicious years. At Gaya, Bengalis and Mahrattas were the largest classes of pilgrims:

> Mahrattas give [to the priests] money, jewels, plate, fine cloth, elephants and horses. The very lowest person performing his devotions at one place cannot spend less including duties than 3½ Rs.; those who worship at two places cannot spend less than 5 Rs.; but many spend 100 Rs. ... almost all the Mahrattas worship at 45 places, and several every year give 5,000 Rs.; while great chiefs expend 40 or even 50,000 Rs.[37]

It was in the elaboration of *shrāddha*, funeral feasts, offerings to the priests and offerings to the deity Yama that Hindu nobles displayed the honour of their ancestors. The notion that the spirit departed rapidly to adjudication and to a new incarnation did not encourage the creation of grandiose 'houses for the dead' like those of western classical antiquity. Nor was there any direct analogy in orthodox Hinduism to the idea of the resurrection of the body from its own tomb. The art of Hindu India did not, therefore, develop a tradition of portraiture and civic commemorative architecture such as we find in the west. Ritual itself was the art-form of pious commemoration.

The ritual specialists also took an active part in spreading the fame and reputation for sanctity of the holy places, emphasizing in particular the great merit to the ancestors derived from performing *shrāddha* there. The orthodox hierarchy was not simply a static 'point of reference', as it often seems to be in ethnographical works; it was an active force shaping society. With a near-monopoly over the written word, Brahmins were able to embroider and build up references to Benares, Gaya and other places in everyday devotional works, such as the *Purānas* which were subject to constant revision and recension. The flow of Brahmins for instruction to the holy cities spread the fame of Kashi (Benares the Illustrious) or Gaya Mahatmya (Place of Great Merit) to a wider and wider audience. Many Puranic interpolations seem to date from the period between the end of the first millennium A.D. and the eighteenth century. In an early interpolation, the *Vishnu Purāna* has a troubled ancestral spirit proclaim,

---

[36] Moti Chandra, *Kāshi,* part II, ch. V.
[37] Martin, *History of Eastern India,* I, 54.

> Would that a wise and blessed person be born in our family who not indulging in stinginess in spending wealth will offer wheat cakes to us, and would donate to the Brahmins for our sake jewels, clothes, a large conveyance, wealth and all enjoyments.[38]

Another adds in a practical frame of mind that the ancestor of anyone who presents a Brahmin with an umbrella during *shrāddha* would be protected from rain and sunstroke during his hazardous journey to the realms of Yama.[39] Echoing the complacency of all ancient seats of learning, a third verse asserts that a Brahmin of Gaya or Muttra who does not 'even know a single verse' of the Vedas is superior to Brahmins in all other places.

Before 1800, *shrāddha* at Gaya and Benares had become large-scale ritual industries. Ledgers still held by the ancestral *shrāddha* priests or *pāndas* (*Prāgwals* at Allahabad; *Gāyawals* at Gaya) illustrate a system of checking and accounting by which the specialists maintained and enhanced their clienteles. If one investigates the streets behind the great bathing *ghats* of Benares, one might encounter Gajendra Nath Phattack. This man calls himself the chief priest of the Manikarnika *ghat* which adjoins the major cremation *ghāt* of the city.[40] He adds the title of 'Royal Preceptor' (*Rājguru*) because his family has acted as *shrāddha* priest and ritual genealogist for fifty-two princely houses over the last twenty generations or so. Like his ancestors before him, Gajendra Nath is the head of a hierarchy of lesser priests and ritual servants on the riverside. His ancestral clientele is of mixed caste but there is a strong bias towards the great warrior-landowner families of the state of Rajasthan who were the most prestigious donors at the holy places during the zenith of the Moghul Empire. Inscriptions on copper plates in the possession of the priest record the visits to Benares of, among others, the Raja of Bundhi and his train in 1658, 1680, 1727 and 1842.[41] On each occasion, the king formally accepted the head of the priestly family as his *pānda*, recognized earlier grants and donations made by his ancestors, performed *shrāddha,* and then gave a further donation to the priest. During the 1842 pilgrimage the then maharaja presented the priest with the revenues of a large area of land in Rajasthan and began the construction of a royal temple in one of the quarters of the city.[42] The visits of persons of lesser status were recorded on sheets of paper, and after about 1680 entered in a ledger book.[43] Here one can see the entries of men from as far afield as Delhi and the Punjab in Urdu, Persian and Hindi. There are also notes on the

---

[38] *Vishnu Purāna* cited P. V. Kane, *History of Dharmashastra,* V part II, 931–2.

[39] *Markandeya Purāna,* trans. Pargiter, canto 68–9.

[40] Family tree in possession of Sri G. N. Phattakh, chief *purohit* Manikarnika Ghat and interview March 1973.

[41] Copper plates in possession of Sri Phattakh dated *Sambat* (Indian Era), 1715, 1737 and 1899.

[42] Copper plate dated *Phāgun Baddi* 11 *Sambat* 1899.

[43] The author holds a microfilm of the record book which is now in the possession of Sri Devi Narayan, Sakshi Binayak, Varanasi.

arbitration of conflicts between the *pānda* and his colleagues over their clients;[44] and records of gifts and grants. Until the present century, the *pāndas* would make regular tours of the distant areas in which their clients were most numerous to remind them of the needs of their ancestors.

Other ritual specialists also benefited from the growth of ancestral oblation at the holy city. Ordinary bathing-priests incorporated their particular *ghāts* and temples into the ever more complex ritual round. Each ritual event required a separate donation to the Brahmins, and since the assertion of prestige required that a prince must be attended by the largest number of retainers, the sums expended became very large. The lower caste Brahmins who presided at the burning *ghāts* and the untouchable Doms who actually incinerated the bodies flourished also. Many pilgrims who came to perform *shrāddha* returned in their last years in order to die in the 'peace of Kashi'. The funerary specialists, manipulating both fear of pollution and fear of death, were able to amass huge fortunes. Some of the largest mansions adjoining the Harish Chandra Ghat on the river front were built in the late eighteenth century by the family of Lakshmi Narayan Dom, reputedly one of the richest families in India. Yet these funerary specialists continued to stand on the very lowest rung of the caste system because of their constant association with the pollution of death. Good Hindus prayed for more male children; the Harishchandi Doms, it was rumoured, prayed for more deaths.

DEVOTIONAL MOVEMENTS: THE INEFFICACY OF RITUAL: 1500–1800

While the elaboration of orthodox ritual around the holy places was progressing in the years 1600–1800, other nearly contrary tendencies were also working beneath the complex surface of Indian religious life. The fifteenth and sixteenth centuries had been a period of revival in all forms of Hinduism, but notably there had been a great burgeoning of sectarian movements which proclaimed the way of total devotion to the Godhead (*bhakti mārga*) as a method of salvation superior to both ritualistic 'works' and 'knowledge'. The origins of these sects were as tangled as their philosophical differences were subtle, but to a greater or lesser extent their beliefs had encouraged ways of looking upon death and transmigration which disparaged display and elaborate ritual. One influence of these sects' view of death was the ancient tradition of Tantric Yoga[45] and mysticism which included the belief that it was possible to overcome physical death and attain beatitude on this earth without resort to the pain of rebirth. It was thought that alchemy or yoga could transform the corrupt human body into an incorruptible 'perfect body'.

[44] e.g., settlement of a dispute between *pāndas* over members of the Kohli Khattri sub-caste, Record Book p. 239 (opposite date 1788 *Sambat*).
[45] S. B. Das Gupta, *An Introduction to Tantric Buddhism* (Calcutta, 1958), also his *Obscure Religious Cults* (Calcutta, 1952); Charlotte Vaudeville, *Kabīr,* I (Oxford, 1974), 127.

One area in which Tantric beliefs seem to have been influential was through the religious movement initiated by the teacher Kabir in the later part of the fifteenth century. Kabir, a social reformer, a bold enemy of Brahminical pride and caste distinction, opposed idol worship and the doctrine of reincarnation. A Muslim weaver by birth, Kabir sought a popular religious regeneration; in modern times he has been sanctified as an apostle of social reform and Hindu-Muslim unity. In his frontal attack on Brahminism, he deprecated holy places and death ritual also. According to him, the Hindu prejudice about Gaya or Benares was 'mere fantasy' as the attainment of spiritual experience does not depend on the sanctity of any given spot.[46] Kabir's doctrines were replete with references to Death as the 'Final Enemy', but in the context of a passionate belief that salvation could be obtained by all in this life:

> Dead is the physician, dead is the patient,
> The whole Universe is dead,
> Only Kabir will not die
> Who had his support in Rām [God][47]

The doctrine implied that *shrāddha* was wholly irrelevant to salvation, and held out promise of the immortality of the 'perfect body'. The legends associated with the death of Kabir are interesting here. The story has it that there was a dispute between the saint's Hindu and Muslim followers as to whether the body should be buried or burned. But when the shroud was examined, there was no sign of Kabir's mortal remains besides a handful of rose petals. The devotees accordingly burned half the petals and buried the other half.[48] Yet in later centuries, the followers of Kabir (the Kabir-Panthis) seem generally to have buried their dead.

The more orthodox Vaishnavite devotional sects which flowered in the sixteenth and seventeenth centuries retained the doctrine of transmigration. Allusions to death in their literature are, however, rather tangential. The aim is to show that life is transitory and that only steadfast devotion to the God can given it meaning. Thus the poet Surdas sings,

> Do not succumb to pride, for jackals, crows and vultures will devour the mortal body—
> It goes three ways; to worms, to excrement, or to the pyre!
> Where will be that freshness and beauty, that lovely form?
> ... Surdas says that unless a man worships the Lord, he squanders his life.[49]

In general, north Indian Vaishnavite devotional cults retained the orthodox rites of cremation and a simplified form of *shrāddha*, but for them, these

---

[46] *Kabīr* I, 266, *sākhi* 21 8 (b) 'Though a man builds his house in the outskirts of Kāsi [Benares] and though he drinks pure [Ganges] water, without Hari's [God's] name there is no salvation'.

[47] *ibid*, 258, 19, 2 (a).

[48] *The Dabistan, or School of Manners,* trans. D. Shea and A. Troyer (Paris, 1843), II, 9.

[49] Surdas, *Sursagar (Vinay)*, 86. I am grateful to Dr. R. S. McGregor of the Oriental Faculty, Cambridge, for permission to use his unpublished translation.

forms could only have meaning if infused with love for the God.[50] Bengali *bhakti* sources in the tradition of the great teacher Caitanya and his school are more precise. Here worship of 'inferior gods and ancestors' is either omitted or given a very low status, and 'service to Krishna is superior to all other acts'.[51] The *shrāddha* feast is reduced to a few acts of prayer and a general commemorative feast for the local community. Indeed in one text, the argument for performing *shrāddha* is turned on its head. The ancient books make the service so complicated, it is said, that no one can possibly get it right and the whole enterprise might as well be abandoned.

The antiquity and outward coherence of Hindu funerary ritual has hardly concealed the ambiguities, not to say contradictions, of their underlying philosophies and implications for society. The doctrine of transmigration and individual moral responsibility sits uneasily with the overt role of *shrāddha* in 'creating' ancestors and helping them achieve Heaven. In the same way, the conspicuous ceremony and expenditure arising from the 'tribal' aspect of the rites stands at variance with the strong scriptural admonition that they should be an austere individual sacrifice concerned as much with the soul of the sacrificer as with that of the deceased. In pre-colonial times, the contradiction was never resolved, even for the priestly and royal elite. The close association of genealogy with the claim to kingship encouraged the extravagant 'tribal' aspect of *shrāddha* and swelled the funerary communities of the holy places. At the same time the austere spiritual individualism immanent in Hindu philosophy continued to feed movements of textual study and devotion which rejected ritual, especially the much-tainted rituals of death, as a way to salvation. But unlike western Europe where competing ideologies were able to eliminate each other and generally modify the rituals of death, these discordant elements achieved a symbiosis in Hindu India. The concept of spiritual hierarchy meant that even the most anti-ritualistic of religious teachers acknowledged that rituals might have value for the spiritually child-like.

As we shall see, colonial rule, superficial as it was in most respects, did create the conditions for a significant change of emphasis in funerary ritual over the last century. At first the security of a continental empire once again resulted in an expansion of 'tribal' display, especially at the holy places. But in the longer perspective, the shock of the colonial and Christian assault on some aspects of funerary practice unleashed a range of newer and deeper movements of reform. Despite their doctrinal differences, these movements were unanimous in emphasising the austere, celebratory aspect of *shrāddha*. Urban and upper caste India at least has widely begun to resolve the ambiguity in this direction. In the villages, less has changed.

---

[50] J. G. Shah, *Shrimad Vallabhacharya. His Philosophy and Religion* (Ahmedabad, 1969).
[51] S. K. De, *The Early History of the Vaisnava Faith and Movement* (Calcutta, 1961), p. 408; see also pp. 531–3.

DEATH AND THE COLONIAL STATE, 1780–1880

Much as missionaries and officials may have wished it, the onset of British rule in north India between 1763 and 1806 did not result in an abrupt period of westernization. In fact, like the Muslim Empires before it, this supposedly Christian Empire presided over a substantial reinforcement of Hindu practice, a virtual reinvention of tradition. One early consequence of British rule was the spectacular growth of pilgrimage to the holy places for *shrāddha* and other purposes.[52] Communications improved with the restoration of political order while the British abandoned the dues which the state had once taken from pilgrims going to the holy places. These dues brought them little financial gain in India, and the odium of 'meddling in heathen religion' at home. Between 1780 and 1820, the number of pilgrims who went to Allahabad, Gaya and Benares each year may have trebled. Further west more settled conditions at the foot of the Himalayan Mountains reinvigorated pilgrimage up to the lofty shrines of Baijnath and Badrinath. New security was accompanied by a redistribution of wealth within the subcontinent. Bengali government servants together with merchant families who grew fat on external trade were conspicuous beneficiaries of the Pax Britannica. Though princely families remained major donors at the holy cities, these new men were emerging as a force. A Calcutta Deputy Accountant-General of the East India Company was active in renovating the Gaya temples.[53] At Benares, Khattri and Agarwala, merchant families erected new cremation *ghāts,* bridges and temples. Pradip Sinha has shown for Bengal how wealthy factotums of the British in Calcutta retired to their native villages to spend large sums on, among other things, competitive *shrāddha* feasts.[54]

The ritual centres also benefited from the creation of an all-India railway network after 1850. They became accessible to prosperous village people who could not previously have afforded the time away from their fields. The Sanskrit scholar Monier Williams was startled to be assured by a Gaya priest in the 1870s that the coming of the railways had seen a sharp decrease in the appearance of ghosts. Speedier travel, he was told, enabled people to get to Gaya faster and move their relations quickly through the malignant phase and on to beatitude.[55]

L. P. Vidyarthi has argued that the nineteenth century saw the 'feudalization' of the priestly communities at Gaya.[56] The term is unhelpful, but the process recognizable. Debarred from warfare, the protected princes of the colonial period continued to lavish their wealth on building, donation and pilgrimage. Pilgrimages became longer and more elaborate and began

[52] Martin, *Eastern India,* I, 53.
[53] *Ibid,* p. 60.
[54] Pradip Sinha, *Nineteenth Century Bengal. Aspects of Social History* (Calcutta, 1965), p. 92.
[55] Monier Williams, 'Sraddha Ceremonies at Banaras and Gaya', *Indian Antiquary,* V, 1876, 200.
[56] L. P. Vidyarthi, *The Sacred Complex in Hindu Gaya* (London, 1962).

to take on some of the characteristics of modern tourism. When the Maharaja of Tanjore visited Benares in 1821, this prince from the far south spent hugely and had prepared an elaborate 'souvenir volume' which contained paintings of the bathing places and temples which he had visited.[57] It was not surprising then that the priests and funerary specialists of the holy cities were able to build more and more sumptuous residences in the first half of the century. A group of Gaya genealogical priests was even admitted to the 1911 Imperial Durbar in Delhi. This curious mingling of the Puranic and Gothic came about because the British tended to see the Gayawals as an equivalent to the College of Arms.

The British elaboration of Hindu tradition was more striking in the area of legal interpretation. We have noted that the Dayabhaga school of law related the right to inherit property to the ritual competence to carry out *shrāddha*. Far from reducing the ritual element, the British courts, including the Privy Council, interpreted the doctrine of 'spiritual benefit' with even greater rigidity and extended some of its provisions to northern and western India where Dayabhaga had never been prevalent.[58] Yet this was a case where Hindu death rituals were embalmed rather than enhanced: the early nineteenth-century judgements made it clear that it was the competence and not the inclination or intention to perform *shrāddha* which was at issue.

In some areas, though, European administration had a sharper cutting edge. In the first decade of the nineteenth century there grew up a sustained assault on certain aspects of Hindu funerary practice which were seen to be 'contrary to nature'. British Protestant missionaries were in the van of this programme. But despite their reluctance to become involved, the colonial authorities also began to see themselves as having rights and duties in an area which had previously fallen wholly within the sphere of the lineage or caste. 'Suicide' at the holy places was the first object of attack in an uncoordinated series of local, provincial and central government ordinances which stretch from about 1780 to the celebrated outlawing of widow-burning ('suttee' or *sati*) in 1829. Jonathan Duncan, the paternalist British Resident at Benares (1786–95) sought to end the suicide or self-mutilation of Brahmins used as a form of coercion in the pursuit of commercial or boundary disputes (*dhārna*).[59] He deplored the 'predisposition of the people of this city to take poison on the slightest of pretexts'. Here the object of suicide was to throw the spiritual blame for the death of a Brahmin on their opponents and thus reduce them to the lowest possible state in the next life, perhaps even 'a worm in ordure for 60,000 years'. In other cases, such as hurling oneself under the celebrated processional car of the god at Juggernaut (Jaganath)

[57] Preserved in the Saraswati Library, Thanjavur.
[58] See, e.g., J. C. Ghose, *The Principles of Hindu Law* (Calcutta, 1903), pp. 31–3, 43; J. D. M. Derrett, *A Critique of Modern Hindu Law* (Delhi, 1970), p. 176, also his *Essays*, III, 81.
[59] Proceedings of the Resident of Benares, 24 October 1794.

171

or the suicide of lepers at Allahabad or in the Himalayas, the aim was to acquire immediate entry into paradise according to the promise of the *Purānas*. While involuntary human sacrifice had disappeared from Hinduism at an early period, self-sacrifice was regarded as a mode of acquiring very great merit, of insuring a good reincarnation or even paradise itself. By contrast in Christendom, suicide was regarded as a sin against the Holy Spirit, and as an offence against Natural Law. The authorities first instituted systems of surveillance of these Indian ritual suicides, but by the mid-nineteenth century had come to forbid them absolutely.

A much more public assault on Hindu death custom was mounted in the 1820s by the Baptist missionaries of Bengal against the so-called 'ghāt-murders'.[60] This practice involved the carrying to riverside *ghāts* (sometimes the burning grounds themselves) of people who were thought to be terminally ill. Lacking food, water and attention, these sufferers passed quickly to the realms of Yama. It is probable, as the missionaries asserted, that such cases of exposure sometimes represented wilful manslaughter by relations who were anxious to get their hands on an inheritance. The missionaries did indeed nurse some of these people back to life.[61] But 'ghāt murder' was not the result of some peculiar viciousness of the Hindu character. Dying people were a desperate liability to a Hindu household since a death inside the house would require expensive and lengthy rites of purification, and death on a bed might expose the family to malignant spiritual visitation. Also, as we have seen, Hindu culture defined death in a different way from the west: continued activity of brain or heart was not necessarily of great significance. Nevertheless, the missionaries managed to have legislation passed which inaugurated formal policing of the *ghāts* and forbade the exposure there of persons considered living according to the tenets of western physiology.

By far the most publicized and bitter dispute about Hindu death ritual, however, concerned the notorious 'suttee' or *sati*, the burning of widows with their dead husbands.[62] Despite the revulsion of the missionaries and many of their own officers, the British authorities trod much more carefully here because the practice had a solid foundation in the Hindu lawbooks. Thus says the law-giver, Brihispati, in a macabre and evocative simile:

> In the same manner as a snake-catcher drags a snake from his hole,
> so does a woman who burns herself draw her husband out of hell;
> and she afterwards resides with him in heaven[63]

[60] E. Daniel Potts, *British Baptist Missionaries in India 1793–1837. The History of Serampore and its Missions* (Cambridge, 1967), p. 143.
[61] *Friend of India*, 30 April 1835.
[62] See also A. Mukhopadhyaya, 'Sati as a Social Institution', *Bengal Past and Present, Jubilee Number,* 1957, pp. 107–22; B. Hjejle, 'The social policy of the East India Company with regard to sati, slavery, thagi and infanticide, 1772–1858', unpublished Oxford D. Phil. thesis, 1958.
[63] Quoted in *PP, 1821, xviii.* 333.

Here then, one encounters the Hindu theme of sacrifice in its most dramatic form. Self-sacrifice is the ultimate form of sacrifice to deities, and according to some texts, efficacious against a vast weight of accumulated evil. But since a man's wife is literally one flesh with him, widow sacrifice has the same value in assuring salvation. To Europeans it was no more than a grisly form of murder.

From 1815 onwards, the authorities implemented a rudimentary system of policing *satis* in order to ensure that they were at least carried out in conformity with the scriptures. Widows could not be forced onto the funeral pyre, they had to be over the age of puberty, and they could not be tending young children—though the definition of 'child' was in doubt. By licensing *satis* in this way, the government hoped to 'confine those sacrifices within as narrow bounds as the rules for their guidance would permit'.[64] But during the 1820s, the growing pamphlet campaign by missionary writers in India and Britain gradually built up public opinion against the practice. Finally, with Regulation XVII of 1829, the Governor-General, Lord Bentinck, had *sati* banned throughout British India on his personal initiative.[65] It flickered on spasmodically in the Indian states and in remote rural areas until the end of the century.

Many impassioned speeches were made about *sati* and full-length studies of this great victory of imperial reform continued to appear until as late as Edward Thompson's work of 1928. What is striking, however, is quite how limited the numbers of *satis* were. Between 1817 and 1827, as few as 4,323[66] were reported for a total population of about 160 million for the whole of British India. The practice was very largely confined to Bengal, and in particular, to the environs of Calcutta. Between 1815 and 1820, the annual average for the Presidencies of Bombay and Madras was under fifty. In fact, the great concern with which the British regarded *sati* reflected a more general movement of Anglo-Indian opinion, rather than its incidence or statistical significance. At the end of the eighteenth century, the regard for Asian civilization which derived from the Enlightenment still prevailed. Commentators were shocked by the fate of individual widows, but did not translate their revulsion into a general attack on Hinduism. By 1820, the mood had changed. *Sati* was simply the most obvious manifestation of the universal degradation, barbarity and corruption of Hinduism which was at that very moment on the point of dissolution before the advancing tide of Christianity. The attack on *sati* also implied a rejection of the 'Hindooisation' of the officials who had countenanced it for so long,[67] especially those who

---

[64] Resolution of the Governor General in Council, 4 July 1817, *PP, 1821, xviii.* 358.
[65] John Rosselli, *Lord William Bentinck. The Making of a Liberal Imperialist 1774–1839* (London, 1974), pp. 208–14.
[66] Calculated from *PP, 1821, xviii,* 370–529; see also *PP, 1825 xxiv,* 120–40.
[67] Edward Thompson, *Suttee. A Historical and Philosophical Enquiry into the Hindu rite of Widow Burning* (London, 1928), p. 76; H. J. Bushby, *Widow Burning* (London, 1853), p. 51.

opposed the anglicization of education and the general missionary assault on Indian culture. Again, *sati* was seen as irrefutable justification for the continued British presence in India. Edward Thompson echoed a long tradition of nineteenth-century attitudes when he wrote:

> Such things as suttee kept back Indian political progress by many years; until the rite was abolished even a beginning in self-government was impossible.[68]

The British obsession with *sati* was boundless. Thousands of pages of Parliamentary papers were given up to 4,000 immolations while the mortality of millions from disease and starvation was only mentioned incidentally—sometimes only because it tended indirectly to increase the number of widows performing the 'horrid act'. The colonial state was prodded into action on a matter which bore on natural morality but mortality which derived from the working of the grain market was treated as a law of nature, in no way amenable to intervention by the state.

One reason for the wave of revulsion amongst the British was *sati*'s notorious prevalence around Calcutta itself. For here 'we find the Hindoo superstition in its most degraded and darkest state, in the very part of our Empire, where the influence of our manners must first be felt and to which we must first look for the dawn of morality and civilisation'.[69] In fact, the geography of nineteenth century *sati* marks it out as a reinvented tradition; it had little connection, for instance, with the heroic self-immolation of the widows of dead Rajput warriors in the great medieval campaigns against the Muslims, though the scriptural authority may have been the same.[70] But neither contemporaries nor more recent commentators have been able to provide convincing arguments as to why certain groups of Bengalis carried out the rite so much more frequently than others. A number of partial explanations can be presented. First, there is the *cui bono* argument which holds that *sati*'s particular prominence in Bengal was a result of the considerable support promised to widows in the Dayabagha (as opposed to Mitakshara) school of law. The Dayabagha school it can be argued, gave the widow a much greater lien on the property of the deceased for support, though it was not favourable to inheritance by females. This might have encouraged heirs to do away with widows or to pressurize them into suicide. The argument may explain the numbers of *satis* in Bengal by comparison with other parts of India, but it hardly explains the great variations of incidence between the different districts and cities of Bengal.

Another explanation relates to the religious beliefs of the population. *Sati*, it was argued, can be connected with the worship of the goddess Kali, a terrible deity who symbolized the destructive forces that were necessary for ultimate recreation, and demanded constant animal sacrifice.[71] This was

[68] Thompson, *Suttee*, p. 131.
[69] Report of H. Oakley, Magistrate of Hughly, 19 December 1818, *PP, 1821, xviii*, 527.
[70] Thompson, *Suttee*, pp. 29-35.
[71] S. Mitra, *Durga-Kāli* (Calcutta, 1878).

certainly the view of Ram Mohun Roy, the Bengali deist reformer, whose personal opposition to *sati* gave the missionaries an important Indian ally.[72] Certainly, *sati* was rare where Islam and less sanguinary Hindu sects were prominent. It was, for instance, practised very little in Dacca and Murshidabad districts where popular Hinduism had early been influenced by the presence of Muslim Sufi saints. As one approached Delhi, the centre of Muslim India, it almost died out and only revived in the Punjab where the militant Sikh Khalsa had inaugurated a consciously anti-Islamic revival in the eighteenth century.[73] Similarly, the centres of the more pacific Vaishnavite branch of Hinduism which preached against the taking of life, and even Benares (which though a Shaivite centre, also supported a Tantric tradition aiming at the immortality of a 'perfect body') recorded very few *satis*. Yet this line of argument seems incomplete. Many parts of India saw the worship of sanguinary female deities but were not associated with widow-burning, while on the contrary, Nadia in Bengal was both a major Vaishnavite centre and a notorious focus of *sati*.

Finally, it is interesting to speculate on some of the sociological origins of *sati*. A scrutiny of the caste and distribution of recorded *satis* shows that the overwhelming number were Brahmins or widows from artisan and entrepreneurial castes. The practice was also very common in the heavily Brahmin Rahti tract of west Bengal. In a district like Birbhum where the major landholders were not high caste and tribal influences were still strong, very few instances were recorded.[74] Widow-burning among Brahmins appears to be closely related to matters of status.[75] Since a widow was perceived almost literally to be part of her husband's body, her presence in a household raised questions of pollution; she was in effect, in a 'liminal' and dangerous state. The highest castes would only tolerate a widow who practised extreme asceticism. When the lower castes pressed for higher ritual status, they often forced widows into perpetual mourning. They also forbade widow remarriage which was regarded as impure, since a man was in effect using the physical leavings of another. *Sati*, like hypergamy and the observation of extreme ritual purity, then, was one of the techniques by which Brahmin families sought to maintain a social and ritual supremacy. Likewise it may be that those caste groups like the merchant and Kayasth (writer) caste which were consciously seeking to raise their ritual status might occasionally have encouraged *sati* in an attempt to associate themselves with Brahmins and the injunctions of the sacred texts; such castes were also well represented among *satis*.[76]

[72] J. C. Ghose, *The English Works of Raja Ram Mohun Roy compiled and published by Eshan Chunder Bose*, 2 vols. (Calcutta, 1885), I, 309.
[73] Thompson, *Suttee*, pp. 73–4.
[74] Hughly Magistrate's report, *PP, 1821*, 527.
[75] Report of J. Master, Calcutta Faujdari, ibid.
[76] Returns of *sati* by caste and district, ibid, 360–73; Ghose, *Works*, II, 345–6.

HINDU REFORM MOVEMENTS AND RITUALS OF DEATH,
1820–80

Perhaps the most significant aspect of the whole missionary and official onslaught against 'depraved Hindoo customs' was the manner in which it galvanized Bengali opinion to a reassessment of its own religious practice, and gave new life to debates on the authority of scripture and the validity of ritual which were deeply embedded in the historical tradition. The government's abolition of *sati* itself provoked a response from a group of more conservative reformers who deplored official intervention in custom and formed themselves into the Dharma Sabha (Religious Association). To this body, which admitted the need for change and yet glorified Hindu tradition, some historians have sought to trace back the origin of the Indian nationalist movement.[77]

The movement for change among Bengali Hindus had, in fact, preceded the *sati* controversy for some years. Debate between Vaishnavites and Shaivites had been fierce towards the end of the eighteenth century.[78] The key figure of the early nineteenth century was to be Ram Mohun Roy, a Brahmin government servant. Roy had begun to rebel against ritualism while living in Benares, but exposure to Christian and particularly Unitarian ideas had forged this awareness into a coherent set of reform prescriptions in the years before 1820. His ferocious opposition to *sati* and the infanticide of female children was only part of a frontal assault on the validity of ritual as a way to salvation which found little to favour in the ordinary rites of *shrāddha* either.

Ram Mohun Roy was a monotheist who based his ideas on the later books of the classical Sanskrit tradition, and in particular, on the Upanishads. He was also heavily influenced by the thought of the south Indian teacher Shankaracharya, who had flourished in the eighth century A.D.[79] In his system, Shankaracharya had retained ritual as an indirect but significant path by which the majority could attain salvation. There were three paths: the path of ritualistic works (*kārma mārga*), the path of devotion (*bhakti mārga*) and the path of direct knowledge (*gyāna mārga*). However, according to him, only a tiny elite of people, purified through many rebirths, had the necessary spiritual elevation to aspire to the latter. For the majority ritual and devotion were appropriate means for purification and preparation. Shankaracharya was neatly able to combine his monistic high philosophy with a justification for Brahminism and ritual.

Ram Mohun's refurbished nineteenth-century Vedantism differed from Shankaracharya's on certain philosophical points, but his most radical

---

[77] cf. D. Kopf, *British Orientalism and the Bengal Renaissance* (Berkeley, 1969).
[78] Ghose, *Works*, introduction, p. 6.
[79] J. H. Killingley, 'Vedānta and Modernity' in C. H. Philipps and M. D. Wainwright (eds.) *Indian Society and the Beginning of Modernisation* (S.O.A.S., London, 1976), pp. 127–40.

contention for practical religion was that ordinary people also 'were capable of adoring the Supreme Being without the puerile practice of having resort to visible objects' (i.e. idols and ritual). This 'puerile practice' was suitable only for the most degraded criminal. Ram Mohun used a scriptural reference to 'the unhappy agitation and wavering of an idolater on the approach of death' because he was unable to arrange the performance of *shrāddha,* as an example 'which should make men reflect seriously on the miserable consequences of fixing their minds on any other objects of adoration but the one Supreme Being'.[80] *Shrāddha* then was not so much pernicious, as the later revivalists thought, but irrelevant. God might assign men to another body after rebirth, just as Christians thought that the soul would again be clothed with flesh at the Last Trump, but on this body God would bestow the 'consequences of its good and evil works' in the past life.[81] Death rituals practised by heirs and successors could not affect the outcome either way. Ram Mohun's beliefs caused his followers in the Brahmo Samaj (Deist Society) to reduce death ritual to little more than a ceremony of commemoration. While the Samaj itself attracted only a small proportion of the Bengali intelligentsia, who were often at odds with orthodox society, this radical attitude to tradition brought the issue to the forefront of the debate not only among the traditionalists, but also among other more widespread heterodox movements.

In fact the Brahmo Samaj never managed to wash away the charge of anglicization and crypto-Christianity. Its refined sensibilities and eclecticism were unable to touch the deeper forces of cultural pride, even chauvinism which were to prove the driving force behind modern Hindu revivalism and tinge the ideology of Indian nationalism. This role was filled more successfully by the Arya Samaj (Aryan Association) which from small beginnings in the Punjab in the 1870s grew to become the most celebrated of the movements of new Hinduism.[82] Essentially a purification movement, the Samaj sought to remove from Hindu belief and practice all elements which could not be traced to the most ancient of the classical texts, the Vedas. Its main target was Brahminical ritual which it saw as an alien accretion on 'pure' Aryan religion. This attack broadened into a rejection of the ritual and social domination of Brahmins and on the modern form of the caste system itself.[83] According to the Aryas, caste was instituted in accordance with the 'merit and capability' of individuals. And since these varied, there could be no justification for inherited caste status. Instead individuals should be ascribed to putative castes in the course of their own lifetime. Thus

[80] Ghose, *Works,* I, 92, note to Roy's trans. of canto 18 of the 'Ishopanishad of the Yajur Veda'.

[81] ibid, 'Reply to the Second Number of the Brahminical Magazine, 1821', pp. 190–1.

[82] Kenneth W. Jones, *Arya Dharm. Hindu Consciousness in the Nineteenth Century* (Berkeley, 1976).

[83] J. R. Graham 'The Arya Samāj as a Reformation in Hinduism with special reference to Caste', Yale University Ph.D. 1943, pp. 269–90.

learned and pure men should 'become' Brahmins; warlike men, Kshatriyas, and so on.

The Aryan message of revival was propagated throughout north India and especially in the cultural frontier zone of the Punjab where there had been generations of conflict between Hinduism, Islam and Sikhism; it was the faith of vigorous entrepreneurs, young literati and, latterly, of independent peasant-farmers. Its methods reflected the transformation of its founder, Swami Dayananda, from a traditional wandering holy man teaching in Sanskrit and engaging in formal debates with local Brahmins, to a 'reformer' who spoke in Hindi, wore western dress, and encouraged pamphlet warfare and railway tours. Aryas were active missionaries in the western sense and they used forms of congregational worship adapted from Christian and Muslim sources. Yet Vedic fundamentalism and the radical attack on hierarchy were themselves recessive features within the Hindu tradition. Dayananda owed as much to traditional Brahminical teaching as to the Brahmo Samaj of Bengal in formulating his new creed. Hindu reform was vigorously nudged by the impact of the west, but its lines of direction were already laid out.

Funeral practice and *shrāddha* ritual inevitably attracted the hostility of the Aryan reformers. No trace of elaborate funerary forms can be found in the first books of the Vedas; worse, the practice itself helped to confirm the dominance of the Brahmins and the perversion of true religion. In the case of funeral practice, Dayananda and his followers mounted a straightforward campaign to reinstitute the simple methods of burning enjoined in the ancient texts. Dayananda's major work *Satyārtha Prakāsh* (The Light of Truth) reiterates the ideal depth of the cremation trench, the quantities of sandal wood required for the pyre, the amounts of saffron and clarified butter (two ritual substances) to be used in the burning, and the nature of the hymns to be chanted.[84] Even these simple instructions, however, implied a covert attack on hierarchy. It had become the practice to reserve the use of sandal wood and clarified butter for the higher castes. Dayananda insisted that sandal wood should be used for all and that 'however poor the deceased, in no case should less than 40 pounds of clarified butter be used in cremating the body'. This vastly expensive commodity should be procured 'by begging or as a gift from his caste people . . . or from Government, if need be'.[85] Here Dayananda was insinuating another of his favourite themes: that true religion could only subsist in the context of a Hindu state. It was obviously absurd to expect the British Government to spend large sums of money in the provision of clarified butter for funerals.

The question of death and cremation also illustrated the Aryas' new and

---

[84] Dayananda Saraswati, *Satyārtha Prakāsha* (Lahore, 1880); trans. and ed. C. Bharadwaja, *Light of Truth—an English Translation of Satyārth Prakāsh* (3rd edn. Lahore, 1927), p. 571.
[85] ibid.

aggressive attitude to Islam and Christianity. The doctrine of the resurrection of the body reinforced the insistence on burial of the dead, but the Aryas vigorously rejected this. Bodily substance was illusion and fragmented back into its basic particles, so the dead could not be raised incorruptible. But besides, burial was degrading. How, for instance, could it be compatible with the Christian idea of love? 'How can it be an act of love on your part to throw earth, bricks, stones, lime and other things, on his [the deceased's] eyes, mouth, chest, and other parts of the body?'[86] More than this, burial was an insanitary method of disposing of the dead 'because the decomposition of dead bodies sets in, which pollutes the air which in its turn gives rise to disease'. Here we have an interesting example of the manner in which revived Hinduism employed the rhetoric of classical theological debate and modern rationalism to reinforce each other. Burial 'polluted the air', 'rendered useless acres of agricultural land', 'caused fear to the timid from the sight of graves' (a psychological argument here), and insulted the dead. But the concept of the insanitary is highly ambiguous. On the one hand, Dayananda has assimilated very recent western medical ideas about the origin of disease, but on the other hand, he is affirming a classical sanskritic notion of the nature of matter, and an injunction against ritually polluting air and earth which are regarded as pure substances.

The blunt notions of Dayananda and other Aryas leaders on the nature and object of *shrāddha* ceremonies also throw light on the modification of Hindu tradition they envisaged. Above all other orthodox rituals, it expressed the essential notion of hereditable purity and impurity which underpinned the caste system itself. Arya preachers made a point of belabouring *shrāddha* and major classical debates on the issue (*shastrārthas*) were held in Lahore in 1878, in Wazirabad in 1896,[87] and in Moradabad in 1898. The object of the Aryas was to reduce the ritual to a mere feast of commemoration, which is what they considered the practice of Vedic times to have been.[88] According to them, the spirits of the ancestors did not physically share in the ritual feast. Indeed, since their merit was assured by acts in their individual life, such rituals could not help them to acquire a more acceptable regeneration or a more rapid transition to Heaven. The chain of hereditable caste would thus be broken because a man's status in the after-life could not be modified by the ritual actions of his family, howsoever pure and pious they might be. The printing presses of the Punjab and United Provinces rolled out contributions to this debate throughout the last two decades of the nineteenth century. But direct Vedic authorities were not the only ones invoked. In a manner typical of Victorian Indian thought, the Aryas at the debate in

---

[86] ibid, p. 570

[87] 'Shastrārtha bich Arya Samaj Wazirābād aur Pandit Ganēsh Datta Shāstri Lāhaur vishye Pitrashrāddha ...' (Punjab Economical Press, Lahore, 1896), India Office Library Hindi pamphlets collection.

[88] J. N. Farquhar, *Modern Religious Movements in India* (Indian edn., 1967), p. 121.

Wazirabad in 1896 attempted to enlist on their side the weighty name of Friedrich Max-Müller, Boden Professor of Sanskrit at the University of Oxford, who was regarded as the leading Orientalist of the period. Max-Müller tactfully refrained from direct polemic but added to Arya Vedic fundamentalism an argument derived from contemporary European notions of 'natural religion'. According to him, ancestor worship was a 'natural' consequence of the universal fear of the dead.[89] The *shrāddha* ceremony in the Vedas had originated, however, as no more than a feast in honour of the living relatives. Again, the Aryas had brought western 'scientific' thought to the aid of indigenous controversy.

Quite apart from direct theological objections, the Arya publicists sought to purify *shrāddha* rites on other grounds also. First, it was not only the ideology but the practice of the ceremonies which helped to maintain the false caste hierarchy. The position of the celebrants, the length of the ceremonies and the rank of the specialists employed all helped to designate and order castes. By reducing funerary ritual to a few simple and uniform acts, a further public manifestation of hierarchy would be removed. This would also undermine the economic basis of much of the priestly class itself, particularly the 'filthy, cheating, fraudulent wretches' of Gaya, Benares and other holy places with whom Dayananda had had early and abrasive encounters. Since to Aryas only pure actions with pure consequences could bring salvation, the whole panoply of ritual activity there brought no benefit—in fact, brought demerit to millions of participants:

> Hundreds of thousands of Rupees are given away in charity to the priests for the good and happiness of the *manes*. These priests of Gaya waste all this money in prostitution and other sinful practices. If this be the merit of offering cakes to the *manes* at Gaya, why can Gaya not be freed from sins like prostitution?[90]

Faced with 'evidence' from the orthodox that the spirits of the dead actually appeared and consumed the cakes of the sacrifice, Dayananda contemptuously dismissed it as trickery. What happened, he said, was that the priests got a man to hide in a specially prepared pit near the point of oblation. When the cakes were presented, this man would surreptitiously help himself to them and have a good meal in his underground hiding place.

At first sight this denunciation of funerary specialists for dishonesty and uncleanliness reads like a reaction to the western critique of Hinduism. But it also had deep roots in indigenous traditions and sensibilities. Funerary and *shrāddha* priests had always occupied a low position amongst Brahmins. Popularly they were seen as manifestations of the spirits they served, not only unclean but also inauspicious.[91] According to the Sanskrit scholar, J.

---

[89] 'Shahstrārtha', pp. 20–1.

[90] Bharadwaja, trans. *Satyārtha Prakāsh*, p. 364.

[91] J. Parry, 'Ghosts, Greed and Sin. The Occupational Identity of the Benares Funeral Priests', *Man*, XV, 1980, 88–111.

180

C. Heesterman,[92] at sacrifice in Hinduism the sacrificer was deemed to be reborn, transferring to the priest the odium of his own death and impurity. Thus the purification and even abolition of the funerary priesthood could be justified by an appeal to one element of the religious tradition itself.

A final Arya objection to *shrāddha* practice sprang from ideas about domestic and political economy. Both marriage feasts and oblations to the dead had become the occasion for notable displays of piety. Expensive rituals were common among poorer people of high caste who needed to maintain their local status, and were reputed to be the origin of much debt and forced land sales. Opposition to conspicuous ritual expenditure had indigenous roots among Vaishnavite devotional reformers; Shaivism also had an ascetic and restrained aspect. At the same time, British revenue officers who deplored rural indebtedness and moral crusaders who abhorred its alleged consequence, female infanticide, came together after the 1840s in a common assault on expensive *rites de passage*. By the 1870s, Aryas and other Indian social reformers had taken up the challenge and mounted a widespread campaign through newspapers and caste associations to limit these practices. Ideal economy budgets for both marriage and *shrāddha* were circulated by a number of publicists.

The influence of Arya opposition to death rites was considerable. In 1900, there were barely one million people who described themselves as Aryas for the purposes of the Census, but the ripples of controversy went far beyond them. In particular, their attitudes had a distinct impact on the various neo-orthodox movements which rose up in opposition to them, especially the *sanātan dhārma sabhās* (societies for ancient religion) which developed in north India in the 1880s,[93] and the contemporary Bengali devotional movements which mixed ecstatic worship with cultural revivalism. It was unlikely that the majority of Hindus would be prepared to abandon the whole of their scriptural tradition since the Vedas. And besides its toughness and resilience as a social system, caste also had its defenders as a moral ordering of mankind. The *sanātan dhārma sabhās* were more a defensive movement by orthodoxy, then, than purification movements in their own right. They appealed indeed to the lower sections of Brahmin society which had little connection with the extreme ritualism of the holy cities, and yet wished to guard the social position of the priestly class against its opponents. The aim of the *sanātan dhārmis* was to frustrate the radicals by reforming Brahminical practice from inside. They were prepared to use modern methods of proselytization, to distribute the sacred books to the lower castes,[94] something which was frowned upon by unregenerate orthodoxy, and to 'reconvert' apostate Muslims, Sikhs and Arya Samajis. Their position on death ritual

[92] J. Heesterman, 'Brahmin, Ritual and Renouncer', *Wiener Zeitschrift f. die Kunde S. U. O. Asiens*, VIII, 1964, 1–31.
[93] Farquhar, *Religious Movements*, pp. 157–73.
[94] ibid, p. 316.

was, therefore, ambiguous. Discriminations of caste could not be abandoned, but some of the intricacy, cost and superstition of the rituals had to be removed.[95] *Sanātan dhārmis* were also prominent in the various associations which developed after 1870 to protect and regulate the holy places, such as the Allahabad Hindu Samaj (society) and the Benares People's Association. Members sought to discipline the bodies of *shrāddha* priests, to compromise their disputes over clients, and to promote commercial morality and sanitation.

The late nineteenth century neo-traditionalist revivalist leaders of Bengal, such as Swami Vivekananda, also adopted positions which contributed to the change of mood among the orthodox. Mixing devotionalism with a highly sensitive cultural nationalism, Vivekananda called ritual 'the kindergarten of all religions'. But because they were part of India's heritage, customs such as *shrāddha* should not be abandoned to placate westerners, let alone the Brahmos and Aryas. All the same, modification and simplification were desirable, and 'new rituals' should be developed to express the spirit of the age.[96]

THE NEW INDIA:
CLEANLINESS, SELF-RESTRAINT AND THRIFT, 1880–

The attitude of the new Indian elites to death ritual was also modified by a partial adoption of western notions of sanitation, public health, and civic responsibility. From the 1860s the British authorities had become somewhat more vigorous in promoting measures of medical and sanitary reform. Control of burning-*ghāts* and Muslim burial grounds seemed particularly important during periods of epidemic. As the price of firewood rose, the poor were less and less able to afford the cost of cremation and the services of attendant Doms. In many cases only the ritually impure parts of the body—especially the mouth—were burnt, and the corpse was simply thrown into the River Ganges, which was anyway considered to be an unequalled purifying agent. This may have given great joy to Rudyard Kipling's English subalterns who made a grand game of potting at the corpses as they floated down river, but it recommended itself less to the tough, and generally Scottish, breed of Medical Officers and Surgeons-Major who began to appear in India after the Mutiny. The need to protect Hindu holy places from the intervention of these energetic foreigners impelled further numbers of ortho-dox Hindus into public associations which could regulate practice at the *ghāts*. The desire to retain charge of pilgrimage centres, bathing and burning places or burial grounds was an important, and little recognized, force behind the growth of voluntary associations in late nineteenth century India. In 1912, for instance, the Allahabad Seva Samiti (Service Club) went so far

[95] See, e.g., *Brāhman Sarvāswa* (Allahabad), I–IV, 1891–93.
[96] S. P. Basu and S. B. Ghosh (eds.) *Vivekananda in Indian Newspapers* (Calcutta, 1969), cites *Madras Mail*, 6 Feb. 1897.

as to hire a champion swimmer to save drowning pilgrims and provide a boat to release and dispose of floating corpses which had got caught in mid-stream. An attempt was also made to cull the gargantuan alligators which waited hopefully on the riverside.[97]

Over the last hundred years, therefore, the funerary practices of even the most orthodox Hindu family have been simplified, standardized and reduced in cost and time-scale. Economy and other material changes have played a considerable part in speeding the decline of the old customs.[98] For instance, the gradual destruction of north India's forests has made the acquisition of scented wood more difficult. Fewer married women are now cremated in the costly red embroidered Banarsi sari, and white silk saris for widows are no longer obligatory. The decline of the old landed and princely families has removed some of the greatest benefactors of the holy places from the scene, and after the Depression of the 1930s, the level of general donations declined, never to revive. Also, the greater physical mobility of the population reduced the role of the funeral rituals as an *ad hoc* council and affirmation of the solidarity of the clan brotherhood. As the tie between the lineage and its area of land-control broke down, and more family members travelled outside the locality or even outside the country for employment, it proved increasingly difficult to assemble the relations to seven degrees. Thus Kayasth (writer caste) families in the United Provinces reduced the length of *shrāddha* rites from forty days to thirteen in the course of the last century. This was ostensibly because brethren in government service were unable to take sufficiently long leaves. But the traditional desire to raise caste status must also have played its part here. As we have seen, the lower the caste, the longer the rituals, and in the eighteenth century Kayasths in this region had evidently been ranked quite low.

Changes of attitude converged with these material incentives to simplicity. Very close observance of caste ranking disappeared at the burning *ghāts* as it disappeared in public transport and on the main roads. Differentials of caste continued to be observed, but without the great rigour of the past. Women and children began to appear at the burning *ghāts* in much greater numbers from the beginning of the present century and the concept of *shrāddha* as a feast of commemoration rather than as the actual embodiment of the soul in a new body appears to have gained currency even amongst those who venerate all the gods of the Vedanta and exercise ritual purity. One particular instance of changing attitudes is the erosion of the distinction

---

[97] *Report of the Sewa Samiti, 1913* (Allahabad, 1913), unpag., misc. collection of Sir Sunder Lal Dave, Allahabad.

[98] The following observations are based on interviews carried out in north India and England, 1979–80; I am particularly grateful to Mr. T. N. Sharma of the Oriental Faculty, Cambridge for his valuable information. It is much more difficult, of course, to measure *attitudes* to death, but Farquhar, *Modern Religious Movements*, p. 432, notes as early as 1909 that 'educated Indians' of that time found it difficult to believe that the ancestral spirit actually ate the sustenance offered in *shrāddha*

between 'unnatural' and 'natural' death following the spread of the western idea that all death is in some sense the result of disease. Previously children or people who died from rotting diseases and had not therefore completed their life-cycle had been buried rather than cremated. But in more recent times, even small children and lepers have been cremated in the towns.

After 1920 a further voice was added to those who denounced the cost and intricacy of death ritual. M. K. Gandhi's attitude to religion was coloured by a personal revulsion against the 'uncleanliness' which he with his one western eye saw in traditional India's holy places.[99] Dirt was a visible manifestation of the pilgrims' 'absent-mindedness, hypocrisy and slovenliness'. Inner cleanliness and outer cleanliness, individual and national purity must go hand in hand. The idea that death ceremonies are a public, even national act, reinforced an innate hostility to elaborate ritual which derived from his western Indian merchant background. He doubted that *shrāddha* had any effect on the moral fate of the spirit of the deceased,[100] let alone on its physical form. *Shrāddha* was even of dubious benefit to celebrants and relatives since they were only helping to perpetuate the spirit's cravings for the attachments of its past life. Gandhi's objections, then, derived not from rationalism but from his austere view of Karma and moral retribution. He urged his own bereaved friends and relatives to recite prayers and offer fruits only after funerals. Spinning homespun thread was also suggested: Gandhi saw in the spinning wheel a symbol of both individual and national salvation.

That all ritual and familial actions must be judged by national standards was a theme that Gandhi also emphasized in his strong opposition to the elaborate funeral feasts for caste-fellows and Brahmins which were often held on the eleventh day after death. In 1930, for instance, he strongly supported some young men in western India who had organized a boycott against a lavish funeral feast.[101] The money thus wasted should have been given to the poor, he considered. We see here the convergence of the tradition of hostility to lavish 'tribal' display with the more recent idea that Indians had duties to the nation which overrode the demands of kin and clan. This itself was a complex response to the intervention of the colonial state and its apologists in some corners of the ritual arena.

CONCLUSION

The history of death rituals in India is difficult to organize into clear epochs. Nearly all the elements of practice and belief which are prevalent in modern India among high caste and urban people were explicit in the great corpus

---

[99] Gandhi, *An Autobiography*, pp. 241–3.
[100] *Collected Works of Mahātma Gandhi*, XXX (Delhi, 1968), 321. 'If it [shraddha] has any spiritual utility, I do not know it. I do not understand too how a departed person is benefited through shraddha'.
[101] *Collected Works*, XXXVI (Delhi, 1970), 55–6.

of Puranic literature, and many can be traced back even earlier. What happened was a series of changes of emphasis rather than a succession of doctrinal and social breaks in funerary institutions and attitudes to death, such as is supposed to have characterized the history of Europe. Over the long term, the most characteristic change in the form of funerary ritual has been the slow assimilation of folk practices, in which the propitiation of spirits was the dominant purpose, to the orthodox Brahminical rite of *shrāddha* in which both living and dead were thought to acquire spiritual benefit. Yet even amongst the orthodox and high caste, *shrāddha* and the ceremonies connected with it has been ambiguous. There remained a strong 'tribal' element which was concerned with the succouring and 'creation' of ancestors, the confirming of the clan and the glorification of genealogy through conspicuous feasting, gifting and pilgrimage. On the other hand, there was the anti-ritualistic and philosophical interpretation of *shrāddha* which insisted on simplicity and held ritual to be largely irrelevant to the fate of the dead soul which was predetermined by the accumulated weight of good and evil actions in past incarnations.

In the seventeenth and eighteenth centuries, the 'tribal' aspect remained strong as new regional rulers sought to glorify their lineages and build up the holy cities which were favoured locations for *shrāddha*. The very wealth and 'corruption' of orthodox ritual, however, kept alive movements of religious teaching which rejected ritual as a way to salvation. In the colonial period, the reaction to Christianity and western notions of morality indirectly strengthened the part of tradition which considered that funerary rites should be more in the nature of an austere sacrifice of commemoration. The growth of towns, economic pressures and programmes of caste reform have tended to point in the same direction.

While the interpretation of the meaning of the rituals among the Hindu elites has shifted over time, there has also been a subtle change in the role of funerary rituals as indeed of other rituals in society at large. Until recent generations, ritual played a positive role in forming the Indian social order; it did not simply 'reflect' economic and social changes outside. We have seen how in the Dayabhaga school of law the ritual rules of *shrāddha* were used to determine inheritance rather than *vice versa*. In the eighteenth century, if not later, doubts about the identity of an heir could be resolved in the ritual arena when the identity of the chief sacrificer at the funeral was known. The ritual circle remained a dangerous place in which statuses could be created or compromised. Again, the priests of the holy places actively enhanced the prestige of their seats and elaborated rites which could affect the disposition of resources in society at large.

In recent generations, however, the potency of events in ritual arenas to alter the status or position in the world has diminished, though it continues to remain strong in the villages. Inheritance legislation has swept away the ritual rules of Dayabhaga law; inheritance and adoption are decided by legal instruments. The priestly establishment at the holy places, now diminished, has ceased actively to build clienteles and has succumbed to the intervention of purely commercial middlemen. We might say that there has been a general progression from ritual to ceremony. Ritual affects statuses in the outside world; ceremony merely confirms them.[102] This change appears to have occurred in European societies also and it has manifested itself in events as various as coronations, civic festivals and wakes for the dead. It is not that Indian, or even European society, has necessarily become more 'rational'. It is simply that the areas in which ritual performance could substantively modify the conduct of social life have been steadily reduced by the growth of a whole range of more specialized institutions connected with the state. Organs as diverse as the registrar's office, the law courts and the newspapers have come to resolve those conflicts which might once have been played out in the ritual circle.

[102] Cf. B. S. Cohn, 'Honour and Honours', unpublished paper presented to the SSRC Conference on Indian Social and Economic History, Cambridge, 1976.

186

VIII

War and Death, Grief and Mourning in Modern Britain

DAVID CANNADINE

The history of death in the Anglo-Saxon world during the modern period seems to be well established, at least in outline. The surveys of Ariès and Stannard, combined with the sociological studies of Gorer and Feifel, and the psychological investigations of Lifton and Olson, add up to an impressively uniform view.[1] During the nineteenth century, so the argument runs, western society was obsessed with death, whereas sex was virtually ignored. At a time of unprecedentedly high death rates, children were introduced to death—their own, their siblings' or their parents'—at an early age. The ceremonial of mourning and the ostentation of cemeteries reached new heights of extravagance: death, grief and bereavement were integral parts of life. But during the last eighty years or so, the position has been exactly reversed. Sex, formerly the taboo subject *par excellence,* has now been brought out into the open, while death, once the centre of attention, has 'become shameful and forbidden'. Patients now die alone and in hospital, instead of at home, surrounded by loving families, as in former times. In England, funerals are now perfunctory in the extreme—an attempt to deny death rather than come to terms with it. And in America, the same prevailing attitude has led to that extraordinary charade of morticians, caskets, embalming and 'Beautiful Memory Pictures' so hilariously sent up by Evelyn Waugh and devastatingly exposed by Jessica Mitford.[2] What was once commonplace has become forbidden; while what was once forbidden has become commonplace. In so far as the history of the western world is the history of the bedroom, the love-bed has replaced the death-bed as the central object of interest and attention.

As well as embodying a beguilingly symmetrical argument, this interpretation enjoys the dubious distinction of enlisting nostalgia in its sup-

---

[1] P. Ariès, *Western Attitudes Towards Death from the Middle Ages to the Present* (London, 1976), pp. 85–103; D. Stannard, *The Puritan Way of Death: A Study in Religion, Culture and Social Change* (New York, 1977), pp. 188–94; G. Gorer, *Death, Grief and Mourning in Contemporary Britain* (London, 1965), pp. 23–9, 171–2; C. W. Wahl, 'The Fear of Death', in H. Feifel (ed.), *The Meaning of Death* (London, 1959), pp. 26–7; R. J. Lifton and E. Olson, *Living and Dying* (London, 1974), pp. 19–21, 36. See also E. Kubler-Ross, *On Death and Dying* (London, 1970), esp. pp. 5–8.

[2] Evelyn Waugh, *The Loved One* (London, 1948); Jessica Mitford, *The American Way of Death* (London, 1963).

port—in the case of death, even if less so in the case of sex. The key work here, to which all subsequent studies are indebted, is Gorer's survey of grief and mourning in modern Britain. For, although his study was of contemporary England, his interpretation embodied a powerful and exceedingly influential historical perspective, which assumed that in the nineteenth century there had been a golden age of grief, in which the carefully structured and universally observed rituals of mourning provided necessary and successful support to those who were bereaved and in need of restructuring their lives.[3] But, he went on to argue, the decline of these important and useful rituals in the twentieth century has resulted in a society which gives little if any support to the bereaved. As a result, mourning, rather than being kept out in the open, is now treated 'as if it were a weakness, a self-indulgence, a reprehensible, bad habit, instead of a psychological necessity'.[4] Grieving has never been as traumatic as it is in modern Britain. The decline of the rituals of mourning, which had prevailed to such good purpose in the nineteenth century, is seen as a development in all ways to be regretted.

To this interpretation of grief the historians have recently added a corresponding argument with regard to dying. For if grieving in the nineteenth century was successful, death was almost pleasurable. Both Stannard and Ariès, in luxuriant, nostalgic prose, picture the Victorian death-bed scene as 'a ritual ceremony over which the dying person presides amidst his assembled relatives and friends', eagerly awaiting the 'sweet glory of salvation' and 'removal to a better world'.[5] By contrast, death in the twentieth century is degraded to the level of 'termination', a mere 'technical phenomenon', characterized by 'loneliness, irrelevance and an absence of awareness', in which the dying patient is cruelly, callously 'ejected from his customary social milieu', and leaves this world drugged, lonely and afraid.[6] In the twentieth century, death is as terrible as grieving is ineffective. Whatever may have happened to sex, the developments on the death front—at the level of dying as much as at the level of bereavement—are regarded with disapproval.[7]

This essay, by examining some aspects of war and death, grief and mourning, seeks to argue that this historical picture may be as mistaken as the nostalgia which underlies it is misplaced—at least in the case of modern Britain. It will suggest that the conventional picture of death in the nineteenth century is excessively romanticized and insufficiently nuanced; that it makes assumptions about the functional and therapeutic values of the elaborate

[3] Gorer, op. cit., pp. 8, 11, 110; J. Hinton, *Dying* (Harmondsworth, 1967), p. 188.
[4] C. M. Parkes, *Bereavement: Studies in Grief in Adult Life* (London, 1972), pp. 8–9, 142. See also: R. J. Kastenbaum, *Death, Society and Human Experience* (St. Louis, 1972), pp. 216–24; Ariès, op. cit., p. 92.
[5] Stannard, op. cit., pp. 174, 188; Ariès, op. cit., pp. 46, 58–68, 88.
[6] Stannard, op. cit., pp. 191–2; Ariès, op. cit., pp. 87–8, 92.
[7] For some well-stated criticism of this view, see: L. Stone, 'Death in New England', *New York Review of Books*, 19 October 1978, 44.

death-bed, funerary and mourning rituals which are unproven; and that it ignores significant developments—both ceremonial and demographic—at the end of the century. It will also maintain that the impact of the First World War on attitudes to death has been underrated by sociologists and historians; that its significance was profound for at least a generation; and that inter-war Britain was probably more obsessed with death than any other period in modern history. Finally, in the light of this alternative historical per-spective, it will argue that, contrary to both the received view and the prevailing nostalgia, the best time to die and to grieve in modern Britain is probably now.

I

The starting point from which the conventional argument is made is the undoubted ostentation of the Victorian funeral, at all levels of society. The last rites of the Duke of Wellington in 1852 were on a scale of grandeur and magnificence which was never attained before and has never been equalled since. 'Nothing shall be wanting in this tribute of national gratitude' observed Prince Albert, who was responsible for the arrangements; and nothing was.[8] Even relatively little-known aristocrats, like the sixth Duke of Devonshire, were made the centre of great pageants, with their coffins extravagantly decorated, and immensely long, solemn and splendid processions. When the fifth Duke of Rutland died in 1857, his lying-in-state was attended by 1,037 persons on the first day and 2,674 on the second, including five labourers who walked twenty-five miles each way.[9] In death as much as in life, the aristocracy was set apart on a plane different from that of ordinary mortals. And, although the middle classes could produce nothing to compare with this, the deaths of great civic or entrepreneurial worthies were commemorated with all possible pomp, as in the case of Robert Milligan, first Mayor of Bradford, M.P. for the town from 1852 to 1857, and the founder of one of its great mercantile houses.[10] Even members of the working class sought, in death, a level of ostentation which had been denied them in life. 'Nothing can exceed their desire for an imposing funeral', noted Edwin Chadwick in 1843. 'They would starve to pay the undertaker.' Indeed, in that year, it was calculated that of the £24 million deposited by the working classes in savings banks, over one quarter represented savings for funerals. As Ariès

---

[8] J. Morley, *Death, Heaven and the Victorians* (London, 1971), ch. 7; Elizabeth Longford, *Wellington: Pillar of State* (St. Albans, 1975), pp. 489–95.

[9] F. M. L. Thompson, *English Landed Society in the Nineteenth Century* (London, 1963), pp. 79–81; W. L. Burn, *The Age of Equipoise: A Study of the Mid-Victorian Generation* (London, 1964), p. 310.

[10] J. S. Curl, *The Victorian Celebration of Death* (Newton Abbot, 1972), pp. 2–8; S. Rawnsley and J. Reynolds, 'Undercliffe Cemetery, Bradford', *History Workshop Journal*, IV (1977), p. 216.

rightly notes, this was the period in which 'mourning was unfurled with an uncustomary degree of ostentation'.[11]

Why was this? What was its purpose? According to most authorities, the ritual and ceremonial of the death-bed, the graveside and of mourning fulfilled important functions, giving the greatest possible comfort to the dying, and meeting effectively the psychological needs of the bereaved survivors.[12] But this argument, influential though it is, is far from proven. To begin with, the assumption that extravagant ceremony and ostentation helped to ease the prospect of death for the dying is more easily asserted than it is demonstrated. As Lawrence Stone has recently argued, the picture of graceful, peaceful death in the bosom of the family is excessively romanticized. All too often, in the nineteenth century, death was painful, agonizing, even foul and embarrassing. In particular, the all-too-frequent death-bed scenes in which children were the central characters can rarely have approximated to that idealized final tableau in which the Victorian paterfamilias took moving and stately farewell of his nearest and dearest. Nor is it entirely clear that all victims looked on death as the road to glory: the fear of hell and damnation was for many as real as it was horrifying.[13]

In the same way, it remains undemonstrated exactly how—if at all—the elaborate rituals of mourning actually helped to assuage the grief of the survivors.[14] Olson and Lifton may assert that there is 'considerable psychological wisdom' in correct rituals of mourning.[15] But the nature of this wisdom remains elusive. At the most trivial level, even the wearing of mourning clothes might be more of a sartorial torture than it was psychologically therapeutic. Contemporaries noted that black veils were 'most unhealthy; they harm the eyes and injure the skin'. Likewise, black kid gloves were described as 'painfully warm and smutty, disfiguring the hand and soiling the handkerchief and face'.[16] More importantly, it might be argued that, far from wishing to make exhibitions of themselves by donning yards of black crêpe, most mourners would have preferred to be treated as normal human beings as soon as possible: something which the ostentatious wearing of black and the need to stay apart from society for a year or more by definition prevented. For the excessive concentration of mourning did not so much help the bereaved to come to terms with their loss and make a new life for themselves, but actually robbed them of the will to recover, and condemned them to spend their remaining years more obsessed with death

[11] Morley, op, cit., p. 11; P. Cunnington and C. Lucas, *Costumes for Birth, Marriage and Death* (London, 1964), p. 198; Ariès, op. cit., p. 67.
[12] Gorer, op. cit., pp. 15, 112.
[13] Stone, 'Death in New England', p. 44.
[14] The best account of the ritual of mourning—as distinct from the ritual of the funeral—is in L. Davidoff, *The Best Circles: Society, Etiquette and the Season* (London, 1973), pp. 54–6.
[15] Lifton and Olson, op. cit., p. 33; Gorer, op. cit., p. 110.
[16] Cunnington and Lucas, op. cit., pp. 250–2.

than was either necessary or healthy—as exemplified most spectacularly in the case of Queen Victoria. When Dr Watson's wife died, Sherlock Holmes told him that 'work is the best antidote to sorrow', and his scepticism of the assumed efficacy of conventional modes of mourning is one which merits further attention.[17]

In other words, it is arguable that the Victorian celebration of death was not so much a golden age of effective psychological support as a bonanza of commercial exploitation. The elaborate funerary and mourning rituals were more an assertion of status than a means of assuaging sorrow, a display of conspicuous consumption rather than an exercise in grief therapy, from which the chief beneficiary was more likely to be the undertaker than the widow. Indeed, in both its extravagance and its ineffectiveness, the English way of death in the nineteenth century may most plausibly be seen as the direct precursor of the American way of death in the twentieth. Then, in England, as now in America, the bereaved were pestered by undertakers whose main aim was to make as much money as possible. The yards of crepe which mourning etiquette required were of more importance in making the fortunes of firms like Courtaulds than they were in comforting the bereaved. The whole obsessive paraphernalia of mourning pin cushions, mourning brooches, mourning aprons, mourning lockets, mourning neck-laces, mourning earrings, mourning parasols, mourning handkerchiefs and even mourning bathing costumes, were more a cause of financial anxiety to the bereaved than a source of emotional solace.[18] 'The terror of inevitable expense' was a very real threat.

Whatever historians and sociologists may think of them now, some con-temporaries in the nineteenth century had no doubt that the excessively extravagant Victorian funerary and mourning customs *did not work* and fulfilled *no useful function*—except that of filling the pockets of the under-takers and other tradesmen who thrived on public bereavement and sorrow. 'We do not hesitate', thundered the *Quarterly Review* 'to denounce the present accumulation of ceremony and outlay at funerals as not only ridicu-lous but sinful.' At a time when between £4 and £5 million was being spent annually on such pursuits, their outrage is understandable. Forty years later, *Woman's World* made the same point even more emphatically:

The customs are neither good in themselves, nor did they command general approval. Mourning made its demands at the worst possible time, when money was short and when grief had enervated the mourners. Relatives met and discussed dress, and sought the shopkeeper's advice in a manner that could only be distasteful; how much crepe should be worn, whether it should be worn in that shape or this, whether an edging, rather than a whole width, would do, and so on. Sometimes,

---

[17] A. Conan Doyle, *The Return of Sherlock Holmes* (London, 1964), p. 16. This book was first published in 1905.

[18] Cunnington and Lucas, op. cit., p. 253.

an illness in a family would, in a very unpleasant, calculating way, restrain relatives from buying new clothes.[19]

Suitably updated, this might be straight from the pages of Jessica Mitford.

Likewise, those great mid-Victorian cemeteries—Highgate and Kensal Green in London, Undercliffe in Bradford, Mount Auburn in Boston and Greenwood in New York—were very much the Forest Lawns of their time, in both their expense and their status consciousness.[20] For these romantic, rural retreats were essentially an analogue of romantic, rural suburbia. Their careful layout, with greenery, gardens, gently curving roads, and restful, contrived vistas, was exactly reminiscent of exclusive, middle-class building estates like Headingley or Edgbaston. Their precisely-graded plots, placing a premium on location, accessibility and view, reflected the same subtle social gradations of suburbia itself. And their family vaults, in which parents and children were once more re-united, reaffirmed that same middle-class belief in the sanctity of family life (or death) that was embodied in that other great bastion of bourgeois values, the middle-class villa. If a house was a machine for the middle classes to die in, a vault was a machine for them to decompose in. In every sense, Kensal Green was the Hampstead of the dead. Within the limits of the technology available, the nineteenth-century way of death was as much of a racket as its twentieth-century successor across the Atlantic. It was not a halcyon era of grief in the sense that it was effectively assuaged, but only in that it was commercially profitable.

Moreover, it was of relatively limited duration, fully established by the 1840s, but already in decline by the 1880s. In 1875, the National Funeral and Mourning Reform Association was founded to campaign for 'moderation' and 'simplicity' instead of 'unnecessary show', and vehemently attacked the excessive cost and cynical manipulation by undertakers of funerals.[21] Equally significant were technological changes. In America, such developments at the end of the nineteenth century merely served to replace one form of ostentation by another—caskets, embalming and the like.[22] But in England, by contrast, technological change served to *lessen* the display. By 1909, thirteen crematoria were operating, and the Cremation Society numbered among its champions such luminaries as the Duke of Westminster and the Duke of Bedford.[23] The advent of the motor-driven hearses from the 1900s was a further nail in the coffin of ostentation. In high society, too, there was

[19] Morley, op. cit., pp. 13, 22, 24, 76.

[20] T. Bender, 'The rural cemetery movement: urban travail and the appeal of nature', *New England Quarterly*, XLVII (1974), pp. 197, 199, 204, 210; Stannard, op. cit., pp. 167–88; Rawnsley and Reynolds, op. cit., pp. 215–20.

[21] Morley, op. cit., pp. 76–8; Cunnington and Lucas, op. cit., p. 198.

[22] Stannard, op. cit., p. 188.

[23] B. S. Puckle, *Funeral Customs: Their Origin and Development* (London, 1926), pp. 126, 228; P. H. Jones and G. A. Noble, *Cremation in Great Britain* (London, 1931), pp. 15–57; C. J. Polson and T. K. Marshall, *The Disposal of the Dead* (3rd. edn., London, 1975), p. 39; Morley, op. cit., pp. 91–8.

revulsion against the excesses of the past. Queen Victoria's funeral, although incomparably better organized than Wellington's was far less elaborate, just as Gladstone's had been less extravagant than Palmerston's. And King Edward VII, on acceding to the throne, ordered that mourning for his mother should not last beyond April, so that the season might be unaffected. And this was in harmony with more general developments. As one contemporary noted in 1901: 'For the last decade or so, the time of mourning for private persons has been considerably shortened, and the mourning garb itself shorn of much of its distinctiveness.'[24] The revolution against ostentatious but ineffectual rituals of dying and grieving was already well under way.

But these changes in taste and technology, which served to place the English way of death on an entirely different evolutionary path to that across the Atlantic, paled into insignificance compared with the massive, dramatic and unprecedented fall in the death rate which took place at the same time. The exact reasons for this still remain in dispute. But it seems likely that medical improvements, better standards of public health, improved housing conditions, higher wages, shorter working hours and a more nourishing diet all played some part in it.[25] The result was a spectacular fall in the death rate itself, from 22 per thousand in the 1870s to 13 per thousand by 1910. And the simultaneous fall in fertility meant that not only were fewer children being born, but also that an even smaller proportion were dying in infancy. While in Victorian England it was a commonplace for parents to grieve for the loss of some of their offspring, and for the children themselves to possess a vivid sense of impending death at an early age, by Edwardian times these experiences were increasingly rare.[26] As life expectancy rose, from 40 for a man in the mid-nineteenth century to 52 by 1910, death became more commonly associated with old age. Parents might, with growing confidence, expect their children to outlive them, and for their part, the younger generation, instead of being surrounded by death, came increasingly to live in the 'intense present'.[27]

Accordingly, it can be argued that some of the changes in attitudes to death which Ariès vaguely dates as belonging to the last thirty years or so were in fact under way in the decades before the First World War.[28] The 'denial of death', so often assumed to date from the years after 1945, had already started well before 1914. Moreover, to some contemporaries then, if not to historians now, these changes were seen as an *improvement*. In

---

[24] Ibid., p. 78.
[25] For a full discussion of this, with a comprehensive bibliography, see: R. Mitchison, *British Population Change Since 1860* (London, 1977), pp. 41–57.
[26] Ibid., pp. 23–5; D. Vincent, 'The Growth of Working-Class Consciousness in the First Half of the Nineteenth Century: A Study in the Autobiographies of Working Men' (Ph.D. thesis, University of Cambridge, 1975), pp. 73–5.
[27] Hinton, op. cit., p. 53; R. Kastenbaum, 'Time and Death in Adolescence', in Feifel, loc. cit., pp. 104–9.
[28] Ariès, op. cit., pp. 85, 87.

1899, for instance, an article appeared in the *Fortnightly Review* entitled
'The dying of death'.[29] 'Perhaps the most distinctive note of the modern
spirit', the author began, 'is the practical disappearance of the thought of
death as an influence directly bearing upon practical life'. In Medieval
Europe, he explained, 'death was king', and 'he not only reigned but
governed'. But recently, he suggested, all this had changed:

> The Church in all its sections is devoting more and more to this life than any
> other. Death is regarded no longer as King of Terrors ... The fear of death is
> being replaced by the joy of life. The flames of Hell are sinking low, and even
> Heaven has but poor attractions for the modern man. Full life here and now is
> the demand; what may come after is left to take care of itself ... Death is
> disappearing from our thoughts.

How did he explain this relatively novel development? In part, he
suggested, the answer lay in the decline of theological interest in the after
life, and in part because of 'the increasing popularity of cremation'. More
generally, he argued that 'the increased age and duration of life' meant that,
compared with earlier times, death was increasingly occurring at an age
which seemed appropriate: 'nowadays', he argued, 'death comes later, with
more warnings of his approach, and takes us less by surprise. We are more
willing to go, less willing to stay.' At the same time, he suggested that the
evolution of a mass, urban society, highly mobile and specialized, meant that
life was too crowded and busy to be dominated, as of old, by thoughts of
death:

> We are cast back for a moment on to our natural, feeling self, when we hear of
> a friend's death; but almost immediately the claims of modern life are upon us.
> Letters have to be written, business or even pleasure has to be attended to; we
> send a wreath, and our friend drops out of our life.

'Thus', he concluded,

> on all sides death is losing its terrors. We are dying more frequently when our
> life's work is done, and it seems more natural to die. We live so hurriedly that
> the final ceasing to be is getting to be regarded as the *summum bonum*.

Other contemporaries agreed in detecting important changes in attitudes
to death at the end of the nineteenth century. Here, for instance, is Freud's
account of prevailing attitudes in the years before 1914:

> We show an unmistakable tendency to put death on one side, to eliminate it from
> life. We try to hush it up ... The civilized adult can hardly even entertain
> the thought of another person's death ... Our habit is to lay stress on the fortuitous
> causation of death—accident, disease, infection, advanced age; in this way we
> betray an effort to reduce death from a necessity to a chance event.

Or, as he put it elsewhere, the 'tendency to exclude death from our

[29] J. Jacobs, 'The Dying of Death', *Fortnightly Review*, LXXII (1899), 264–9.

calculation' was already commonplace.[30] Indeed, Geoffrey Gorer's own lack of experience of death in the years before 1914 offers exact corroboration of this view. None of his close relatives had died. He had witnessed no death-bed scenes. Nor had he seen any corpse. And when, in 1915, his father went down in the *Lusitania,* he recalls that 'I cannot remember anyone, master or boy, talking seriously to me about death in general or the death of my father in particular'.[31]

But if the *celebration* of death was on the wane from the 1880s onwards, the *glorification* of death—of death on active service, in battle, in the front line, for one's country—was markedly on the increase. The growing inter-national tensions of these years, combined with the ever-widening appeal of ideas of social Darwinism, and the stridently athletic ethos of the late-Victorian and Edwardian public school, produced an atmosphere in which soldiering and games were equated, in which death was seen as unlikely, but where, if it happened, it could not fail to be glorious. In the pages of *My Early Life,* for instance, Churchill recalls how, at Harrow and in India, war was treated by masters and soldiers alike as merely an extension of games. The Dulwich school song—'Fifteen fellows fighting full, out for death or glory'—embodies the same sentiment, as does Newbolt's 'Vitae Lampada', where the solution to difficulties in cricket or in soldiering is 'play up, play up and play the game'.[32] As Osbert Sitwell recalls:

> We were still in the trough of peace that had lasted a hundred years between the two great conflicts. In it, such wars as arose were not general, but only a brief armed version of the Olympic Games. You won a round; the enemy won the next. There was no more talk of extermination, of Fights to a Finish, than would occur in a boxing match.[33]

Once more, Gorer himself provides corroboration, in describing his own attitude to death in his pre-war, schoolboy days:

> The only death that I contemplated was natural death. Violent death was exotic, a thing which happened in books—I was an avid reader of Conan Doyle and, particularly, of Rider Haggard—and did not represent any sort of domestic threat.[34]

In other words, the assumption which underlay the late-Victorian and Edwardian glorification of death in battle was that there would not be very much of it. How else can one explain the patriotic *naïveté* of this comment by Sir Garnet Wolseley, on the death of one of his soldiers: 'I envy him the manner of his death—if I had ten sons, I should be proud if all ten fell as

[30] Sigmund Freud, 'Thoughts for the Times on War and Death: II: Our Attitude Towards Death' (1915), in J. Strachey (ed.), *The Standard Edition of the Complete Psychological Works of Sigmund Freud,* vol. XIV (London, 1957), pp. 289–91.

[31] Gorer, op. cit., p. 3.

[32] G. Best, 'Militarism and the Victorian Public School', in B. Simon and I. Bradley (eds.), *The Victorian Public School* (London, 1975), pp. 142–3.

[33] Osbert Sitwell, *Great Morning!* (Boston, 1947), p. 199.

[34] Gorer, op. cit., p. 2.

he fell.'[35] As the First World War was to show, once this possibility became real, the empty bombast of such shallow rhetoric was soon exposed as offering neither comfort nor consolation. But until then, such attitudes remained paramount. In 1905, for instance, General Sir Ian Hamilton unveiled a Boer War memorial at a minor public school, and announced—with evident approval—that soldiers who died for their country met death 'as a bridegroom who goes to meet his bride'.[36] Indeed, by this time, the cult of 'manliness and good learning' had produced a code of living 'so robust and patriotic in its demands that it could be represented as reaching its perfection in the code of dying'. Certainly, this was the moral to be drawn from H. A. Vachell's *The Hill* where, in the finale, Henry Desmond's death while fighting for his country is made the occasion of this moving exhortation:

> To die young, clean, ardent; to die swiftly, in perfect health; to die saving others from death, or worse—disgrace—to die scaling heights; to die and carry with you into fuller, ampler life beyond, untainted hopes and aspirations, unembittered memories, all the freshness and gladness of May—is not that cause for joy rather than sorrow?[37]

At that time (1905), not only the public-school elite, but also those lower down the social scale who aped its values and absorbed its attitudes, would have answered 'yes' unhesitatingly.[38]

II

Such was the prevailing attitude towards death at the outbreak of war in 1914. The English were less intimately acquainted with death than any generation since the industrial revolution. The death rate had fallen markedly. The ostentation of mourning had been in decline for over thirty years. Dying was increasingly associated with old age. At the same time, death on the battlefield was seen as something noble, heroic, splendid, romantic—*and unlikely*. As A. J. P. Taylor has rightly noted, in 1914 'no man in the prime of life knew what war was like. All imagined that it would be an affair of great marches and great battles, quickly decided.'[39] Indeed, it was this universally-held presupposition which in part explains the extraordinary enthusiasm with which men of all classes volunteered. 'Our one great fear', Sir Oswald Mosley recalls, 'was that the war would be over before we got there.' 'Our major anxiety', agrees Harold Macmillan, 'was

---

[35] J. Morris, *Pax Britannica: The Climax of an Empire* (London, 1975), p. 465.
[36] Best, loc. cit., pp. 144–5.
[37] D. Newsome, *Godliness and Good Learning: Four Studies on a Victorian Ideal* (London, 1961), p. 238; H. A. Vachell, *The Hill* (London, 1937 edn.), p. 236.
[38] J. Springhall, *Youth, Empire and Society: British Youth Movements, 1883–1940* (London, 1977), p. 40.
[39] A. J. P. Taylor, *The First World War* (Harmondsworth, 1966), p. 158.

by hook or by crook not to miss it.'[40] Indeed, for most soldiers in their early days at the front, the public-school attitude held up surprisingly well. 'It's all great fun', Rupert Brooke kept repeating in his letters home. 'You wouldn't think it was war', noted another officer. 'There is a fine heroic feeling about being in France', agreed Wilfred Owen, 'and I am in perfect spirits.'[41]

But such feelings—'young, clean, ardent' in the best H. A. Vachell tradition—could not long survive the reality of life (and death) at the front. Only two weeks after writing the missive just quoted, Wilfred Owen sent his parents a very different sort of letter. 'I can see no excuse for deceiving you about these four days. I have suffered seventh hell.'[42] All those naive beliefs—that war was a game; that death was unlikely; and that, if it came, it would be experienced 'swiftly and in perfect health'—were devastatingly destroyed by the first experience of bombardment in the trenches. 'Men of whatever age', Harold Macmillan recalls, 'are not often confronted with death—certainly not violent death. Now we lived with death, day by day.'[43] On the first day of the Battle of the Somme, 20,000 soldiers were killed, the greatest loss ever suffered in a single day by the British army, and the equivalent of all British losses in the Boer War. All in all, some 722,785 British citizens died as a direct result of the war, and the total losses of the Empire as a whole were over one million.[44] In an attempt to render such incomprehensible figures meaningful, Sir Fabian Ware calculated that if the Empire's dead marched four abreast down Whitehall, it would take them *three and a half days* to pass the Cenotaph. With no exaggeration, Leon Wolff rightly describes the First World War as a 'carnival of death'.[45]

Altogether, some six million men from the United Kingdom fought during the First World War, so that roughly one in eight were killed (to say nothing of a further one and a half million who were disabled).[46] And when broken down, the figures become even more extraordinary. Of the men who were aged 20–24 in 1914, death came to 30.58 per cent, and of those aged 13–19, the figure was 28.15 per cent which, as Rosalind Mitchison notes, 'meant grief and shock for almost every family in the country'.[47] In 1842, when campaigning for better sanitation, Edwin Chadwick had noted that 'the annual losses of life from filth and bad ventilation are greater than the loss

[40] Sir Oswald Mosley, *My Life* (London, 1968), p. 44; Harold Macmillan, *Winds of Change, 1914–1939* (London, 1966), p. 59.
[41] P. Fussell, *The Great War and Modern Memory* (Oxford, 1977), pp. 25, 81.
[42] Ibid., p. 81.
[43] Macmillan, op. cit., p. 98.
[44] J. M. Winter, 'Some Aspects of the Demographic Consequences of the First World War in Britain', *Population Studies*, XXX (1976), 541.
[45] J. Morris, *Farewell the Trumpets: An Imperial Retreat* (London, 1978), p. 201; L. Wolff, *In Flanders Fields: The 1917 Campaign* (Harmondsworth, 1979), p. 11.
[46] J. M. Winter, 'Britain's "Lost Generation" of the First World War', *Population Studies*, XXXI (1977), 450.
[47] Mitchison, op. cit., p. 59.

from death or wounds in any wars in which the country has been engaged in modern times'.[48] But the subsequent improvements in sanitation and nutrition, combined with the sudden catastrophe of 1914 meant that, for the next five years at least, that proposition was spectacularly reversed. Once more, the angel of death had been abroad throughout the land; but this time the beating of his wings was not so much inaudible as deafening.

But in one sense, at least, Bright's Crimean War speech was appropriate to this later conflict. For once again, it was both 'the castle of the rich and the cottage of the lowly' that the angel of death visited in these years. Anthony Eden, the second son of a landed baronet, lost his elder brother John in October 1914, and his younger brother Nicholas was killed at Jutland two years later. Like many others who received such news, Eden at first was incredulous:

> In my wretchedness, I could hardly believe it . . . Of course I knew that Nicholas ran some risks, but I had never doubted for a moment that he would come through all right, whatever happened to the rest of us. . . . It was fortunate for me that during these weeks I was heavily occupied.[49]

And yet, compared with Mrs Elizabeth Ann Butler of Leicester, the Eden family was relatively fortunate. All her eight sons served in the army, of whom three were killed in France, one died from consumption following exposure at the front, one was wounded twice, and another once.[50] It is doubtful whether Wolseley's words would have been of much comfort. As Harold Macmillan recalls, the 'shadow of death had begun to darken all our young lives':

> The list of dead piled up, month by month and year by year, to a frightful sum. There were the great names of those to whom I had looked up in my childhood . . . There were those whom I had met in my short Oxford life . . . Then there were Eton friends, Oxford friends and regimental friends, friends of my own age, and now, alas, friends even younger than I. Day by day the list grew. One scarcely dared to read the newspapers, especially if a new battle had begun to rage.[51]

As this quotation implies, although the aggregate losses suffered by the working class were the greatest, the largest proportional loss was among the elite—landowners, businessmen and members of the great professions. They joined up first and, as the backbone of the officer class, ran a far greater risk of death than did the rank and file. As early as December 1914, six peers, sixteen baronets, six knights, ninety-four sons of peers, eighty-two sons of baronets and eighty-four sons of knights had been killed. Of the twelve Eton scholars elected in 1906, five did not return from the war. Nor did 578 of the 2,100 Old Cliftonians who volunteered. The death rate of Balliol

---

[48] Morley, op. cit., pp. 9–10.
[49] S. Aster, *Anthony Eden* (London, 1976), p. 5; Anthony Eden, *Another World, 1897–1917* (London, 1976), pp. 82–3.
[50] F. Armitage, *Leicester 1914–1918* (Leicester, 1933), p. 348.
[51] Macmillan, op. cit., pp. 78, 95.

graduates who joined up was precisely twice the national average. Of the Oxford generation which matriculated in 1913, 31 per cent were killed.[52] What this meant in personal terms is well evoked by the reminiscences of the second Lady Curzon, who vividly recalls the labour which she and her husband undertook in writing letters of condolence to their friends:

> Reading through the personal letters addressed to George at this time, . . . I am impressed once more by the terrible toll of young lives exacted by the First War. There was scarcely one of our friends who did not lose a son, a husband or a brother. Among George's correspondence there are countless letters written in reply to the condolences he had sent his friends on the loss of their sons. There are letters from Lord Shuttleworth, Lord Albemarle, Lord Falkland, Lord Barnard, Lord Denbigh, Lord Trewern, Lord Kinnaird, the Bishop of Derby, Dr. Pember, the Warden of All Souls—to mention only a few . . . Truly, England lost the flower of her young men in those terrible days.[53]

Here, indeed, is the origin of the belief in that 'lost generation' of poets, philosophers and politicians, men of brilliance, promise and innocence, who were snuffed out in the carnage of the First World War.[54] 'Nobody, nothing', argues J. B. Priestley, 'will shift me from the belief, which I shall take to the grave, that the generation to which I belong, destroyed between 1914 and 1918, was a great generation, marvellous in its promise.'[55] F. A. Simpson, in his commemoration sermon at Cambridge in November 1932, made the same point even more emphatically:

> Our true leaders, as well in literature and the arts as in public life—but most of all, I think, in public life—our true leaders were taken from our head now nearly twenty years ago: when a generation was not decimated but decapitated; not mauled at mere haphazard, but shorn precisely of its grace and glory, of its most ardent, its most generous, its most brave. . . . Our born leaders are dead.[56]

Stanley Baldwin, the most dominant political figure between the wars, certainly agreed. 'There is nothing', he observed on the occasion of the unveiling of a war memorial, 'in the first twenty years after the war that can make good to this country the loss of so many men of that age.'[57] As his most recent biographers note, throughout his years of fame, power and office, Baldwin retained a sincere, abiding belief that 'he was in command only because better men lay underground. . . . He held power by the sufferance

[52] Winter, 'Britain's "Lost Generation" ', pp. 457–65; idem, 'Balliol's "Lost Generation" ', Balliol College Annual Record (1975) p. 23; D. Winter, Death's Men: Soldiers of the Great War (London, 1978), p. 31; R. Hyam, Britain's Imperial Century, 1815–1914 (London, 1976), p. 378.

[53] The Marchioness Curzon of Kedleston, Reminiscences (London, 1955), pp. 85–6.

[54] Winter, 'Balliol's "Lost Generation" ', p. 26. For the best summary of the 'lost generation' argument, see: R. Wohl, The Generation of 1914 (London, 1980), pp. 85–6.

[55] J. B. Priestley, Margin Released: A Writer's Reminiscences and Reflections (London, 1962), p. 136.

[56] F. A. Simpson, 'A Sermon Preached in Great St. Mary's Church at the Commemoration of Benefactors, 2 November 1932', Cambridge Review, November 1932.

[57] Stanley Baldwin, On England (London, 1926), p. 64.

of the dead'.[58] And the young R. A. Butler, who owed his early promotion to Baldwin, was of the same opinion: had it not been for the disasters of the war, 'those of us who were called to office would not have come to the front so early and with so little experience'.[59]

But, while it cannot be doubted that there was, to some extent, among the elite groups a 'lost generation', the degree to which it was a 'demographic disaster' is much less clear.[60] To begin with, it is important to stress that, even among the elite, the majority of men who served *did actually come back*. Moreover, Britain's losses were, proportionately, far less than France's or Germany's.[61] In addition, it is a mistake to suppose that the men in the age groups which suffered the heaviest losses of life would have risen to positions of power and leadership in the mere twenty-one years of peace which separated the two wars.[62] Men of Anthony Eden's generation were still relatively young in 1939. The levers of power would only have been theirs in the 1940s and 1950s, the period when, appropriately, all Britain's Prime Ministers (with the exception of Neville Chamberlain) had served in the trenches. Baldwin may have believed that he held power on 'the sufferance of the dead'. But none of those whom he defeated in the inter-war years—Curzon, Macdonald, Lloyd George, the press lords—had been front line soldiers in the great conflict.

In demographic terms, too, the loss must be put in perspective. Fewer men were lost as a result of the war than had emigrated from Britain in the decade before 1914.[63] And, although the birth rate had declined during the war, with so many men away, the compensatory fluctuation in the years immediately afterwards meant that the losses were soon made good. In Leeds, for example, the birth rate stood at 23.6 per 1,000 in 1914, and then fell to 17 per 1,000 in the war years. But in 1920 it was 25 per 1,000, and in 1921 22 per 1,000, so that the town's total losses were made good in one year. And the figures for the nation as a whole are almost identical.[64] Even the myth of the maiden aunt—those millions of women condemned to eternal spinsterhood because their would-be husbands lay dead in the fields of Flanders—has recently been shown to be fallacious. Among the women aged 20 to 44 in England and Wales in 1921, 40.7 per cent were unmarried, whereas for the same group in 1911, the figure was actually larger at 41.6 per cent.[65] Even in France, where 1 in 28 of the population died compared

[58] K. Middlemas and J. Barnes, *Baldwin: A Biography* (London, 1969), pp. 53–5.
[59] Lord Butler, *The Art of the Possible* (London, 1971), p. 8.
[60] Hyam, op. cit., pp. 378–9.
[61] Wohl, op. cit., pp. 113–5.
[62] H. Pelling, *Britain and the Second World War* (London, 1970), p. 273; A. J. P. Taylor, *English History 1914–45* (Harmondsworth, 1970), pp. 165–6.
[63] Ibid., p. 165; Mitchison, op. cit., p. 59.
[64] Winter, *Death's Men*, p. 255; A. S. Milward, *The Economic Effects of the Two World Wars on Great Britain* (London, 1970), p. 15; M. Howard, *Studies in War and Peace* (London, 1970), p. 108.
[65] Mitchison, op. cit., pp. 59–60.

with 1 in 66 in England, the demographic effects were less than expected.[66] As Dennis Winter rightly notes, 'the carnage of the Somme, Ypres, Arras and all the set battles of the western front was of little long-term consequence, *provided* that one can ignore the grief associated with loss'.[67]

But that, of course, was impossible. For in the inter-war years, the myth of the 'lost generation' took on a life of its own.[68] Baldwin may have been in error in supposing that he ruled on the sufferance of the dead; but the fact that he believed it sincerely cannot be doubted. The abiding sense of loss throughout the land was as real as it was unassuageable.[69] When writing his classic survey, *England their England* in 1933, A. G. Macdonell included this piece of dialogue between Donald Cameron and a villager:

> '. . . There's no one between them and the old chaps like us'.
> 'All the rest were killed, you mean?'
> 'Most of them, sir. Forty two were killed from this village, and they'd be men of thirty five and forty by now'.
> 'Ah! That War didn't do any of us any good', said Mr. Stillway. 'Nothing's been the same since.'[70]

Above all, it was in those public schools and universities, from whose pupils and alumni the officer class had largely been recruited, that the sense of loss was most acute. The mood is well caught in this unpublished poem by E. W. Hornung written in the 1920s:

> Who are the ones that we cannot see,
>   Though we feel them as near as near?
> In chapel we felt them bend the knee,
>   At the match one felt them cheer.
> In the deep still shade of the colonnade,
>   In the ringing quad's full light,
> They are laughing here, they are chaffing there
>   Yet never in sound or sight.[71]

Even Churchill, often accused of glorifying war and gore, sensed the deep melancholy that underlay the euphoric rejoicings on Armistice Day in 1918:

> These hours were brief, their memory fleeting; they passed as suddenly as they had begun. Too much blood had been spilt. Too much life-essence had been

[66] For the effects of the First World War on France's population, see: L. Henry, 'Perturbations de la Nuptialité Résultant de la Guerre 1914–1918', *Population*, XXI (1966), 273–332.

[67] Winter, *Death's Men*, p. 255.

[68] Winter, 'Britain's "Lost Generation"', p. 465.

[69] This seems to be the central point missed by Wohl (op. cit., pp. 210–11), who writes off the 'lost generation' as an élite myth. Having examined the First World War through the eyes of Brooke, Sassoon *et al.*, he is almost bound to reach this conclusion. But the *responses* to the First World War in the inter-war years which, significantly, his book ignores, show just how widespread this sense of loss was. The fact that the élite suffered disproportionately, and that their fate was stressed disproportionately via memoirs, is of little help in explaining that *mass* appeal of the Cenotaph, or the cult of the *Unknown* Warrior. See below, section VI.

[70] A. G. Macdonell, *England, Their England* (London, 1971 edn.), p. 196.

[71] Morris, *Farewell the Trumpets*, p. 411.

consumed. The gaps in every home were too wide and empty. .... There still remained the satisfaction of safety assured, of peace restored, of honour preserved, of the comforts of fruitful industry, of the homecoming of the soldiers; but these were in the background; and with them all there mingled the ache for those who would never come home.[72]

For Churchill, war had not only been stripped of that 'glitter and glamour' about which he had learned in public school: it had also reached such a level of technological refinement and sophistication that death, already of unparalleled magnitude in the conflict just ended, had now become a part of life as never before:

> Mankind ... has got into its hands for the first time the tools by which it can unfailingly accomplish its own extermination. This is the point in human destinies to which all the glories and toils of men have at last led them. They would do well to pause and ponder upon their new responsibilities. Death stands at attention, obedient, expectant, ready to serve, ready to sheer away the people *en masse*; ready if called upon, to pulverize, without hope of repair, what is left of civilisation. He awaits only the word of command. He awaits it from a frail, bewildered being, long his victim, now—for once only—his master.[73]

Although few would have expressed their ideas on the subject with quite such rhetorical luxuriance, there can be no doubt that the fear of further—and even greater—death by war, and the desire to avoid it at almost any cost, bulked large in the conduct of Britain's foreign policy during the 1920s and 1930s.[74] The 'shadows of Passchendaele' cast their gloom and melancholy far into the next two decades—shadows to which historians and sociologists writing about death in twentieth-century Britain have paid peculiarly little attention.

III

Such was death in general during the First World War: what was it like in particular?[75] Among those six million men who served—over half the adult male labour force of the United Kingdom—there was one fundamental division, between the death of others and the death of self. And, in most cases, it was the death of others which evoked the most sustained and varied responses: for that was the product of experience, whereas death of self remained something which could only exist in the imagination. Those doctors and psychologists who have analysed death have argued that there is a limit

[72] Winston S. Churchill, *The World Crisis: The Aftermath* (London, 1929), p. 19.

[73] Ibid., pp. 450, 454–5.

[74] Pelling, op. cit., p. 273.

[75] In the sections which follow, I have deliberately avoided using the evidence from the poetry of the First World War, largely because this has been so thoroughly analyzed already. For the most recent anthology of the poetry, see: J. Silkin (ed.), *The Penguin Book of First World War Poetry* (Harmondsworth, 1979). For analysis, see: J. H. Johnston, *English Poetry of the First World War* (Princeton, 1964); H. D. Spear, *Remembering We Forget: A Background Study to the Poetry of the First World War* (London, 1979).

to what human beings can witness without becoming immune to those normal feelings of horror, sorrow and revulsion which the sight of the dead usually evokes. 'Too frequent losses in war', notes Hinton, 'can blunt the expression or even the feeling of grief. The saturation with sorrow and the bitter necessity to adapt and carry on reduce the intensity of grief over repeated tragedies.'[76] And Lord Moran, analysing the behaviour of soldiers during the First World War, reached the same conclusion:

> The annihilation of thousands of his own people, the death of many of his friends, may shake the foundations of all but the most stable. His faculties may be numbed, his will frozen by the appalling carnage. A torpor affecting all his thoughts and actions may fall upon him, or his sense may be left raw by the horrid slaughter.[77]

'The dead', agrees Dennis Winter, 'appeared to be quickly forgotten, certainly in conversation.'[78]

Assuredly, there is much evidence in support of such a view. 'The dead were the dead', Siegfried Sassoon noted; 'this was not time to be pitying them or asking silly questions about their outraged lives. Such sights must be taken for granted, I thought'.[79] To the question 'what of the dead and wounded?', Guy Chapman returned a similar answer: 'The dead no longer count. War has no use for dead men. With luck they will be buried later.'[80] No doubt this was, in part, the result of the surfeit of death, in which sympathy was stupefied and the senses were numbed. Maze admitted that he was 'indifferent to the sight of our own dead', and when convalescing in hospital, he discovered further evidence of his own insensitivity:

> All these men in the ward, with the exception of myself, are bad cases; they have been here some days, and I have watched them with the eye of a man who observes but cannot feel—I can feel no more; I am not callous—I am merely immune from reaction to wounds, blood, bandages, suffering, even to death.[81]

'The more men die,' agreed Graham, 'the easier it becomes to die. Death becomes cheaper and cheaper. It becomes a matter of the everyday.'[82] But in addition, this feeling arose from the awareness that to bring the dead back from the battle zone only involved further (and worthless) risk to life and limb. In the words of Guy Chapman:

> They remained a long time without burial, for who was going to risk lives for such a task? The weather was no longer hot, and the dead would keep. They lay out there at the side of the track in the drizzle, yellow or grey or blue with blood dried black on their skin and clothes; sometimes a shell would hasten the indignity of slow decomposition. They were certainly not worth another life.[83]

[76] Hinton, op. cit., p. 174.
[77] Lord Moran, *The Anatomy of Courage* (London, 1945), p. 43.
[78] Winter, *Death's Men*, p. 56.
[79] Siegfried Sassoon, *Memoirs of an Infantry Officer* (London, 1966), p. 208.
[80] G. Chapman, *Vain Glory* (London, 1968), p. 328.
[81] P. Maze, *A Frenchman in Khaki* (London, 1934), pp. 251, 324.
[82] S. Graham, *A Private in the Guards* (London, 1919), p. 9.
[83] G. Chapman, *A Passionate Prodigality* (London, 1953), p. 252.

Cloete put the same sentiment even more abruptly: 'Though we would risk our lives for a wounded man, the dead, even our friends, were not unduly mourned. There was, in our unconscious minds, the feeling, "better them than me." '[84]

So, after any major offensive, the combat zone might remain littered for weeks with bodies—gradually decomposing and giving off a nauseous, unforgettable stench. New trenches might be dug through them; parapets might be made of them; even bodies decently buried might come to the surface again.[85] Almost every soldier's memoir contains a horrifying passage like this:

> The sun swelled up the dead with gas and often turned them blue, almost navy blue. Then, when the gas escaped from their bodies, they dried up like mummies and were frozen in their death positions. . . . There were sitting bodies, kneeling bodies, bodies in almost every position, though naturally most of them lay on their bellies or their backs. The crows had pecked out the eyes of some, and rats lived on the bodies that lay in the abandoned dugouts or half buried in the crumbled trenches. . . .
>
> Burial was impossible. In ordinary warfare the bodies went down with the limbers who brought up the rations. But then there were seldom more than three or four in a day. Now there were hundreds, thousands, not merely ours, but German as well. And where we fought several times over the same ground, bodies became incorporated in the material of the trenches themselves. In one place, we had to dig through corpses of Frenchmen who had been killed and buried in 1915. These bodies were putrid, of the consistency of Camembert cheese. I once fell and put my hand right through the belly of a man. It was days before I got the smell out of my nails. . . .
>
> The only previous experience I had had of rotting bodies had been at Serre, where, as a battalion, we dealt with the best part of a thousand men who came to pieces in our hands. As you lifted a body by its arms and legs, they detached themselves from the torso, and that was not the worst thing. Each body was covered, inches deep, with a black fur of flies which blew up into your face, into your mouth, eyes and nostrils, as you approached. The bodies crawled with maggotts. . . . We worked with sandbags in our hands, stopping every now and then to puke.[86]

It was even worse when soldiers were literally 'blown to pieces'. For the fragments of their bodies would be gathered together and put in sandbags—which might then be mistaken for the real thing, and be incorporated into the parapet.[87]

Thus hardened to the fate of their comrades, it is hardly surprising that English soldiers—at least, the few of them who have discussed this delicate subject in their memoirs[88]—regarded killing the enemy with enthusiasm or

[84] S. Cloete, *A Victorian Son: An Autobiography, 1897–1912* (London, 1972), p. 252.
[85] S. Rogerson, *Twelve Days* (London, 1933), p. 5; H. S. Clapham, *Mud and Khaki* (London, 1938), pp. 38, 145–6.
[86] Cloete, op. cit., pp. 236–7.
[87] H. Allen, *Toward the Flame: A War Diary* (London, 1934), pp. 45–51; H. Dearden, *Medicine and Duty* (London, 1928), p. 93.
[88] But see Winter, *Death's Men,* ch. 13.

indifference. 'We are out to kill, and kill we do, at any and every opportunity', one officer in the light infantry wrote to his parents with evident relish in December 1914.[89] 'We killed them in heaps like flies on paper', crowed another. 'It was terrible work, but we glorified in it.'[90] But such public-school enthusiasm was soon blunted, either by the reality of combat:

I had sniped a couple of Germans with telescopic sights but they had not seemed real—just little mannekins who stood in the circle of my telescope doubly bisected by the crossed hairs that centred it. But this was real. This one I had killed. I think it would not have been difficult for me to have scalped him, as some of the Italians among the French Canadians were said to have done. But I couldn't do it. I began to laugh. It was against the king's regulations and the Geneva convention. But it was a pity. It is easy to understand how atrocities are committed as men revert to savagery under pressure. He had tried to kill me. The bastard. I left my German with regret and turned my back on the war;[91]

or by feelings of numbness combined with callousness:

The German dead had no interest. They lay about everywhere unburied, for our own dead had precedence with the burying-parties. All along the devastated village streets the Germans lay dead as they had been shot down in action of flight, the look of running in fear was still on the brown faces, and the open mouth and white teeth seemed to betoken calls to their comrades as they ran. In the debris of the houses . . . the dead lay too.[92]

And yet, as this passage shows, the enemy dead did exert a peculiar fascination. In part, this was because they seemed to be physically different: 'porcine' is Paul Fussell's word for them. Blunden, for instance, noticed that a 41-year old officer who lay dead was 'pig-nosed and still seemingly hostile'. Sassoon observed the enemy's look of 'butchered hostility'. And a third soldier summed it all up: 'There's no doubt about it, they're a dirty lot of bastards.'[93] But in addition, callousness was reinforced by acquisitiveness, for the enemy dead were regarded as an inexhaustible quarry for souvenir hunters. The British might refuse to risk their lives to bring German bodies back; but they would happily run the gauntlet to get their guns or watches. Leon Wolff's account of Passchendaele makes this clear:

After each attack, the souvenir hunters got to work. Gradually the corpses were kicked over, the whites of their pockets turned out, their tunics and shirts undone. Revolvers were the best prizes; but money, watches, rings and the crosses of Catholics were also in demand. An artilleryman examining German corpses for revolvers observed, . . . giving one a vicious kick and snarling 'The dirty bastard, somebody's bin 'ere before me'. Front line soldiers were quickest in pursuit of loot; artillery and labour troops were slower and more methodical.[94]

[89] Quoted in T. Moult, *Cenotaph: A Book of Remembrance in Poetry and Prose for November the Eleventh* (London, 1923), p. 157.
[90] Winter, *Death's Men,* p. 26.
[91] Cloete, op. cit., pp. 241–2.
[92] Graham, op. cit., p. 239.
[93] Fussell, op. cit., pp. 77–8.
[94] Wolff, op. cit., p. 287.

It was with such activities and attitudes in mind that, in 1915, Sigmund Freud offered this comment on the outlook of soldiers: 'When the furious struggle . . . has been decided, each one of the victorious fighters will return home joyfully to his wife and children, unchecked and undisturbed by thoughts of the enemies he has killed.'[95]

But this was only part of the picture. As the agents of death, the British soldiers may have been unfeeling or callous.[96] But among their own comrades, their apparent indifference was more a defence mechanism than an indicator of true feelings. Quips such as 'There go the cemetery reinforcements' and 'There's a shortage of coffins up there', with which retiring troops might bombard those about to go up to the front, were not so much expressions of callousness, as attempts to render horror and death bearable by making them funny.[97] Maurice Bowra explains this phenomenon well.

> On the surface, they had developed what seemed to be a callous indifference to death, and if someone was killed, might say 'he's had it', or 'that's another gonner', but this was their defence against feelings which they might otherwise not have been able to master. They looked after one another with protective care.[98]

Even if, in the short run, the pressure of events meant that there was no time to assimilate the news of the death of a comrade, its impact dawned sooner or later. Christopher Edmonds, for instance, recalls how, initially, when his servant Stanley was killed, he felt only 'rage and horror'. But later the full impact of his death hit him: 'Now that we had an opportunity to think clearly, I began to realize how much was lost on me.'[99]

So, while the monotonous carnage of war dulled the senses in general, and made soldiers indifferent to death *en masse,* the well-attested cameraderie of the trenches meant the loss of particular colleagues was always painful, something which, however often it happened, could never be looked upon with indifference. In a letter in October 1916, Vere Harmsworth explained to his family what it was like to see his men killed:

> The awful nightmare of seeing one's own men—that one has been with for so long—being struck down all round one, will never move from one's mind. One gets attached to one's own men, and their loss hits one as hard as dear friends.[100]

Among close colleagues, whether officers or in the ranks, the loss could be even more terrible. Lord Boyd Orr recalls his reaction to the carnage among his fellow officers on the Somme in 1916:

---

[95] Freud, 'Our Attitude Towards Death', p. 295.
[96] The ambiguity of the soldiers' position, as both the agents and the victims of death, is well discussed in A. Corvisier, 'La mort du soldat depuis la fin du Moyen Age', *Revue Historique,* CCLIV (1972), 5–6.
[97] Wolff, op. cit., p. 213.
[98] C. M. Bowra, *Memories, 1898–1939* (London, 1966), pp. 89–90.
[99] C. Edmonds, *A Subaltern's War* (London, 1929), pp. 141, 180.
[100] R. Pound and G. Harmsworth, *Northcliffe* (London, 1959), p. 510.

My officer friends were nearly all dead. While what was left of a first-class battalion travelled back I heard the piper of a Highland regiment which had suffered a similar fate, playing 'The flowers of the forest . . .'. I have never in my life felt so unutterably sad. My friends and comrades were nearly all gone.[101]

Indeed, those whose friendships were closest were, on occasions, unable to grasp the reality of loss at all. Some soldiers would eat meals for their dead comrades. Others, as Plowman explains, remained simply incredulous:

I miss Connor. Every day his pal Mathieson asks me if I've any news of Connor, and when I say no he shakes his head and adds 'No, sir, I'm sure he's killed. I said so when he didn't come in.' But every day he repeats the question.[102]

In part, it depended on how they died. Some, like Connor, simply vanished without trace, which made the realization of their death all the harder to accept. Some were literally blown to pieces and, as Rogerson explains, 'men do not easily or soon throw off the shock of seeing all that could be found of four of their comrades carried down for burial in one ground sheet'.[103] Some died alone in the combat zone, snuffed out while attempting pathetically to bandage their wounds. And some died publicly, slowly, in excruciating agony:

Pratt was hopeless. His head was shattered. Splatterings of brain lay in a pool under him; but he refused to die. Old Corporal Welch looked after him, held his body and arms as they writhed and fought feebly as he lay. It was over two hours before he died, hours of July sunshine in a crowded place where perhaps a dozen men sat with the smell of blood, while all the time above the soothing voice of the corporal came a gurgling and moaning from his lips, now high and liquid, now low and dry—a death rattle fit for the most bloodthirsty novelist.[104]

However death came, it was customary for soldiers to give their comrades a decent burial, even if they might ignore men whom they did not know. Many memoirs bear witness to the zeal with which officers and men went searching—often in the greatest danger—for missing comrades. Anthony Eden, for instance, recalls how, after his commanding officer, Lord Fever-sham, had been killed in action, and his body had been located, he and some colleagues set out, equipped with a wooden cross and a prayer book, so as to give him a decent burial:

Sadly we set about our task. I read a few lines from the burial service, which someone had lent me at headquarters, Dale set up the wooden cross, we gave our commanding officer a last salute, and turned away, leaving him to Picardy and the shells.[105]

---

[101] Lord Boyd Orr, *As I Recall* (London, 1966), p. 71.
[102] M. Plowman, *A Subaltern on the Somme* (London, 1927), p. 204; Winter, *Death's Men*, p. 56.
[103] Rogerson, *Twelve Days*, p. 7.
[104] Winter, *Death's Men*, pp. 56–7.
[105] Eden, op. cit., pp. 116–17; Moran, op. cit., p. 59; Dearden, op. cit., pp. 100–2.

On occasions even the unknown could be buried with such tenderness and feeling, as this account, quoted by Edmund Blunden, makes plain:

> We finish the grave, a shallow one, and three or four of us take up the stiff body and lower it into the hole. We have no ropes and have to stoop well down with our arms in the grave. The body slips from our hands, and falls the last inch or two, stiffly and in a lump. We put in the first few shovelfulls of earth gently, and then rapidly fill up the grave. One of the party finds a couple of slips of wood and trims them with his jacknife. He fastens them into a cross with a piece of string and, after printing on to it the name and regiment with an indelible pencil, sticks it at the head of the grave. There is nothing more to do, so, with a few trite remarks, but mostly quiet, we set off on the long march to where the battalion is.[106]

IV

Such varying scenes of death experienced by the six million men who served in the First World War are not easily summarized. Most generalizations have some validity, but few are universally applicable. Callousness and revengeful feelings towards the enemy could co-exist with the tenderest solicitude for one's comrades. Irreverent, ghoulish, macabre badinage might be the sign of heartlessness, or merely a cover for inner feelings almost too sorrowful to be recognized. Revulsion at the sight of rotting and decayed bodies was mingled with real and abiding grief that colleagues and comrades were gone for ever. Instant numbness on hearing of the death of a friend might later be replaced by a more painful and vivid realization of what had been lost. But whatever might be the reactions to death, the reality, the presence of death, was inescapable. Any soldier would see more of it in a week at the front than he might reasonably have expected to have witnessed in a lifetime.[107] And, at the same time, the presence of death all around him would oblige him to confront the prospect of his own death—at an age when, for civilians, death had become unlikely, and in a manner which, for those not in the trenches, was literally unimaginable. How did the soldiers react to this? If the experience of death of comrades was painful, how did they confront the prospect of the death of self?

Some, in well-meant attempts to give comfort to their relatives, or because they actually believed it, spoke of death as fulfillment in a manner that Vachell would have appreciated. 'If I fall', wrote Vere Harmsworth to his uncle, 'do not mourn, but be glad and proud. It is not a life wasted, but gloriously fulfilled.'[108] J. L. Garvin's son took an identical attitude. 'If I die',

---

[106] Quoted by Edmund Blunden, introduction to P. Longworth, *The Unending Vigil: A History of the Imperial War Graves Commission, 1917–1967* (London, 1967), p. xviii.

[107] For a subtle analysis of the way in which the omnipresence of death at the front shattered the conventional view of life and death as exclusive categories, see: E. J. Leed, *No Man's Land: Combat and Identity in World War I* (Cambridge, 1979), pp. 18–24.

[108] Pound and Harmsworth, op. cit., pp. 510–11.

he wrote, 'I couldn't die for a better cause.'[109] Anthony Eden, on learning of the death of his brother Nicholas, expressed a similar view in a letter to his mother. 'We must all die some day, why not now by the most honourable way possible, the way that opens the gates of paradise—the soldier's death.'[110] In the same manner, an officer from Watford contemplated the prospect of his own death in words that would have made Newbolt proud:

> If one does take a toss, there's always the satisfaction of knowing that one could not do it in a better cause. I always feel that I am fighting for England—English fields, lanes, trees, good days in England, and all that is synonymous with liberty.[111]

But few were able to contemplate their own death with such heroic, self-consciously romantic, patriotic equanimity. The most that many would admit was that the prospect that this day, this hour, this minute might be the last resulted in a heightened perception of the world around them. Here, for instance, is the reaction of one soldier to a clear, crisp November morning of 1915:

> With the possibility of speedy death before me, I understood more clearly than ever before that I had got from this particular impression all that could be got, that it was perfect, and could not by longer living be at all improved or developed.[112]

Others found life in the trenches so ghastly that death was looked upon with selfish pleasure, as offering the certain prospect of release from earthly torment. 'Death must at times have been eagerly desired and sought,' recalled Graham. 'Life in the trenches was not just called hell: it was hell.' A. G. West agreed. 'When we were wet in the trenches and it was very cold and dull', he recalls, death was looked upon as a 'welcome thing'.[113] And Siegfried Sassoon took the same view. 'As for me', he noted, 'I had more or less made up my mind to die, because in the circumstances there didn't seem anything else to be done.'[114]

Between these two extremes—savouring each day in case it might be the last, and hating every minute of life as postponing the release brought by death—were a variety of other opinions, often held at different times by the same soldiers, depending on how they felt, and how the war was going, at a particular moment. On occasions, life was seen as a gamble with 'the twin gods of war, Mr Luck and Mr Death'.[115] If soldiers survived their round of duty at the front, they felt that they had cheated death. As Plowman explains: 'It is marvellous to be out of the trenches: it is like being born again . . . Instinctively we feel as if we have earned the right to go home. We gave Death the chance. Death did not take it, and we've escaped alive.' Or, as

[109] K. Garvin, *J. L. Garvin: A Memoir* (London, 1948), p. 85.
[110] Aster, op. cit., pp. 5–6.
[111] Winter, *Death's Men*, p. 32.
[112] A. G. West, *The Diary of a Dead Officer* (London, 1919), p. 6.
[113] Ibid., p. 9; S. Graham, *The Challenge of the Dead* (London, 1921), p. 74.
[114] Sassoon, op. cit., p. 11.
[115] Cloete, op. cit., p. 297.

Churchill put it, 'In war, chance casts aside all veils and disguises, and presents herself nakedly from moment to moment as the direct arbiter of events.'[116] But, at other times, soldiers regarded death not so much as a gamble, but with fatalistic resignation: if a bullet had your name on it, then there was little that could be done about it. One soldier, before going out to search for the body of his friend, paid his servant the last wages he owed him. Sure enough, he was killed. 'Who shall say that he did not know his fate was upon him?' asks a brother officer. 'Those who had been with him from the morning have little doubt about it'.[117]

Others responded differently, regarding death with anxiety and alarm, not so much because they feared it for themselves, but because they wondered what would become of their dependants once they were gone. Here, for instance, are the last thoughts of Sergeant Fine:

> 'I believe in God and all that; I'm not afraid to die', said he, 'but the question I ask is, if I die, what are they going to do? What will the army do for them? Why, nothing, of course. There are too many widows and orphans.'[118]

Alternatively, death might be feared because soldiers dreaded their own bodies being subjected to the indignities of decomposition. Plowman, for example, recalled a conversation with a friend on the Somme who 'simply could not stand the thought of his body being left on the wire to rot, and he extracted from me a promise to do what I could if he were killed'.[119] But the majority, it seems, were indifferent to what became of their bodies afterwards. If it came to a choice between death and hideous mutilation, death was definitely to be preferred as the lesser of two evils. Anthony Eden put this most eloquently:

> Please God, if I am to be hit, let me be slightly wounded or killed, but not mutilated. I cannot explain what prompted this dread of the loss of limbs or other mutilation for life. To be killed did not seem all that bad. It did not seem a business to make such a fuss about, especially if it was quick and with little suffering.[120]

Or, as Cloete put it even more pithily: 'I was not afraid of death, only pain. I had seen too many people die. They died calling on God, asking for their mothers, cursing God, or grimly silent.'[121]

There were, of course, many ways of dying. Lord Moran, on the basis of his observations in the trenches, thought that most soldiers died easily:

[116] Plowman, op. cit., pp. 56–7; M. Gilbert, *Winston S. Churchill*, vol. III, *1914–1916* (London, 1971), p. 585.

[117] E. Hopkins, *A Social History of the English Working Classes, 1815–1945* (London, 1979), p. 211; Rogerson, *Twelve Days*, pp. 43–4.

[118] Graham, *Private in the Guards*, p. 131.

[119] Plowman, op. cit., p. 101.

[120] Eden, op. cit., p. 138.

[121] Cloete, op. cit., p. 260.

Dying men rarely experience pain or apprehension, or terror or remorse; their lives peter to an end 'like their birth, their death is a sleep and a forgetting'. When death is not very far off, when a wounded soldier lies very still on his stretcher, when old age or mortal illness have laid their hands on men, nature with a kindly gesture dulls the senses, and death like a narcotic comes to steal men almost in their sleep.[122]

Certainly, those soldiers who sincerely thought themselves to be dying, but later survived, shared the same opinion. Here, for example, is R. H. Tawney's account:

I thought—if that's the right word—'This is death', and hoped it wouldn't take long. . . . Not that I much minded dying now, or thought about it. By a merciful arrangement, when one's half dead, the extra plunge doesn't seem so very terrible. One's lost part of one's interest in life. The roots are loosened, and seem ready to come away without an agonising wrench.[123]

Cloete's response was similar, if less elegantly phrased:

I was sure I was dying. . . . This is when I decided that the parsons talked a lot of damn nonsense about death. There was nothing to it. Easy as falling off a log. I thought this in those actual words.[124]

Indeed, those who came round after being wounded, convinced that they had been dead, regarded retrospective death in a somewhat mystified manner:

Something has happened, but I can't remember what. There's been a great nothingness, and I cannot remember what happened before it. I seem to have been dead, and death, apparently, is nothingness.[125]

But not all of those who actually did die were able to regard life's last great adventure with such serenity. Some were unaware that the end was in sight, regarded their wounds as superficial, and died assuming that they would soon recover. Some, on the brink of death, announced that they felt a great deal better; and then promptly expired. In many cases, as Jack Seely recalled, the last thoughts which soldiers entertained were of their mothers.[126] But for others, death was as terrible to endure as it had been frightening to contemplate. Nurse Millard gives this harrowing account.

I could see he was going fast. . . . His look was deep with terror. . . . He seized my hand and gripped it until it hurt. His breath was coming in gasps, and his pallor became more intense. 'Don't let me die', he whispered thickly. 'Please don't let me die . . . Do something . . . give me something. I don't want to die.' He looked up at me, desperately, hanging on to my hand in his panic.[127]

This was not death 'young, clean, ardent'. Still less was it to 'die swiftly, in perfect health'. For this soldier as for thousands of others, death was a

[122] Moran, op. cit., p. 154.
[123] R. H. Tawney, *The Attack and Other Essays* (London, 1953), p. 18.
[124] Cloete, op. cit., p. 295.
[125] Plowman, op. cit., p. 237.
[126] Ibid., pp. 60, 180; J. Seely, *Adventure* (London, 1930), p. 267; Dearden, op. cit., p. 9.
[127] S. Millard, *I Saw Them Die* (London, 1936), pp. 69-70.

hideous, haunting nightmare. There was none of that ardent nobility which Vachell had depicted: only an agonized, prolonged, degrading, undignified end to life.

In this hell-on-earth, where daily 'death wandered up and down ... and fed on life', few generalizations are safe except this: that, *pace* Freud's prediction, those millions of soldiers who witnessed such scenes and survived never forgot what they had experienced.[128] Even Anthony Eden, who concluded his wartime reminiscences on an unusually optimistic note, conceded that the effects of the war were as lasting as they were terrible: 'Grief, and the sadness of parting, and sorrows that seem eternal, are mitigated by time, but they leave their memories and their scars, and we would not have it otherwise.'[129] And for others, the torment lingered unabated. 'I felt,' J. B. Priestley notes, 'as indeed I still feel today, and must go on feeling until I die, the open wound, never to be healed, of my generation's fate, the best sorted out and then slaughtered.'[130] Or, as Maurice Bowra recalled, even more succinctly: 'The memory of the carnage and the filth has never left me.' Hugh Quigley was even more tormented: 'That cry of dying men will ring in my ears a long time after everything else will be forgotten.'[131] And, as Harold Macmillan explains, to these grotesque memories of the past were added ineradicable feelings of guilt, because while some comrades had died, others had lived who, genuinely, thought themselves to be unworthy:

> Few of the survivors of my own age felt able to shake off the memory of these years. We were haunted by them. We almost began to feel a sense of guilt for not having shared the fate of our friends and comrades. We certainly felt some obligation to make some decent use of the life that had been spared to us.[132]

V

But the soldiers who returned home after the war were not the only group everlastingly to be affected by the 'carnival of death' in which they had been participants. It has become a commonplace to stress the extent to which, both during and after the First World War, there were two nations in Britain. 'By the end of 1918,' note Robert Graves and Alan Hodge, 'there were two distinct Britains ... the fighting forces, ... and the rest, including the government.'[133] In large part, this was because there was no way for those at the front to explain to those at home *what the war was like*. As Guy Chapman recollects: 'It was—I think it still is—impossible to make those who had no experience of this war understand it, as it must be understood,

[128] Winter, *Death's Men,* p. 248.
[129] Eden, op, cit., p. 150.
[130] Priestley, op. cit., p. 139.
[131] Bowra, op. cit., p. 91; Chapman, *Vain Glory,* p. 462.
[132] Macmillan, op. cit., p. 98.
[133] Robert Graves and Alan Hodge, *The Long Weekend* (London, 1971), p. 10; Hopkins, op. cit., p. 211.

through all the senses.'[134]More particularly, in the light of the argument being developed here, it is important to stress the difference between those at the front, who saw and purveyed *death,* and those at home, who saw no death, no carnage and no corpses, but who experienced *bereavement.* Freud summed this up well: 'A distinction should be made between two groups—those who themselves risk their lives in battle, and those who have stayed at home, and have only to wait for the loss of one of their dear ones by wounds, disease or infection.'[135]

For it remains a truism that, however many people may have done well out of the war, there was scarcely a family in Britain which, by 1918, had not suffered the loss of a father, a son, a brother, a cousin or an uncle.[136] But whereas on the battlefield death took the form of cascades of corpses, at home it merely announced itself as a laconic message. Christopher Tennant went to France on 10 August 1917, got up to the front line for the first time on 1 September, was killed on 3 September, and his parents were informed three days later.[137] In his autobiography, Sir Harry Lauder gives a harrowingly vivid picture of what it was like to receive such news:

> On Monday morning, the first day of 1917, I was handed a telegram. My heart started to beat double time. I could not bring myself to open the telegram. I knew what it contained. God! the agonies I suffered that bright New Year's morning. They cannot be written about. But hundreds of thousands, aye, millions of fathers and mothers will know just what I passed through for many hours and for many weeks. My only son. The one child God had given us.[138]

But the most graphic account of such a disaster is this description by Margot Asquith of the news that Raymond, the Prime Minister's son, had been killed in 1916:

> On Sunday, September the 17th, we were entertaining a weekend party . . . While we were playing games, Clouder, our servant, . . . came in to say that I was wanted.
> I left the room, and the moment I took up the telephone I said to myself, 'Raymond is killed'.
> With the receiver in my hand, I asked what it was, and if the news was bad.
> Our secretary, Davies, answered, 'Terrible, terrible news. Raymond was shot dead on the 15th. Haig writes full of sympathy, but no details. The Guards were in, and he was shot leading his men at the moment he had gone over the parapet.'
> I put back the receiver and sat down. I heard Elizabeth's delicious laugh, and a hum of talk and smell of cigars came down the passage from the dining room.
> I went back to the sitting room.
> 'Raymond is dead', I said, 'He was shot leading his men over the top on Friday.'
> Puffin got up from his game, and hanging his head took my hand; Elizabeth burst into tears . . . Maud Tree and Florrie Bridges suggested I should put off

[134] Chapman, *Passionate Prodigality,* p. 165.
[135] Freud, 'Our Attitude Towards Death', p. 291.
[136] Hopkins, op. cit., p. 212.
[137] Winter, *Death's Men,* p. 256.
[138] Sir Harry Lauder, *Roamin' In the Gloamin* (London, 1928), p. 184.

telling Henry the terrible news as he was happy. I walked away with the two children and rang the bell: 'Tell the Prime Minister to come and speak to me', I said to the servant.

Leaving the children, I paused at the end of the dining-room passage; Henry opened the door, and we stood facing each other. He saw my thin, wet face, and while he put his arm around me, I said:

'Terrible, terrible news.'

At this, he stopped and said:

'I know it . . . I've known it . . . Raymond is dead.'

He put his hands over his face, and we walked into an empty room and sat down in silence.[139]

But in two respects at least, the Asquith family was relatively fortunate. In the first place, they were spared the protracted agony which resulted from the 'missing, feared killed' telegram, which all too often raised hopes unrealistically, only to make the subsequent news of death even harder to bear. In April 1917, for instance, Bonar Law learned that his second son, Charlie, was missing after the Battle of Gaza. For many weeks, on the strength of a German newspaper report, it was thought that he might be a German prisoner of war, and this frail hope seemed to have been triumphantly substantiated in June when a message was received from the Vatican saying that he was a prisoner in Turkish hands. But jubilation and relief turned to dust when it later transpired that the crucial word 'not' had been omitted from the Vatican telegram.[140] For Kipling, the agony was even more protracted. His only son John was reported missing after the Battle of Loos in October 1915. But for two years, despite the obvious conclusion to which they knew this pointed, Kipling and his wife refused to abandon hope. Not until the end of 1917, when it was clear that John's body would never be found, were the last glimmers of hope extinguished.[141]

The second, and even greater, disaster which Asquith was spared was the loss of more than one close relative. Once again, Bonar Law was less fortunate. In September of 1917, only three months after the final news about Charlie, he learned that James, his eldest son, had been shot down. Lord Blake describes Law's reactions thus:

This second bereavement, following so soon upon the fluctuations of hope and despair over the first, came as a terrible, almost an overwhelming, blow . . . Night seemed to have descended upon him. For the moment he was incapable of work, and could only sit despondently, gazing into vacancy. All those dark clouds which were never far below the horizon of his thought came rolling up, obliterating light and happiness.

[139] Margot Asquith, *The Autobiography of Margot Asquith* (2 vols., London, 1920), II, pp. 242-4.

[140] Robert Blake, *The Unknown Prime Minister: The Life and Times of Andrew Bonar Law, 1858-1923* (London, 1955), pp. 354-6.

[141] Lord Birkenhead, *Rudyard Kipling* (London, 1978), pp. 267, 277; C. Carrington, *Rudyard Kipling: His Life and Work* (3rd. edn., London, 1978), pp. 508-9, 512.

Only after a visit to his son's old squadron in France, where he sat in the cockpit of a plane, alone for two or three hours, 'sunk in a sombre reverie', was he able to pull himself together and carry on his work.[142] But for those denied the distracting and dutiful treadmill of endeavour, the news of one death after another seemed to empty the reservoirs of grief beyond replenishment. For, as Lord Rosebery explained, on hearing the news that the second of Lord Rothermere's sons had been killed, there was a point beyond which it seemed impossible to assimilate such tidings: 'Speaking metaphorically, the fountain of tears is nearly dry. One loss follows another till one is dazed.'[143]

However illustrious or insignificant were the bereaved, it seems that their basic reactions were similar, namely numbed incredulity. A Hunslet housewife, who lived in the poorest quarter of the town, on learning of the death of her son, could only say 'I've lost my boy', and then became dumb with grief.[144] Kipling was 'numbed' by his son's death, and poured out his sorrow in 'My Boy Jack', with its desolate refrain:

> 'Have you heard news of my boy Jack?'
> *Not this tide*
> 'When d'you think that he'll come back?'
> *Not with this wind blowing, and this tide.*

When John Buchan lost his brother, he suffered a 'terrible blow'. Jack Seely, when his son was killed, admitted he was 'heartbroken'. For Lord Rosebery, the death of his favourite son Neil was 'almost mortal'.[145] Robert Vansittart, on hearing that his elder brother had been killed, left the Foreign Office for a solitary walk:

London seemed suddenly void. I locked up my papers, lurched across Horse Guards Parade, plunged into the mutilated plane trees of the Mall, as far as possible from light or sight, and sobbed my heart out. If disaster really were an impostor, how gladly would we treat triumph 'just the same'.[146]

J. L. Garvin's grief for his son was even more terrible:

He died a thousand deaths for those in the trenches, including his own son. I have no doubt that this was true, for he stayed awake night after night, groaning in his half wakefulness, and evidently living through unimaginable scenes of the battlefield.[147]

[142] Blake, op. cit., pp. 354–6.
[143] Pound and Harmsworth, op. cit., p. 621.
[144] Winter, *Death's Men*, p. 257.
[145] Birkenhead, op. cit., p. 269; Carrington, op. cit., p. 495; J. A. Smith, *John Buchan: A Biography* (London, 1965), pp. 205–6; Seely, op. cit., p. 262; Robert Rhodes James, *Rosebery* (London, 1963), p. 478.
[146] Lord Vansittart, *The Mist Procession* (London, 1956), p. 146.
[147] Garvin, op. cit., pp. 84–5.

And Asquith, in his moving lament for Raymond, summed up in one symmetrically-heartbroken sentence the grief of bereaved parents throughout the land:

> The War has sucked up so much of what was most loveable and full of promise that I have always been haunted by a fear that a toll would be exacted of me also ... *Whatever pride I had in the past, and whatever hope I had for the far future—by much the largest part of both was invested in him.* Now all that is gone. It will take me a few days to get my bearings.[148]

But, for Asquith as for thousands of others in his position, it took far longer than 'a few days' for them to 'get their bearings'. Letters of condolence, as he himself admitted, were of little comfort. However great were the immediate distractions of high politics, the death of Raymond was a 'shattering blow' which left 'an inexorable scar'.[149] In the same way, for Lord Lansdowne, the death of his second son was a 'blow' from which 'he never entirely recovered'. For John Buchan, the loss of his elder brother was 'a deep and enduring grief'. And Kipling, once John's death was finally established beyond all doubt, never again wrote with exhilaration of battle and war, but became obsessed with pain, fear and death.[150] Indeed, in his poem for Armistice Day, 1923, he expressed in desolate verses the unassuageable grief of all the bereaved:

> When you come to London stone
>   (Grieving—grieving!)
> Bow your head and mourn your own
>   With the others grieving.
>
> For the minutes let it wake—
>   (Grieving—grieving!)
> All the empty-heart and ache
>   That isn't cured by grieving
>
> Where's our help from Earth or Heaven?
>   (Grieving—grieving!)
> To comfort us for what we've given
>   And only gained by grieving.[151]

And J. L. Garvin's daughter, in describing her father's sorrow, only showed how well Kipling's poem caught the prevailing mood:

> The loss of a son, an only son, is something that no other person can assess. I do not think that anyone, anyone at all, can fully know what the loss meant to my

[148] Earl of Oxford and Asquith, *Memories and Reflection, 1852–1927* (2 vols., London, 1928), II, pp. 158–9. My italics.

[149] J. A. Spender and C. Asquith, *The Life of H. H. Asquith, Earl of Oxford and Asquith* (2 vols., London, 1932), II, pp. 226–7, 279; H. H. A., *Letters of the Earl of Oxford and Asquith to a Friend, 1st Series, 1915–22* (London, 1933), p. 10.

[150] Lord Newton, *Lord Lansdowne: A Biography* (London, 1929), p. 443; S. Tweedsmuir, *John Buchan, by His Wife and Friends* (London, 1947), pp. 85–6; Morris, *Farewell the Trumpets*, p. 200; Birkenhead, op. cit., p. 273.

[151] *The Times*, 10 November 1923.

father, and increasingly as he grew older. Only the millions of other fathers who suffered in the same way can realise it. It was always in Garvin's heart; but he could seldom speak of it.[152]

This outpouring of grief must be set in the context of those demographic changes which had been taking place since the 1880s. From that time onwards, the death of children and adolescents, previously commonplace, has become less frequent, as children increasingly tended to outlive their parents. One consequence of this may well have been to make the death of such young ones the hardest form of bereavement to bear.[153] For sons and daughters not only give adults a parental role: they provide a way of fulfilling ambition vicariously, they satisfy cravings for immortality, and they give a meaning to life as a whole which it might otherwise lack. Under normal circumstances, these feelings have become increasingly commonplace from the 1880s. But the First World War brutally shattered such recently-developed attitudes, as an older generation which had dared to believe that their children would live on after they themselves were dead and gone were obliged to watch these hopes disintegrate. To say that parents 'never got over' the death of their sons in the first war was as true as it was platitudinous. Indeed, the most famous lines of Lawrence Binyon's poem 'To the Fallen'—'At the going down of the sun and in the morning we will remember them'—were more a description than an exhortation.

VI

These were the diverse experiences of death which were so unforgettable for so many of those alive in Britain between 1914 and 1939. Those six millions who had served at the front had seen more death in their relatively brief spell of armed service than they might reasonably have expected to encounter in a lifetime. And the deaths which they saw were violent, horrible, bloody, degrading and brutal, when, if they had been civilians all their lives, they would probably have limited their repertoire of death to old age and natural causes. At the same time, the soldiers themselves had been the agents of death, killing, maiming and wounding in a manner which would be unimaginable in civvy street. Shock, guilt, anguish, grief, remorse: these were only some of the emotions which such an experience left behind: above all, a desire to forget, and yet also a recognition that such experiences could not be, must not be, forgotten. At the same time, bereavement had become a more universal experience than ever before, as nearly every family in the land experienced the untimely death of one or more of its younger male members.

[152] Garvin, op. cit., pp. 84–5.
[153] Gorer, op. cit., pp. 61, 116–9; Hinton, op. cit., pp. 75–6, 82, 84, 88; Parkes, op. cit., p. 123; I. O. Glick, R. S. Weiss and C. M. Parkes, *The First Year of Bereavement* (New York, 1974), pp. 46–51.

As Sigmund Freud noticed early in the war, neither prevailing attitudes to death, nor the customary rituals of mourning, would be able to cope with these experiences:

> It is evident that war is bound to sweep away this conventional treatment of death. Death will no longer be denied; we are forced to believe in it. People really die; and no longer one by one, but many, often tens of thousands in a single day. And death is no longer a chance event. To be sure, it still seems a matter of chance whether a bullet hits this man or that; but a second bullet may well hit the survivor, and the accumulation of death puts an end to the impression of chance.

'We are unable to maintain our former attitude towards death, and have not yet found a new one', he added.[154] How, then, in the inter-war years did grieving parents and sorrowing soldiers come to terms with this unprecedented 'carnival of death'? If, as Baldwin claimed, mourning for the war dead 'will last all our lives', what form did that mourning take?

Significantly, it did not lead to a return to the excesses of Victorian mourning customs, nor to a revival of religion. On the contrary, the reverse happened. As grief became more intense, and bereavement more widespread, the ostentation of mourning declined even further, so that by 1917–18, what remained of Victorian mourning costume after the changes of the preceding thirty years largely disappeared.[155] This fundamental change in mourning customs well illustrates the danger of supposing that wearing yards of black crepe was somehow psychologically beneficial. For in this case, death had become so ubiquitous and tragic, and grief so widespread and overwhelming, that even those remaining Victorian rituals—probably never effective even in the mid-nineteenth century—were now recognized as being inadequate, superfluous and irrelevant. What point was there in donning widow's weeds when the husband probably lay mutilated, unidentified and unburied on the fields of Flanders? What comfort could crepe or black-edged notepaper bring in the face of bereavement at once so harrowing, so unnatural and so widespread? As John Morley rightly notes: 'Mourning succumbed before the vast numbers of the dead; faced with this, family mourning and its conventions were an insufficient comment.'[156]

At a more general level, the established church—concerned, like all Christianity, with explaining the significance of death in this world and life in the next—seemed unable to cope when confronted with so much mortality and grief. At the front, chaplains were often unable to give soldiers a decent, Christian burial. And what did it matter whether they did or not: for how could one realistically continue to believe in the resurrection of the body when all that was left might be a few rat-bitten pieces of rotting flesh? At home, the Church's response was similarly inadequate, as Church leaders were unable to give clear and satisfactory answers to the questions asked

[154] Freud, 'Our Attitude Towards Death', pp. 291–2.
[155] Gorer, op. cit., p. 6.
[156] Morley, op. cit., p. 79.

incessantly by the bereaved and the suffering. Was God on Britain's side or Germany's? Did all soldiers who were killed go to Heaven automatically? Why and how could a loving, omnipotent God allow such killing and carnage? If the Church had been able to answer such questions, then it might, indeed, have experienced that great revival for which some of its leaders hoped. But to neither the soldier at the front, nor to the bereaved at home, baffled and numbed by the cataclysmic events in which they were caught up, could the Church offer plausible explanation or abiding comfort.[157]

Under these circumstances, where traditional ceremony and traditional religion seemed inadequate in the face of so much death and bereavement, alternative attempts were made to render such losses bearable in the years after the war. Two responses in particular merit attention: the one official, public and ceremonial; the other private, spontaneous and individualistic. The first was the construction throughout the country of war memorials, and the gradual evolution of the ritual of Armistice Day.[158] The second was the massive proliferation of interest in spiritualism. For all their differences of form and style, these two attempts to come to terms with death in inter-war Britain share one important characteristic: they were in large part spontaneously generated by the bereaved for their own comfort. In the case of spiritualism, the upsurge of popular interest in the years immediately after 1918 was quite remarkable. And the Armistice Day ritual, far from being a piece of consensual ceremonial, cynically imposed on a divided and war-weary nation by a cabinet afraid of unrest and revolution, was more a requiem demanded of the politicians by the public. *Pace* Ariès, this 'cult of the dead' was not so much 'an expression of patriotism' as a display of bereavement. It was not a festival of homage by the citizens to the state, but a tribute by the living to the dead.[159]

Early in 1919, after the riotous jollification of Armistice Day itself, when joy and happiness had temporarily rolled away the clouds of grief and bereavement, the War Cabinet began to consider how to celebrate the successful outcome of the Versailles Peace Conference which it was hoped would reach agreement during the summer. A committee was set up, under the chairmanship of Lord Curzon, whose talent for organization and love of pomp and pageantry were proverbial, to make the arrangements.[160] By May 1919, it had decided on four days of celebrations early in August,

[157] For a much fuller treatment of this problem, see: A Wilkinson, *The Church of England and the First World War* (London, 1978).

[158] The only thorough account of this so far published is: E. Homberger, 'The Story of the Cenotaph', *Times Literary Supplement,* 12 November 1976, pp. 1429–30. My indebtedness to his work and agreement with his conclusions, will be apparent.

[159] Ariès, op. cit., pp. 74–5. The interpretation of Armistice Day advanced here is in close agreement with the analysis of the equivalent French festival in A. Prost, *Les Anciens Combattants et la Société Française 1914–1939* (3 vols., Paris, 1977), III, pp. 6104. See also O. Chadwick, 'Armistice Day', *Theology,* LXXIX (1976), 325.

[160] Public Record Office (hereafter P.R.O.) CAB 23/9, 19 February 1919.

including a victory parade through the streets of London, a day of thanks-giving services throughout the land, a river pageant on the Thames, and popular festivities mounted by local authorities. But, under pressure from the King, it was agreed to simplify the programme, and bring it forward so that the celebrations might come as soon as possible after the treaty was actually signed.[161] Finally, it was agreed to hold a Thanksgiving Service in London on 6 July, and the victory parade on 19 July. It was at the Cabinet meeting at which these decisions were taken that Lloyd George proposed—as was to be the case in France—that there might be 'a catafalque at some prominent spot along the route selected for the military procession, past which the troops would march and salute the dead'.[162] And, he went on to suggest, 'some prominent artist might be consulted on the subject'. Curzon's response was distinctly unenthusiastic, but he agreed to refer the matter to his committee: 'If the idea were properly carried out, it should prove very impressive; it was, perhaps, however, more essentially suitable to the Latin temperament.'[163]

Three days later, by which time Curzon's committee had carefully con-sidered Lloyd George's proposal, the Cabinet discussed the matter again.[164] Curzon reported that his committee as a whole shared his scepticism:

> There was considerable feeling against the idea of adopting the French proposal to have a catafalque on the processional route which would be saluted by the troops as they passed in honour of the dead. The king was not in favour of the idea, and objections had been raised in other quarters.

Curzon then went on to enumerate them more fully:

> The reasons against the proposal were: that it was foreign to the customs and temper of the nation; that it might not be easy for the public to assume the properly reverential attitude; and, as the structure would be of a very temporary character, it must be carefully safeguarded or it would be overturned and trampled in the crush.

But Lloyd George—the only vociferous champion of the scheme in Cabi-net—would not be moved: 'He deprecated a national rejoicing which did not include some tribute to the dead.' Accordingly, his proposal for the construc-tion of a 'temporary pylon' was carried, and the same day Sir Edwin Lutyens was asked to design a non-denominational, temporary shrine, made out of wood and plaster, which could be constructed within two weeks. By the following day, full-scale drawings were available, and on 8 July he was announced in *The Times* as the designer of 'a temporary but fitting monu-

---

[161] P.R.O. CAB 23/10, 15 May, 30 June 1919.
[162] Ibid., CAB 23/11, 1 July 1919.
[163] Cf. the two published accounts of Curzon's part, which assume all the ideas and enthusiasm were his: Marchioness Curzon, op. cit., p. 99; the Marquess of Zetland, *The Life of Lord Curzon* (3 vols., London, 1928), III, p. 200.
[164] P.R.O. CAB 23/11, 4 July 1919.

ment'.[165] It was at his suggestion that its name was changed from catafalque to Cenotaph: the empty tomb.

The celebrations held in London and the provinces on Saturday 19 July were a great success. But the high point of the London ceremonial was the quite unexpected appeal of the Cenotaph itself. The salutes of Pershing, Foch, Beatty and Haig to dead comrades were captured in unforgettable photographs which appeared in newspapers throughout the country, and at the end of the day, many of the bereaved placed wreaths at the base of the Cenotaph in remembrance of dead relatives or comrades.[166] No such response had been anticipated: the Cenotaph was envisaged as a temporary monument, which would soon be dismantled, after which no further official, ceremonial recognition of the war dead was intended. But public opinion decreed otherwise. As *The Times* noted on 21 July: 'The Cenotaph ... is only a temporary structure made to look like stone, but Sir Edwin Lutyens' design is so grave, severe and beautiful that one might well wish it were indeed of stone and permanent.'[167] So insistent was public pressure that at the end of July—only eleven days after the Cenotaph had been unveiled—the Cabinet agreed to replace it with a permanent and identical structure on the same site, and to ask Parliament for the £10,000 necessary to finance the work.[168] Lutyens' own account of these developments remains the best:

> The plain fact emerged, and grew stronger every hour, that the Cenotaph was what the people wanted, and that they wanted to have the wood and plaster original replaced by an identical memorial in lasting stone. It was a mass-feeling too deep to express itself more fitly than by the piles of good fresh flowers which loving hands placed at the Cenotaph day by day. Thus it was decided, by the human sentiment of millions, that the Cenotaph should be as it now is.[169]

Accordingly, the old structure was dismantled early in January 1920, and work on its permanent replacement was immediately begun.[170]

Before that, however, there was the problem of how to commemorate 11 November 1919, the first anniversary of the Armistice. For the lesson of the Cenotaph affair was that there could be no once and for all salute to the dead but that, on the contrary, some annual act of remembrance seemed to be required. In the first few years immediately following the end of the war, awareness of bereavement grew rather than abated. In October 1919 Lord

---

[165] *The Times*, 8 July 1919. For Lutyens and the Cenotaph, see: S. M. Alsop, *Lady Sackville: A Biography* (London, 1978), p. 221; A. S. G. Butler, *The Architecture of Sir Edwin Lutyens* (3 vols., London, 1950), III, pp. 37-8; C. Hussey, *The Life of Sir Edwin Lutyens* (London, 1953), pp. 386-95. Hussey is mistaken in supposing that, because Lutyens' earliest sketches are dated July 19, this was the day on which he drew them. In all probability it was two weeks before, July 19 being the day for which the Cenotaph had to be completed.

[166] *The Times*, 21 July 1919; P.R.O. CAB 23/11, 22 July 1919.

[167] *The Times*, 21 July 1919.

[168] Ibid., 31 July 1919; P.R.O. CAB 23/11, 29, 30 July 1919.

[169] Quoted in Butler, op. cit., III, p. 37.

[170] *The Times*, 14 January 1920.

Milner wrote to Lord Stamfordham, George V's private secretary, passing on an idea of Sir Percy Fitzpatrick's suggesting that the war dead might be commemorated by the observance of a period of silence throughout the land at 11 o'clock on Armistice Day. The king conveyed the suggestion on to the Cabinet which, in spite of Curzon's objections, supported the proposal and settled on a period of two minutes' silence.[171] Not everyone approved the innovation, as this extract from the young Evelyn Waugh's diary makes plain:

> At 11 a.m. today we had the king's amazing proposition of two minutes' silence to commemorate last year. It was really a disgusting idea of artificial nonsense and sentimentality. If people have lost sons and fathers, they should think of them whenever the grass is green or Shaftesbury Avenue brightly lighted, not for two minutes on the anniversary of a disgraceful day of national hysteria. No one thought of the dead last year; why should they now?[172]

But Waugh was almost alone in that view. For the vast majority of the population, the observance of the silence was as total as it was effective. Not only in Britain, but throughout the Empire, traffic came to a halt, telephone operators stopped their work, department stores ceased to trade.[173] This account of the observance in Manchester catches the flavour well:

> The first stroke of eleven produced a magical effect. The tram cars glided into stillness, motors ceased to cough and fume and stopped dead, and the mighty-limbed dray horses hunched back upon their loads and stopped also, seeming to do it of their own volition. . . . Someone took off his hat, and with a nervous hesitancy the rest of the men bowed their heads also. Here and there an old soldier could be detected slipping unconsciously into the posture of 'attention'. An elderly woman, not far away, wiped her eyes, and the man beside her looked white and stern. Everyone stood very still. . . . The hush deepened. It had spread over the whole city and become so pronounced as to impress one with a sense of audibility. It was . . . a silence which was almost pain. . . . And the spirit of memory brooded over it all.[174]

Waugh may not have remembered the dead; but countless millions of the bereaved certainly did. They may indeed have thought of their loss 'whenever the grass is green'. But what Waugh did not appreciate was that this was not enough. As *The Times* realized, the key to the extraordinary success of the silence was that it made public and corporate those unassuageable feelings of grief and sorrow which otherwise must remain forever private and individual:

> The great silence is bound to have a permanent effect. Since the Armistice so much has happened that the wonderful body of sacrifices made in the war has

[171] Harold Nicolson, *King George V: His Life and Reign* (London, 1967), pp. 446–7; *The Times*, 7 November 1919; P.R.O. CAB 23/18, 5 November 1919.

[172] R. Davie (ed.), *The Diaries of Evelyn Waugh* (Harmondsworth, 1979), p. 37.

[173] *The Times*, 8 November 1919.

[174] *Manchester Guardian*, 12 November 1919.

been liable to be publicly forgotten. Grief has been private. The great result of the two minutes' homage yesterday will be to teach the nation its general loss.[175]

So successful was this innovation that it was immediately clear that it must become permanent. And, although the king did not lay a wreath on the temporary Cenotaph in person, the cascades of flowers with which it was once more deluged only served to confirm the wisdom of making it a permanent monument.

It was arranged that the king should unveil the new structure on Armistice Day 1920, and in October that year the Cabinet again turned its attention to the matter.[176] Once more, a committee was set up to make the arrangements, and again Curzon was put in charge. Since the Cenotaph was seen as 'an Imperial monument, commemorating men of many races and creeds', it was thought 'undesirable that the unveiling ceremony should have any distinctive denominational flavour'. Accordingly, it was decided that the National Anthem should be played when George V arrived in Whitehall; that he should unveil the Cenotaph 'without ceremony'; that the two minutes' silence at 11 o'clock should be followed by the hymn 'O God our help in ages past'; and that the 'Last Post' should then be sounded. But no sooner had this been agreed by the Cabinet than it was confronted with a further proposal, emanating from Dean Ryle of Westminster Abbey.[177] His suggestion was that the body of an unknown soldier should be disinterred from Flanders, brought by destroyer to England, and receive a state funeral in Westminster Abbey on the same day that the new Cenotaph was unveiled. This time, even the king was unenthusiastic, on the grounds that 'a funeral now might be regarded as belated, and almost, as it were, re-open the war wound which time is gradually healing'. But after some debate, the proposal was agreed to, and Curzon's committee took over responsibility for the arrangements.[178]

As with the Cenotaph and the two minutes' silence, despite initial mis-givings on the part of the authorities, the appeal of the ceremonial on the day itself far surpassed expectation. 'The ceremony of yesterday', noted *The Times,* 'was the most beautiful, the most touching, and the most impressive that in all its long eventful story, this island has ever seen.' In Whitehall, the king and his family, the Cabinet and representatives of the Empire, the service chiefs and a tremendous throng of the bereaved were gathered, and the emotion of the occasion was so overwhelming that even *The Times* abandoned itself to lachrymose and extravagant hyperbole:

> The first thundering strokes of Big Ben boomed out, louder it seemed, than ever one heard it even in the stillness of dawn. The King turned to face the Cenotaph and, by a touch on a button, released the flags . . . They fell away, and it stood, clear and wonderful in its naked beauty. Big Ben ceased, and the very pulse of

[175] *The Times,* 12 November 1919.
[176] P.R.O. CAB 23/22, 14 October 1920.
[177] M. H. Fitzgerald, *A Memoir of H. E. Ryle* (London, 1928), p. 311.
[178] Nicolson, op. cit., p. 447; P.R.O. 23/22, 15, 26 October 1920.

time stood still. In silence, broken only by a nearby sob, the great multitude bowed its head ... Then, suddenly, acute, shattering, the very voice of pain itself—but pain triumphant—rose the clear notes of the bugles of The Last Post ... We were made one people, participants in one act of remembrance.[179]

The first part of the ceremony having been completed, the coffin of the Unknown Warrior was conveyed down Whitehall on a gun carriage to the Abbey, with the king as chief mourner, and with Haig, Beatty, French and Trenchard among the pallbearers. In the Abbey itself, where again the bereaved formed the largest part of the congregation, the Unknown was laid to rest amid further scenes of intense solemnity:

The great service virtually formed part of a single ceremony with the unveiling of the Cenotaph. In all its history, the Abbey can have witnessed no such moving spectacle. The congregation of nearly one thousand of those bereaved in the war, and one hundred nurses wounded or blinded in the discharge of their duty; the lines of soldiers, sailors, and airmen who had won the Victoria Cross 'for valour' stretching down the Nave, fifty on either hand; the long procession from the North Transept to the West End of the Nave in which, as chief mourners, the King and Princes of the Blood followed the coffin with its nameless burden—a procession, blessed, as it might seem, at its entry by the effigy of the great Earl of Chatham, and greeted as it reached the graveside by the figure of his famous son: all this was to stir such memories and emotions as might have made the very stones cry out. The popular feeling matched the occasion. Outside the Abbey for a distance of a mile or more stretched a long line of people eager to enter and pay their tribute to the heroic dead. For over ten hours, till it was necessary to close the doors at 11 p.m., they passed through the Abbey, in a ceaseless stream; and day by day throughout the following week, the grave was visited by thousands of those whom the Unknown and his friends had died to save.[180]

Indeed, by the end of the week, it was estimated that one million people had visited the Cenotaph and the graveside, and that no less than 100,000 wreaths had been laid either in the Abbey or in Whitehall. *The Times* produced a special, four-page *Armistice Day Supplement,* and the papers were filled, not only with accounts of the ceremonial, but with fanciful essays in which the life of the Unknown Warrior was re-created.[181] The Cabinet did not exaggerate when, in formally tendering its thanks to Curzon's committee, it spoke of the 'remarkable success' of the ceremony. As *The Times* put it more fully: 'The authorities frankly admit that the extent to which the public imagination has been stirred has exceeded all their expectations.'[182]

Elsewhere throughout the country, the two minutes' silence was once more observed and, where war memorials had already been constructed and dedicated, wreaths were placed by local dignitaries. Throughout the 1920s, in towns and villages, schools and universities, in Eastbourne and Southport, Liverpool and Leicester, Cardiff and Edinburgh, war memorials were

[179] *The Times, Armistice Day Supplement,* 12 November 1920.
[180] Fitzgerald, op. cit., pp. 311–12.
[181] *The Times,* 16 November 1910; *Evening News,* 11 November 1920. .
[182] P.R.O. CAB 23/23, 17 January 1921; *The Times,* 15 November 1920.

dedicated, and immediately became the centre for local ceremonial on Armistice Day every bit as poignant and intense as that in Whitehall.[183] There might be conflict over the type of memorial, and criticism of the design finally chosen; but without exception, all communities sooner or later followed the example of the Cenotaph, and constructed monuments to their dead. At the same time, from 1921 the British Legion (formed in May that year by combining disparate ex-servicemen's associations) began to sell its Flanders Poppies, and from 1924 the wreaths laid by the royal family at the Cenotaph were made in the Legion's factory. From 1923 onwards, the Legion also staged an annual Festival of Remembrance at the Albert Hall, which was attended by the Royal family, and in 1928 the Empire Field of Remembrance was established at Westminster Abbey for the first time.[184] With these final developments, the ritual of Armistice Day was completed and it remained, throughout the inter-war years, the most universal and emotional annual event, its appeal enhanced by the fact that it was broadcast live from 1928. As *The Times* noted as early as November 1923: 'There is nothing artificial in the annual observance at the Cenotaph. It has become part of the expected order of things.' Two years later, by which time some thirty million poppies were regularly sold, it added: 'Poppy day has now become firmly rooted in the heart of the British nation.'[185]

Indeed it had—so much so that, in 1928, Dorothy L. Sayers was able to build the entire plot of *The Unpleasantness at the Bellona Club* around the ritual of Armistice Day. At one point in the story, Wimsey deduces that General Fentiman, who is supposed to have died on November 11, in fact expired a day earlier, for the simple reason that among the deceased's clothes, no poppy was found:

> 'Is it conceivable' (Wimsey asks) 'that, if the old man had been walking on the streets as a free agent on Armistice Day, he would have gone into the club without his Flanders poppy? A patriotic, military old bird like that? It was really unthinkable.'

[183] For the building and dedication of the local memorials cited, see: H. W. Fovargue, *Municipal Eastbourne, 1883–1933: Selections from the Proceedings of the Town Council* (Eastbourne, 1933), pp. 98–106; J. E. Jarratt, *Municipal Recollections: Southport, 1900–1930* (London, 1932), pp. 66–70; V. E. Cotton, *The Book of Liverpool Cathedral* (Liverpool, 1964), pp. 65–9; Armitage, op. cit., pp. 347–9; J. B. Hilling, *Cardiff and the Valleys: Architecture and Townscape* (London, 1973), pp. 152–3; C. Hussey, *The World of Sir Robert Lorimer* (London, 1932), pp. 91–6; Cmd. 279 xxi (1919), *Report of the Committee on the Scottish National War Memorial*. For general comments on war memorials see: A. Whittick, *War Memorials* (London, 1946), chas. 5, 6; G. Stamp, *Silent Cities* (London, 1977), pp. 16–18; H. Baker, *Architecture and Personalities* (London, 1944), pp. 93–102; Butler, op. cit., III, pp. 38–41. For London see: Lord Edward Gleichen, *London's Open-Air Statuary* (London, 1928), *passim*.

[184] *The Times*, 29 October 1921, 5 November 1924; G. Wootton, *The Official History of the British Legion* (London, 1956), pp. 37–41; A. Brown, *Red For Remembrance: The British Legion: 1921–1971* (London, 1971), pp. 77–81; M. Macdonald, *John Foulds: His Life in Music* (Rickmansworth, 1975), pp. 26–31.

[185] *The Times*, 23 October 1923, 12 November 1925.

And, later in the book, Wimsey establishes that it was during the two minutes' silence that Fentiman's body was transferred from a telephone booth into the lounge of the club—'the one period when one could be certain that everybody would be either out in the street or upstairs in the big balcony ... looking out—and listening'.[186] Even Curzon's doubts that the British would be too reserved and embarrassed to 'assume the properly reverential attitude' towards the Cenotaph, were shown to be without foundation. Not only in Whitehall, but at other large memorials such as the Hall of Memory in Birmingham, throughout the 1920s and 1930s, men respectfully and unselfconsciously removed their hats as they walked by. As one history of English customs explained in 1938, the ceremonial aspect of the reverence for the dead had long since become traditional:

> Nearly twenty years after the end of the Great War, we take it as an established custom that November 11th should see the king and the representatives of the services, the veterans, and the government, gathered together with the people of England in Whitehall, and at other memorials all over the country, to pay tribute to those who fell ... Surely the deriders of tradition would not see such things decay, or the memory of their fathers, brothers and cousins pass away.[187]

What is one to make of this extraordinary annual display?[188] What does it tell us about attitudes to death during the inter-war years? How did this ritual, so tentatively proposed by the politicians, but so avidly seized upon by the public, assist those millions of bereaved in coming to terms with their loss? It seems clear that those millions of bereaved wanted some ceremony, some reassurance that their loved ones were not forgotten and that they had not died in vain. As *The Times* explained, the particular appeal of the Unknown Warrior was that he 'might be the child of any one of a million mothers. Therefore all could mourn him the better because he was unknown'. But in addition, the annual ceremonial thereafter was certainly seen as easing that grief of which Kipling wrote so eloquently, by providing the opportunity for making private and individual sorrow for a time public and corporate. 'It brings us face to face with death', noted *The Times,* 'and with the tremendous meditations that death presents to man.'[189]

---

[186] Dorothy L. Sayers, *The Unpleasantness at the Bellona Club* (London, 1977 edn.), pp. 117–18, 124.

[187] Taylor, *English History,* p. 217; Morris, *Farewell the Trumpets,* p. 201; F. J. Drake-Carnell, *Old English Customs and Ceremonies* (London, 1938), p. 110.

[188] Apart from the works by Homberger and Prost already cited (notes 158, 159), the only *historical* analysis of such festivals is K. S. Inglis, 'The Anzac Tradition', *Meanjin Quarterly,* XXIV (1965) 25–64. There is, however, a considerable amount of sociological literature, in England and America, which analyses the *contemporary* meaning of the ceremonial. See: R. Bocock, *Ritual in Industrial Society* (London, 1974), pp. 18–20; W. L. Warner, *American Life: Dream and Reality* (rev. edn., Chicago, 1962), pp. 5–19, 30–4; idem, *The Living and the Dead: A Study of the Symbolic Life of Americans* (New Haven, 1959), pp. 248–70, 274–9. For a critique of the theory in Warner's analysis, see: S. Lukes, *Essays in Social Theory* (London, 1977), pp. 52–73.

[189] *The Times,* 12 November 1920, 10 November 1923.

VII

But this was not the only attempt made, in the inter-war years, to render grief and bereavement bearable. In a book entitled *Life Beyond Death, With Evidence,* published in 1928, the Rev. C. D. Thomas concluded with these comments on 'Armistice Day, 1927':

> Some suppose their dead to be extinct, gone out of being like some glad song which died away in silence, only surviving as a memory. Others hope that they may meet again with those they lost. Many add faith to that hope, looking with confidence for re-union on the morrow of death. And yet, even these are often unaware of the whole glad truth. . . . We say, your departed certainly return, they often stand at your side as in former days, though not being clairvoyant you fail to see them. They speak to you, but not being clairvoyant you do not hear them. They try to impress you with an awareness of their presence, though you deem that sudden thought of them just a fancy of your own and nothing more.[190]

The objective of this book was to 'call to memory those who have risen to the life beyond, and especially those who sacrificed themselves for others at duty's call'. It was, in short, a propaganda exercise on the part of the Spiritualist movement, offering hope to those who had lost relatives in the war—hope that their dead still lived, if in a different world, and hope that contact with them could be established. If Armistice Day was the *public recognition of bereavement,* the Spiritualist movement, by contrast, was the *private denial of death.*

Before the First World War, the Spiritualist movement in Britain was as diverse as it was ineffectual.[191] At a popular level, interest had originally been stimulated in the 1850s, as the movement which had originated in the United States in the previous decade crossed the Atlantic. The great popularizing work of Daniel Douglas Home, the most famous English medium, resulted in the holding of the first Convention of Progressive Spiritualists at Darlington in 1865. Three years later that movement collapsed, as did its successor, the British National Association of Spiritualists, which was set up in 1873, but was defunct within a decade. At the end of the century, however, there was considerable local development, so that in 1891, the National Federation of Spiritualists was founded, with forty-one local societies as members. By the time that organization was transmogrified into the Spiritualists National Union, in 1902, there were altogether 125 affiliated societies, a figure which, by the outbreak of the war, had grown to 141. Development had been slow and intermittent, and there was no evidence to suggest, in 1913, that the National Union was on the brink of unprecedented expansion.

But this was not the only area of interest in the after-life. In 1881, the Society for Psychical Research was founded in Cambridge by Frederick Myers, Desmond Gurney and Henry Sidgwick 'for the purpose of inquiring

[190] C. D. Thomas, *Life Beyond Death, With Evidence* (London, 1928), pp. 194–5.
[191] For the background to the Spiritualist Movement, see: G. K. Nelson, *Spiritualism and Society* (London, 1969), esp. pp. 89–111, 127–48.

into a mass of obscure phenomena which lie at present on the outskirts of our organised knowledge'.[192] The members shared a belief that realities existed which could not be accounted for or described by existing scientific methods, and at the same time they sought to prove the existence of such realities by means which were, in themselves, scientifically acceptable. So, in its early years, the Society was ruthless in its exposure of fraudulent mediums, and its publications—the *Proceedings* and the *Journal*—were meticulously scientific in tone. Although a small body, the society drew support from some of the greatest luminaries of the late Victorian and Edwardian intellectual establishment: Arthur Balfour, Leslie Stephen, Lewis Carroll, Lord Rayleigh and Sir Oliver Lodge.

Before 1914, therefore, the Spiritualist movement had two aspects to it. At one level, it was a small, unpopular movement, concerned with the evidence for life after death, indulging in private seances and table-tilting sessions. At another, it was an elite intellectual activity, patronized by men searching to restore the consolations of religion which Victorian scientific advances had so effectively denied. As a result of the First World War, however, its characteristics, functions and appeal were all markedly changed. Instead of being regarded as an inaccessible elite intellectual activity, or as the popular pastime of cranks and crooks, spiritualism suddenly assumed a widespread and urgent relevance for those seeking to come to terms with their bereavement brought about by the First World War. As one authority on the subject later explained:

> The whole question of Survival became invested with a new meaning. Were all the brave lads dead, who had gone forth buoyantly to fight for their country? If they lived, where were they, and what were they doing? These were the questions that many a mother pondered in her heart . . . It was really the bereaved mothers of Britain that lifted Spiritualism out of the dust, and who have made London the greatest centre in the world for Spiritualism and Spiritualistic activity. If the Church had no definite answer for the inquiries of these mothers, they began to inquire for themselves. If the church could not give them the information they desired, they were resolved to find that information elsewhere.[193]

Initially, however, Spiritualism did not prosper. During the latter stages of the war, the press mounted a violent campaign against it, giving great publicity to the exposure of fraudulent mediums and fortune tellers.[194] 'It is surely nothing less than criminal,' thundered *The Umpire* in August 1916, 'that these harpies of humanity should be permitted without practical protest to trade upon the mental crucification of those whose loved ones have fallen, to die upon the war-wasted fields of France and Flanders.' But by the end of the war, the undoubted popularity of the movement caused the press to

---

[192] S. Hynes, *The Edwardian Turn of Mind* (Princeton, 1968), pp. 139–45.
[193] J. Lamond, *Arthur Conan Doyle: A Memoir* (London, 1931), pp. 169–70.
[194] Nelson, op. cit., pp. 155–6; J. McCabe, *Spiritualism: A Popular History from 1847* (London, 1920), p. 236.

take a more tolerant attitude. By 1919, there were already 309 societies affiliated to the SNU, exactly double the pre-war figure, and by 1938 the number had risen to 530. In fact, by the mid-1930s, there were reported to be over 2,000 properly-constituted local spiritualist societies, and it was estimated that the total number of committed members might be in excess of a quarter of a million. Spiritualist books gushed from the press: some were histories of the movement; some described spectacular evidence of life after death; some were accounts of the intellectual pilgrimages of individuals.[195] In 1938, when the movement was still expanding, three book clubs were founded for its members: the Occult Book Society, the Psychic Book Club, and the Spiritualist Book Society. Jews, agnostics and Anglicans founded their own societies, for grief-stricken widows and mothers who sought 'the touch of a vanished hand and the sound of a voice that is still'.[196]

Two people in particular were of great importance in furthering the cause of Spiritualism. The first was Sir Oliver Lodge, an eminent scientist in his own right, who had become a committed Spiritualist during the 1880s when he was a professor at Liverpool. In September 1915, his youngest son Raymond was killed at the Battle of Ypres, and during the following year messages were received from Raymond via a medium which reinforced Lodge's own belief in the survival of personality after death.[197] In part to express his grief, and in part to offer to others the prospect of the consolation he had himself found in Spiritualism, he recorded these psychic experiences in a book, *Raymond,* published at the end of 1916:

> It may well be believed that it is not without hesitation that I have ventured thus to obtrude family affairs. I should not have done so were it not that the amount of premature and unnatural bereavement at the present time is so appalling that the pain caused by exposing one's own sorrow and its alleviation, to possible scoffers, becomes almost negligible in view of the service which it is legitimate to hope may thus be rendered to mourners, if they can derive comfort by learning that communication across the gulf is possible.[198]

In fact, as he had no doubt expected, the book did Lodge's scientific reputation a great deal of harm, as many readers found it at worst banal and at best unconvincing. In particular, the passage in which Raymond described the types of whisky and cigars consumed in the next life aroused widespread ridicule. But even so, as Lodge had hoped, the book proved to be extraordi-

[195] See, for example: H. Carrington, *The Story of Psychic Science* (London, 1931); J. A. Hill, *Spiritualism: Its History, Phenomenon and Doctrine* (London, 1918); C. Richet, *Thirty Years of Psychical Research* (London, 1923); A. C. Holmes, *The Facts of Psychic Science and Philosophy* (London, 1925); H. Leaf, *The Psychology and Development of Mediumship* (London, 1926); C. L. Tweedale, *Man's Survival After Death,* (London, 1920).
[196] Nelson, op. cit., pp. 161–2; A. Conan Doyle, *The History of Spiritualism* (2 vols., London, 1926), II, p. 225.
[197] W. P. Jolly, *Sir Oliver Lodge* (London, 1974), pp. 199–226; Oliver Lodge, *Past Years: An Autobiography* (London, 1931), pp. 170–88.
[198] O. Lodge, *Raymond* (London, 1916), pp. vii-viii.

narily influential, and went through twelve editions between November 1916 and December 1919. In the following year, Lodge went on a tour to the United States, and throughout the 1920s a stream of articles flowed from his pen.

But even Lodge was far surpassed as a propagandist by the movement's most spectacular recruit: Sir Arthur Conan Doyle.[199] The creator of Sherlock Holmes had flirted with Spiritualism from the 1880s, but only became firmly committed at the end of 1916. Like Lodge, he had lost a son in the war and again, like Lodge, he wrote a book—*New Revelation* (1918)—which was as influential as it was derided. From 1918 until his death in 1930, Doyle worked tirelessly in the cause of Spiritualism, often holding meetings in five different towns a week. His tours to all parts of the country were widely reported; his meetings were extremely popular; and many new societies were set up in towns after his visits. He visited Australia and New Zealand in 1920–21, the United States in 1922 and again in 1923, South Africa in 1928, and northern Europe in 1929.[200] He defended William Hope, the spirit photographer, when he was accused of fraud in 1922, and led a mass resignation by 84 members of the Society for Psychical Research when he came to believe that it was biased against the movement. In 1926 he published his two-volume *History of Spiritualism,* which was dedicated to Sir Oliver Lodge, and he is reputed to have spent over a quarter of a million pounds in support of the movement. In the words of one of its earliest historians: 'St. Paul's missionary work was ... quite paltry in comparison.'[201]

The history of psychic photography, of stories of the return of dead soldiers, of seances, mediums and table-tilting, does not bulk large in descriptions of inter-war England. Yet there can be no doubt that, just as the Cenotaph and the local war memorial were a permanent reminder of death and bereavement, so the Spiritualist movement offered the most persuasive case for the denial of death, and the hope of being reunited in the future. In private seance, as in public ceremony, inter-war Britain was obsessed with death. The easy transition, so often depicted, from a death-dominated, sex-denying nineteenth century to a death-denying, sex-dominated twentieth completely ignores this massive, all-pervasive pall of death which hung over Britain in the years between 1914 and 1939, and also the inventiveness with which the grief-stricken responded to their bereavement. Even the greater sexual freedom of the 1920s, far from being *inversely* related to death, was *directly* related to it, as soldiers who had survived tried to forget by bouts of frenzied self-indulgence, and those who had been too

[199] Lamond, op. cit., book II; J. Dickson Carr, *The Life of Sir Arthur Conan Doyle* (London, 1949), chs. 20–2.
[200] See Doyle's own accounts in : *Our American Adventure* (London, 1923); *Our Second American Adventure* (London, 1924); *Our African Winter* (London, 1926); *The Wanderings of a Spiritualist* (London, 1928).
[201] McCabe, op. cit., p. 239.

230

young to serve tried to assuage their guilt by aping their elders.[202] At a more precise level, pilgrimages by widows and parents to the war graves were running at 140,000 a year in 1931, and 160,000 eight years later.[203] Even detective novels, rarely concerned with violent death in the years before 1914 became, at the hands of Agatha Christie and Dorothy L. Sayers, more murderous and macabre. As George Mosse rightly notes:

> The new interest in the history of attitudes to death has not yet considered the cult of the fallen soldier. This is a curious omission, not only because this cult is central to the development of nationalism, but also because it changed men's views of death itself.[204]

It is possible to catch in these last words an echo of Freud's prediction that the war would make it impossible 'to maintain our former attitude towards death'. Any investigation of death, grief and mourning in modern Britain which ignores the impact of the First World War is incomplete.

VIII

But this is by no means a full picture of the inter-war years in Britain so far as death is concerned. For while the First World War left a shocking legacy of grief and bereavement of unprecedented ubiquity, it was also true that those trends which had been discernible in the years between 1880 and 1914, and which in part had furnished the context within which war death seemed so agonizing and incomprehensible, were themselves becoming ever more pronounced in the years which followed. Eight more crematoria were opened between 1922 and 1931, and the ostentation of funerals and mourning costume lessened still more.[205] Improved diet, better medical facilities and rises in real wages meant that the death rate further declined and life expectancy rose. Even among children, deaths from tuberculosis, typhoid and scarlet fever became increasingly rare. By the 1920s, the death rate for women aged between 25 and 44 had fallen to 39 per cent of its level in the 1840s, and for men the corresponding drop was to 51 per cent.[206]

---

[202] Fussell, op. cit., p. 110.

[203] Wootton, op. cit., pp. 104, 128; Longworth, op. cit., pp. 79–81, 104–6, 126. For the activities of the Imperial War Graves Commission, see *The Times*, War Graves Supplement, 10 November 1928; Longworth, op. cit., chs. 1–6; Stamp, op. cit., pp. 8–16. The work of individual architects is discussed in : Hussey, *Lutyens*, pp. 372–6; Butler, op. cit., III, pp. 41–2; Baker, op. cit., pp. 88–93; Hussey, *Lorimer*, pp. 98–101; Sir R. Blomfield, *Memoirs of an Architect* (London, 1932), pp. 173–80. For war graves in Germany, see: G. L. Mosse, 'National Cemeteries and National Revival: The Cult of the Fallen Soldier in Germany', *Journal of Contemporary History*, XIV (1979), pp. 7–20. The most recent study of war graves and memorials is in J. S. Curl, *A Celebration of Death: An introduction to some of the buildings, monuments, and settings of funerary architecture in the Western European tradition* (London, 1980), ch. 11.

[204] Mosse, op. cit., p. 1. My italics

[205] Morley, op. cit., p. 91; Jones and Noble, op. cit., pp. 59–77.

[206] J. M. Winter, 'The Impact of the First World War on Civilian Health in Britain', *Economic History Review*, 2nd ser., XXX (1977), p. 389, 497–8, 500; Mitchison, op. cit., pp. 41, 50.

So, in trying to evaluate attitudes to death in inter-war England, it is necessary to examine the problem at two distinct levels. As far as pre-occupation with death and bereavement as the result of war is concerned, it seems likely that inter-war Britain was more obsessed with death than any other period in recent history. The 'lost generation' may in some ways have been an elite myth. But the widespread bereavement which prevailed in inter-war England, allied with the rituals of remembrance and the success of spiritualism, leave no doubt that it was also a mass reality. On the other hand, at the level of particular, domestic, individual experience, death from natural causes, as an integral and accepted part of family life, seems to have been less significant than in the period before the first war (with the conspicuous exception of the influenza epidemic of 1918). Death in the past from war was unprecedentedly widespread; death in the present in peacetime was markedly diminished.

It is in this curiously ambiguous context that the impact of the Second World War on British attitudes to death must be set. This time, with the recollections of the earlier conflict vividly in mind, there were no cavalier assumptions that the war would be 'over by Christmas'. On the contrary, it was fully expected to be protracted and bloody: 'victory however long and hard the road may be' was the best hope that Churchill could offer. Once more, the angel of death appeared, and in a guise which closely resembled the outfit she had worn a generation earlier. Investigations into the attitudes of those who fought reveal the same mixture of feelings as before when observing the death of others and while confronting the prospect of the death of self: fear, resignation, grief, compassion, anguish, enthusiasm, indifference, callousness and guilt.[207] And for those at home who lost close friends or relatives, the same responses of numbness, incredulity, and heart-broken desolation which the passing of time could not assuage, which had been so widespread after the First World War, are once more well-attested.[208] For the second time in only three decades, European civilization abandoned itself to the 'carnival of death', and for performers and spectators alike, the feelings which it evoked were strikingly similar to those in the previous war.

In at least two ways, however, experience of death in the Second World War differed markedly from that in the First, at both the individual and at the global level. In the first place, although the experience of death in the

---

[207] J. D. Teicher, ' "Combat Fatigue" or Death Anxiety Neurosis', *Journal of Nervous and Mental Disease*, CXVII (1953), 236–40; R. Grinkler and J. Spiegel, *Men Under Stress* (London, 1945), pp. 25, 33–5, 113–7, 360–3; J. G. Gray, *The Warriors: Reflections on Men in Battle* (New York, 1970), pp. 47–53, ch. 4.

[208] See, for example the reactions described and recorded in: James Pope-Hennessy, *Queen Mary, 1867–1953* (London, 1959), pp. 607–8; Lord Birkenhead, *Halifax* (London, 1965), pp. 542–3; A. Boyle, *Trenchard: Man of Vision* (London, 1962), p. 729; C. Weizmann, *Trial and Error* (New York, 1949), p. 427; Nigel Nicolson (ed.), *Harold Nicolson: Diaries and Letters,* vol. II, *1939–1945* (London, 1967), p. 458; C. P. Snow, *The Light and the Dark* (Harmondsworth, 1962), ch. 39.

two conflicts was similar, its actual impact on the British between 1939 and
1945 was undeniably less than it had been between 1914 and 1918. The
reaction to the casualties and fatalities of the first war had been stunned,
stupefied, incredulous amazement that they could possibly be so large. But,
with this experience still vividly in mind, the response to the losses of the
second war was heartfelt relief that they were, relatively speaking, much
less. Only 270,000 members of the British armed forces were killed: less
than one half the number for the First World War. Even with the 60,000
civilians added, who died as a result of air raids, total fatalities were markedly
down. So, while experience of loss and bereavement was still widespread,
it was less all-pervasive than after the First World War. And the losses
were, perhaps, made easier to bear by the realization that they had been
made for more worthwhile goals, both strategically and morally. Compared
with the First World War, when a few pathetic yards of trench were won
at an appallingly high cost in human lives, the scale and speed of conflict
in the second war was much greater, and the ground covered in attack or
in retreat was much larger. Above all, the cause in which lives were
sacrificed—the destruction of Nazi tyranny and Japanese imperialism
—seemed far more noble and significant than the defence of Belgian
neutrality.[209]

Accordingly, the pall of death which had hung so sorrowful, stagnant and
static over Britain between 1918 and 1939 did not descend again as
completely after 1945. No second Unknown Warrior was brought from
some foreign field to keep the older hero company in Westminster Abbey.
Discussions took place between 1944 and 1948 concerning the construction
of new memorials to the fallen in this second great conflict: but the government
was unenthusiastic, and public opinion was less concerned, than had been
the case between 1918 and 1921.[210] The fact that the two wars were seen as
different episodes in the same conflict, combined with the post-war lack of
men and materials for such 'unnecessary' construction work, were further
arguments against a new spate of monuments. So, at the Cenotaph, the dates
1939–45 were added to 1914–18 and, at most local memorials also, the
names of those who had died in the more recent conflict were merely tagged
on to the earlier list.[211] In keeping with the welfare-state ethos of the post-
war world, the National Land Fund was established as the principal national
monument in the budget of 1946, with a capital of £50 million, which was
to be used for the acquisition of great houses or areas of outstanding national
beauty, which might serve as worthy monuments to the dead and give

[209] Pelling, op. cit., p. 273; Taylor, *English History*, pp. 726–7.
[210] Whittick, op. cit., chs. 1–3, 11, 'Conference on War Memorials, 9 June 1944', *Journal of the Royal Society of Arts*, XCII (1943–4), pp. 322–41; *Hansard*, Lords, 14 February 1945, cols. 1016–54; *The Times*, 28 April 1944; 29 June 1944; 15 February 1945; 23 January 1947; 6, 9 July 1948.
[211] Pelling, op. cit., p. 274; Taylor, *English History*, p. 257; *The Times*, 9 August 1946; 19 February 1948.

pleasure to the living at the same time. But even this most utilitarian of monuments has rarely been used for the purpose originally envisaged, as the funds set aside have been constantly plundered by other government departments short of cash.[212]

In the same way, the rituals associated with Remembrance Day and the Cenotaph never recovered their inter-war level of intensity or significance. During the war, the public ceremony in Whitehall on November 11 was curtailed and, although it was restored in 1945, the government announced in January 1946 that in future there would be one Remembrance Day, to be held on the Sunday immediately before 11 November, at which the dead of both world wars would be commemorated.[213] But as a result, the two minutes' silence which in the inter-war years had brought all weekday activity to a halt for five years in every seven, was never again so intense, as the silence on Sunday found most people at home or in church, rather than about their normal, everyday business. The passage of time only served to weaken the hold of Remembrance Sunday still further as, from the late 1950s, the balance of population increasingly tilted towards a younger, post-war generation, to whom the First World War was history, and the Second only a vague recollection, if that. As a result, attendances at Whitehall and at local memorials declined, and demands for the reform or abolition of Remembrance Sunday became ever more widespread.[214] Eventually, in 1968, a new service was devised 'in response to criticism that the older form of service was too patriotic and warlike in tone, and too narrow and retrospective in its import to engage the interests of any but the elderly'.[215] How long, even in this revised form, Remembrance Day can last in the future is not at all clear.

In other ways, too, the shadow of death from war was diminished after 1945. There was no second, massed recourse to Spiritualism, as there had been in the inter-war years. The only famous proselytizer to emerge from the second war was Lord Dowding; but by 1951 he was forced to admit that his campaign and propaganda had met with little success.[216] Indeed, since the 1950s, the membership of Spiritualist societies has consistently fallen, in marked contrast to the trend of the 1920s and 1930s.[217] In the same way, there was no repetition of the idea of a 'lost generation', partly because the pre-1914 innocence had been lost for good, and partly because it was, after

[212] *The Times*, 10 April 1946; Stamp, op. cit., pp. 18–19.
[213] *The Times*, 1 November 1940; 20 June 1946; P.R.O. CAB 128/5, 28 January 1946.
[214] *The Times*, 9 November 1953; 12 November 1956; 13 November 1963; 9 November 1964; 16 November 1967. See also: R. Coppin, 'Remembrance Sunday', *Theology*, LXVIII (1965), esp. p. 530.
[215] Brown, op. cit., pp. 76–7; *The Times*, 8 November 1967; 22 August 1968; 28 August 1968.
[216] B. Collier, *Leader of the Few: The Authorised Biography of Air Chief Marshal the Lord Dowding of Bentley Priory* (London, 1957), ch. 23. Dowding's books on the subject were: *Many Mansions* (London, 1943); *Lychgate* (London, 1945); *The Dark Star* (London, 1951), esp. p. 8.
[217] Nelson, op. cit., pp. 167, 286.

all, the survivors from that 'lost generation' who actually managed to win the second war, and who stayed in positions of power until the early 1960s. Even the revenue derived from the sales of poppies remained stagnant at about £1 million, which meant that in real terms the British Legion's income in the 1950s and early 1960s fell by over one-third.[218]

But if the shadow of death was lightened at a personal level *despite* the Second World War, it was intensified at a global level *because* of it. For the first time, humanity in general was brought into the front line. The first war, however unprecedented its scale, and however great its use of conscript armies, remained for the British largely a soldier's war: the civilian population was not directly involved. But the bombing of Coventry and Plymouth, London and Glasgow, brought ordinary men and women into war in a new way between 1939 and 1945. Even more horrifyingly, the Germans used 'the lights of perverted science' in an attempt to bring about the total extermination of one race. Reports such as that by Richard Dimbleby, who entered Belsen with the liberating allied forces, presented an unforgettable picture of mass extermination and atrocity, as death became part of life in an unprecedented and terrifying manner.[219] Yet even this was eclipsed by the use of the atomic bomb against Japan. At Hiroshima, estimates of those killed at once varied from 100,000 to 200,000, and as many again were doomed to live baffled, diseased, half-human lives as a result.[220]

Here was 'total immersion in death' of a new and horrifying kind, which surpassed even the greatest atrocities of conventional warfare. In the words of Robert Jay Lifton:

> When we hear reports about the Hiroshima bomb, our emotions are not exactly the same as when confronted with equivalent evidence of bomb destruction in London, Amsterdam, Hamburg, Dresden or Tokyo. These cities, to be sure, convey their own messages of man's capacity and inclination to assault himself. But with Hiroshima (and her neglected historical sister, Nagasaki) something more is involved: a dimension of totality, a sense of ultimate annihilation—of cities, nations, the world.[221]

Thus have the 'shadows of Passchendaele' been superseded by the clouds of Hiroshima. When President Truman described the dropping of the first atomic bomb as 'the greatest thing in history', those words were true in more senses, perhaps, than he realized. For the first time ever in recorded history, global, total death has become, since 1945, a very real possibility. As in the medieval world, death once more not only reigns but rules. But this time it is the bomb, not the bacillus, which is his emissary. 'The dark

[218] *The Times*, 5 November 1966.
[219] J. Dimbleby, *Richard Dimbleby* (London, 1977), pp. 180–4.
[220] R. J. Lifton, *Death in Life: The Survivors of Hiroshima* (London, 1968), pp. 20, 115. For the background to the dropping of the bomb, see: H. Feis, *Japan Subdued: The Atomic Bomb and the End of the War in the Pacific* (Princeton, 1961).
[221] Lifton, op. cit., p. 14.

235

powers of destruction unleashed by science' have brought mankind to the brink of total destruction.[222] Churchill might have been wrong in making such a prediction after the First World War: but the aftermath of the second war showed that he had erred only in the timing, but not in the substance, of his prophecy.

As a result, death in the second half of the twentieth century has taken on a global aspect which renders studies of it in modern times which are confined to one particular country somewhat myopic. For the threat of mass, accidental death, and the desire to avoid it, has permeated all our lives and experiences and expectations, to some extent. High politics, for example, is now dominated by the thought that one mistake, one rushed decision, or one breakdown in communication, and catastrophe might ensue. 'Mankind', Kennedy noted in his inaugural address, 'holds in his hands the power to abolish all forms of human poverty and all forms of human life.'[223] Increasingly, the key to world peace has lain in the recognition that, if global conflict comes again, there will be no winners. 'Safety', Churchill observed in his last great Parliamentary speech, on the hydrogen bomb, 'may be the sturdy child of terror, survival the twin brother of annihilation.' Or, as Kennedy put it six years later, it was only the 'uncertain balance of terror that stays the hand of mankind's final war'.[224]

But it is not only political life and international diplomacy which have been transformed by this 'constant risk of universal death'. Psychologists like Lifton have attempted to come to terms with the implications that such absurd and arbitrary death has for the way we look at life. But, as he himself admits, while 'our perceptions of Hiroshima are the beginnings of new dimensions of thought about death and life', it is not at all clear as to what, exactly, these new dimensions of thought should be.[225] Alvarez has taken the argument one stage further, accepting the importance of Hiroshima, but doubting whether any new dimensions of thought on life and death are feasible, as mankind totters beneath the crushing burden of knowing that he has the power to destroy himself completely. 'Death', he argues, 'is everywhere and on such a vast scale that it becomes indifferent, impersonal, inevitable and, finally, without any meaning.' For him, it is the presence of a 'ubiquitous and arbitrary death' which is the key explanation to the sense of chaos and futility which he sees as the distinguishing mark of creative endeavour in the second half of the twentieth century. How is it possible, he argues, for anyone to write in an appropriate vocabulary of death which is at once arbitrary and omnipresent? 'The growth of modern technology', he asserts, 'has made death itself absurd by reducing it to a random

---

[222] G. W. Hibbitt (ed.), *The Dolphin Book of Speeches* (New York, 1965), p. 285.

[223] Ibid., p. 284.

[224] Robert Rhodes James (ed.), *Winston S. Churchill: His Complete Speeches, 1897–1963* (8 vols., London, 1974), VIII, p. 8629; Hibbitt, op. cit., p. 285.

[225] Lifton, op. cit., p. 14.

happening, totally unconnected with the inner rhythms and logic of the lives destroyed.'[226]

In Britain, these twin facets of the problem of the bomb—its political dimension and its philosophical implications—converged in the person of Bertrand Russell, who in 1958 began the Campaign for Nuclear Disarmament. Obsessed with the threat of 'universal death' which he believed now hung over the world, Russell devoted much effort in his declining years to bringing home to the leaders of the world the real magnitude of the risks of nuclear warfare.[227] For four years or so, the CND, followed by the Committee of 100, was a powerful pressure group, with its Aldermaston marches, mass meetings in Trafalgar Square, and a stream of propaganda, much of it written by Russell himself. But by the mid-1960s, it was clear that such activity would meet with little success. The British public as a whole was singularly uninterested in the bomb—as a threat to humanity or as an 'independent deterrent'. Nor was the British Government swayed by the campaign. Indeed, even if it had been, it was not at all clear what influence, if any, it could have brought to bear on other nuclear powers.[228] Even Russell, increasingly disenchanted by the tactics and personnel of the CND and the Committee of 100, felt obliged to admit that his efforts had failed, and turned his attention, in the last years of his life, to American war crimes in Vietnam. 'My views on the future', he wrote in the concluding chapter of his autobiography, 'are best expressed by Shelley in the following poem:

> Oh, cease! must hate and death return?
>   Cease! must men kill and die?
> Cease! drain not to its dregs the urn
>   Of bitter prophecy.
> The world is weary of the past,
> Oh, might it die and rest at last!'[229]

IX

Such global, galactic gloom brings us a long way, in time as in subject-matter, from the Duke of Wellington's funeral, with which this essay began. Clearly, the history of death which looks at the death of individuals as part of the normal, expected course of events is very different from the history of death which is concerned with the danger of mass extermination. The literature on nuclear holocaust takes little note of other work on contemporary death, just as the literature on contemporary death takes little note of other

[226] A. Alvarez, *The Savage God: A Study in Suicide* (London, 1971), pp. 199–203.
[227] Bertrand Russell, *The Autobiography of Bertrand Russell*, vol. III, *1944–1967* (London, 1969), ch. III. See also his polemics: *Common Sense and Nuclear Warfare* (London, 1959); *Has Man A Future?* (Harmondsworth, 1961).
[228] H. Pelling, *Popular Politics and Society in Late Victorian Britain* (2nd edn., London, 1979), pp. 177–8; L. D. Epstein, 'The Nuclear Deterrent and the British General Election of 1964', *Journal of British Studies*, V (1966), p. 159.
[229] Russell, *Autobiography, 1944–1967*, p. 172.

work on nuclear holocaust. The subjects may be related, but they are also distinct: death as analysed in the second half of the twentieth century is either general and in the future, or individual and in the present. It is rarely, if ever, both together.

Indeed, it is not at all clear how it can be, if only because, for most of us, the prospect of mass death from nuclear war is something we choose not to think about. In Britain as elsewhere, we may live in the shadow of the bomb; but the sun still keeps on shining. As Alvarez himself admits, for the majority of the population, 'life, after all, goes on, empirically and as rationally as possible, whatever the ultimate insecurities'.[230] So, it is perhaps most appropriate, in the interests of completeness and consistency, to return to the more local issue of individual death in modern Britain, and to see what historical perspective this essay offers on the problems and analysis of death, grief and mourning in our society today.

If one ignores the danger that we may all die too young, exterminated by means beyond our control, and denied the fulfilment of earlier and more long-lived generations, then the picture of death in Britain today is relatively optimistic. *Provided* the shadow of global death is lifted, or ignored, we seem to have before us the prospect of longer lives than any generation which has gone before. Improvements in health, housing, hygiene and the standard of living have continued since the Second World War, giving young people today a life expectancy of which their grandparents could not have dreamed. In the years 1901–71, the death rate for young adults has fallen between 75 and 90 per cent. From 1936 to 1956, mortality of women at the age of fifty fell by 33 per cent, and of men by 25 per cent. The reason why so many people seem to die today of heart attacks, strokes and cancer is that there is, literally, little else to die of, as most of the killers of the nineteenth century have been eliminated. Indeed, men and women are more likely today to die of being overfed than under-nourished. Whether these improvements and developments will continue in the future, or whether there will be a reversal, is unclear. All that can be said with certainty is that a higher proportion of people die old in Britain today than ever before.[231]

These are the basic demographic facts concerning death in modern Britain. At the emotional level, however, the picture is less serene, as death from old age brings with it its own particular problems. The indignities of geriatric wards and the dangers of euthanasia and premature termination are well known. So are the problems of talking to doctors or even close relatives about the prospect of one's own death. With fewer people believing in the resurrection of the body and the life everlasting, the contemplation of death is for many as terrifying as the experience of death is lonely. And for those who are left, grief-stricken and bereft, the traumas of adjustment remain severe.

---

[230] Alvarez, op. cit., p. 197.
[231] Mitchison, op. cit., pp. 250–6.

Accounts of anguished, unassuaged loneliness, and the descriptions of the misery which some endure before death, are eloquent reminders that in the second half of the twentieth century, death and bereavement remain two of the most awesome experiences of life.[232]

But how does all this appear when put in a historical perspective, as has been attempted in this essay? What light does the historical account given here throw on that nostalgic view of the past which governs so much analysis of contemporary grief and mourning in Britain? It has tentatively been suggested that many of the assumptions of such writers about the nineteenth-century way of death are unfounded or mistaken: what does that imply about their perspective on the present? It has been argued that dying in the nineteenth century was more often wretched than sublime: does that support the widely-held view that dying in Britain today, which is undoubtedly *different,* is also *worse?* A case has been made here that ostentatious mourning in the nineteenth century was probably more a display of status than a successful means of assuaging grief: does that mean that there is any historical justification for the widespread view that, because such rituals have now become much attenuated, grief today is *therefore* harder to bear?[233]

In response to these questions, two general, if tentative, conclusions seem to emerge. In the first place, the evidence marshalled here suggests that in the years since 1945, dying has *certainly* been *different* but has *arguably* been *better,* not worse, than in any earlier period of modern British history. Assuredly, the shadow of ultimate catastrophe broods dark, menacing and horrifying. But, to quote Alvarez again, 'this sense of disaster is, for the moment, mercifully peripheral to the lives most of us lead'.[234] And, on the credit side, since 1945 there has grown up the first young generation this century which has not had to join up and then be blown up. More than ever before, death now occurs at what is, psychologically, the most satisfying time: in old age. Neither youthful nor violent death is as widespread in Britain as it was: it is largely, and appropriately, experienced by the elderly, and frequently occurs in a relatively peaceful form. For the dying, the need to put on a good show, the fear of hell, the pain of protracted illness, the indignity of suffering, and the gnawing anxiety about the financial vulnerability of those left behind, have all been markedly (and thankfully) lessened. In Britain, in the present, opportunities for people to take leave of life 'as painlessly as possible and with the minimum of fuss', are more widely available than they have ever been before.[235]

In the same way, bereavement and mourning are certainly different from what they were in the nineteenth century: and they may, actually, be easier

---

[232] See, especially, Kubler-Ross, op. cit., pp. 160–218.

[233] As argued in Gorer, op. cit., p. 110.

[234] Alvarez, op. cit., p. 203.

[235] J. McManners, 'The history of death', *Times Literary Supplement,* 14 December 1979, p. 112.

to endure today than they were in the past. There are fewer parents grieving over children whose lives were prematurely snuffed out by disease (as in the nineteenth century) or by war (as in the first half of the twentieth). The excessive and exploitative extravagance of nineteenth-century English funerals has disappeared, and has not been replaced by the costly and preposterous charade of the twentieth-century American way of death.[236] The decline of elaborate, stylized mourning rituals, which so successfully cut off the bereaved from life-enhancing society, may actually make it easier for those who mourn to come to terms with their grief, as the demands of ordinary, daily life encourage them to pick up the threads once more. And the fact that the majority of people in this country can reach maturity without the experience of widespread death or widespread war is surely more a cause for thankfulness than for nostalgic regret.

If these tentative conclusions are valid, then they have significant implications for the historical perspectives on contemporary death which at present are so popular among those many historians, sociologists and doctors who have analysed the subject in the present, and which are so powerful in influencing their suggestions as to what should be done in the future. Assuredly, these authorities are quite correct in saying that more work needs to be undertaken on the subjects of death and bereavement. But there is little evidence to support their *historical* explanation as to why, now, dying and grieving are so traumatic, or their suggestions as to how these difficulties might best be alleviated. For if, as has been suggested here, dying and grieving today are certainly different and arguably easier to endure than they were in the nineteenth century or in the years up to 1945, then it follows that it is no solution to our very real contemporary problems to try to put the clock back to some idealized, mythical and non-existent nineteenth-century golden age, where it is erroneously supposed that these matters were coped with so much more effectively than they are by us today.

On the contrary, the arguments developed here suggest that the best way to help those who face death or suffer bereavement in the present is not to draw attention to some nostalgically-distorted image of a past paradise which never actually existed, but rather to stress that dying and grieving in the present bring with them their own problems which must be faced, analysed and (if possible) solved here and now. Assuredly, dying may still be, as H. G. Wells observed, a messy business.[237] But the very real traumas associated with it are not at all lessened *either* by assuming that an earlier society had found the correct solutions which we have, foolishly, somehow lost or disregarded, *or* by arguing that the best way to solve our problems is to return to these past practices. The sooner studies of contemporary death,

[236] For a recent (and excessively jargon-ridden) analysis of the modern American funeral, see: R. E. Turner and C. Edgley, 'Death as Theater: A Dramatalurgical Analysis of the American Funeral', *Sociology and Social Research,* LX (1976), 377–92.
[237] C. P. Snow, *Variety of Men* (Harmondsworth, 1969), p. 74.

grief and mourning liberate themselves from this distorted and distorting straitjacket of the past, the better.

X

This essay is no more than a preliminary, tentative foray into a very large subject. Indeed, in many of the areas it has covered, it has exposed more puddles of ignorance than pools of information. We still know quite extraordinarily little about attitudes towards death in the nineteenth century. At all levels of society—working class, middle class and aristocracy; rural and urban; Anglican, Catholic and Dissenter—much more research needs to be done. As with so many examples of ostensibly 'total' social history, this essay rests far too extensively on the diary-keeping, letter-writing, reminiscence-producing, much-biographied elite, and the assumption that what they felt about death and bereavement during the First World War may be taken as representative of society as a whole is easier to assert than it is to prove. Likewise, it shows that additional work must be done on the varying rates of change in attitudes towards death among different social groups and in different regions. Above all, it suggests how important it is to provide a more complete and rigorous historical framework within which to set contemporary analysis of death, grief and mourning.

Assuredly, the history of death in Britain over two centuries seems a relatively small-scale subject compared with the broad sweep of Ariès. And, if the suggestions outlined here are to be followed up in detail, the focus of research will only be narrowed still further. For while these grand generalizations are stimulating and provocative, they often conceal and distort as much as they reveal and illuminate. At least, that seems to be the case as far as death in Britain in the modern period is concerned. For, with all the caveats that must be entered about the sources used and arguments made in this essay, several important conclusions do emerge, which substantially modify the conventional wisdom on the subject. To begin with, it is time to re-assess the view that the Victorians, by their publicized ostentation, had successfully come to terms with death and bereavement. There is a need, when writing about death in the twentieth century, to pay due regard to the extraordinarily significant impact of the First World War, which has hitherto been too much neglected. And at the very least, the assumptions that contemporary death is uniquely terrible and contemporary bereavement is unprecedentedly hard to endure, need to be treated with some scepticism.

Most importantly, it may be necessary to re-think that beguiling and nostalgic progression from obsessive death and forbidden sex in the nineteenth century to obsessive sex and forbidden death in the twentieth. For even if that model is of some relevance in the realm of public attitudes, it says little of value about the world of private experience. Recent research suggests

241

that the Victorians were interested in sex as much as we are.[238] And, in the light of the evidence advanced in this essay, it seems possible to argue that they were not particularly successful in coming to terms with death. The twentieth-century part of the argument can be equally criticized. To begin with, the increased amount of public discourse on sex does not necessarily mean that people are more obsessed with the subject in private than were the Victorians. And the fact that people do not talk about death in public does not mean that it is ignored; on the contrary, ever since Freud wrote his seminal article, there has been an endless spate of studies, which has reached epidemic proportions in the last three decades.[239] Viewed in this light, the conventional wisdom on the subject of sex and death in Victorian and modern Britain with which this essay began seems neither intellectually convincing nor a worthy object of nostalgic, romanticized veneration.

At an even more general level, this essay suggests some considerations which might usefully be borne in mind when writing about death at any time, in any country, and among any social group. It suggests that even in countries as superficially similar as Britain, France and the United States, there may be fundamental differences in chronology, in technological developments and in general attitudes. It suggests that the history of dying, of death, of grief, of mourning, of bereavement, of funerals and of cemeteries are all distinct subjects, the relationship between which is at best complex and at worst obscure. It suggests that any attempt to trace the evolution over time of an emotion like grief, or even to generalize about such an emotion at a given time in a given society, is an extraordinarily difficult, if not impossible task. It suggests that any investigation of death which ignores the impact of war and killing—be it murder, suicide or death by violent means—misses out a crucial dimension. In other words, the most important—if predictable—conclusion which this essay reaches is that the history of death is at least as complicated as the history of life.

---

[238] For some recent work, see: I. Gibson, *The English Vice* (London, 1978); S. Marcus, *The Other Victorians: A Study of Sexuality and Pornography in Mid-Nineteenth Century England* (London, 1966); R. Pearsall, *The Worm in the Bud: The World of Victorian Sexuality* (London, 1969); B. Harrison, 'Underneath the Victorians', *Victorian Studies*, X (1966–7), 239–62.

[239] See especially, S. Anthony, *The Child's Discovery of Death* (London, 1940), and the many pre-1939 works cited in the books by Hinton, Gorer and Parkes.

Index

ACHILLES: death of, in *Odyssey*, 24
Ackermann, Rudolph, 135, 137
after-life, 11, 194, 227–31; *see also* **Paradise**, **Purgatory**, **Hell**
Alanbrooke, Viscount, funeral of (1963), 79
Albemarle, Duke of (General Monck), funeral of (1670), 68
Alexander IV, pope, 57
Alexander VII, pope, monument to, 139–40
Alfieri, Vittorio, monument to, 139–40
Allahabad, Hindu pilgrimage centre, 161–2, 163, 164, 165, 166, 170
Alvarez, A., 236–7, 238, 239
American way of death, 3, 120, 187, 191, 192, 240
Anderson, Hamburg *Bürgermeister,* avoids public funeral, 92, 102
Anjou, attitudes to death in (17th and 18th centuries), 11, 124
Anne, Queen, funeral of, 61, 71–2
Ansbach, 11 grades of funeral in, 84
Apollo, Greek idea of death (often premature) from arrows of, 19–20
Aquinas, St Thomas, 48
Ariès, Philippe, on history of attitudes to death, 3, 4–7, 40, 115, 116–21, 188, 193; limitations of, 123, 124; problems raised by, 8–10, 13, 81, 193; quoted, 110, 189–90
Armistice Day ritual, 219, 221–4, 234
Arsenius, patriarch of Constantinople, 58
Artemis, Greek idea of death (often premature) from arrows of, 19–20
Arya Samaj (Aryan Association), organ of new Hinduism, 177–81
Asquith, H. H., 216
Asquith, Margot, 213–14
atomic bombs, 3, 235–6

attitudes to death, historical sequence of (Ariès): natural acceptance, 3, 118; preoccupation with fate of individual, 3–4, 118–19; reaction against elaborate burials, triumph of reason, 4–5, 119; surviving family as focus of attention, cult of the tomb, 5, 119; suppression of idea of death, 5, 120
Augustine of Hippo, St, 40, 52, 58

BACON, John, monument designed by, 138–9
Baldwin, Stanley, 199–200, 218
Banks, Thomas, monuments designed by, 136, 148–9
banners, at royal funerals, 64, 65, 66
Baring, Sir Francis, with wife and two grandchildren: monument to, 151
Baroque monuments, 132
Bartolini, Lorenzo, statue of Charity by, 146–7
Bavaria, burials in cities forbidden in (1803), 105
Becket, St Thomas, 53, 58, 59
Bede, 43
bell-ringing, at Hamburg funerals, 89–90, 99
Benares, Hindu pilgrimage centre, 159, 161, 162, 163, 164, 165, 166–7, 170
Berlinghieri; monument to, in Campo Santo, Pisa, 151–2
Bernard of Clairvaux, St, 44
Bernini, G. L., monument designed by, 142
bishops: burial of, 44; at royal funerals, 63
Bloch, Marc, of *Annales* school of historians, 115–16, 130
Blunden, Edmund, 208
Boase, T. S. R., 40
Boccaccio, *Decameron* by, 55

INDEX

mourners at Hamburg funerals, for placing in, 88, 95

poor men: burial of, in Hamburg, 91, 95, and in Victorian England, 189–90; interred free as one of the seven works of mercy, 82; at royal funerals, 47, 48, 64

Pope, Alexander, 149

popes: monuments to, in St Peter's, Rome, 132

pornography, subject of death as a form of, 2, 117, 187

pregnancy, burial of women dying in (Middle Ages), 55

Priestley, J. B., 199

Privy Council, and royal funerals, 65–6, 68–9, 71, 78

processions, part of funeral formula, 82; at Lutheran funerals, 83; numbering thousands at Hamburg funerals, 88–9, declining with introduction of carriages, 98; at royal funerals, 48, 51, 62, 63, 65

Protestants, in France, 81–2, 126, 127

Provence, attitudes to death in (18th century), 12, 13

psalms, seven penitential, 42, 56

Psychical Research, Society for, 227–8, 230

Purānas of Hindus, 161; on death rituals, 154, 161, 165, 184–5

Purgatory, doctrine of, 60 118; Protestant denial of, 107; prayers of survivors, and period spent by soul in, 45, 83

Puritanism, in New England, 121

QUIGLEY, Hugh, 212

REINCARNATION of souls, doctrine of, 37; for Hindus, 156, 167, 185

Reitendiener (personal guard of honour of Senate), on horseback at Hamburg funerals, 89, 100, 101, 103

Remembrance Day, replacing Armistice Day, 234

Requiem Mass, 42, 83, 119; for kings, Offertory in, 48, 63, 64

resurrection of the body, 5, 58; burial rite and, 43, 44; medieval funeral founded on belief in, 82; new Hinduism and, 179

Reynolds, Sir Joshua, P.R.A., 36

Rich, Edmund, Archbishop of Canterbury, body of, 52, 54

Richardson, Samuel, *Clarissa Marlowe* by (1748), 147

Ripa, Cesare, *Iconologia* by (1593), 142

Roberts, Earl, funeral of (1914), 79

Romanticism, and deathbeds, 119, 121, 123

Rosebery, Lord, 215

Rousseau, J. J., 110, 122, 123

Rowell, Geoffrey, on the liturgy of Christian burial, 123

Roy, Ram Mohun, Brahmin reformer, 175, 176–7

Russell, Bertrand, 237

Rutland, 5th Duke of, funeral of (1857), 189

Ryle, H. E., Dean of Westminster, 223

SADE, Marquis de, 121

saints: deathbeds of, 51–2; translation of bodies of, 52–4, 60

Salisbury, Richard Neville, Earl of, heraldic funeral of, and of his son (1462–3), 75

Sanātan dhārma sabhas, neo-orthodox Hindu societies, 181–2

Sassoon, Siegfried, 203, 209

sati (widow-burning) by Hindus, 164, 172–5

Saxe, Maurice Maréchal de, monument to, 131, 132–3, 134, 137–8, 141

Sayers, Dorothy L., 225–6

scavenger caste of Hindus, handling of corpses by, 159, 167

Schultze, Gottfried, Hamburg bookseller: details of expenditure on funeral of (1680), compared with those for funeral of Frantz von Bremen, 93–5, 96–7

Seely, J., 211

sensibility in the visual arts, seen in Nelson's monument, 138, 144

sermons: at home of deceased, in Hamburg, 89, 90; at Lutheran funerals, 83; at royal funerals, 48, 62; at translations of saints, 53

sex: death changes place with, as taboo subject, 187; after First World War, 230–1

Shankaracharya, S., Indian teacher (8th century), 176

shrāddha, oblations, for the dead, by N.